CLEMENT ROSS
(AKA RANGER IGUANA)

SEVENTH
SON
TO SURVIVE

Library of Congress Control Number: 2025904251

ISBN
978-1-964488-62-2 (Paperback)
978-1-964488-63-9 (eBook)
978-1-964488-61-5 (Hardcover)

"The question has not been settled whether madness is a higher form of intelligence."

Edgar Allan Poe

Dedication — Part One

This book is primarily dedicated to Mister Michael T. Hall. U.S. Army retired.

When I met him, he was SGT Hall, E-05. Platoon Sergeant of Weapons Platoon of Alpha company, 1st Ranger Battalion, 75th Infantry. That was October 1980.

Mike Hall was from Avon Lake, Ohio. I was from Mentor, Ohio. We were on opposite sides of Cleveland, but we had that connection.

In 1999, I saw Mike again at the Ranger Rendezvous at Fort Benning. He was still active duty and the Command Sergeant Major of the Ranger Regiment.

We met again in 2014, Savannah for the 40th Anniversary of the 1st Ranger Battalion.

Mike told me he tried to retire after 30. Army called him back. They could do that to me until I turn 60. Ranger Tab goes a long way.

Mike Hall is and always will be the most squared away soldier and the most squared away Ranger I've ever known or met.

In 2020, I asked his permission to add him to this dedication. I was blessed to hear his reply that he would be honored. The honor is all mine.

SGT Hall made me the Ranger I became. It goes beyond that. The person I became was a result of the Ranger I became.

Define this. Code. Ethics. Honor. Morals. Courage. Bravery. Intestinal fortitude. What do these terms mean? Nothing without Mike Hall. Thank you.

Dedication — Part Two

This book is also dedicated to Lynn Ann Ross (nee Frick) – my wife -- who picked up the pieces. How she dealt with the shards I'll never know.

I also dedicate this book to Betty Frick, mother-in-law extraordinaire. She knows me and understands my weirdness. And she would probably say that she loved me more for it.

Also dedicated to Mark Vocca, Reggie Richards III, Tod Ross, and Rod Schaffter. Four great friends who know me, accept me -- as I love them and accept them. As brothers.

Also to Chris O'Connor, my unofficially adopted son (and his lady, Dani).

TABLE OF CONTENTS

THE RANGER CREED

Recognizing that I volunteered as a Ranger, fully knowing the hazards of my chosen profession, I will always endeavor to uphold the prestige, honor, and high esprit de corps of the Rangers.

Acknowledging the fact that a Ranger is a more elite soldier who arrives at the cutting edge of battle by land, sea, or air, I accept the fact that as a Ranger my country expects me to move further, faster and fight harder than any other soldier.

Never shall I fail my comrades. I will always keep myself mentally alert, physically strong and morally straight and I will shoulder more than my share of the task whatever it may be, one-hundred-percent and then some.

Gallantly will I show the world that I am a specially selected and well-trained soldier. My courtesy to superior officers, neatness of dress and care of equipment shall set the example for others to follow.

Energetically will I meet the enemies of my country. I shall defeat them on the field of battle for I am better trained and will fight with all my might. Surrender is not a Ranger word. I will never leave a fallen comrade to fall into the hands of the enemy and under no circumstances will I ever embarrass my country.

Readily will I display the intestinal fortitude required to fight on to the Ranger objective and complete the mission though I be the lone survivor. Rangers Lead The Way!

— Ranger Handbook SH 21-76[1]

1   https://web.archive.org/web/20150315100040/https://www.benning.army.mil/infantry/rtb/content/pdf/2011%20rhb%20final%20revised%2002-11-2011.pdf

AMENDMENT 1

Congress shall make no law respecting an establishment of religion, or prohibiting the free exercise thereof; or **abridging the** *freedom of speech*, or of the press; or the right of the people peaceably to assemble, and to petition the government for a redress of grievances.

THIS MUCH I KNOW IS TRUE

I have written this book during scotch #3. Never #4.

[And that's not, scotch number three but I really mean five. Three means three. Like Mark Vocca told me, "Hey pissing in the closet is on my resume." I've used that verbatim. Because it's true and matches my history.]

This is a testimony, an account of facts. Nothing has been altered. Although I have allowed omissions. Memory presents an interesting challenge. Reliability. As clearly as I remember, I will report the facts. Do I trust myself? No. I'm sixty years old. Some memories are not reliable. Sometimes I have partial memories. Sometimes I have stark raving mad memories. And sometimes, I have no memories at all. Of the latter, Bunny used to say that.

Sir Arthur Conan Doyle taught us that there is observation, fact and deduction. Speculation might entertain, but it counts for naught. When I was interested in writing the "Ross Family" history, I asked Veronica (Aunt Baby), "What is the first thing that comes to mind when you think of your father?" She said, "go and get me something to beat you with."

Shrinks talk about parts of our history that we "Block Out." Yes, I can attest that some of that is involuntary. But I also block out events intentionally because I don't want to remember it. Then other events are branded into my hide so that I'll never forget.

There are parts to be omitted to protect those who did no harm. Or did harm. I must also say. I am not innocent. I caused harm. One day my reckoning will come.

A book can document the history of memories. The smell of custard brings back a time of comfort and safety. Why does baked dessert have that effect?

I have an Alter Ego. His name is James Kennedy. I will not reveal the secrets of his past. But he committed decadent acts. Compartmentalization is a gracious tool that allows for separating. If I met someone and we were to engage in carnal activities, then my name was James Kennedy. Sorry Dale. I borrowed the last name from you.

If I ever tell the sins of James Kennedy, it will come out as a separate book. Perhaps with allusions to this one. It would be a book of pain, degradation, fornication, -- a book of self-loathing. Thanks, Bunny!

I have emailed people I love and told them what James Kennedy has done. They forgave me. No need to repeat the sins here.

Goethe called his autobiography, "Dichtung und Wahrheit." That translates to "Poetry and Truth." Poetry implies poetic license to alter. I make no such claims. If I tell a truth, it's the truth. If I omit facts or elements out of context, it's deliberate. Is it lying by omission? Probably. This book is my writing. I have control. Therefore, I determine the content.

Hell, I've got a ton of garbage that I'm ashamed of. Ask any of my exes. Actually, don't ask. They are masters of hyperbole. Well, the first two were. To clarify – Lynn is not my ex. She is my current wife. And the best of all. ("Good things come to those who wait"?)

#1 – kept a journal. Subjective document of events. One sided. Biased. There are two sides to every story.

#2 – Had Tourette's, Was a pathological liar. A new term, "Spend-a-holic." And collected Barbie Dolls. She had a son with Tourette's and a daughter who wanted to be a punk rocker. I loved Megan.

#3 – that's Lynn. I love her with all my heart.

Some would call this a journal. My first wife kept what she called a journal. She recorded her thoughts, feelings, truths and lies. A true journal would document my sins and the sins of others. A true journal would start with "I'm not proud of this but…" THAT's a Doug Enkler line. Doug will thank me for my discretion.

In this "journal," I pick and choose which of my sins I reveal and which sins are hidden. Am I biased? Absolutely. And that is not fair. But it remains my choice. It's subjective.

I also hide or reveal the sins of others. Those revealed deserve to be exposed. I'll explain it this way. In 1981, I got a unicorn tattoo. It was for Martha Alexy. The unicorn meant the protector of innocents. Martha needed protection. Russ DeGidio was her enemy. But she would not learn that until 1980.

There is also the expression of the Johari window. I learned this in 11th grade high school at Lake Catholic. Communications Class.

Johari Window

	Known to self	Not known to self
Known to others	Arena	Blind Spot
Not Known to Others	Façade	Unknown

Is that public domain? May I use it? Perhaps 1977 or 1978.

My sins include sex, drugs, theft, and lying. I don't think I hide any of the sins about drugs. But it's too early to tell. Some will be revealed and some will not. That is my prerogative. So, this is not a tell "all." It is a tell "some." It's January (now October), 2020, as I begin this. How many people will I piss off and how many will forgive me?

Update for the review... February 16, 2022. We continue the "review."

On January 3, 2020, I was laid off. I had three boards of directors that became hateful. I was a community association manager (CAM).

Let me start over. I've been a CAM for the last sixteen years (as of January 2020). When I told my wife I'd been laid off, she rightfully said something that it must be your fault. I have no idea what it is but she's usually right. I started writing this book at that moment... well, after she went to bed and I poured scotch number #3. That's my limit.

My wife Lynn once asked me early on in our marriage or perhaps before we were married. "You tell me you're a writer, but you never write. Sure an occasional poem to me. But where's the novel? Or the book?" Back then I would tell her, because I'm not in pain.

I'm writing now because I am in pain. Again. It overwhelms me. Perhaps she does not think it's real. But it's not emotional. It's physical. My lower back and my neck are bad... I have to create this record before I'm in so much pain that I can't physically get the words on paper.

Comically, Lynn, is oft "inaccurate" with words... we call them Lynneeisms... Metaphors like Dim-Bat, Guinnea Goat and Ejaculation Seat. They are mixed metaphors. Brilliantly creative. Albeit funny as hell.

It took me from 1961 to 2004 for me to meet Lynn. Forty-three years. Billy Joel captured it when he wrote "and I have to laugh when she reveals me." Lynn does.

She knows me better than anyone. Period. And she honestly loves without condition. That adverb is quite deliberate. But I won't explain. It's in the past where it belongs. Once you realize a bad mistake, let it go. Discard it in the past where it belongs. It holds no relevance in the present or future – unless you repeat it. [See Santayana.]

This is non-fiction. The editor might tell me when I can and cannot use real names. No. I thought about it. Did Anne Frank change the names so she wouldn't offend the Nazis? No. My testimony stands as is. This is a memoire. Not written as events happened but in retrospect years later when memories are selective and subjective. And details... little things like names... I will recall some, but many will be lost in the trenches of time.

I will not address wife #1 Lise Stevens and wife #2 Patti Glaser because fingers can point on both sides and it would only be hateful. Let those flames ebb to ash and fade to black. Technically, Michaela Becker was technically wife #1. But she was an eleven-month mistake made by a desperate and lonely soldier in a foreign land.

I anticipate jumping back and forth between past and present or near present in the process of writing this piece. Lynn hates that... when we're watching movies. I hope she doesn't hate this.

At age sixty, I've had three wives (four if you count the eleven months with Michaela Becker) and no children. To the latter part I say... "tongue in cheek"? I can't think of the best metaphor. I practiced birth control using coitus interruptus. It might have been Mark Vocca or Mark Ross who said, "Don't be surprised if one day there's a knock on your door and some teenager, sez: 'Dad?'"

Lithuania and Bohemia

The family of grandma Ross came from Conus, Lithuania. The biggest Jewish settlement in the country. That was told to me by Stella Rosenfeld. I told Doctor Rosenfeld that my grandma's name was Muscowicz. She said, "a Jewish name."

The family of grandpa Ross came from Bohemia. Bohemia is near Prague. The country does not exist anymore. It's now part of the Czech Republic. Borders are curious. The last name was Hrachovina. Kliment Hrachovina was the great grandfather who came over in the 1880s.

Pittsburgh, PA

The beginning. My father met my mother when he was in Dental School in Pittsburgh. He went to Hiram college in Ohio and got a BS in chemistry. Mom said his grades were all C's.

I struggled with chemistry in high school and got a D and an F. Too bad there wasn't a tutor at home who could have couched me. Sarcasm intended and deliberate.

Mom at that time was a registered Nurse working at among other places in a mental hospital. She told me that all the mental patients were obsessed with either religion or sex. "But so little has changed." Intended Frank Zappa allusion. Not that it has anything to do with television...

Sometimes I like to taper off with ellipses.

Religion – the existence of God or the reality of Satan? Why is one existence and the other reality?

Sex -- is my identity straight, gay, bi, trans or other? Whoever knows for certain? I know for some; it is absolutely certain. I know others including myself that it a grey area. Uncle Barry was gay. Not one – except Mom and Tanja -- accepted that he was gay. On the farm. Mom did. But she was in Cleveland. Barry would have been better off in Ohio. He chose to stay in the area around Pittsburgh.

He would have been better off in NYC or Frisco. But he may have also died sooner.

Neurologists told me a vaccine is nearly impossible for HIV because the virus mutates. That was in the 1980s. And here in 2020, we still don't have a vaccine for COVID-19. Yes they can render HIV symptoms untraceable. Meaning, someone who gets HIV from you can't trace it back to you. That's great. Like a Fuck bot who can impregnate every woman he meets but won't get linked due to a paternity test.

It's October 30, 2020, and the current president claims we're close to a vaccine for COVID-19. Corona virus mutates, just like HIV. We are so far from close.

I'm now on revision number 4 or 5 and it's January 18, 2021.

Mark wants me to never publish. I can't think of a person I praise higher.

I'll tell Lynn, ask Lynn to publish this when I'm dead. I'll honor Mark that way.

Audra Jean Lindley

My mother, Audrey Lindley, grew up on a farm in Eighty-Four, Pennsylvania. Eighty-Four was outside of Washington which was outside of Pittsburgh. Some called her Audrey and some called her Audra. She was born November 4, 1937. Uncle Ron, her older brother told me that she was the rebel. She listened to Elvis Presley and wall-papered her room. None of the other kids did that. She wanted to improve everything about her life. She saw her destiny beyond the farm.

No one could have predicted it but… the farm would have been a better or a safer place than what her life became with this dentist. And her children.

The dentist may have paid for three of her children's college educations, bought many Christmas presents and paid for private Catholic school. But the cost. What was the trade-off for safety? Security? Shelter from abuse?

My college at Cleveland State University was paid for with grants because I was an Army veteran.

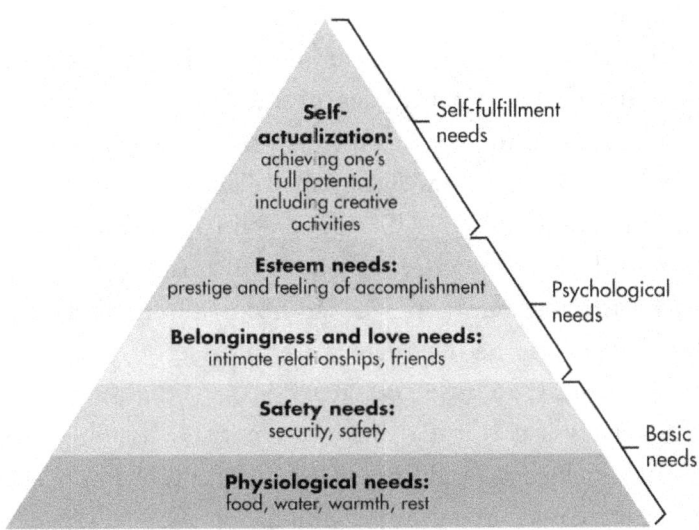

Maslow's Hierarchy of Needs. We – mom and the kids -- had the purple level Number One. The "rest" [2-5] are questionable. How many nights where we woken after the witching hour because the drunken bunny wanted company while he consumed Manner's big boy burgers or some other fast food fattening meal. That's not a question. It was a regular routine.

All of the other levels are cast aside. We had friends. My friends were sliced away by changing schools when it wasn't necessary.

I wonder if I had stayed at Ridge, where would I be now?

But the choices made brought me to Lynn and so I have no regrets. My path here took many turns astray. But the fact is that it got me here.

This isn't a teaching book or a text book. But every human being needs to understand Maslow. I learned it in high school psychology… then it was forgotten. Until I went to Cleveland State University and took social work classes. They also had Erickson. But Maslow was the one I identified with.

My siblings and I -- we were the children of a successful dentist. He had a great reputation in Mentor for being a painless dentist and for being really friggin' cheap.

At some point, Mom took over the books and quickly ascertained that the rates Bunny established in 1962 were the same in the mid- to late 1970s. Good dentist; bad businessman. He would have been better off joining an existing practice.

And their accountant? He had been ripping them off for years. Every time he did their tax return. Jerry. They should have sued him. Too little, too late.

Bunny was a horrible business man. A horrible father. Cyndy, Chucklehead and Princess Cathy will probably disagree. So, let's leave it as my humble opinion.

The Lindley Family

Mom said that Jacquie traced her (our) heritage back to the daughters of the American revolution. I asked for a copy. I never got it.

The Ross Family

In the Ross family, I was the second child, born September 14, 1961. Chris Overbaugh was the first. I'm ashamed to admit, I do not have his birthday. Sorry, Chris.

My father was the only boy with Veronica (aka Baby), Temple, Charlotte (aka Chicky), and Catherine (aka Kitty), his four sisters. Only Temple had no nick name. The story goes (so much of this is second hand, hearsay), that grandma Ross loved this Jewish temple so much, she named her daughter "Temple."

Grandma Ross was the one who came from Conus, Lithuania.

Grandpa Ross was from Bohemia. The original last name was Hrachovina.

Grandma Ross was from Conus, Lithuania. The original last name was Muscowicz.

Professor Stella Rosenfeld at CSU told me that Conus was the largest Jewish settlement in Lithuania. She herself was Lithuanian and spoke the language (and German) fluently.

Hrachovina and Muscowicz to then Ross

There are stories that build around truth, but no one ever knows if the stories and the truth are the same.

Grandpa Ross was supposedly born Edward James Hrachovina. He was too young for World War I and too old for World War II. But he served six years Army and six years Marines. Which came first and which came second, no one knew. But the story goes that in between, he got into a horrible fight with his father and re-enlisted and changed his name to James Edward Roche (based on Hrachovina).

One of my aunts, most likely Temple told me that they teased him in the military calling him Roach and Cockroach, which led to changing the name from Roche to Ross.

Temple gave me documents, photocopies of records when she learned I was trying to piece together family history.

At some point, Francis Muscowicz married a Japanese man whose last name was Mitsui. Ink had been spilled on the certificate of married to hide details.

The marriage was short lived. Somehow the divorce changed her last name to Muscus.

James met Francis and were wed.

The Bunny was born in November 1933 somewhere close to Kankakee, Illinois. McKees Rock? But that's PA?

At some point from there, they moved to Cleveland, Ohio and settled in an eastside suburb called Eastlake where they bought a home on Woodstock road.

Sometime around 1951 or 1952, Bunny went to Hiram College in Ohio. I remember coming across some paperwork that gave him an exemption from the draft so he did not have to go to Korea. Vietnam draftees were not so lucky. He graduated with a degree in Chemistry and then applied for dental school at Penn State.

Cyndy would also attend Hiram college in 1981. She stayed one year and then transferred to Northwestern in Illinois. I feared that Cyndy was condemning herself to a lifetime of servitude of pleasing the Bunny.

The family of the Bunny lived in Eastlake. The only boy got the most privileges including drinking the liquor from the top shelf. That would be the top shelf of the bedroom closet. His parents' bedroom. Where the booze was stored. Mom told me about that.

None of us were ever witness to it until years later in Mentor. The Bunny kept his liquor bottles above the stove in the cabinet there. There was usually at least one bottle of Canadian Mist.

Eastlake -- where grandma and grandpa lived was a suburb along lake erie. I would say, half-way between Mentor and the border of Cleveland on East 185th Street.

Grandpa and Grandma Ross

My grandparents loved to spend time with me. Eastlake was a peaceful suburb of Cleveland. I rode my tricycle up and down Woodstock road. I loved that at the end, where it intersected with other roads, there lived Mrs. Carpenter and her dog. Was its name "Rags"? Something like that. I think that was right.

Mrs. Carpenter had lots of Tchotchke. Knickknacks that were on the shelves. I studied them – why would someone want them?

1969 – The Summer of Love – the concert at Woodstock. Temple told me that the house in Saugerties where she and Tom lived was the same house that Janis Joplin stayed in when she performed at Woodstock. I was too young in 1969 to know anything about the rock concert.

But it made me curious why suddenly the street sign at the corner of Lakeshore Blvd and Woodstock road, the Woodstock road sign was now painted with flowers. They were colorful on a white background. Most street signs were green background with white lettering.

It would be years before I made the connection.

School in Mentor

At an age before school, from my perspective, the Ross family was a normal family. Normal meant, went to kindergarten. We ate, took naps (or pretended to), played, read books, watched television. Flew kites. Then came kindergarten. As far as I knew, all was still normal. However, Cathy was born in 1967. I was six years old in first grade. Mom told me later that the bunny would get drunk and rape Mom. Given that her last two children were born in 1964 and 1967, each rape must have occurred prior to 1966.

I would be inclined to believe that the rapes stopped after 1967. Not because he stopped drinking. Because there were no more children born after 1967.

This must be said. Bunny is dead. Died in 2006. So this is not revenge. Bunny died with his sins. And no accountability. But he wanted it that way. He never admitted to any act of violence or torture. In his mind, it never happened.

How pleasant to float through life like that.

Paul Simon has a song. "So I'll continue to continue that life will never end and flowers never bend with the rainfall…"

<u>Mom, I forgive you.</u>

My mom early on was a rebel, she listened to rock and roll from Elvis when the farm was all about Hank Williams and Patsy Cline.

The rebel was broken into subservience. Eventually conformed to being a docile zombie abiding by his rules.

To her credit, she endured and survived torture, beatings, belittlement, rape, condescension, humiliation, broken bones, broken cartilage, a barrage of insults and disrespect, -- bottom line – it was treatment that no human being should ever be subjected to. And it lasted for years. Not four years. It lasted many years.

What mom endured; it was never treated as sadistically. In comparison. She was treated far worse. That needs to be said here early. Because eventually the Shell of Mom became a puppet. Mindless. "You're the son of a dentist! Do you understand? You don't dress that way!" Brain washed. Stockholm syndrome.

She eventually broke that pattern. But the rebel?... the Bunny did his damage for so many years. Mom was the rebel. The rebel was in shards of broken glass.

In a utopia, I'd take a time machine back to meet the rebel. I'd tell the rebel, you will meet a brutish ogre disguised as Gregory Peck. Run away. His semen and bank account are not worth the years of abuse inflicted upon you and your children.

<u>Dale R. Rice Elementary School</u>

Then came Rice Elementary, and things started to change.

Normalcy? That didn't last long. I was shielded or sheltered from the truth. Perhaps (most likely) mom tried to hide the truth from the kids. But that barrier would crumble and dissipate. East of Eden would haunt me for most of my life.

Berliners called it "Jenseits von Eden." A better description. But it basically means "beyond Eden." Or as Milton called it, "Paradise lost."

Grandparents' home for Sunday dinner

Growing up, we spent a lot of time in my Grandparents' home for Sunday dinner which typically was roast pork and dumplings, a bohemian recipe my Lithuanian -grandmother learned from her mother-in-law (Bohemian). Just like she taught my mother.

But time and again, my father would say something off color and grandma would say (forgive the spelling... I've never seen it written)... "Tu Rupuze." I asked what does it mean. They told me, "You ugly toad." It sounded like "Too **Rupe** Rah Zhah."

Jump ahead to 1990. My German professor at Cleveland State University was Stella Rosenfeld. We talked about how grandma Ross was Frances Muscowicz from Conus, Lithuania. She said that's the largest Jewish community in Lithuania. They left in the late 1880s so they never had to deal with the Nazis. I asked if she could explain an idiom and she said sure. I told her my grandmother used to say to my father, "Tu Rupuze." Google translate has accent marks over the "U," "Z," and "E." Two dots, a V and one dot. In that order. She pronounced it "too rupe rah zah."

Professor Rosenfeld slapped both palms across her mouth and looked left and right. She said, "Never ever say that." I said, "What? What? My grandmother said it meant 'you ugly toad.'" She said "yes, that's the literal translation. But think about the worst, most profane expletive in the English Language... now multiply that by 100."

Grandma called my dad a cocksucking motherfucker. Times one hundred.

PART ONE: MENTOR, OHIO

This is a story told in snap shots. Don't follow the bouncing ball – it goes forward and backwards.

1960s

I remember our black and white television – Saturday morning cartoons… cartoons with Astroboy and Popeye. Bugs bunny and Daffy Duck and Porky Pig from the 1940s. A lot of WWII era cartoons that featured stereotypes of Nazis and Japs. All were black and white. Racist as hell.

The TV had rabbit ears. Those were control antennas -- it also had control knobs for vertical, horizontal, hue and tint. Early days we fidgeted with all six to get a good picture.

Eventually, all the cartoons were in color. In the living room, we had a Magnavox. It was huge. The TV repair man was always fixing it.

As the years progressed, we had more than just the Bugs Bunny/Road Runner Hour. The Banana Splits came on the scene with Live action and animation. The Arabian Knights. Sean Kelly used to do, "SIIIIIIIIIIZZZZZZZZEEE of an Amazing Yak!

Mentor was an east side suburb of Cleveland. Lake County. Along Erie's shore. I've heard all the jokes. Mistake by the lake. Armpit of Ohio. I loved Cleveland. Let me clarify. I loved the Cleveland Zoo. I loved the Cleveland Museum of Art. I loved the Cleveland Museum of Natural History. Yes, the Cuyahoga river caught on fire from the pollutants. More than once. Shame on Cleveland. Shame on the polluters. Shame on the overseers. Cleveland was so much more.

Yet it should have supported the historic society better when they wanted to name a landmark, a historic site. The stadium for the Cleveland Browns. The historic society wanted it named a historic landmark. Cleveland Politicians said no, tear it down and build a new one. And someone's pockets got filled with kickback money.

Mentor, Ohio

Mentor was like "Mayberry, R. F. D." No people of color allowed – but that was wrong. Mentor allowed Hawaiian families (Jeff Ficke) and Native American (Teri Pealer), but no Black or Latino.

Emmett Till

Mentor would not be kind to Emmett Till. If you don't know the name and have to look it up, then by all means do so. Every human should know the name, Emmett Till. And know his story and the tragic torture committed by white racist sadistic psychos in Mississippi. Psychos who got away with kidnap, mutilation, torture and murder of a 14-year-old child. IN AMERICA.

Emmett allegedly whistled at a white woman. He was from Chicago visiting his family in Mississippi. Some said he also had a white girlfriend in Chicago.

The white racists in Mississippi, they captured Emmett Till. A 14-year-old child. They mutilated him.

His mom refused to do a closed coffin. She wanted the world to see what they did to Emmett.

I want the world to see what they did to Emmett.

Remember Emmett Till.

In Mentor, we went to the roller rink, now called Joy's Roller Rink on Andrews Road. I took Karate lessons at Mentor Beach Park Pavilion. We had a dairy queen on Lake shore Blvd Between Dawson and Brooks. And a Putt Putt golf behind Dairy Queen.

In Mentor, we didn't have a ghetto, a slum, homeless, junkies, mafia, or serial killers. "Well Maybe…" Angie Baby.

Mentor was like living in Tom and Huck's world. How do you explain, you enter the woods at Eckley's corner and come out at Granger's pond? It was a bike path through the woods. Now it's all developments. I could not navigate there now.

Mentor had this program that they called "Helping Hands." Some very smart person was concerned about bullies. Whoever started this program, God bless you. What she (or he) did was photo copy a hand. The photocopy showed white all around the hand and black where the hand was pressed against the glass. Copies were distributed to parents. Anyone who wanted one. The deal was if a child was being harassed or pursued by a bully, if the child saw the zerox of the hand, that meant the door was open. Walk in and the family would protect you. You did not have to knock. Just walk in and you were safe.

My dealings with bullies were at the schools. I never got the benefit. But I'm glad that others could. Some walks home were perilous. But I was white. So I only had to be concerned about the bullies who targeted white kids. I would not want to be black kid in Mentor in the 1960s or 1970s. We had none.

I walked along Lake Shore Blvd. The side streets were questionable. But not Lake Shore.

The YMCA

In the 1960s mom took me to the local YMCA for swimming lessons. I think it was on Mentor avenue (aka Route 20) west of 306.

I think they kept the chlorine levels high for kids who peed in the pool.

There was a day when we had to count fingers under water. I couldn't see. The chlorine burned. My vision was blurry.

The YMCA also had an Automat. The only place I ever knew to have an automat.

The world's first automat was named Quisisana, which opened in Berlin, Germany in 1895.

The YMCA had one. You could get sandwiches – egg salad, chicken salad, ham and cheese, and ice cream. Ice cream sandwiches and drumsticks.

Tim Deegan

Tim Deegan and I were best friends. Until he left for Kansas. His dad was a chemist. Tim had an older sister Jacquie and a younger sister Annie.

Tim was proud of his Irish heritage. He told me his name said it all; he was "Timothy Patrick Deegan." He might as well have said, "Boris Yeltsin" if he was Russian. I didn't know Irish names. I knew Saint Patrick's Day, so I suppose "Patrick" was recognized. My family did not celebrate ethnic heritage. What heritage did we celebrate? Nothing.

Tim's Dad was a chemist. All I knew about his mom was that she was older. Tim had two sisters. Jacquie who was older and Annie who was younger.

Tim and I would ride our bikes to Granger's Pond and sit there on a dirt mound listening to CKLW from the motor city,

Windsor and Detroit. They played the best rock and roll. It was AM. On the AM radio dial, it was eight point zero… they called it the Big Eight.

If we swam, we went home with wet clothes and dirty white t-shirts. Usually dry by the time we reached Mentor. It was at least a thirty-minute bike ride.

The record store on 615 had hand-outs of the Big 8's top 40 songs. 4th grade was in 1970 to 1971.

One of our favorites was "You could have been a lady" by April Wine. They were a Canadian band. Windsor?

At one point, Tim told me his all-time favorite rock song was "Layla" by Derek and the Dominoes.

Jacquie probably had the 45.

Tim and I each had Genesis, "Nursery Crimes" and something like "Best Rock of the 1970s." A four album set.

My friend Matt Zolnay reminded me that we also listened to WIXY 1260. He said he heard Yellow Submarine the first time it aired in Ohio on that station. As soon as he mentioned it, I remembered it.

Mark Vocca told me about the WHK Auditorium where he saw the show when Brian Eno was in the audience to the see DEVO. Johnny Dromette pulled the Pagans from the roster. He wanted Brian to see the Kent State students.

Matt and I met in 1997 when I moved to Ohio City. We became best buds and have remained hermanos ever since.

Tim Deegan's dad gave him this kit for his birthday. It was to make paperweights. We had a pyramid and a cube. In the first one, we placed a nickel. Thomas Jefferson's profile.

In the second, we placed a live grasshopper. That was in the pyramid. The grasshopper struggled against being submerged. We killed it.

I don't think we had a concept of death back then.

Did I realize the insect died? I don't know.

1973

I had a little box on my window sill to save for a big purchase. And it was for the Beatles, 1962-1966. It was a double album of their best songs of that time span. I saved my lawn mowing money to buy it. It came out in 1973.

As far as I was concerned, 1973 was the best year for music. I just didn't know it yet. I was 12 years old in the seventh grade. I would discover them in a few years. That was the year of: David Bowie, "Aladdin Sane;" Mott the Hoople, "Mott;" Roxy Music, "Country Life;" Iggy and the Stooges, "Raw Power;" New York Dolls, Debut album, Alice Cooper, "Billion Dollar Babies." Lou Reed, "Berlin;" Frank Zappa, "Over-nite Sensation." Elton John, "Good-bye yellow brick road." Pink Floyd, "Dark side of the moon." Beatles, "1967-1970." Chicago VI. And the Rolling Stones, "Goats Head Soup."

And somewhere in there was the K-tel single, "Hocus Pocus," by the Dutch band Focus. Who knew yodeling would be so popular? I would discover those albums after 1973. But they would stay with me forever.

I will reference and mention music often. In the Bunny years, it was my escape. My mind could shut off the torture if I filled my senses with music.

In elementary school I had a radio with an ear-phone. I listened to CKLW on AM radio and loved Motown and Beatles. Those two were the prime goals of 45s at garage sales. And Marvel Comic books.

As the years progressed, the music parents hated was my focus. I sought it because they hated it. Ironically, I loved it. Not because they hated it. Because it was good. David Bowie, Alice Cooper. They were the start. And I sang my heart out. Memorizing the lyrics and matching every syllable.

Ridge Junior High and Art Class

At Ridge Junior High, Mrs. Gooding, the art teacher told us to bring in music to play while we created art. I brought in the Beatles, 1962 to 1966. She played it (from me) and the album "Tapestry" by Carol King (her album). I heard her Tapestry so many times, I fell in love with it and had to buy it. And to this day, I have it on CD. She also played two 45s. "Free Ride" by the Edgar Winter Group and Bachman-Turner Overdrive "(Would you) let it ride."

Carmen Glenn

8th Grade art class. Miss Gooding taught this method of art. You pick a starting point and do not lift your finger. Without ever looking at the paper. You capture every detail. In one long line. Carmen Glenn posed as the model. My portrait was framed and on display at Ridge Junior High. Carmen's parents loved it. They asked me for the art. I gave it to them gladly.

Mentor

Mentor was like Keats' Ode to a Grecian urn. We had a farmers' market fruit and vegetable stand about 200 yards from our house. Most of the terrain was farm land or undeveloped wood land. The homes on the side streets that led to the shores of lake erie were small. It was like they were summer cottages for the wealthy Cleveland executives.

The "Woods"

We lived on the north end of a "block" of Lakeshore boulevard, Tall Oaks, Magnolia, and Cole Street. South of Cole there were the woods. They were acres of undeveloped woods that were our playground. They're gone now.

"The Woods" spanned south of Cole drive to Jeremy Avenue on its southern border. Route 306 aka Reynolds was its western border and Clearair Drive where Tim Deegan lived was its eastern border.

About 200 yards south behind the Bachovsky house was a frame of what must have been a Cessna that crashed into our woods. Or a helicopter I could never be sure. There were no wings nor helicopter blades.

The nearby fruit and vegetable stand was owned by a farmer. Young boys who ventured into his fields were trespassing and the punishment was a salt gun. Salt pellet shot into the skin burns. The salt-gun shot penetrates below the epidermis. You can't scratch it out. You have to wait until it dissolves.

Our Neighborhood

Growing up in Mentor, some things were normal. Karen and Kim Parker lived on Magnolia. Their bassett hound was named "Corey." They were our baby-sitters. The Dumanski family were on Tall Oaks – with Glenn, Brad, Joellen, and Paul. Joellen baby sat. I was probably five when I started to roam up to their home and knock on the door. Mr. Dumanski would always greet me saying, "Well look who it is… Clem Kadiddlehopper" (Red Skelton's character on his show).

BTW – Karen Parker was every teenage boys' dream girl crush.

She was the baby sitter and taught me "the hearse song" by Harley Poe. I was five or six and loved it. Google is amazing. She didn't teach me all the verses. Most of them, but I read others in my late 50s due to Google.

Change of subject: I would watch in wonder as Glenn Dumanski and his friends traded baseball cards and called out stats like computers. How did they record all that data in their minds?

I had no interest in cars or sports. I loved movies, music, comics, art, literature, theatre, and history. In my twenties, thirties and even forties, my lack of interest in cars and sports often prompted the question: "Are you gay?"

But I knew comics like an encyclopedia.

Also, I loved books. In the beginning, I loved ghost stories. Grandpa Ross and Grandma Ross had a home full of books. Art books, history, literature. I'm sure my passion for books came from them.

I got my library card in second grade. Salida Library across from Dale R. Rice Elementary. I would carry home books with arms weighted down. I didn't know it then, but I was like Roald Dahl's Matilda. Just no magical powers. And I couldn't do math in my head thanks to Bunny. Still can't to this day. Early on he punished me with multiplication tables. All he accomplished was a mental block. I can do math on paper or with excel. But not in my head. Whack came the palm. Like the school marm in *The Wall*, "Wroooong... do it again." My head still hurts.

Our house was converted to make room for the dental office and practice. There was a waiting room, reception, the patient room where work was performed. An office in the back and a lab in between. The narrow hall to the kitchen/dining room had all his dental record files. The entire front yard was a parking lot.

Eventually my job would be: mow the lawn, trim the hedge that spanned the parking lot flanks (front, left and right), and scrub the dental office floor on hands and knees with a bucket and a wash rag. For that, I got an allowance that I would spent on Comic books until music became the priority.

As a young boy, if I had to go to the dental office at night, I pretended I was a werewolf so the other monsters wouldn't touch me. I had forgotten that. Memories are like bubbles under water. One never knows what triggers will allow them to float back to the surface and be revealed.

Bunny was a monster. To protect myself, I became a werewolf so the other monsters would not touch me.

I admit. I am damaged. Who isn't?

I once had a friend who taught me not to use the passive voice. "It was ambiguous and lacked commitment." Like writing I am damaged... it fails to state who the cause of the damage was. However, within the context of this book, it is most likely pretty damn clear who the cause was. I still agree with the wise advice as a rule of thumb.

The Elk's Lodge

Back then, we were frequent visitors of the Elk's Lodge on Route 20. That's where the Bunny would get inebriated then drive home along route 306 barely missing the ditch.

Where were the Mentor Police? Elk's bartenders: what was the standard of "you've had too much... Let me call you a cab." Cops turned a blind eye on 306 and the bartender did not stop pouring.

But the Elk's was also the place of the Christmas Show. Members' kids would dance on stage doing pantomime to songs just like the parents did on 50/50 nights.

Digression: if you lived in Mentor, Reynolds road was route 306, Andrews road was route 615 and Mentor avenue was route 20. Everyone knew the names of Reynolds, Andrews and Mentor. But nobody called them that. It was always 306, 615 and 20. Lakeshore Blvd would have completed the square, but no one called Lakeshore anything but Lakeshore. Perhaps because Munson connected Lakeshore to 615.

Newberry's and the record store

One time, mom went to Newberry's at the Great Lakes Mall and found a 45 rpm of Alice Cooper doing "Hello Hurray / (I wanna be) Elected." She bought it for Cyndy or Cathy to perform pantomime at the Elk's Christmas party. She thought Alice was a girl. When she played the 45, she did not like it. She said, "All it was was screaming."

She gave me the 45. I ended up trading it to Tim Deegan for "Come on people now shine on your brothers everybody get together try to love one another right now." It was Jacquie's 45. She signed it.

Early on, I suppose my musical taste was stuck. Young Bloods were hippies. I dug Melanie Safka who was a flower child ("Ring the Living Bell") and Donovan Leitsch who was… Donovan. But "Atlantis" was one cool song.

Many years later, for music, Newberry's would become my favorite record store for cut outs like Roxy Music – Viva! -- but moreso for bootlegs. There I found David Bowie's "Dollars in Drag – the 1980 Floor Show." "Soft in the Middle" by Bowie. And "Resurrection on 84th Street" from the 1976 tour. "Iggy and Ziggy," the tour in 1977 of Iggy Pop with Bowie on keyboards.

But I'm getting ahead of myself.

Eastlake and Grandpa Ross

Grandpa Ross had a reel-to-reel and a book of 10,000 jokes. We would sit and record our voices reading the jokes. I always got the part of the punch line.

Grandma Ross taught me the only way to eat cottage cheese was loaded with pepper. I shake it on my cottage cheese to this day.

They had a huge library of books. As a child, I loved the art books and the New Yorker magazine cartoon collections.

Most of the art books were in the living room on a book shelf next to the sofa. The basement was filled with rows and rows of bookshelves, and so was the bedroom as you came up the stairs and turned left then right. The books smelled like time and dust. My grand parents taught me to love books.

Bunny never read. Mom never read.

So why did I read? Grandpa and grandma Ross. They read.

In the dining room, there was my grandfather's bookcase, behind the chair where he sat for dinner. I inherited that bookcase. I always loved books.

I combed garage sales. I found and read Victor Hugo's "the Hunchback of Notre Dame" when I was nine or ten years old. And John Howard Griffith's "Black Like me" in the fifth grade.

One day in the late 1990s, I was in an art and framing store in downtown Cleveland and found a framed piece of art. It was called "the Bookworm" by Carl Spitzweg from 1850. I bought it and hung it in my apartment next to my grandfather's bookcase.

Many years later, I received some photos from my mom who developed slides into photos. At first I didn't notice. There was a photo of my grandfather sitting in his chair at the dining room table. Behind him, the bookshelf.

One day I looked closer. Over his left shoulder was something hanging on the wall. It was "the Bookworm" by Carl Spitzweg.

Road Trip to Wallkill

1967. My grandparents (paternal side) drove to Wallkill, NY to visit Temple Shields and Kitty Mooney. They took me along for the ride. I loved my grandparents.

Charlotte (aka "Chicky") and Lee Haywood lived on a side street off Lost Nation Road in Willoughby. They eventually moved to Wallkill – while I was in the Army? Not sure.

On the road trip we went to Niagara Falls. I-90 takes you right to it. Words do not describe them. You have to see them in person. Just saying "its water tumbling over a cliff..." -- that does not do it justice.

We visited Temple Shields and then I stayed with Kitty and Bob Mooney. Bob had a younger brother who was visiting. He had a race car track/game. We played it for a while and then I suggested, let's make our own track. He asked can we do that? I said I don't know. Let's try. It'll be fun. And we did.

The day we drove to NYC for my flight back to Cleveland, we went to a head shop in Manhattan. I remember the hookahs and black light posters and jewelry... a lot of turquoise.

On the flight heading back to Cleveland, when I was alone on the plane without Kitty or Bob, I cried. The stewardess asked me if I was afraid of flying. I lied. I told her yes. The truth was I was missing Aunt Kitty and Uncle Bob. I would have rather stayed with them. Mentor meant more Bunny.

Kitty and Bob had a farm with berries and spearmint.

Uncle Bob had his mom in a hospital bed with all kinds of tubes connecting her to machines. When I first saw her I was afraid because I didn't understand. But they told me she has a condition and that she would be okay.

I didn't know what "okay" meant.

During that visit, Aunt Kitty and Uncle Bob showed me the stars. We looked at the Big Dipper and Orion and they showed me his belt. I think that may have been the moment when if I cared about something; when I learned it, I did not forget it.

Years later when I lived in the Ohio City and Tremont neighborhoods, any time I had a visitor from out of town, out of state, I made the road trip with them to Niagara Falls. And we had to do the Canadian side. The American side said, "We couldn't care less." The Canadian side said, "Holy fuck -- would you look at this?"

The I-90 corridor was amazing with the maple trees in the autumn. They looked like they were ablaze with red and orange flames. I would imagine that fire fighters have a different appreciation. But I could care less. They were beautiful.

Ashtabula, Ohio... That was camping. With the Overbaughs. Veronica and Ken were the aunt and uncle. My father's sister Veronica aka "Baby." She married Ken Overbaugh. The kids were Chris and Kenny, Becky and Noel. Chris was the first born of the Ross grandchildren.

Kenny and I were the same age and went to the same Kindergarden. But I was am and he was pm.

During the time when Kenny and I were in Kindergarten, the Overbaugh family lived in this big house on Lakeshore Boulevard. Mentor or Willoughby? I forget. I just recall that it had stairwells hidden like a haunted house. And all the kids would play. Chris, Kenny, Becky and Noel. With my brother and sisters and me.

At night, Uncle Ken would smoke a pipe with cherry tobacco. I loved the smell. They had a home that was peaceful. I realized their normal was what normal was supposed to feel like.

Veronica was nicknamed "Baby." I never knew why. After the Army I stopped calling her Aunt Baby and just called her Veronica. It seemed more respectful.

In Ashtabula, my male cousins, Chris and Kenny and I would find a tree and sleep there underneath it.

Sometimes we would throw rocks at the bats that came out at night. Not to hit them. I loved bats. It was to watch them soar down and then realize it wasn't a mosquito and soar back up.

Before bedtime, the adults built a camp fire and Aunt Veronica would play guitar and we sang songs. She had sheet music with the lyrics. I remember standing over her shoulder so I could read the lyrics and sing along. Bob Dylan's "Blowing in the Wind." Peter, Paul and Mary's "Puff the Magic Dragon." I wish I could recall the other songs. Little green apples and Clear waters? They were songs from the 1960s. I loved to sing. So I learned the songs and sang them.

The meaning – it escaped me. Until I was older. Dylan was prophetic.

Chris and Kenny and I took BB guns and shot bullfrogs. In Mentor, I was used to toads which were tiny. Bull frogs were huge. My uncle Ken would skin them and fry the legs with butter. They were delicious.

Never lie to kids. They always remember promises. Bunny promised a motorized mini-bike and a BB gun.

My Overbaugh cousins gave me a broken mini-bike. Bunny promised to fix it. Bunny was not a mechanic. Uncle Lee was a mechanic. He would have known how and would have fixed it.

The mini-bike rusted and rotted in the outdoor shed.

After all I'd been witness to, why did I believe a promise from the Bunny? Children become jaded after once bitten twice shy.

The Gibbon with the Hatchet

Back in those days, I was having nightmares about a gibbon with a hatchet who wanted to kill me. Was it due to Edgar Allen Poe? I have no idea. Poe never wrote about a gibbon with a hatchet.

It may have been brought on by Alice and Herb Malone… not them, but their nephew. We – the children of Bunny and Audrey – called them Aunt Alice and Uncle Herb, even though they weren't blood relatives.

This one asshole nephew of Alice and Herb hated me because I used the terms of endearment, aunt and uncle. He should have been flattered that I cared that much. I don't know. I never did know and I never found out. But I took his threats seriously. He wanted to kill me and perhaps in my dreams he was the gibbon. He was an unevolved primate so that would make sense.

My father had a sister named Charlotte who was nicknamed "Chicky." She married Lee Haywood. Lee was a mechanical genius. But the bunny who was a dentist had to insult him every chance he got.

Bunny used to say," you'll grow up a gas pump jockey just like your uncle Lee." And I thought, you've never taught me mechanics? I didn't even know how to change a flat tire until Steve Koleszar showed me.. Learning from Lee would be a blessing. Fifty years later, I'm still paying to have basic mechanical things done for my car that Lee could have taught me.

Lee and Charlotte let me stay in their home when Tom Beechum died [Tom was Temple's second husband after Jim Shiels]. We held hands and prayed each night before dinner. That was not a practice in our household. We never prayed at all.

What would we have prayed for? Intervention from God? Perhaps for the Archangel Michael to come down and slay an evil worse than Lucifer. The metaphor "wildest dreams" comes to mind.

Bunny used to load his own buck shot rounds. Please allow me to qualify that – he had this device that loaded black powder and ball bearings – like little bee-bees into a sleeve with a copper bottom. He never told any of us what it was called or what it was used for.

When the master bedroom was upstairs and he had his gun room in the storage closet next to the bedroom. It was a big closet. It held all the Christmas decorations. It had shelves. A table with his gun reloading device.

One day I found his porn stash. No idea how old/young I was. His porn stash wasn't playboys with nekkid women with pubic bushes that resembled afros on Angela Davis. These were Swedish erotica with penetration photos. I hid them in the Woods. He never asked where they went and I never told.

I used to think one day, he'll teach me about guns and rifles and ammo. I was so naïve. I still am. That's the one trait of "innocence" that I wish I could scrape off of my hide.

The Bible says that the sins of the father run unto the son for seven generations. The seventh son breaks the mold. I doubt my father was ever naïve. I did not inherit that trait from him. I can say that I never abused my wife. I never abused children.

Perhaps I used to think that my father would teach me things he knew that were important to him. Here is my naivete... a dentist was a doctor. He went to college. Medical school. He had to be smart. Had a knowledge base that would be impressive.

Someone taught him to degrade and humiliate and dehumanize. If he himself were subjected to it, "one would think" he would hate it and never want someone else to go through what he went through. It was just the opposite. The chip on his shoulder said he had to do it better.

At Tom Beechum's funeral, there was a guy. I met him at the bar we went to. He was jewish and a writer. He praised the Bunny for his ability to express emotion. I told him, "You've met Doctor Jekyll. You haven't met Mister Hyde."

He said, I understand. Then he said, I never knew my own father until I wrote a book about him. Perhaps you should do the same. He was right. The process of writing this book has taught me more about the Bunny than I ever knew.

The truth is he had no interest in what his children liked – we liked and were interested in art, music, theater, history, and film – me, personally I also liked books. I loved to read but I don't recall the others ever reading.

The Bunny had no interest in sharing interests other than his own with anyone. Mom wanted a garden. We had one eventually in Concord.

I suppose he tried to teach us fishing. Boring. That lasted perhaps from age five to eight. If that. Bait a hook with a worm that you'd kill with a harpoon. The sinker would drag it to its death. The fish would bite and the bobber would sink. Yank the pole and the fish was caught.

Fish live on air from gills. We "cleaned" fish -- fully alive and suffocating. The lower jaw would gasp for breath that did not come. That would be like me slicing from the scalp to the breast-bone, then under the ribs, then driving the blade through the anus. That's how you clean a blue gill or trout.

The Bunny taught by his example. It was okay to be arrogant and always overly selfrighteous -- I learned that definition from Neil Allen. Bunny made it okay to be self-absorbed by his example. His priorities were the only priorities. It was okay to intoxicate. It was okay to condescend. Bad habits I wish I could unlearn.

It is with great difficulty that I struggle to unlearn – I'm not always successful.

The Bunny went to Hiram college, and then to Penn State for medical school. The Bunny had four sisters. Veronica, Temple, Charlotte and Catherine. I think Catherine went to college. Veronica and Charlotte did not. Why?

What Audrey tried...

Mom was the Rebel. That's what Uncle Ronnie said. I believed that when she told me she had 45s of Elvis.

Mom signed me up for art classes at Willoughby Fine Arts. She signed Cyndy and me up for Drama and we did the Marvelous land of Oz. She allowed me to buy a black G.I. Joe.

When I went to convenient across the street and bought what she asked for, I also bought a rubber bendable skeleton for close to five dollars. I used to buy a candy bar for less than a dollar and she forgave that. The five-dollar toy was too much. She said I would not get the plastic dinosaurs that I wanted. Why? Because I lied. I did not tell the truth about buying the five-dollar toy skeleton.

Mom was my hero when she said, "I want a divorce" when the bunny broke her nose. That day when Veronica came over. She recanted. I suppose I forgave her because she was trying to make it work. It would never work with the Bunny. He was a tyrant who would always put himself first.

Mom pissed me off one day at Lake Catholic. She picked us up one day. I asked her about throwing out my favorite jeans. She defended it saying, "You are the son of a dentist."

Fuck that noise. That's all I needed to hear. I opened the car door to jump out.

A dentist? Yes, he was a dentist. Why should I curb my behavior because I was the son of a… What was he in reality? Sure. He was a dentist. He was also a wife beater, a wife rapist, a child abuser, a family pet killer, a drunk, a racist, a misogynist, a bully, a cheat,… is that enough?

Bottom line is I forgave mom. I was angry that day. She revealed her superficiality. She revealed her delusion of how the world of Bunny was painted a palatable color. Accept the tip of the ice berg. Deny the existence of what threatened below the surface.

To me, the bunny ceased to exist as a person. I never felt hate. I felt a void. Perhaps I felt the bunny's shadow. The darkness of where he was. But the essence was gone. That was good because the essence was vile.

Friends have asked me, "do you hate your father?" I say no. He ceased to be. Ask Hamlet. Read his soliloquy. And don't wait for a celebrity to recite it in a grad school English course because she chose to share with an audience who had baited breath. Sarcasm intended.

Bunny could have been. Could have been real. He chose not to be. For him, it was better to exist in the realm of "not being."

Not being a husband, a father, simply not being.

Apology

Bunny never said, "I'm sorry." Would all have been forgiven? I don't know. Never had the chance to broach that subject.

Eighty-Four, Pennsylvania

Outside of Pittsburgh, was a town called Washington. Locals called it "Warshington." That's like redd up a room. Or put things up.

Mom was Audra on the farm. She was the rebel. That's what Uncle Ron called her. She listened to Elvis Presley records and wall papered her bedroom.

Ron Lindley was her older brother. He said she's going to leave the farm and come back successful.

Mom tells the story about "Buck-shot." He was a black man who was employed as a farm hand. The Lindley family had ten kids. But they needed to employ a farm hand? Perhaps it was charity because Buck-shot was black. Buck-shot got his nickname because he was afraid of rifles. And this was eighty years before Trayvon Martin, George Floyd and Breonna Taylor.

Mom said that Buck-shot got the idea that he was going to be fired and so he hung himself in the barn.

What was never mentioned is how he got that idea. Did an uncle taunt him with the hint? And what was Buck-shot's real name?

Grandma Lindley was skinny, bashful, full of smiles. She hugged like she was doing the twist. She was always in the kitchen.

Adjacent to the kitchen was a wash-room. There was a strainer and washboard there. And there was a wringer. I'd never seen a real wringer. Like two long cylinders that rolled in opposite directions to press and drain water out of clothing,

Gran-pap was a man with arms like beef jerky. They were leather or close to it. He rode the tractor and then spent the evening in the living room.

When the grandkids were there, he liked giving us 50 cent pieces.

2003

In 2003, I was at the farm. I visited with mom. I stayed with Ron and his new wife Joann and I told Ron of all the stories of what the Bunny did. He said we could have stayed with him. He was so distraught. Secret Shame. The family in Eighty-Four, PA never knew the truth about Mentor. They knew the sister was married to a dentist and had four children. But the terror was never revealed.

My parents called it "visiting the farm." We would make the road trip to outside Pittsburgh, outside Washington, to Eighty-Four along Sugar Run road.

On the road, Cyndy and I would sing "Black Water" by the Doobie Brothers and "Thank God I'm a Country Boy," by John Denver.

We spent the first night in the motel. That was so Bunny could inebriate. We'd watch Chilly Billy on the local Pittsburgh station. It was a Ramada inn.

The next day, we would drive to the farm house.

The farmhouse was so beautiful. The foyer had a staircase that went up to a second-floor balcony on three sides. Entrances to the bedrooms. All made of beautiful wood.

To the right was a family room. Coach, sofa and TV. To the left was a parlor with a piano. Past the family room was the kitchen with a back patio. Past the parlor was a bedroom stacked from ceiling to floor with junk. Grandma was a pack rat. A hoarder.

My cousins and I discovered a foot locker with Army uniforms. The name tag said "Lindley" so we assumed it was ours. To this day, I don't know if it was an uncle that died in Vietnam or an uncle who crashed over the cliff.

We played a game called the lost patrol. We dressed in our Uncle's fatigues from Vietnam and walked around the farm. Like soldiers.

My cousins told me that I tried to teach them how to jump off a telephone pole. Climbing up and then jumping off – hit the ground and roll.

In the 1970s, one visit, we ordered a dumpster and cleaned the bedroom – filling the dumpster. When we returned the next summer, the bedroom was as full as if we never touched it.

Mom's family was huge. Uncle Bob... he had Tanya and Robbie. Uncle Junior (Jesse): he had Britt and Brian. Britt joined the marines. Uncle Ron had a son named Barry who was medically schizophrenic. Uncle Barry died from AIDS. He was my favorite uncle. Aunt Jacquie... Lou killed her dog.

Lou needs to go. I'll do it.

I took home a field jacket from one of my uncles. It had the embroidered name tag of "LINDLEY." I wore it proudly.

I think the Bunny was a bit jealous. He waited for an excuse to throw it away.

For breakfast, I was sent to the hen house to get eggs. My family had a chicken coop that had little shelves with hay for the chickens to lay eggs. I would copy the sounds they made. I thought it would make them feel more comfortable. Like saying, hey I'm not here to steal your babies, I'm a chicken just like you. Great plan. It didn't work.

I used to say Barry was my favorite uncle and I was just like him. The others would say, "Barry is the eternal Bachelor."

My uncle Barry was gay and died from complications of the HIV virus.

My cousin Tanya was not happy with how the family treated him at the funeral.

Mom and I drove to see the farm and to see Barry when I was separated from Lise in 1994. I took my portfolio of pastel works and let Barry pick out the one he liked. He chose the little fox.

I drew that to honor the Little Prince. The secret of the fox: "It is only with the heart that one sees rightly; what is essential is invisible to the eye." That is from Antoine de Saint Exupery. I have cited that often. Recited to give credit where credit is due. I have lost track of how many copies I've purchased and given away of the Little Prince. Even to total strangers.

Junior Lindley praised the Bunny at the bar we would frequent close to Sugar Run Road. It was a honky tonk. A redneck bar that played country music on the juke box.

Junior was slobbering over his beer. Was it 1994? I don't recall.

He muttered "your father is a good man."

Junior aka uncle Jesse attempted to rape my mom when she was 13. If I had known that then, I would have choked the life out of him.

Britt and Brian. Sorry. I would kill him if I had the chance. He died a broken wretch.

Back in Mentor, next door were the Jewarts: Eddie and Brian

Eddie was my age. Brian was older. They taught me "running bases," a game that's part of baseball. They taught me flying kites in the field next to their house.

They taught me, the following song: "Dan'l Boone was a man / " was a big man / "But the bear was bigger / "So he run like a nigger / "up a tree..." Grammatically it evinced an ignorant composer.

I am ashamed to admit, that I laughed. I was ignorant and had no clue what the n-word even meant. It would be years before I would realize that the n-word meant black human being. And it was used to put them down, make them feel less that whites. How ridiculous.

This was no dilemma. Eddie Jewart was my friend. Was he a racist? We were seven or eight years old. It was the late 1960s. There were no black families living in Mentor, Ohio. Conclusion: Yes he probably was. But he didn't realize it. I tolerated it. So what was I? Probably.

Eddie's mom, Phyllis Jewart was a hoot. One day Eddie and I were listening to 45s. Phyllis came in and said, "May I play one?"

She played David Rose, "the Stripper." Then Phyllis did what I did not expect. She danced. I think perhaps I was five. Maybe seven.

But his mom doing the Oh-Lah-Lah?? I was not ready for that and got red faced.

Eddie and I watched "Shane" on Big Chuck and Houlihan and loved it. Sometimes we would sleep in sleeping bags on his back porch. In preparation we'd go to the convenient store across Lakeshore blvd and buy a bag of penny candy. They were literally one cent apiece. Hence the name. Try to find penny candy now.

The Uncle who played the Badger Game

Once upon a time, I had an uncle or maybe he was my father's uncle.

He died in the electric chair. I used to have a google print out of the exact date.

His name was Edward Muscus. Check me on that because I didn't find it on-line.

He would hide in the closet. His girlfriend would pick up a married man from the bar. She always looked for the ring. She promised him sex. But once in the apartment, he would spring from the closet and beat the guy up – hence the name the badger game. The badger hid in the closet. Once the guy – the victim – was senseless from the beating he took, they would steal everything.

Because they were married men, they would not tell the police.

One night, the inevitable happened. He punched some poor guy so hard he killed him.

My uncle was tried and convicted of killing a man. He was electrocuted in the Ohio chair in 1966 or 1967.

Angelisa Boykin

My grandmother had a sister and in the 1940s she ran away and married a black man. Today we call them African-Americans.

One of her daughters was Angelisa -- my cousin. First or second removed, I don't know. Just call her cousin. Her husband was called "L.B." I never learned what the initials represented.

Aunt Temple told me about their existence. Temple said the white Ross family scorned them. They -- not Temple -- said, "How could we accept black relatives?" Easy. You just shake hands and hug. They are family.

Angie and I wrote to one another sending letters and photos and every year a Christmas card.

Recently, Angelisa passed away. Her daughter Brenda stays in touch with me.

I was in Chicago in the summer of 1999. BP bought Amoco and I was in Chicago to train my counterparts.

The guy doing my job was ironically named David Clement. He had five direct reports. I had one. My direct report did the QDRO analysis and letters. David's direct reports did everything. That was my first experience with a delegator who took credit for other peoples' work. I would meet many delegators in future years.

One night I planned to board the train to travel to Kankakee to visit my family. The family of Angelisa.

I had to work late and I missed the train. In the hotel lobby, I had martinis and shrimp cocktail and watched the news. That train, the one I planned to take to Kankakee to visit my family – that night it derailed killing most of the passengers.

Brenda Euell is Angelisa's daughter. She and I stay in touch. She works for the IRS. One day we'll meet. I'll give her one overdue hug.

Billy and Keith

My introduction to black anybody came from television and Marvel Comic books... until years later when Mark Vocca introduced me to two guys he worked with at his record store: Billy and Keith.

Mark Vocca said that Keith used to call his brother Billy, "the nigger with freckles."

Billy and Keith treated me like any other human being.

Mark made me realize a point I missed. Mark played sports in Columbus and Cleveland. As a result, Mark was always around kids – some happened to be white and some happened to be black. To him, color didn't matter. To Mark, the priority was could you play ball and hold your own.

Marvel had the Black Panther (1966), the Falcon (Captain America's partner starting in 1969), Luke Cage (1972), and Blade (1973).

Around 1972, 1973, I started collecting Jungle Action featuring the Black Panther and Luke Cage Hero for Hire. I'd been a comic fan and collector for at least three years prior to that. About the time when I earned money from mowing lawns, was when I also started buying and reading comic books.

Back to Eddie

I have no recall of why Eddie Jewart and I fought. It was stupid at best. But Eddie and I got into a fight. He said, "Your dad is a fat slob." I said, "Your dad is a pretzel." I did not have a comeback. It was a stupid fight.

Eddie took a piece of wood and swung it like a baseball bat and broke it on my arm. I stood unmoved. He looked shocked.

Fists started swinging.

We were in the field next to his house. He ran. He went to his mom and I followed. Phyllis shouted, "What are you two boys fighting about?"

We both said, "I don't know."

This should stand as a metaphor for all fights. They are stupid.

I said fight. I did not say "Noble Cause."

<u>Rice Elementary</u>

We lived on Lakeshore Boulevard. Rice Elementary was also on lake shore boulevard. We walked to school. No, it wasn't "uphill both ways in the snow." I think perhaps mom drove when it rained. I don't recall. But walking in snow and slush were memories. And eating road salt. The salt trucks came around and I couldn't wait. I loved salt and still do.

The thing I remember most about elementary school was being bored. If something wasn't a challenge, I lost interest.

Miss Pope taught first grade. We did calisthenics to a song called "Go you chicken fat go."

We had a field trip to the Cleveland Zoo. I remember the gorilla stuck out his tongue. That was the coolest thing. After wards we were asked to write about the most interesting thing about the zoo. I asked, "how do you spell 'tongue'?" Miss Pope said sound it out. Instead I wrote that his fur was black like a bat. I didn't want to sound it out. I knew I had read it somewhere and the spelling was weird.

Mrs. Tate had second grade. Miss Carlyle taught third grade. Miss Carlyle's father had a clothing store in Painesville. It was high-end. I have scattered few memories of those years. The teachers were nice and I did good because I had a good memory and Bunny's asshole activities were random. On one hand that was worse because I couldn't predict them. When it became every fucking Saturday and Sunday night, we dreaded what new surprise? What new torture? When I visited kids and met their parents, that devasted me. This is how it's supposed to be? Their normal became my envy. Or back then I called it that they were lucky. I did not deserve "normal."

Mrs. Heisner in fourth grade – that was fun. It was a split class. Half fourth graders and half fifth graders. Fourth graders were supposedly the nerds. The smart ones. But so were the fifth graders. It lasted one year. The experiment was cancelled.

If we had recess indoors due to rain, the record player was brought out. It was 1970-71 and the hot song was Don McLean's American Pie. The song was so long, the 45 had part one on side one and part two on side two.

In fourth grade, I was nine. I did not have many 45s. I had the ballad of Davy Crocket by Bill Hayes and when I tried to play it, the other kids said flat out, "No."

[For the kids who only know compact disks (CDs) or digital music: 45 RPM – rotations per minute – that was the speed you played a record. And it had music on both sides. The other options were 33 RPM and 78 RPM. Albums were 33 or technically 33-1/3. 78 was for the old Victrola. I once owned a Victrola and had records to go with it. But Cathy decided it was hers and took it with her to Raleigh. I did not protest.]

A Fifth grader named Jeff. I think. He was my friend in 4th grade. When he was a fifth grader. We built a planetarium together. We painted ping pong balls hung around the sun.

All that changed the next year. Jeff treated me like I was an untouchable when he was in sixth grade

Substitute teacher of 5th Grade. Miss Lutz. Mike DeVito could whistle with each finger. Two index, two social. And so on. Mike taught her to whistle the same way. We, the others in the class, were envious of Mike because he got more attention from Miss Lutz than we received.

We loved having Miss Lutz substitute. Clarifier – the boys did. Miss Lutz was Raquel Welch with blonde hair. The similarity of Lutz and "lust" were more than ironic or coincidence.

But in the fourth grade, I met Tim Deegan and Melanie Digevonie (Spelled correctly?). Melanie was the smartest girl in the school. She aced every test. Her papers came back 100%,

A++. She lived south of Lake shore Boulevard so after Rice Elementary, I never heard what happened to her.

But Melanie was our biggest challenge. "Our" – the rest of the smart kids, especially Tim and me. She challenged us to be better than our potential. She was the brass ring. Just out of reach. No one resented Melanie. We revered her. At least I did. I was never jealous. I didn't envy. I admired another person's mind. I knew it didn't rub off. But I wanted to be better like her.

Tim Deegan moved to Kansas in Eighth grade. I kept losing friends who moved away or disappeared.

Mrs. Hayes taught fifth. We rode our bikes to visit her. Way east of Mentor. Headlands pershaps.

Mr. Farley taught sixth grade. Rice Elementary was a major construction project then because they were building Bellflower elementary on Reynolds road (route 306).

Sadly there were bullies. I don't remember the names of the bullies as much as I do the victims.

Christie Leeper was tormented cruelly. Boys would surround her and chant "Fish eyes and frog guts." The chant repeated until she threw up. In defiance of those boys, Christie became my very first girl friend in fifth or sixth grade.

I bought her a bottle of perfume from Medic Discount Drug store.

One day, while visiting, her older sister told me that going steady leads to engagement and engagement leads to marriage… she scared the hell out of me. I was only in fifth grade.

I broke up with Christie.

[I'm sorry Christie. If you ever read this.]

She was so pretty.

Jeff Ficke was a new kid from Hawaii. Jeff was a nice guy, but this was an all-white suburb. One day all the bullies surrounded him. Jeff said, "You better watch out. I know some tricks." That was enough to back the bullies off.

I witnessed this but did not help. I held my head in shame.

Jeff brought a record to class that the teacher played. It had a song called "Here comes Santa in a red canoe." Hawaiian Christmas songs. How cool was that?

In sixth grade, Mister Farley gave me swats. That should not be plural. It was only one. There was one day, Mister Farley left the class. He was a weird teacher. Known for corporal punishment. Swats. And supposedly his swats hurt like the devil. Boys would cry or bawl.

In his absence, we had an eraser fight. Sixth graders, yeah, you think you're badass because next year, you're going to ridge junior high. During the eraser fight, everyone saw when Mister Farley came back into the classroom. Everyone, except me. He called me out, into the hallway with his paddle. "He said bend over and grab your ankles." I complied. Whack. It didn't hurt. It didn't hurt at all. We walked back into the classroom and everyone looked at me surprised that I wasn't crying. Bunny made me cry. Farley was a joke.

When Tim Deegan and I became friends, he had this white orb that was an AM radio and we would bike to Granger's pond and listen to CKLW from Windsor and Detroit. The Big 8.

Tim told me his mom said, "You can go to Granger's pond. But not to Red Oak." Tim said okay. Well, you could not bike to Granger's pond without travelling to Red Oak which was the name we gave to a ravine that tossed you if you didn't control your bike. My parents did not know what "Granger's pond" or "Red Oak" even meant.

I realize how clueless my parents were. My mother tried. I had an interest in Art. She enrolled me in art classes at Willoughby fine arts.

Tim Deegan had an older sister named Jacquie and she introduced us to so much music. Jacquie had the stones "exile on main street" album and we marveled at the album cover.

Around 1979, I was at an Iggy Pop concert at the Cleveland Agora and found Jacquie's portfolio of photography work on an empty table. She had photos of Iggy and Tim Curry. Beautiful work.

My family life was becoming a living nightmare. Every time I saw Teri Pealer, she took me out of that angst. I looked forward to seeing her every time she was there. That started at Rice Elementary and continued through 1979. I love you, Teri. Always will.

The real bullies showed their faces at Mentor Ridge Junior High, St. Joe's, Lake Catholic and Mentor High.

Why did it take me so many years to understand that bullies are cowards? Anger is the mirror reflection of Fear. That's why bullies never win. But I'm getting ahead of myself.

One day – at Tim Deegan's house -- I demonstrated my ability to create the sound of a cat and a monkey. The monkey was Corey from Aunt Alice and Herb Malone. Jacquie said we have to have two of her friends come over. One could do a chimpanzee and the other could do a lion.

Parents were supposed to teach us. Good examples. We'd go to Weslaco Fishermen's Club or Cloverdale and my father with his beer buddies would sit and sip and tell jokes that insulted black human beings. They called them "nigger jokes."

I'd like to know from my black friends if they ever sit around and tell "whitie jokes." What a waste of time.

Marvel Comics

I started to buy Marvel comics in 3rd Grade. That was the first time I had my own money.

The Amazing Spider-Man, the Incredible Hulk, Captain America, The Mighty Thor, the Avengers. That started it. The bunny never understood. He called it wasted money on "those goddamn funny books."

Back then the heroes were mostly white. Then I learned of black heroes. The black panther, the falcon and then Luke Cage. My father was an Archie Bunker wanna-be. That's why initially I embraced black Super-heroes. But then it was the stories and the art.

Art – comic book art was over the top. Museums had Van Gogh, Edward Hopper, Da Vinci. Comic book art had Jack Kirby, Jim Starlin, John Buscema, Johnny Romita, Todd McFarlane... The list goes on and one.

Comics taught me about racism, sexism, Vietnam, College campus protests, Hallucinogenic drugs. Social mores. The caste system.

Comics taught me morality. But that it comes at a cost. Heroes win, but at a cost that was personal. Usually some sacrifice. "For the greater good."

By the 1995-time frame, my collection was worth $55,000. I sold my collection of DareDevil from issue #1 to #300+ to a lawyer from a westside suburb for $1,200.

That paid for our water-proofing our basement at the Manor Park home in Lakewood.

In 1996-1997, I sold the rest to the comic bookstore at Shoregate for $50. I gave wife a check for $25 and a copy of the receipt and said here is your share of marital property.

I'm not sure why... but look at any male Marvel superhero who wears no shirt. The Hulk, the Sub-Mariner, the Silver Surfer. None of them have nipples.

Some comedian once wrote: "Why do men have nipples?"

I guess Marvel answered that.

One of the Bullies

There was a bully at Rice Elementary. Eddie Jewart and I hated him. You would think, that since he stole our lunch money, made us give up our lunch snacks, that we would still know his name. I do not. But we knew which bike he rode.

One night during a school function, we found his bike in the bike rack with no lock. We took it and walked it to the nearby woods and left it there. Unfortunately, the janitor saw us and busted us. He caught me while Eddie fled. I had to tell the story of what we did. Not why. Just what. I had to ask... why didn't anyone care about "why?" He was a bully. A bad one. If I could remember his name, I'd hunt him down.

1974 – Cheech and Chong's "Earache, my eye."

In 1974, I was 13 and in 8th grade. The comedy duo of Cheech and Chong had a radio hit about a slacker who played loud music and tried to tell his dad that he had an earache. The music he played during the comedy skit was from a band called "Alice Bowie."

Three years later, I was 16 and sophomore year at Saint Joseph High. Alice Cooper and David Bowie had each released Greatest Hits albums. Bowie's was called "Changes One."

I was a stereotype. "What music would my parents object to the most?"

Based on Cheech and Chong, it had to be David Bowie and Alice Cooper. The Alice Cooper record had the two songs mom hated when she bought Hello Hurray backed with I wanna be Elected. The 45 I traded to Tim Deegan for the hippy song, come on people now – that he got from Jacquie.

I fell in love with Bowie and Cooper.

1975 – Maninno's Drug Store

Norman Redenshek was the stock boy at Maninno's. I was in class with is sister Sue. He asked me to fill in for him so he could join his family on summer vacation. Mannino's had comics… I was glad to do it. I spelled Mannino's two different ways because it's gone now and I don't recall the correct spelling.

I was 14 and working a real job. I had to vacuum every aisle. That was tedious and boring but I did it. My attention to detail helped.

I had to restock the Semulac formula for newborns.

The delight was I got to shelve the new Comic books. I started by organizing them by publisher. Charleston, DC, Gold Key, Harvey, and Marvel. Then alphabetized by title.

To be honest, when the Penthouse porno magazines arrived, I put one copy in a box that went into the dumpster. I went back after the store closed and did dumpster diving. I was 14. Sorry Mr. Mannino.

My next job would be at Bob Evan's restaurant on Route 306 aka Reynolds road. I was there from age 16 until I joined the army in 1980.

Bunny and the dental office helper

I think her name was Karen Carpenter. Like the singer with her brother but not the same. She lived on a hill in Willoughby. Bunny would finish the dental work and sit in the kitchen with Karen. They would share a six-pack of beer. Then Bunny would drive her home.

Mom thought he was sleeping with her.

Bunny sent mom to therapy. In the 1960s, that's what they did to women. It HAD to be their fault. The men decided it was all in her head.

The therapist said it was her imagination.

Consider the etymology of hysterectomy. It literally means to surgically remove the hysteria from the patient. If a woman was depressed or angry or going through menopause or the least bit out of sorts, legit or not, the medical solution was a hysterectomy. Surgical removal of the "hysteria" – i.e., all the reproductive parts. Womb, uterus, fallopian tubes… all gone. And to this day, we still call the procedure by the same name. The medical community needs to wake up and smell the coffee. Rename it was it is… Ectomy (surgical removal) of the womb, uterus and fallopian tubes. And any parts that I've omitted by my lack of anatomy knowledge.

I credit a neurologist, Bob Daroff, for teaching me in science, a body is dead, when the brain is dead. Hence, the body is alive, when the brain is alive. This should be the standard for abortions. Once the brain is alive, no abortion. Prior to brain activity, it is not alive. It is a parasite and can be aborted. My words, not Bob's. Bob and Jane Daroff were great friends. I respected and admired them.

Grand Pap and native American

He told us he was Native American. We were too young to ask, "Which tribe?" I wish I had asked. I plan to do a DNA test. If I do it before I submit this manuscript, I'll report the results.

If you buy, "Bury my heart at Wounded Knee," by Dee Brown, there is a photo in the back of a Sioux chief who looks identical to my Uncle Ron. Doppelganger.

Mom never told us to lie

But mom never said, "Don't tell the truth." But all we knew was "Don't tell nothing." Why? All the years, all the abuse, Silence. And I abided. In high school, I told Brandon and I told Mark. I never told the Police.

Can you imagine, if I told the mentor police? "Is wife beating a crime? Isn't that assault? How about driving drunk? Endangering the lives of minors?"

Spare the rod, spoil the child. I was not spoiled.

How many charges there would have been? Bunny committed the acts. That is not questionable.

What's weird is that she never said, "Don't tell the truth." Somehow, we all abided. Maybe it was that unspoken rule that you never tattle.

That could explain it. But the Bunny broke the law. Forgive us for not knowing the law. Each of us, in our hearts, we knew what he was subjecting us to was wrong.

But there was no store front advertising... "IF a parent is abusing you, come inside! We'll fix it."

Mom once said, in the 1960s, there were no women's shelters. Women had no options. Tolerate abuse or die. Men were entitled to be and allowed to be as cruelly abusive as they wanted to be. Caveat -- some men. Not all.

Back to the story...

2nd Grade with Mrs. Tate or
3rd Grade with Mrs. Carlisle

The teacher had three of my friends confront me.

One said, "We want you to stop wiping your boogers on the side of your desk." I said, "I do not do that." He said, "yes - you do... look." And he pointed at the left side of my desk and the evidence was there.

But that didn't stop me. I put them on the bottom of the desk.

I told you. I am not without sin.

Music from my parents

I would be remiss if I didn't mention the music that my parents introduced me to. The point is that Bunny was more than a tyrannical bully and sadist and mom was more than a domestic violence victim.

Bunny had albums that he played. Jim Croce's "Photographs and Memories." Herb Alpert and the Tijuana Band's "Going Places." Harry Belefonte's Live album. Johnny Cash "Live at San Quentin." Blood, Sweat and Tears. And a Hank Williams album. The Kingston Trio's Greatest Hits, especially "Tom Dooley." He also had albums by Jackie Gleason called "Music for lovers" that cracked me up.

Now Mark Vocca told me his orchestrations are brilliant. They were slow versions of classic renditions. I only knew Jackie Gleason from the Honeymooners. Mark has been a musician all his life. I was only a singer. I studied lyrics and singing.

Redemption?

Does this mean that the Bunny had redeeming qualities? Hear me on this please. Every human has elements of good and bad. Lynn taught me that and I struggled kicking and screaming all the way to the conclusion. Yes, I fought the black and white notion that had no grey area. I did not like grey areas. I fought them in Mentor, I fought them in Berlin. And I fought them as a civilian after the army.

The bunny was a good dentist. The bunny had friends who loved and respected him. His sisters loved him, sort of... they made overtures that they did. I would guess some were genuine and others were not.

Veronica came over the night of the broken nose and blouse ripped open. He was exposed. He could not deny it anymore.

There were four children terrified. And all he showed was a cocky, arrogant, unsympathetic attitude. He could have said, "Yeah? So what?" Yeah I did that... So what?

How much effort to say, "I'm sorry." Those words never came.

The bad... to me, there are certain lines you – one – does not cross. And once crossed, you can never go back. Some of his deeds, I cannot "unsee."

Chris Rock does this classic comedy routine. He says some people are proud of stupid shit. I'm paraphrasing. But then he says (mocking some speaker), "I've never been to jail – you're not supposed to go to jail. I've never beat my wife – you're not supposed to beat your wife."

Certain Lines: beating another human. Now sometimes it's justified. Not beating a spouse. But beating a husband who beats a spouse? Yes gladly.

Certain Lines: using a broom stick to break a dog's ribs that's cowering and whimpering under a child's bed? That beating of the bully is long overdue.

You never cross certain lines. Once you do, you can't go back. I can't unsee mom on the floor begging for mercy while Bunny kicked her ribs and broke them out of anger. Because she dared defy his authority asking him not to beat the dog. She had that act of defiance. Who needs to be told, "don't beat the dog"?

I seriously wanted to beat the Bunny to death or near death. With all I witnessed, he deserved it. I would have to ask that question again in 1986 when I left the army. After Ranger Training. I was capable. I chose not to ever be as bad as he was/is.

Non-Sequitur... I hope Audra -- my niece-person reads this manuscript of this book. I know my youngest sister, rhymes with blister, decided sometime after 1997 that she hated me. I was never told why.

I was told very harshly, "Catherine must never know that you and I prepared her condo for the carpet cleaners." Was that 2003 or 2004? Dunno.

In 2003, I lived in mom's double in the basement. Only 13 months. And I drank wine and scotch and had sexual relations with two Raleigh women.

But I also went to Audra's mom's town house and prepared it for the carpets to be cleaned. Mom asked me to promise I would not tell Audra's mom. Really? I didn't have her email or cell… how was I going to tell her? Oh, I know. In a book written nearly twenty years later. This is how absurd family arguments are.

YMCA on route 20

Mom took me there for swimming lessons. I could not see underwater. The chlorine was too strong. Too many kids peeing in the pool. I've opened my eyes underwater in the gulf of Mexico in salt water and had no burn.

At the "Y," They had an Auto Mat. They don't have these vending machines now. The Auto mat had ice cream sandwiches, candy, ham and cheese sandwiches.

I read that the auto mat was invented in Berlin in the 1870s.

Why Berlin?

When I re-enlisted, I did for Berlin Brigade.

Mom taught me the soundtrack to "Cabaret." I loved that movie and the music. Not the Nazi theme. I liked decadence. I liked degrading myself. Bunny taught me that.

In 1977, David Bowie moved to Berlin and had a nightclub called "Der Djungel." He also recorded three albums there:

"Low," "Heroes," and "Lodger." The Eno trilogy. Overall, I liked Low the best , but the song Heroes was monumental.

Music from my parents – continued...

The albums were played on a Magnavox stereo system. Large as a dresser. It was about six feet long, four feet tall and three feet deep. When I inherited it, I had to tape two pennies on the needle to keep it from skipping across the record.

Mom had one album that she played all the time. Barbra Streisand's "The way we were." Barbra's movie with Robert Redford. She played it so many times that I memorized all the lyrics. Especially the day she was faux painting the kitchen cabinets with Phyllis Jewart.

Mom also loved musicals. We watched "the Music Man" and "Cabaret." Cabaret introduced me to Berlin. I think that was why I ended up re-enlisting for Berlin and living there for four years. Well, that and because David Bowie moved there in 1977 and did three albums with Brian Eno, Robert Fripp and Iggy Pop. Not all musicians (except Eno) were involved with all the albums. Or all the songs.

At some point, I watched the musical of "Li'l Abner" with Julie Newmar as Stupifyin' Jones. I don't have many "lust objects." But all of them are from old movies. Julie Newmar in "Li'l Abner." Cyd Charisse in "Singin' in the Rain." Lauren Bacall in "To have and have not." Shirley Jones in "Elmer Gentry." Natalie Wood in "the Great Race." Sally Ann Howes in "Chitty Chitty Bang Bang." And Teresa Graves in "Get Christie Love." The only modern lust object I have is Helen Mirren. She gives new meaning to the term Hot Dame. Google, "Helen Mirren Nude" and look at the images section. She was red pepper hot.

The children of James Edward Ross and Francis Muscowicz

To us, they were Grandpa and Grandma Ross.

Edward James Hrachovina was born in Bohemia. Francis Muscowicz was born in Lithuania, in Conus, the biggest jewish community in the country.

Bunny went to college. He went to Hiram and graduated with a bachelor of science in chemistry. He then went to Penn State and got his doctor in dentistry.

How did Bunny pass English 101? Did Hiram exempt science majors from English? How did he write term papers? Mid-term and Final? I explain this later on... he asked me to write the letter of recommendation for Paul Endres to go to Choate or some prep school. He asked me because he couldn't write. I never realized it back then. I realized it for the first time when I had the audacity to demand a letter from my father. The bunny was illiterate. He could not construct a sentence to save his life. I was a junior high school student and wrote a letter of recommendation to a child in Chuck's grade (four years younger than me) for high school. That must have made me in junior high.

Temple and Veronica and Charlotte did not go to college.

But Kitty did. Catherine ("Kitty") Ross went to college. She would have breaks from college and visit me at the parents home on Woodstock. She taught me the Encyclopedia song, that taught you how to spell, "Encyclopedia."

It there was a plastic Frankenstein or a plastic Spiderman, she bought it for me.

I'm glad Kitty went to college.

I don't know why Temple, Veronica and Charlotte never went to college. So Bunny went (only boy) and Kitty went (youngest girl).

Perhaps this book is an attempt to understand the family dynamics.

In the Ross family – Veronica said it was all about, "go and get me something to beat you with." That says to me children living in constant terror. I can relate. Bunny implemented the same strategy.

In the Lindley family – you were sired to be farm hands. So you better work. Girls are useless. Go get edjumacated. Audra – you get your RN and marry a dentist who will give you a better life. Hah! Jacquie, you marry that Peninsula Mediterranean who kills your dog. Audra, your husband will only beat and torture your dogs until they eventually die.

In the Lindley family, the boys had no limits. Junior decided it was okay to rape Audrey. She fought him off and he only partially succeeded. My cousin Tanja had to put up with her cousins touching and trying to fondle her breasts and crotch because she was the only female in miles.

Horny guys need to suffer. If they are so desperate to pull that shit on a cousin… then they need to feel pain. Tanja is a result of that. Let's start with the Taser.

Temple married Jim Shiels because she wanted to move to New York City. She told me she had a map of New York City on her bedroom wall.

Veronica married Ken Overbaugh. He was a master home builder and would restore homes and resell them.

Charlotte married Lee Haywood. He was a mechanical genius whom Bunny always insulted. Uncle Lee became the metaphor. In reality, he was a kind, decent, religious man who treated people with decency and respect. The Bunny, the asshole called him a "gas pump jockey" and said if you don't get better grades, you'll end up just like your Uncle Lee. That would have suited me just fine.

Better like Lee than like Bunny. Lee was a good man. Bunny was a shit for brains. Bunny was a sadistical bully. Lee was kind. Lee cared and treated others with decency and respect. Bunny berated and tormented.

Whom would you rather be like?

Mentor – More – Part One

Mom and the Bunny left for a night at the elks' lodge. That meant the Bunny drank and mom waited. I was the baby sister. There were worst nights. Define worst?

Sequence is screwed up. I did not document dates and times. I didn't keep a diary or a journal. My apathy was that I didn't care to write things down. My apathy was I didn't care to study. My apathy was I didn't care. Period. It wasn't apathy. It was fear. If the Bunny found my notes. But I wasn't a journalist.

My father was called "Bunny." What grown man allows himself to be called Bunny? Ralph Bush called him Bunny. He was a high school friend. One of his sisters (Veronica) told me that he got that nickname, because when he was a baby in the crib, grandma Ross said he looked like a scared rabbit. Yeah, I'd be proud of that simile.

Elks' Lodge Night

Bunny came home drunk and called all the kids to the kitchen table. Oh, look, he brought Manner's Big Boy burgers to everyone, not *for* everyone. To.

He'd been at the Elk's lodge. Manners was at 615. That meant he had to drive eight to ten miles passed our home to the restaurant. Wait for them to pack up the to-go order. Then drive eight to ten miles back to our home.

By the way, this was not a one-time incident. It was a repeat event. I lost count. Needless to say it happened too often.

It was Sunday. A school night. We -- the kids -- had already gone to bed. He woke everyone up. Demanded a gathering at the dining room table. "I provide for you." Like a commandment. "Now you will eat." Voice of a tyrant. Oh, sorry, I didn't mean to interrupt. You'd already figured that out for yourself. My bad.

He didn't work Sundays or Mondays which meant that Saturday and Sunday nights were for getting toxically drunk. That's probably not a legal term but it should be. Legally, there is a category of "intoxicated." I think there should be one further called "toxically drunk." That's the stage where the consumer commits acts of rage, violence and abuse on women and children. The Bunny did that like a pro. And had amnesia of the event. Never remembered one incident.

How in the hell did he not ever get a DUI?

On this night, Cathy cried first. Then Cyndy cried. He dismissed the girls. Sent them to bed.

Chuck tried to cry but he was told to shut up and eat.

The Bunny made those awake and present eat the bounty of Manners Big Boy Burgers. He ate which sobered him enough to comment about the pig sty of our bedroom. Mom tried to protest. I remember the shout and the look, "Audrey!" His facial expression conveyed, you've already been taught what happens if you defy me. Then the sinister, "Do you really want to go there again?" Intimations of the coming of the sadist.

Next step was into our shared bedroom. Not to defend myself, but I was a neat freak and orderly. My brother was a slob.

Bunny went to the boys' shared room. All toys, games, and plastic models were swept off shelves and stacked into a pile in the middle of the room. He also emptied the dresser drawers. The drawers themselves were added to the pile. Then he began stomping. He stomped on everything -- until every toy, game, model and item were broken and in pieces. Every piece smashed and worthless. Any protests resulted in smacks to the head. His big bohemian/Lithuanian hands would pack a wallop. He taught me that I can take a hit.

"Now clean it up," he demanded. How could he have derived pleasure from that act? They say the Russians love their children too. Sting sang that in 1984.

I try to write this objectively. I omit "that made me sad" or "that made me angry." I think that those adjectives are up to the reader to decide. With a document like this, it should be uninfluenced by the writer.

After he passed out, Mom would come in and say go to bed, I'll tidy up in the morning. She was a saint who was as broken as we were. Fist broke will. Fist broke defiance. Fist broke dignity. Fist broke integrity. Fist broke individuality, humanity. Again and again. Next…

Mentor – More – Part Two

Elk's Lodge. It was where drinks were cheap, the bar was dark, kids were babysat by bowls of peanuts and the juke box. Mom later told me he would drive home drunk with the kids in the back of the car. Swerving the whole time barely staying on the road. From 1962 when he moved his family to Mentor, until he died in 2006, he never had one DUI (driving under the influence). Never got pulled over.

At some point, they assigned me baby-sitter duties. I can't tell you how old I was when this happened.

One night, all four kids were in the living room watching television… so since Cathy was born in 1967, this must have been at least 1971.

Mom burst through the front door. She was crying. She had a black eye and a broken nose. Her cheek was severely bruised. The blouse and bra were ripped half across her chest exposing one breast. She fled to the bathroom. Cyndy and Cathy followed. Chuck cried. I ran to the parking lot... our home was the dental office. What probably had been the garage was converted to the dental office. I expected to find a maniac in the parking lot. I did not think about what I would do. But the maniac who hurt mom had to be prevented from causing more harm. In the parking lot, there was our family van – no other vehicle. Bunny was walking out of it heading to the front door. I stood paralyzed. No lunatic. Just HIM. He rubbed my hair and said, "Hiya Bud." I understood in that moment who the lunatic was.

I ask myself. Why didn't I ever question the cause. I could have said, "why did you beat her and break her nose?" Would any answer justify the violence?

"Hiya Bud" explained his personality. His nature.

In the realm of Marvel Comics, he would have been a villain. But there was no Spider-Man, no Thor, no DareDevil to stop him. It went on and on.

Digression: Was it before or after? "It" was the night mom wanted him to stop hurting our dog. Forgive me if I repeat myself. Other details come to mind. The dog was cowering under the bed. Mine or Chuck's. I don't recall. Bunny had ferocious anger. Like a beast uncaged. Like someone with a vendetta. But against a dog? He thrust the broom stick with force to wound, kill or at least break its ribs. Each strike produced whimpers that howled in pain. What sticks in my memory -- he enjoyed it. He knew what he was doing to that animal and he liked it. Sadistically.

How do I explain the look in his eyes. It shifted. It went from rage to satisfaction. It began angry when the dog was still alive. It went to satisfaction when the corpse stopped whelping.

But then -- that wasn't good enough.

Mom had intervened. "She had to be punished."

She begged him to stop. Bunny tossed her to the kitchen floor and kicked her ribs. Again and again. Each time more viciously. She sobbed and cried and pleaded with him to stop.

I saw this that night. In the hallway, I witnessed the savage and brutal beating of mom. In my mind, he stopped being "dad." He was only the ogre, the Bunny.

He enjoyed being the sadist. I learned that later. When it was my turn.

Back to the story...

I followed my father into the house. From the parking lot. The night of the horrible beating. Mom stood behind a chair in the living room. Cyndy and Cathy on each side sobbing. She said, "I want a divorce."

Damn. Finally. An end to the brutal cruelty. No more torture at night. She told me and Chuck to go to Phyllis Jewart's house and ask to call aunt Baby (Veronica Overbaugh). Chuck remembered the phone number, I had forgotten it in the trauma. I called and she came.

Phyllis wanted to know what was going on. "Secret Shame." No one was allowed to tell.

I was fully prepared to go to Aunt Baby's home (Veronica's) and stay there. I looked forward to it. A new life. But we were told to go to bed. In the Mentor home.

The next morning, there was the "Sunday morning chocolate box," a metaphor of what was done must now go away. Forget it happened.

Mom took weeks of healing and required plastic surgery to fix her nose.

Cathy and Chuck forgot about this when the divorce came in 1996. Easier to forgive the Bunny than recall what damage. Was inheritance a motive? I'll never know. It's not fair for me to comment or judge either of them. I haven't seen either one since the Christmas incident of 1995.

Mom never said to lie. She never said don't tell the truth. But we all knew – don't say nothing. I know… that's a double negative. Deliberate. Man who beats wife is white trash.

All the years, all the abuse. Silence. I abided. It was an unspoken agreement. The terms were never discussed. But compliance was expected. The Secret Shame.

In 1987 after the Army, my father and I were sitting in the family room upstairs in Mentor. Some movie was on. I told him about my memories of the events I have described in this book. He said, "you must have imagined that or dreamt it. That never happened. I never did those things."

I have heard from many others that alcoholics employ this strategy to deflect. But the Bunny was worse than an alcoholic. Alcoholics attend meetings. The Bunny was just a drunk.

I concluded, it was hopeless. I would never penetrate the shield to reach the core. Paul Simon wrote: "So I'll continue to continue to pretend. And flowers never bend with the rain fall."

At fifty-nine, I must admit that I have had episodes of amnesia after scotch. But my episodes involved reheating and eating leftovers. Not torturing a spouse and children.

Mom got a nose job to fix her broken nose.

As a child, seeing mom with a broken nose from Bunny punching her in the face was traumatic. And it wasn't just a broken nose. It was a black eye. Blouse ripped off exposing a breast.

One day she came home from the hospital. She said it was "a nose job to fix her broken nose." It looked just like when

Bunny punched her and broke it. I saw it as déjà vu. Already seen. That's a literal translation.

I hated seeing mom with bruises to her face, arms, anywhere. I knew Bunny made the bruises. I hated the bunny. Mom never committed acts of violence against the Bunny.

Bunny constantly committed acts of violence against her and us.

Who does that?

Who tortures women, children, dogs and cats?

The Bunny.

Lynn Ann Frick (now Ross)

I interrupt this story to interject a passage about Lynn. I need to explain why she is so important to me. I had been previously married twice – three times if you count eleven months with Michaela. I should have become jaded and wanted nothing to do with women. When we met, I was not looking and was not even interested. I essentially made the decision to become a hermit and focus on writing my first novel. That didn't work out when two wayward boys tazed my computer tower and monitor.

In 2004 I moved to Florida and worked for WCI, a local home builder. This is a digression.

I was at Tarpon Bay, an HOA with condos. I was on-site as the community manager working under another manager's license. I could do everything except approve invoices. Lynn worked for WCI -- in the warranty department. That meant she coordinated the repairs. We emailed and reading one another's emails, we had a rapport. A rapport as colleagues. Potential to become friends but neither one pushed it.

Once I realized she had a sense of humor and I liked her intelligence, I would use inter-office mail to send her – not gifts. Things that I thought would crack her up. After one email when she told me she liked asperagus, I went to publix and bought a can and channeled it through inter-office mail to her. She liked Jujyfruits and good and plenties and red liquorice. Those packages followed… But sometimes the mail room intervened and removed candy sent to her.

We both liked the Harry Potter movies. Back then "Borders" book store was still around. At the check out they had Harry Potter Bertie Botts Jelly Beans. They had flavors like ear wax and vomit. Lynn put them in a bowl and set them out for the warranty people to sample without a warning. Ed was a warranty technician and painted all the ceilings in our home at Country Creek. Ed came in from the field and took a handful of Bertie Botts and started chewing. He gagged and spat them out.

Lynn and I had been emailing during the summer of 2004 before we met. Our first meeting was at the WCI Employee Expo at Pelican Preserve on October 4, 2004.

Evelyn Bennet introduced me to Lynn. I knelt and looked at her. I realized in that moment, what ever she needed, I would be there.

She bought the home at Country Creek in May 2005 and we moved in together Memorial day weekend. Her father, Charlie, he was skeptical at first. He came down from Cincinnati for a visit. After that, Charlie called me son from then on.

Over the years, Lynn has taught me many things.

About the music of Andre Boccelli. We both loved the Beatles.

One night at Tallowood where she lived when we met. We were singing Beatles songs on the back lanai. Suddenly a scraggly voice shouted, "Will you turn that radio down!" We cackled with laughter.

One mention: Blue icing wedding cake. Lynn knows what that means.

Lynn taught me cooking. Smoked pork butt with cabbage, chicken divan, the best beef stew I've ever had. We both love crablegs and do the cost co crablegs for any special occasion.

This is skimming the surface. Deep down, Lynn taught me to forgive. I don't hate anyone. Before Lynn, I probably hated Bunny. She taught me even a scoundrel like him must have some redeeming qualities. I doubt that he did but I give her the benefit of the doubt.

I have been able to let many things go... **where** do they go? They go somewhere. Poof – they are gone. I have Lynn to thank for that. I held anger to the chest. "Never let it go – feed it when its hungry." That's a reference to the two wolves. The angry and the good. At war. Which one wins? The one you feed. Native American parable.

Bottom Line: I don't know what kind of man I would be today, if it weren't for Lynn Ross. Would I be alive? Would I have committed suicide? Tendencies are certainly or were there. Or would I be a druggie or a drunk?

There are so many negative paths I would have followed. Might have followed.

I read or heard "the innermost part of my consciousness says to me, 'I am a failure.' " That applies.

Lynn challenges me. She engages my brain and never lets me turn it off.

"And I have to laugh when she reveals me." -- Billy Joel. Lynn led me to become the 7th Son.

Matt and I used to brag that we were the seventh sons.

I had many more things to discover before I could make that claim.

Anger destroys relationships.

[Passage written 9/15/2020 and 11/05/20].

There is a poem by Ernst Jandl that applies. He captured it beautifully. This is what Lynn brings to me.

"Liegen bei Dir."
ich liege bei dir. deine arme
halten mich. deine arme
halten mehr als ich bin.
deine arme halten, was ich bin
wenn ich bei dir liege und
deine arme mich halten.

"Laying, or Lying next to you."
I lie next to you. Your arms
hold me. Your arms
hold more than I am.
Your arms hold, what I am
When I lie next to you and
Your arms hold me.
This holds true with Lynn.

Chuck and "Bambi"

Mom took us to see Bambi by Disney in the 1960s. Bambi came out in 1942. We saw it in the theatre in Willoughby at the matinee in 1968 or later. Chuck was four or five. As the story goes, Bambi's mother runs out into the meadow and the hunters shoot her. Chuck is four. Maybe five. What he sees is real. He has a sense of urgency. He runs up the aisle of the movie theater. He feels compelled to warn Bambi on the screen. To Chuck, the cartoon deer was a real and live person.

He yells, "Bambi, your mother is died." Not a typo. That's how he said it. Come on, he was four.

Did Bunny's abuse inspire that? On one hand, there was concern that a deer was distressed. On the other hand, there was a four year old child who thought the cartoon deer was real.

Watchek's

Mom did grocery shopping at Watcheck's at Lost Nation Road and Lakeshore Blvd in Willoughby. It was a mom and pop supermarket with fresh produce. Mostly we went in with her inside. Watchek's gave out Green Stamps. As kids we filled books with green stamps. At least Cyndy and I did.

One day at Watchek's, Mom left Chuck and I in the Impala station wagon and went inside. "Just wait here. I'll be right back."

Chuck wanted to play, "driving the car." Mom walked in and left us alone. Chuck said, "vroom, vroom," as he sat in the driver's seat holding the steering wheel. Suddenly he grabbed the gear shift. I didn't think you could change gears unless the car was with the brake pedal fully compressed.

Chuck shifted gears and put the car in neutral. The car drifted backward into traffic on Lost Nation Road. The incline wasn't steep, but it was sufficient to back us up by about ten feet.

I beeped the horn and Mom came out. I did not know where the emergency brake was. We did not get hit. Pure luck.

Bunny and Dinner at McDonalds

Bunny took the kids to McDonalds. It was new at that time.

He asked all the kids "What do you want?" It was an invite to ask for anything,

Cyndy asked for a cheeseburger and fries. I probably asked for a fish sandwich and fries. This was before they had the quarter pounder with cheese.

Chuck wanted TWO big macs. Keep in mind that Bunny was a glutten – of food and alcohol. Chuck became his mirror. He resented Chuck for most of his life. Chuck represented the things about himself that he hated. He loathed himself and took out that loathing on Chuck.

Chuck ignited Bunny and Bunny berated Chuck. He punished and humiliated him. He called him a glutton and told him he had to eat both Big Macs.

Chuck was a child. If his eyes were bigger than his stomach, you move on.

I think Bunny craved an audience. He needed witnesses to observe him punishing. When it was the kids. Power?

Kafka's Hunger Artist needed an audience to witness his art.

Bunny needed an audience when he punished children. I saw all the families in the McDonald's parking lot were looking at the Bunny. Watching shamefully as he humiliated Chuck. He made him eat both.

It was different with mom. He wanted no witnesses then. Because that would have been shame. Or getting caught.

I was a witness. But Bunny said, I imagined that or dreamed it.

Religion

Religion in my family was not taught. We did not go to church. We followed no church's rules. I learned religion from movies: "The Ten Commandments." "Barabbas." "Samson and Delilah."

Let me correct that... After baptism and first communion and confirmation in eighth grade, we did go to church. Saint John Vianney parish in mentor off of Route 306 aka Reynolds road.

All the years until I turned 13 in 1974 – there was no church or religion. To prepare me for Catholic high school, all four children would get baptized. Cyndy and I would get the First communion rite and the Profession of Faith.

Mom also got baptized. She said she didn't want us to do anything that she was unwilling to do herself. Like take a good beating? To her credit, she didn't force us to do anything she wouldn't also go through herself.

The problem with this was the profession of faith. A commitment to a religion. And mom didn't believe a word of it. She was just jumping off the cliff so we would feel safe in following. I did not.

This was a huge move. Religion when there was none. Let me figure this out. Bunny said he wanted no more religion because he had had enough – raised protestant. He wanted no more. If he had had enough, why was it good for us?

Mom said, I don't know this. But if the kids go through it, damnit so will I.

Bravo Mom. At least you led by example.

The Bible

I went through all the rites to become a Catholic without ever reading the Bible. Believe a book word-for-word that I never read? How can anyone do that?

Father Kline showed Cyndy and I a slide show. Cartoon sketches of biblical stories. Adam and Eve, Cain and Abel, Noah and the Flood. Moses and the Ten Commandments. Abraham and his son. Then jump to Birth of Jesus, water to wine, Pontius Pilate, and nailed to the cross.

Forget the tower of Babel which was bullshit. Forget Job. God and Satan arguing… "Let me test Job" – Satan says. And

God sez, "okay." Okay? Seriously? Yeah read that part. Satan fucked up Job and his family in so many ways. And God said yup, this is a test that you can put him through.

Fuck that noise. Satan won that battle. God gave Satan a pawn and let Satan hit him with everything he had. To his credit, Job never gave up. Oh, but what a cost.

At Cleveland State University, I would read parts as assigned from professors of the philosophy department.

In the 1970s, DC comics released a compliment to the Marvel Treasury Editions. These were oversized reprints for special occasions. The size was about three-foot tall and two foot wide. The first one from DC that I bought reprinted early comics of the Batman in Detective Comics from the 1930s. Joker was a psychotic fiend.

The next DC comic I bought was called "the Bible" and told illustrated versions of stories from the Old and New Testament. Joe Kubert did the artwork. I bought it out of curiosity.

For me it meant, "Oh, so that's where it comes from..." But it also meant, "Oh that's bullshit." Tower of Babel? Seriously? I studied languages. God changed the languages so the tower could not be completed? Really? So French, Spanish, Italian, Portuguese and Romanian were not Latin based?

Bloom County was a newspaper comic strip by Berkley Breathed. One in particular had the two white boys talking on a hill and Milo asked "Did Adam have a navel?" I loved questions like this. Like where did Cain and Abel get their wives? Can't take it literally. This planet has evidence in museums of Natural History that support what the Trump administration coined as alternative facts. It's a new moebius strip. One side is a lie and the other side is true. This paradox cannot have both.

My family needed morality something fierce. Any code of ethics.

Correction. My father. The Bunny. He needed morality and a code of ethics. My family – mom, brother and sisters – we would have gained from the benefits.

But I knew it would not come from the Bible. Perhaps from the Law. That would never happen. If only we could go to the Great Lakes Mall and buy a code of ethics. That would have been money well-spent.

I was essentially a heathen or an infidel. But I knew the Charlie Brown Christmas Special… even though Linus's speech was lost to me.

In first and second grade, I was friends with Steve Jordan. One year, we spent Christmas eve and Christmas morning together. After breakfast, Sandra his mom said let's go. I said where are we going? She said to church. It's Jesus's birthday. You have to go to church on Jesus's birthday. I wanted to ask "who is Jesus" but I was afraid that it should have been obvious but it truly wasn't. I had no idea who this person was and why his birthday was on Christmas morning.

Back home, the torment and torture continued. Why didn't mom escape? She could have left and never looked back. The bunny would not have known what to do with four children.

I don't know how Cyndy did it. But she excelled in Junior High and High School with straight A's.

I poured myself into depression, anger, and self-loathing. Self-loathing because I must have been at fault. At least in part. I had to be wrong. I sought to be punished. Or to escape. Escape came with drugs. Pot, hash, opium, valium, speed, LSD, and crank. Everything but coke and heroin. Cocaine was what we called the rich kids' drug. Now we call "them" the Trust Fund Babies.

Heroin was scary. Some say it's great. But there were too many images of strung out junkies willing to do anything for a fix. I never wanted to try it or do it.

But there was one night on New Year's Eve in 1996/1997 I was in Ohio City. I like Ohio City because it didn't matter if you were black or white, straight or gay. We were all friends. We all treated one another with respect and genuine civility. I saw some of that at CSU but it was feigned or forced. Like when I wanted to be a columnist for the vindicator, the student newspaper that was done by the black students. I showed up and announced my interest. To write a column about racism. They saw me as a white boy. What could I possibly contribute. I went back to the Cauldron. I wrote five articles about racism and called them "Notes from the Zebra Monastery."

A black woman on the Cauldron staff told me that "Zebra" was a derogatory term for someone who was bi-racial. Fyodor Dostoevsky wrote, "Notes from Underground" about existentialism. I was following his lead with the title. I considered it a uniting term, not a dividing term.

I thought that monastery was the perfect choice, because it's where you study.

Back to the story… I was at this new year's eve party and the wife of the host asked me if I wanted a bump. That was slang for a line of coke. I said sure. But this powder was mustard colored. I did the line expecting coke, and then the downward spiral. I finally understood the title of the Nine Inch Nails album.

Coke is like speed in a happy, let's party sort of way.

She denied it was heroin when questioned the next day. I went down a spiral and found myself puking in a toilet. I went outside and walked about because I was afraid to go to sleep. I walked until dawn.

Why does a father have so much power and control over children? The child wants love, acceptance, and security. Safety. I never felt any one of those.

Back in High School, Bunny used to ask me, "Do you want me to send you to a mental hospital?" I'd say no. He'd say, "Then what excuse do you have for your shitty grades?"

The tyrant bully is over you. Intimidating. I waited for the fist. I sobbed. I am embarrassed to admit that. Where was my courage? Where was my bravery?

Looking back, I want to say where was my childhood?

My answer should have been "Stop beating my mom. Stop beating me and my brother. Stop bringing home Big Boy burgers on Sunday night at eleven and forcing us to eat. Stop bringing my mom home with black eyes and broken nose. And stop killing our dogs."

That should have been my answer. But he broke me and I was a coward. I became a shell just like my mother. My grades? I could have had straight A's. I didn't care. And worse. When I was home, I would dwell on what he was doing to damage us all. Focus on homework? That was not going to happen. I wrote poetry that I was the evil one and had to be punished. How fucked up is that?

Bunny taught me:

Treat women with respect. Never beat women. Love women with kindness. ***Not by his example.***

Cookie Monster

Went to PA one summer. My cousins had a finger puppet of cookie monster from Sesame Street. I wanted it. I wish I still had it.

Somehow I talked my cousins into giving it to me. It was three inches tall and made of plastic.

Mom that year asked me if I wanted anything special for Christmas. There was a cookie monster hand puppet. I said I wanted it. I paused. Then I asked her, "Do you think that's weird?"

She said no. Can you say regression?

I was a fifth, or maybe a sixth grader... and a Sesame Street hand puppet wasn't weird? No red flags?

I slept with it like a child sleeps with a stuffed animal.

Years later, in Savannah, there was a stripper who did her dance with a hand puppet of the muppet "Animal." She did her puppet routine to the Oak Ridge Boys' song, "Elvira." I was perhaps 21 and I wanted a hand puppet of Animal. I could not find one.

Hogan's Heroes

One night in Mentor, we were watching Hogan's Heroes. It was sometime between 1965 and 1971. Bunny said, "who plays sergeant Schultz?" I said I don't know. He said, John Banner.

The next night, he said, "Who plays Sergeant Schultz?"

I said I don't know. He said, "Go to bed right now."

I was scared. I didn't know what I did wrong.

But here's the thing that was so fucked up. To this day... I know that Bob Crane was Colonel Hogan, Larry Hovis was Carter, Robert Clary was LeBeau, Richard Dawson was Newkirk, Werner Klemperer was colonel Klink, Ivan Dixon was Kinchloe and Sigrid Valdis was Hilda. I never attempted to commit this to memory. It just happened. Causality? I don't know.

Bunny taught me many things that my mind cannot account for.

Bunny

My father had a nickname. They called him Bunny. I would be embarrassed to be called Bunny. Why did he accept that nickname?

There was a trip to New York, 1968?

Aunt Temple's first husband was Jim Shiels.

Temple told me when she was a little girl, she had a map of New York City on her bedroom wall. She told me as soon as she had an opportunity to live there she would jump at the chance. That chance came with Jim Shiels. I don't recall – maybe he was Army and stationed there? That's possible. But Temple and Jim got married and moved to New York.

Temple and Jim had their first daughter. Named Kitty after Catherine ("Kitty") Mooney nee Ross.

Kitty and I were at a zoo. I only know that because there are photos.

During the New York trip, Uncle Jim took the kids to the drive in. The drive in often had two movies. Double feature. Now I know that the first movie was "Chitty Chitty Bang Bang" with Dick van Dyke and Sally Ann Howes. So the year would have been 1968. I was seven years old in second grade.

The second feature was likely played with the anticipation that the kids would be asleep. It was "Barbarella" with Jane Fonda. I was awake in the back of the station wagon and sitting up watching it the whole time. The mechanical dolls gave me nightmares.

I used to wonder which movie was the second feature. Sometimes I thought it was the James Bond movie, "You only live twice." I saw both at the drive in. Too young to recall correctly.

Cleveland Television in the 1960s and 1970s

Friday nights at 11:30 p.m., it was Big Chuck and Hoolihan (aka Bob Wells). Monster movie night. It would end with pyjama party and the Peggy Lee song, "Is that all there is?"

Or on Saturday nights, there was the Ghoul on channel 61. That was Ron Sneed. We were too young for Ghoulardi (Ernie Anderson).

Or on Saturday afternoons, there was Marty O' Sullivan on channel 43 as Super Host. Super Host had a monster movie double feature. Back then it was Channel 3, 5, or 8. And VHS -- 25 for PBS and 43 or 61.

I suppose that Ron Sneed did a good job filling in for Ernie Anderson. But wouldn't know. I never saw Ghoulardi.

Monsters

Boyhood, all throughout, I loved monster movies. Very few scared me. Fewer gave me nightmares. Monsters had urges that they couldn't control. Dracula had to have blood. Wolfman had to kill. The Creature from the Black Lagoon had to have a mate. Frankenstein's monster? Well, he wanted to be normal and accepted – he is the most complicated. He killed or struck back when he was rejected. Shunned. Feared. He killed the little girl by accident.

Bunny became a monster by choice. Something drove him to believe that he "had to teach a lesson." They were wrong and he was right. "They" were us.

Were Rangers "monsters"? I'd say no. Nazis carried out orders immoral or not. Rangers carried out orders. To save, liberate. We never trained to punish, eradicate or any form of genocide.

Bob Bailey

Bob Bailey and I were friends in fifth and sixth grades at Elementary school. His father was a truck driver. Their basement was full of "boxes that fell off the truck."

Bob talked about a game called "cave man." We would go into the woods and get naked. Nothing else happened. I never understood the nature of the game. He had a younger brother. I think his name was Greg. And he would join us.

One day, we were at my house in Mentor and Bob, Cathy (my youngest sister) and I were in the pool in the back yard. It was an above-ground pool that we would scrub every spring to clean the mold.

After swimming, we were wrapped in towels in the bedroom I shared with Chuck. I went in to take a shower to wash off the chlorine. When I left, Bob was sitting on Chuck's bed and Cathy was sitting on my bed across from Bob.

If this was fifth grade, then I was eleven in 1971. Cathy would have been five.

When I came out of the shower, Cathy and Bob were still sitting where they had been. Calm, talking. Like kids do. No drama. Nothing suspicious.

Time lapse of maybe minutes. Bob went home, Cathy did whatever her thing was and mom came home. Somewhere in that, Cathy and mom talked.

Mom called me to the kitchen. There was a sense of *dire* urgency. The first thing she told me is that Bob Bailey is NEVER welcome here again. I didn't understand, but I accepted it and I said "okay."

She said, "Did Bob Bailey tell you anything about wanting to put his *worm* into Catherine?" I said no. I did not really know what she was talking about. She said Bob asked her if he could put his worm into her and Cathy said no. I was ignorant about the mechanics of sex. Must have been before the discussion of the birds and the bees which mom one day had with me.

When she did tell me -- it was an embarrassing event. She was an RN. So she explained everything clinically as if out of a medical text book. The subject of emotion was not a part of the conversation.

How should you feel? How should she feel? When do you know if it's right? Does Love play a part?

Those were my questions. I'll be damned if I even knew how to ask them. Back then.

Back to Cathy and Bob Bailey...

In 2019, this scenario came up again. Cathy said or accused me of standing by while Bob Bailey raped her. I said that's not true.

I came out of the shower and went into my bedroom and Cathy and Bob were sitting exactly as they were when I left to shower. If there had been a rape, there would have been blood. All over the sheets. Cathy would have been in a fetal position curled up and shaking. Or something. She was still in her bathing suit that she was wearing before I went to take a shower.

I came into the bedroom to find the two of them talking jovially.

Bob Bailey is certainly a scum bag pedophile. But Cathy is a drama queen with a bad memory.

Andy Luptak and the two-speed Huffy bike

Andy Luptak was Joey's older brother. Joey comes up in conversation later when I was at St. Joes (Ken Templin Letter). The Luptak brothers all worked at the Super market across the street from Royal Blue in Mentor. The name escapes me but they used to play Mason Williams' song, "Classical Gas" all the time. The cool version that has the horn section like they used on the Wrestling show.

The Luptak family were all dental patients of my father.

Andy had a two-speed Huffy bike that he wanted to sell. He trusted the Bunny and asked him what was it worth. Bunny said, "Fifty dollars." I was in Elementary school then so it had to be late sixties, or early seventies.

My father bought the bike for me.

When he showed me the bike, I was excited. It was a cool bike.

But then he bragged. He said that Andy asked him what the bike was worth and he said fifty bucks. He laughed and said he could have got one hundred and fifty for it. He said, "but I knew the next question would be, 'would you buy it for fifty?'"

He cheated a child. Likely a teenager. But still a child who trusted him. Bunny's code of ethic was like that.

But there was a day in Jack Even's yard at the corner of Cole and Magnolia that Andy took a branch from a weeping willow and whipped me until I cried. I never knew why he did that. Because he could? Do I wear a sign that says, I love pain?

But that memory was still with me and so when Bunny admitted he ripped off a child over his bike, I didn't say any objections. I should have.

Sometimes I praise something and sometimes I condemn an action. I'm told that that's what Virgos do. September 14th. Guilty as charged.

Steve Grosser

Steve's family moved into our rental home just behind ours. Cyndy befriended Chrissie and I befriended Steve.

His Dad was weird. He told us as fifth graders, we could look at any porn we wanted that only showed boobs. No bush. We were not allowed to see bush. Why? All you saw was pubic hair. A (usually) brown fuzzy, curly patch of pubic hair. No vagina.

Steve taught me how to shop lift. I had always thought that stealing was wrong. Steve justified it saying they don't miss it, the inventory isn't kept, they even add extra to allow for snatch and grabs. He taught me at Mannino's Drug store. We stole Partridge Family bubble gum cards.

Steve taught me more than that. Someone had sexually abused him. Therefore, he sexually abused me. Just like Steve Jordan did five years earlier.

The Grosser family moved and the sex assault ended.

But I continued to shop lift until I got caught at the Convenient Store along the route from Rice Elementary to Home.

I tried to deny it. But when the store owner confronted me, I admitted it.

I never stole again. And I would develop a deeply-rooted disdain for liars and thieves. Perhaps due to being guilty of being both.

Jimmy King and the Mentor Comics Administration (MCA)

Jimmy and I met in the fifth grade when we were both in drama school in Willoughby performing in a play called "the marvelous land of oz." My sister Cyndy was also there and Jimmy's sister Heidi.

We learned that we both loved comics and that bonded us. That was Fifth Grade in 1971.

We started to draw our own comic book super heroes and write stories. Jimmy started it with Omega Man. Then I did the Squirrel. Then he did the Protectors. And I did the Protectors.

Then we switched to comedy in comics. He did Bill the Dill based on Bill Link from his elementary school. And I did Chong based on my brother's creation of a super hero. Other than the name, the comparison ends.

I did a newsletter for MCA that I distributed to our fellow comic enthusiasts. The newsletter included mazes that I designed. Comic trivia, cross-word puzzles, mazes and new cryptic codes. One of my codes went like this...

"The quick brown fox jumped over the lazy dog." Rewritten like so:

TQ UK BW NX JP EV EH EZ YG
EH CI OR OF MU OD TR AL OD

After I taught the code, I would add cryptic messages to my newsletters.

At Mannino's drug store, they had a zerox machine. It photo-copied for 10 cents a page. I got the idea "why not tape all the pages together end-to-end?" The copies were shiny and all came out on one sheet long. I would use scissors to slice at the break and staple.

A five-page newsletter cost me one dime. Not fifty cents.

Later... music would be the bond. I loved the Beatles and David Bowie. Jimmy loved Elton John and Chicago. He played trumpet so the latter made sense. I was a singer.

Jimmy King revealed my naivety that I would not realize (to what extent) until years later

Jimmy and I met in fifth grade. I was ten in 1971. He moved to Florida permanently in eighth grade. I was thirteen in 1974. So our time together spanned those three years. Between 1971 and 1974. Those were important years.

One day there was a rope. A really long rope, looped onto itself and hung from a telephone pole at the southwest corner of Lakeshore Blvd and Reynolds road (route 306) in Mentor.

Jimmy was my best friend and so I trusted him.

I never trusted my father. He could not be trusted. So when I made a friend, my trust was without conditions. Without questions. I took him at face value and believed anything he told me. Hindsight, I should have been suspicious from the get-go.

Jimmy said the rope was left there for kids like us to cut it down and use it. It was around dusk. What Rangers called early evening nautical twilight. The sun is past the horizon, but enough still shines over the earth to provide some illumination.

Jimmy lifted me up to the first rung of the telephone pole and I climbed up to the where the rope was secured and cut it down with my pocket knife.

Jimmy and I build a tree house on the vacant lot at Lakeshore and Tall Oaks Drive. We connected the rope to our tree house and the next tree on the north side.

We did not get caught stealing that rope. So willing to trust. Naïve as hell. That would be a trademark all my life.

Any cop car pulling up would have busted us.

Jimmy stole from Tim Backovsky

I recite this incident with apologies to Tim Backovsky. Tim and Tami Backovsky were twins who moved into the home at the cross roads of Cole drive and Magnolia drive on our block.

Jimmy was an avid fan of the Fantastic Four comic from Marvel. I collected Spider-Man, DareDevil, Thor, Avengers, Marvel Team-Up, Luke Cage and Black Panther. Among many others. The John Buscema Conan the Barbarian stories were great and John Buscema's artwork was the best.

Interesting to note: John's brother Sal used to draw Captain America and the Falcon. I collected those as well. Until Frank Robbins took over the artwork. I don't recall that the writer changed. But I hated the artwork so much I stopped buying the issues. Back to Tim Bachovsky…

I think it was Tim's older brother who had a collection of Fantastic Four comics from the 1960s. All 12 cent issues. We used to group comics according to the price tag. Fantastic Four #1 was a ten cent issue. 12 cent issues were common in the 1960s but rare to find. 15 cent issues were less rare and garage sales had the occasional. When I started collecting, 20 cents was the cover price. I probably had 15 cent issues from grandpa Ross and uncles and aunts. Never from the Bunny. Bunny called them those goddamned funny books. Eventually those "goddamned" funny books had a value of $50,000. And they were collectors who were willing to pay. But things did not work out that way.

Tim Backovsky pulled the comics out to show us. They were in mint condition. Here's the thing… collectors nowadays use card stock backings and plastic bags to preserve the comics (after you read it of course). Back then no protection was employed. Seeing comics from that long ago in mint condition was a rarity. Where he stored them made all the difference.

Jimmy and I thanked Tim for showing us his brother's collection. We were both huge fans of the art work of Jack Kirby and his artwork was in all the issues of the Fantastic Four from issue #1 to #101. Tim had some great issues – great examples of Jack Kirby's artwork and Stan Lee's story telling. I was impressed that Tim's brother had preserved them so perfectly.

While Jimmy and I walked home to my house, Jimmy pulled out a comic from under his jeans and t-shirt. It was a

Fantastic Four comic book that he stole from Tim Backovsky. I never noticed that he stole it when it happened. He had amazing or desperate "slight-of-hand" skills that I never knew about.

I wanted to say we have to take it back. This is wrong.

Jimmy said, and this is a quote I'll never forget... "By hook or by crook." He was proud and gloating. Tim pulled them out of hiding because he trusted me. He didn't know Jimmy and would not have pulled them out to show him. Jimmy relied on Tim's trust of me to give him the opportunity.

One other incident. Mind you... I remained loyal to Jimmy. I never told Tim about the theft. And I should have told him so shame on me.

The "Woods" were south of Cole drive and east of Tall Oaks all the way to Clearair Drive where Tim Deegan lived.

I don't recall when. Jimmy discovered a log cabin-style fort. It was basically a box. Had a tarp roof for when it rained. And a mighty long rope up a tree next to the fort for swinging. The box was constructed like Lincoln logs. Notches cut to fasten. It stood about neck high.

Jimmy said it was abandoned and we should relocate it closer to our woods. He got all the neighbor boys involved. Jeff Piatela, Cory and Cass Warren, and my brother Chuck.

Dumbass me volunteered – because I was the best climber – to get the rope down. As much as I admired Sherlock Holmes, I didn't pay attention. If the cabin or fort had been abandoned the rope, it would have been rain soaked and dry-rotted. But it wasn't – it was like a brand new rope... probably because it was.

I don't know where the relocation site was. I never found out. I'm up a tree and suddenly there were four or five high school age teenagers storming around their clubhouse and they were pissed. And we were scared.

I was scared. I told them we were told that it was an abandoned clubhouse.

One of them shouted, "Does this look like it's abandoned?"

The block kids were sent to get Jeff Pietala's dad.

The boys who built the fort were walking around it saying, "this is great. Just fucking great."

Next the block kids were back. And who was with them? Not Jeff Pietila's dad. It was the Bunny.

He told me get out of the tree.

He negotiated with the Clearair kids and said it was a shame. And he was sorry it happened.

I don't remember what happened after that.

But I used to have nightmares of that day. To relive over and over again.

Who the fuck was Jimmy? His father screamed and he twitched. His sister Heidi was (to me) Maureen McCormick. My sister Cyndy was Marie Osmond (to Jimmy). Jimmy was allowed to have a crush on Cyndy. Any intimation of affection toward Heidi was banned.

In future years, I felt sorry for Jimmy. He had a habit of banishing people from this life. He banished Heidi. Then he banished Carl, his baby brother. Then he banished his wife's son (his wife Renee). Then he banished me. Good luck on your throne. Rhymes with alone…

Guitar Lessons in 4th or 5th grade

I took guitar lessons because I loved the Beatles. The problem was every time I came home from guitar lessons, the Bunny was there. I could not practice guitar. The Bunny made life miserable. "Oh, this -- a child making up stories?" No. I don't play guitar now and I never will.

Mom emailed today 4/05/2020

She said that Uncle Ron had died from the cancer. When I told Lynn she said, when did it happen? I said I don't know. She said, your family is so fucked up. She's right. In her family, if someone dies, everyone finds out. Immediately. Not weeks or months later to say, "oh by the way…"

Writing this book has taught me many lessons. One lesson is "normal" -- is not my family.

Since April 2020, I've worked at CVS. It's February 2021, and customers come in buying Valentine's day cards for daughters and sons. I've never got a valentine's card from a parent, sibling or a cousin or aunt or uncle. But people buy them all the time. Is that what normal people do?

I have been realizing, there are things that "normal people do," and things that our family does.

The rest of the Lindley Family

Uncle Junior died of alcohol. I don't know the date. He had a keg in his trailer and had beer for breakfast. He lived and died in a double wide. His wife was called "Aunt Toots." I never learned her real name. They had two sons. Britt and Brian. Britt became a career marine. Has a wife and family and a house – Montana? I have no idea. I met his wife and kids in 2003 when mom and I did a road trip to Eighty-Four.

Brian had a home across the street and a short distance from the farm-house. Grandma Lindley gave him the land. He built a huge three-story home with a full basement. His wife was like punk rocker with dyed hair… was it blue, green or purple? I don't recall. I liked it.

Brian had his dad's "illness" or uncontrollable need to saturate with beer. His punk rock wife left him. And Brian drowned his sorrows.

All the brothers of mom lived in Trailers. Initially. Some of them built homes on the land they were given from Grandma and Grandpap Lindley. Ron and Bob built houses. Junior was the drunk. He died from Alcohol and only had a trailer.

I should clarify. I was never judgmental of living in a trailer. You had roof, A/C, heat in the winter and a stove and fridge for food.

"Back woods" – that's a term of Pennsylvania or of Ohio referring to PA. Those who live way out where city infrastructure had yet made its way. Eighty-Four was like that in the 1960s and 1970s.

This is probably wrong. Mom had two brothers that died during Vietnam. One at the war and one after ETS driving home and rolling down a mountain.

Mom was born in 1937. Her brothers were all younger and so many were subject to the draft in the 1960s.

Uncle Ron has a beautiful home on Sugar Run Road in Eigthy-Four with a huge barn that he used for his tractors to mow the farm. 180 acres was no small task. At least that was the acreage at one point. Uncle Ron had one son named Barry – named after his brother. Cousin Barry was a wild one. Children want to connect to family. When Barry visited the farm, I used to approach him and want to connect. His time for children was limited and brief. You were dismissable. Sadly cousin Barry was diagnosed as a schizophrenic. Like most with that condition, when on his meds, "I feel great! I don't need these fucking pills." So he would stop taking them and then the trouble started. Tanya told me he died. Probably alone.

Mom's brother, my Uncle Barry died from AIDS. I don't know the date. But no one wanted to admit that he was gay or had a permanent lover. When Lise and I were separated for most of 1994, I went to the farm with my mom to see the family. It was really to see Barry after he had been diagnosed. To see him before he died.

I took my pastel drawings so I could ask him to pick one that he wanted. He chose the portrait of the little fox. Here we now are in 2020 and they have essentially rendered HIV non-detectable and non-transmittable. Does that mean you can transmit HIV to your partner but his test will be negative? That's scary.

There remains no vaccine. HIV mutates. Just like Covid-19.

In the 1980s and 1990s, I was in touch with neurologists because of Lise's job. She was the English editor for the journal Neurology (aka the Green Journal). Tarves Tucker was doing AIDS research and she predicted that a cure might be impossible to find because the virus mutates.

Now they have commercials that say if you're HIV positive, we have a drug for you so the virus will be undetectable... That means, you have the virus, it just won't show up in blood tests.

And there was another uncle who rolled down the mountain in his car. Post-vietnam. I don't know the date. Or his name. Maybe it was Dennis.

Mom was one of ten children. Back then they "sired and reared" farm hands.

Cloverdale

I did not make note of the year or date, but at some point, the Bunny stopped going to the Elks' lodge to get drunk and started going to Cloverdale. Cloverdale had another name... something like East Lake County conservative or conservation community. It was right across the street from Auburn High School in Concord Ohio.

These were old fishermen. They owned cottages around a lake. There was a waiting list to get membership.

Summer of 1972 and before 1973. Between 6th and 7th grade. We spent the summer at Cloverdale at someone's cabin on the lake.

The bunny was always around.

The next year, between 7th and 8th grade, I stayed in Mentor. Mom said are you sure? I said yes. Because I would never be anywhere near the home at 7398 Lakeshore Blvd. I could roam and Bunny would not matter. He didn't care. No witnesses to his drinking. I did not embibe back then. But if I did, I wouldn't join him. Bunny was a mean drunk and violent. The chip on his shoulder said, "You don't like me... Well I'm bigger than you and so I'm going to punish you and make you sorry for feeling like you're better than me because you're not."

I don't know when I wrote that, but it's so true... the Bunny wanted you to know that and never forget it.

Bunny taught lessons that one never forgot.

<u>Stevie at Cloverdale</u>

Her dad was Dick Hladik. And yes he was a dick. He was a member of Cloverdale.

Stevie Hladik was a girl whose father was a member of Cloverdale and had a farm for corn in the area.

Her father wanted a boy. Stevie eventually came out of the closet as a lesbian

Stevie told me be wary of age 13. "It's when you question everything." Stevie and I spent one summer acting like boyfriend and girlfriend. We kissed and held hands. It must have been before I was 13 because she gave me that advice. Thirteen was not the expiration date. I still question everything. And I'm 59. Read my poetry.

Stevie was – I had a crush at 12. In my mind, she was beautiful. Was that horny and 12 or romantic and observant? I remember most our conversations about emotions and how to treat other people. Did I carve our initials into a tree at the picnic grounds?

How should she read this? If we made love, we would be married. Would that mean you would not discover you're gay? Who made these questions? There was a time I questioned if I was gay.

Stevie and I never had sex. We kissed. We never broke up. If we did would that mean I rejected her? I don't have answers.

Emotionally I was stagnant. An object floating in a pond that didn't flow or move. Who taught me what feelings meant? Sadly, no one. It really made me feel all alone.

"How is this scenario supposed to feel?" Ask that to the stars in the night sky. I got the same answer that God gave me. Silence.

Others at Cloverdale...

Wally Mapes made the best waffles and mom got him to write the recipe for her to continue making them for us. Laurel Mapes was his daughter and a temporary short-lived crush (unrequited). I was probably 12 and she was 15? Go figure.

Frank Zagar. Frank had a cottage on a corner of the lower lake. There was a man-made upper lake and the original lower lake. They farmed fish. Frank had a brother Albert who lived in Mentor. Mom was close to Vera Zagar, his wife.

Once Frank taught me that you never keep your hand flat on any surface. You always arch it. He told me how a sledge hammer came down on his hand. He said that if his hand had been flat, the bones would have been broken. But because it was like a cup, it bounced the hammer. Like a coiled spring would do.

Frank used to build bird houses out of PVC. I commissioned him to build one for my friend Brandon Zart when he and April lived in Parma. Frank helped me install it.

Frank had a son who was a hell's angel. According to the Bunny, Frank's son killed a person. Bunny said that Frank paid the judge ten or twenty thousand to acquit. That's Lake County.

Lake County is biased against women.

When my parents got a divorce, the magistrate made the final decision.

This is public record so check it out.

Mom made X amount as a nurse in a nursing home. Her GROSS amount. The Bunny made X amount as dentist. A medical doctor. His X amount was his NET amount.

The fucking idiot magistrate said since his GROSS amount and her NET amount were only $13,000 different, then she go no spousal support.

Let me repeat that – the GROSS and NET amounts were $13,000 apart. Does any one need a math lesson?

Gross and net and not comparable.

Aino Kangas. As a child, he was my favorite. He was funny and had the most hilarious wit. When I was older, mom said he was a mean drunk. I never saw that side of him.

Matt Scoff was a pig farmer. The story goes that he was struck by lightning twice. The second time killed him. He made his own Shlivovitz. Technically, it's plum brandy. But most likely it was 180 proof.

My mom tells the story about how we visited Matt Scoff at his farm. According to the story, I was the only one brave enough to climb the fence and jump into the mud with the pigs and Matt. Everyone else could not stand the smell. I did not notice.

Matt Scoff died. Not after the first lightning bolt hit him, but after the second.

Breezewood Lane

Bunny bought a property that was going to be the site of our new home. I dreaded the idea because Steve Jordan moved to Concord.

It sloped up until you reached the wooded area where it had a sheer drop off to a ravine below.

He had a lake built in the front of the property and continued to have well-witches use their divining rods to locate water. Well-Witches were hocus pocus. But I thought they were real. I believed in Magic. Or I wanted to believe.

We had a garden. I think that was mom's idea. She told me how she'd go into the garden on the farm in PA with a shaker of salt and have lunch.

The strawberries sent runners all over the place.

Mentor Home Remodel

I think it was in 1973 when the Bunny started to remodel the Mentor house. He didn't want to pay the landfill fee so he dumped all the debris from remodeling into the ravine behind the lot in Concord. That had to be illegal. And what a scumbag to dump construction debris like that?

Back to Breezewood

Adjacent to the Breezewood property, there lived Ernie and Dorothy Nicka. As a kid, they were kind, loving, dear people. After the Army, Ernie told me about how he served in World War II under General George Patton. Ernie said we hated the cold showers and wearing a neck-tie into combat, but we would have followed General Patton anywhere.

Bunny built a garage on the property and had the driveway covered in gravel. I used to take girls there to have sex.

Jimmy King and Art

Jimmy and I had an interest in art. I introduced him to Chas Addams. He did cartoons for the New Yorker. Jimmy introduced me to M.C. Escher. I loved his art. Jimmy comes up again and again.

Years later at BP, I would spend lunch hours at Cleveland Public Library in the Art book section.

Jimmy King loved to test me

One day we were playing "Scrabble." He put down tiles that spelled, "IHIS." I said, "What's that?" He said that's what Jane said to Tarzan. I said take it away – there's no comma.

One day, he said "jump ya ornery pardnor." He was doing a mock Yosetime Sam voice. And threw darts at my ankles. One stuck.

Deer Hunting Trip to south Ohio

Bunny took me on a trip to go deer hunting. I don't know why. He never said, do you want to join me in the forest and track down and kill an animal? By the way, a beautiful animal.

Caveat – he never taught me how to fire a rifle. I didn't know how to load, turn the safety off or how to aim. I was a straggler. A follower along for the ride. I had no purpose. Was the lesson to reinforce that fact?

We drove god knows how long. To somewhere south. We stopped for dinner at a Red Barn fast food place.

Once we arrived, I set up my sleeping bag.

The next day, there was a lower branch that Jack Kernoodle hit his head on and so I made it my point of chopping that branch down. With a hatchet. Manly. To prove I was equal. What a joke.

Most of the time I was left on my own. The men left during the day. I should have brought more books.

They had these magazines called "Sex to Sexty" with porn cartoon left in the cabin. My curiosity opened the cover and read them while I was alone.

I remember going out to hunt. Once. Now, I'm a little kid. And I did not know shit about fire arms.

Wouldn't the point be to say, here's the safety, here's how you load, and here's how you pull the trigger?

Why was I there? To prove to his friends that he included his oldest boy?

The day before we left to drive back to Mentor we visited a farm and I watched how the cows were lined up and hooked to the milking machines. The Bunny was obviously friends with this dairy farmer. I didn't know cows were so passive.

Weslaco

Weslaco was a club that Bunny belonged to. As far as I knew he shot clay pigeons there. It had a huge clubhouse. We would sleep in the flat areas for sleeping bags. There was a huge painting of General Custer getting slaughtered by the native americans led by Sitting Bull. Way to go, Sitting Bull! I read Bury my heart at Wounded Knee. I didn't know it then. But I learned it later.

Weslaco had this summer fest for kids. Mostly I remember the Little Tom sodas. There were games like three-legged race. But Little Tom sodas made it an event.

Suicide

The thought of suicide never occurred to me. I learned in class that suicide is either anger – I'm gonna show you how much you don't care about me. Or despair. The state of such hopelessness that nothing matters.

Neither scenario applied to my angst. My pain meant punish me; I deserve it.

I had friends who were suicidal. They were cries for help and I listened. I quoted Bowie and didn't even know it. "Oh, no, love, you're not alone. You're watching yourself but you're too unfair. You've got your head all tangled up, but if I could only make you care."

And "Give me your hands."

I said the same words and didn't know it was a Bowie song. Look it up. I learned it later.

Ridge Junior High School

Seventh grade English. Miss Cipolla had us read the Diary of Anne Frank and 20,000 leagues under the sea. She also took us to see the play of Anne Frank. I asked myself, why jewish people? They were just people. I did not understand and would not understand for years to come. My naivete allowed its first glimpse of sunlight.

That year, we read the Diary and Twenty Thousand Leagues and she also had us read short stories. The anthology included "The cask of Amontillado," by Edgar Allen Poe, "Cat bird Seat," "A Most dangerous game," "The Landlady," by Roald Dahl, and "The gift of the magi, " by O. Henry. Classic short stories.

I tried my hand at short story writing inspired by Harlan Ellison. It was pretentious and arrogant. That was in Berlin from 1983-1986.

French Class & Bea Andrews

Bea Andrews taught us French. She was a delight. Desks were formed in two arching rows. First chair was to her left. If you answered correctly and the person to your right did not, you moved to the next seat. If everyone answered correctly and you did not, you went to the bottom.

Miss Andrews taught us that you can't learn a foreign language if you don't know your own language's grammar. This lesson was so important to me.

Day one she handed out a quiz. This was seventh grade French. She wanted to know: What is a pronoun? What is an adjective? What is an infinitive? How do you conjugate a verb? What is an adverb?

No one passed.

English grammar had not been taught. We had six years of school and how did that happen without even one year of grammar?

Learning a foreign language requires that your English grammar skills are top notch. I learned more about English grammar by studying French than I ever did in any English class.

Or to be fair – perhaps I never paid attention in English class. But I certainly paid attention in Miss Andrews' French class.

Bea Andrews was not loved by her neighbors. The story goes that a dog saved her life. A dog somehow pulled her to safety to the shore when she was drowning in a lake. As a result, she refused to let any dog at the pound be euthanized. I was told she had over fifty dogs in her home. Apparently they barked a lot much to the chagrin of her neighbors.

One day she asked, "Quel jour est au'jhourd'hui?" and for a week we were stumped. It was not me who finally got it right. The question was "What day is today?"

There was a French restaurant in Shaker Heights. It was called the Wagon Wheel. Miss Andrews took her class there for a French meal.

I was brave enough to try escargot. Snail. It mostly tasted of garlic so I didn't mind. I ordered frog legs. I had had frog legs cooked by Uncle Ken. They were great.

These frog legs were too peppery and slimy. Does Connie Tirpak remember that night?

Connie Tirpak

Connie was my friend all through French class. And in eighth grade, we went to France together. Hindsight? Connie would have been an excellent choice as a girl friend. I just wasn't there yet. Yes, I thought about girls.

But me? What was called "low self esteem" – I had it. Consider the Bunny.

How would I court Connie? No car. No job. In 8th grade I was 13 in 1974. I never understood how kids went steady back then.

What was called an "ID Bracelet.' Guys bought one and had it engraved. My ID bracelet was engraved with "CLEM" – upside down it looked like it read, "WEED."

Connie was smart. She was kind and considerate.

I realize in writing this that the young women I respected were all smart and kind. Most considered me a weirdo who liked monsters. I really didn't like monsters. But monsters were more tolerable than the bunny.

Bathroom in Junior High School

I don't know how… but I never went to the bathroom at Ridge. Never peed, and never had a bowel movement. Rumor was -- the ninth graders waited in the boys' room to give you a swirlee. That meant your head in the nasty toilet. Flushed so that shit stains circulated around your head and face. No thanks.

To my recollection, I never saw one kid show up for class with wet hair. But I was convinced of the threat. I did not need further convincing.

Mr. Gooding's Science Class

I was usually pretty good in science. I thank Tim Deegan for that since his dad was a chemist. But in seventh grade we had to do a leaf collection from trees.

The problem for me was that it required parent's help.

Mom was not helpful. She was beaten down back then to submission.

Lynn and I recently watched the Handmaid's Tale by Margaret Atwood and the character "Janine" who lost an eye for being defiant is so much a metaphor for my mom.

The Bunny was going to the Elk's lodge or Cloverdale. The location for libations blurred. I could not tell them apart.

I turned in no leaf collection and got an F on that project.

Mr. Gooding chose that moment to announce that the only student who got an "F" was Jim Ross who turned in no leaf collection.

He humiliated me. Not a teaching moment.

Mr. Gooding also never stopped Patrice Nerone from stabbing me with a thread puller in eighth grade. She penetrated my coccyx.

Bunny

Bunny never beat me with his belt. Perhaps he thought that meant, he treated me better than his father treated him. I would have rather been beaten with a belt and have it over with. The Bunny tortured with pain. Psychological was worst. The Bunny's torment continued. It was sober and drunk. That made me realize, he wasn't just a drunk sadist. He was also a sober sadist.

What does that say about the human condition? Diddley squat.

My damage is that I believed I was wrong. Bunny punished me for it. The truth got lost.

Tim Deegan

When Tim and I did homework together in seventh and eighth grades, we both got A's. After Tim moved to Kansas, my grades slipped. I did my own work. But Tim and I - we checked each other.

It wasn't like Tim did my work for me. But together we were stronger.

Runt

I was a runt in 7th grade at Ridge. Jim Cessna was my friend at Dale R. Rice. I don't know what happened. Suddenly he was a popular jock and I was a runt, a nerd.

Jim became a bully and I became HIS target.

I used to be his friend.

How did he become my enemy? Slaps to the side of the head were normal. The Bunny did that. Whap!

I hope one day Jim Cessna realizes that he tormented a former friend. Shame on him.

Joke Book

It was 7th or 8th grade. This book came out. One side was pollock jokes. You flipped it over and it was Italian jokes. I wasn't polish or Italian. The book was about stupid people. It had nothing to do with ethnic origin. I realized. Black jokes were identical. But they didn't call them Black jokes. They called them "Nigger" jokes.

Tell me what's the joke?

Tell me what degrades a human being to the extent that we are supposed to laugh at that person's expense?

Bunny loved nigger jokes.

He laughed. Why were nigger jokes so funny? Because they put down people. Belittled them as if they were less. Less than what?

Less than the Alt – Right. Less than -- the white supremacist. Less than the Ku Klux Klan. I didn't laugh. I was sad. Black lives matter started in 2013 with Trayvon Martin among others. George Floyd. Breonna Taylor. Never forget the names. Or Emmett Till. Or so many others.

Nerds

In Elementary school, we were all just kids. We learned and we played. Some times a bully emerged. But they were rare. At least from my perspective.

The smart ones began to band together. Tim Deegan and I.

Nerds was not a label then. I think they called us Brains. That changed in Junior High. Suddenly there were all these labels. The jocks played sports. The burn outs smoked pot. The nerds were smart kids into honor society, science, math, and good grades. There were the popular kids. Some were cross-over kids. Maybe a jock, maybe a brain. And there were the wallflowers or nobodys. The kids who just were not noticeable and did not stand out. I think I was my own category. I was a weirdo. My classmates knew of my affinity for monsters.

Seventh and Eighth grade, I was a 3.5 GPA B student. Excuse the conceit, but I was as smart as any 4.0 student. But home life with the Bunny was horrible. And this isn't whine whine whine… it was Saturday night and Sunday night domestic terror. The drunk asshole tormented wife, children and dogs.

I remember once how I wanted to learn to play guitar. The teacher would give me lessons. I'd go home and not touch the rented guitar for a week.

I could never practice at home. Why? Aunt Veronica played guitar. She taught my cousin Chris. He tried to teach me the chords to Wild Thing by the Troggs. That was as far as I got.

She's a dog but Wendy was hot

At Ridge, the worst insult to a woman was to say she was a dog. Decades later and calling someone a dog meant your brother or your sister, it was ceremony. Not derogatory. "Whassup, Dog?"

1981 or 1982 when I was home on leave, I met Suzanne Stiffler at a bar in Painesville. The Brass Rail. Suzanne Stiffer was there with Carol Neiman. Joanne Southwick was also there.

Joanne was "the Cheryl Tiegs"… my metaphor. Joanne sat at the bar. She was practically in tears. Suzanne said "please tell her she still looks like Cheryl Tiggs."

I did. It didn't work. Joanne cried at the bar. My poetry has recurring themes. The demon brothers, Regret and Resent are primary.

When we left the bar, we drove to Wendy Fisher's apartment. Along the way, Suzanne asked which was more important – girth or length?

Wendy Fischer went out nightly. I knew her at Ridge. The other boys called her a dog. I didn't know why. She was slender, athletic. And all so sexy. Wendy was like the porn star you craved. She was the Marilyn Chambers of Ridge Junior High.

I was unacceptable because Wendy went out in search of someone. I was not an option.

I never insulted her.

American Institute of Foreign Study (AIFS)

Spring Break of eighth grade for me, seventh grade for Cyndy, we went to France. Bea Andrews made the arrangements. Back then it cost $650 per person and that covered the flight, hotels, meals, the bus, the train and the tour guides. We had ten days in France. Half in Paris. The other half was a bus trip all the way to the riviera and into Italy for a lunch meal. Then a train trip back to Paris for the return flight.

The Bunny bought me a camera for the trip that required no flash. But you had to stay perfectly still until enough light entered the aperture. That was fine in a hotel or all alone. But we were most often in a crowd on tour of a location and standing shoulder to shoulder, you got bumped.

In Paris, the Louvre was closed. Was that when they built the pyramid with I.M. Pei.

I wanted to see Notre Dame Cathedral. I loved the gargoyles. In the gift shop, I bought a gargoyle that to this day, hangs in our living room.

In some gift store, I bought a black beret and wore it every day.

How ironic that six years later I would wear a different kind of Black Beret – the Ranger Black Beret. "Earned, not issued" (hear that Shinseki?).

Our parents had to sign a waiver if we were going to see a show at the Moulin Rouge. That's because the famous can-can was done without underwear. Commando as it's called now.

One evening we had French Onion soup for dinner at a place that had musical entertainment with an accordian.

You had to peal your fruit in order to eat it because the French used human feces to fertilize. I forgot this one evening and ate an apple. I spent the night puking my guts out. I was sharing a hotel room with the students from North Carolina. Tim Kline, Manley "Brit" Mills and one other guy. I think I puked on some of their clothes.

Brit and I went shopping for a music box for his sister. We ended up in a French department store. It reminded me of the May company or Higbees. I was not expecting Brit's next action and it caught me completely off guard.

Let me start it with this. American accents of foreign languages are the worst. Americans laugh at the Spanish accent of Speedy Gonzales. No Mexican talks that way. It's like the exaggeration of "Treasure of the Sierra Madres."

"Badges? We don't need no stinking badges..."

Brit walked up to this young unsuspecting French girls and said, "Avez-Vous une boite de musique, you know, do y'all have any music boxes?"

I loved Brit. He was my companion and friend. Brit was from Shelby, North Carolina. Sorry Brit. Your French accent sounded like Gomer Pyle. And adding the English question with "y'all" made it all the more humorous.

I had tears streaming down my face.

I loved the students from Shelby and Charlotte, North Carolina. I had a crush on Colleen Hill. WTF, I was an eighth grader. Crushes are turnstiles.

Tim Kline was a riot. He was really funny. I was thirteen but he insisted on calling me, "Mister Ross." It wasn't a southern charm thing. He took it upon himself to show me that I was special among the ranks.

Cyndy had Connie and her older sister as her room mates. Connie was in my class. They came to me to complain that Cyndy did not like how they tidied the room.

I said talk to her. I don't know if they did or did not.

One day on the bus, driving south through France, Cyndy was sobbing in the back of the bus. She had to pee and there was no bathroom on the bus.

She was afraid to speak to Miss Andrews. I spoke to Miss Andrews and we made an emergency stop.

She was my sister. I protect the ones I love. She was 12.

When the Bunny developed my photos, he called me "Shaky" and was pissed about how many blurry pictures there were. I thought let me shove you around and see how still you would remain. But one didn't challenge the Bunny. He was right and you were wrong. Always.

That's why lies came easily.

The Bunny taught us to lie to avoid punishment. You didn't want punishment. "Did you do this?" No. Well, if he couldn't prove it, you were clear. If he could, you got his form of punishment. Most of the time, I would have preferred a beating. A beating was easy to tolerate. Once done, it was over. The other was retaliated again and again ad nauseum.

ID Bracelets

At Ridge, if you were a guy, you had to have an ID Bracelet. It was a chain with a flat piece to engrave your name. This was 1972-1975.

This was so if you wanted to go "steady" with some girl... You would ask her to wear your ID bracelet. Going Steady meant that she – the girl you asked – would not go out with any one but you.

"Go Out" – that was never defined.

The norms of these years were so fucked up.

Girls didn't have some jewelry to pin on a guy.

Seventh and Eighth grade -- we were twelve and thirteen – we didn't have a job or money. But we were supposed to have an ID bracelet.

I don't know how or who paid for it but I had one.

It had my name – the short version. But upside down, it looked like it spelled "WEED." Must have been the font.

I also had a belt buckle of David Bowie from his 1976 tour as the Thin White Duke. Kids at Lake Catholic would ask me where I got a belt buckle with my own photo on it. That was cool. A one sided compliment. You mean, I look like Bowie?

Catholic Youth Organization (CYO)

Frank Zappa does a hilarious song about the CYO. It's from Joe's Garage and it's called "Catholic Girls."

Cyndy and I were in the CYO. We shoved snow in the winter to raise money for the church.

We had meetings. I eventually became the treasurer. Patty Aranavage would sit in front of me on the floor and blink her eyes. I thought she was mocking me. Patty was a crush but I introduced her to Bob who rode Husquavarna bikes. Missed opportunity.

In the CYO, We had retreats.

CYO retreats seemed more like let's match potential couples who will marry and contribute to the church.

My next crush was Donna Kovach. We were on a retreat, and one night, she was really high and confessed to me that I was too good and she was so bad… she had sex and did drugs.

She imagined me as someone pure and innocent. I told her otherwise. She didn't believe me. How ironic. Donna rejected me because she thought I was wholesome and she was the sinner. The opposite was true.

Her best friend, Denise "Dinny" Moore invited me to be her date to the South High School fall dance. I forget which year. But I think I might still have the photo. I was a gentleman and kissed her good night after the formal dance. I don't think she expected anything more other than a chaperone and dance partner. Dinny was sweet. I'm sure she has become someone's "best love."

Further on the CYO

CYO – another retreat – Brandon Zart from St. Joe's came along. I still had a crush on Donna Kovach. Joey Del Vecchio teased me about it. He saw how I looked at her…

Cyndy liked Joey and his older brother. The other Del Vecchio

Brandon and I smoked pot together. Brandon was more Catholic than me.

I didn't know that until later.

While in the shower, Brandon sang "Death Trip" by Iggy and the Stooges. I could not have done it better. We smoked a lot of pot that retreat

Driving to the location, Brandon drove himself. Me and one other guy in the CYO, we had the cop and his wife. They drove. I asked him to play Bowie. He scoffed at the suggestion. He played Simon and Garfunkel the whole way. I listened and realized that I recognized the music. Cecilia, the Boxer, Bridge over troubled waters… So many songs that I knew by heart. But I did not know the name. Except for "Cecilia." I had the 45. Perhaps backed with "Bridge."

Here's the funny thing. I don't know when the green light came on – I'm sure it was when I started paying attention to lyrics. Due to Mrs. Schaeffer at Lake Catholic.

I tried several times to get back in touch with Mrs. Schaeffer. Included going to Lake Catholic. I was blocked every time.

Every Brothers' "Wake up little Susie." It didn't occur to me that it was about having sex and falling asleep. Naivete again.

But this one should have been obvious. "Cecilia" by Simon and Garfunkel. I had the 45 and knew all the lyrics... I just didn't connect to the meaning.

"Making love in the afternoon with Cecilia up in my bed room"

Background chorus sings, "Making Love..." That means sex.

"I got up to wash my face (cunnilingus).

"When I come back again, someone's taken my place."

So having sex with Cecilia... Perhaps it started as coitus, switched to oral. Cecilia must have orgasmed, because that's the only time one would stop to wash one's face. Was Cecilia a squirter? Or maybe she didn't like kissing a face covered in "pussy juice." Okay, I do not write that with any disrespect. I personally love that.

Yeah that's crude. But the point is that the lyrics need to be interpreted.

So the narrator leaves and when he comes back, there is someone else – gender is not identified. Someone else who is now doing oral or fornicating. With Cecilia.

As a student in elementary school, I had no idea how sexual these songs were.

Now that said, I never condemned them. Once I realized the sexual nature, I loved them more. How clever to disguise the meaning with the lyrics.

Billy Holiday did that with "Strange Fruit." But that wasn't about sex. It was about illegal lynchings. And black men being hung for no reason. A song that TIME magazine called the "Song of the Century."

Again, Ridge Junior High School.

Ridge Junior High School. I had been with these people… most of them through the six years at Dale R. Rice Elementary. I had many close friends.

Teri Pealer, Connie Turpek, Tim Deegan, Chris Delly, Jeff Ficke, Wendy Fisher… these were all my friends. There were more. Bunny told me to leave them. I did not want to leave them. They were my friends.

There were others. I'll name them later.

After eighth grade, my parents decided: I should become a catholic and go to catholic high school "because the catholic high schools had no drugs." Hah!

I did not want to leave my friends. I did not want to go to Catholic School. I do not like them Sam I am. I will not eat green eggs and ham. Yeah, that's flippant. Sorry.

At Saint Joe's, I bought my first nickel bag of pot in ninth grade from Bob Lopez. He thanked me for helping him pay for his college tuition. At least, that's what he wrote in my year book.

First Joint

Jimmy King and I built a tree house out of scraps of lumber we found. It was in the corner tree by the vacant lot where Eddie Jewart, Brian Jewart and I would play running bases.

I went into the larger chamber of the tree house and rolled my first joint. I did not know you were supposed to remove the stems and seeds from the bag and only use the "shake." The joint kept popping. Flames hit a seed, and POP.

95

Beverly Krofta happened to walk by. "I know what you're doing up there. My older brothers smoke pot. I can tell by the smell." I do not recall how I responded, but obviously I was busted. Perhaps I said, "do you wanna come up and join me?" But probably not. It would only be a few more years and she would blossom into a beautiful young woman. It didn't flirt with Bev. Her sisters Vickie and Karen were gorgeous. Model material. But I did flirt with Perry.

Perry Warren

Perry Warren lived on Clearmont in Mentor. Perry was a smart woman. Insecure like me. I didn't know about her family life.

Perry didn't get the attention the "pretty girls" got. Let me explain. There were girls who were barbie pretty. They looked like orangutans, but so did Barbie.

Perry was a face that needed no make up. She was pure.

Perry studied everything, There was not a subject she could not answer.

Why did Perry like me? I know why I liked her. She was delicious.

One day on the bus to Ridge Junior High, she quoted Bill Cosby better than I ever could. I thought I had all his records from the 1960s memorized. Perry beat me hands down. She did the sound effects. She did the voices. I was so impressed.

Perry was a young woman who wanted to be accepted. As a person, as a woman.

I have to ask Perry what may I tell about us? I will not betray confidence.

I wanted to tell in this document about our bat mitten match. That is between Perry and me and no one gets that detail.

I saw Perry again when she worked at the convenient store across Lake shore blvd after I got out of the Army. 1987. She was as beautiful as ever.

I was too insecure to ask her out.

If I could just talk to Perry Warren again... There are certain girls who are fuckable. One night. Others who are "This feels good for about five times." Then there are those who are "just right" – like the three bears in Goldilocks.

Perry Warren was just right.

We never had coitus. Oh, that would have been lovely... but it did not happen.

I wonder if Perry would want me to reveal this. I cherish my memories of her. What Perry and I learned without trying was with intimacy, it is the one who gives who achieves the greatest pleasure. Not the one who gets. Giving grants the greatest pleasure.

If I were to write a love letter to Perry. I would want her to know: our intimacy was genuine. We were just too immature to know the words to convey it. I know it wasn't love. What child understands that concept? But the intimacy was not fake or superficial. There was a deep caring that we each felt. But our brains could not put the words in our mouths. Where we lacked the words, we expressed physically. You showed me love. Thank you. Did I show you it back? I hope so. It was pure and genuine.

My genuine side probably ended with Perry.

CYO and Jeri Jauch

Jeri and I met on a retreat (that's Catholic term for we go camping and pray and do religious stuff. The purpose was to develop moral teenagers. The outcome was to fire the flames of lust – then marriage). To become good catholics and give 10%.

I was the weirdo. I never wanted to lie about wanting sex. But I did. I wanted to be known as the gentleman who respected women.

When I met Jeri, I was impressed with her intelligence. She was so smart. So confident. I was a totally insecure nerd.

I think I was flattered that she was even interested. There's a song, "she's so high above me..." – that's a lyric, not a title. Maybe from James.

Jeri and I made out at the retreat. Sexual touching but nothing more. We could have done more. Desire was there. I don't know. Saving it for marriage?

Had she been willing. But I paused to understand limits. If initiated, I participated. Gladly and gratefully. I loved the intimacy.

Jeri and I... it was different. Sometimes I thought she had our entire future plotted out from engagement to marriage to children to old age and retirement to adjacent plots.

Jeri was a planner. She knew what she wanted. And she would make sure every "T" was crossed and every "i" doted... I had no goals. I was lost. Family life sucked so bad. Jeri deserved a decent kind man.

My family life – my father was a tyrant bully. How could I ever be normal?

If I wanted to be true to protecting my mother, then I had to be true to protecting Jeri and any other decent woman. I didn't know about the seventh son back then. All I knew was "the sins of the father run unto the son for seven generations." That doomed me to repeat.

I had to protect Jeri from me.

One day she saw me at Mentor High School talking to Sue Heeter. Jeri told me she was a slut. I said she was my friend. We both loved the Beatles and she introduced me to Mott the Hoople.

I used to talk on the phone in the dental office. When I wanted a private conversation.

It wasn't that night. It was many nights later.

Jeri and I talked about Sue Heeter. I asked her, "So do you think you're better than her?" Jeri said, "yes."

Was that the excuse I needed? I don't know. I'm 58 now. I write this remembering – with a 58 year old brain. How much is accurate and how much is tainted by memories?

Jeri, I broke up with you to protect you. Or so I tell myself. But I can't lay in your arms now and ask you to forgive me.

The demon twins, Regret and Resent, they haunt me to this day.

Bob Evans Restaurant in Mentor

At age 16, I worked at Bob Evans. Bus Boy, then dish tank. Then grill chef. I worked there until I joined the army.

I had many friends at Bob Evans.

John Tozzi who much later went to Kent State and sent me a photo of a party in the dorm room. I connected with him on face book before I deleted my account due to a stalker. John was now a sports writer. I think in Pittsburgh. I introduced John to Devo.

Mike Taylor and I smoked a lot of pot and went to some pretty cool concerts. We saw Alice Cooper's "From the Inside" tour.

Denise Dugger. We tried to date and went to a show at the Painesville Agora. My friend from Lake Catholic referred to Denise as the girl that everyone wanted to date. He was the biggest Rush fan I ever met. Denise lived in his neighborhood. Wickliffe? Perhaps. Denise was gorgeous. She was sweet and kind.

Peggy and Amber Womack. Amber was Peggy's daughter. We all considered her our little sister. Amber and her wife Lisa visited Lynn and me in 2018. Amber reminded me that I never let her lift the lower bus cart tray onto the dishtank surface. I had a strong back back then. It wasn't that Amber wasn't strong. She carried her own as a "bus boy." I just felt protective of her. She called me a gentleman. Yes, with Amber.

Bobby Stevens. Actually Bobby grew up on our block. On Magnolia Drive a short distance from the Carpenters but on the other side of the street. His family moved some time in the 1970s. Bobby used to do "Whippits" in the cooler and piss off the waitresses. Whippits were the act of taking a can of ready whip and holding it vertically and turning the nozzle in your mouth. You got no cream, just the gas that gave you a brief high.

Anita was a hostess. One night, I do not recall how it started or who initiated it, but we ended up in my parents' van in the parking lot of John Vianney parish and in the back of the van we had sex. Restaurant workers all fuck each other. I talked to Lynn about that and she said the same thing when she was the manager of an R.J. Gators in Fort Myers.

Rusty Thomas worked there until he joined the army. I tried to talk him out of it. Rusty and I met two college girls and took them to Cedar Point in Sandusky. I don't know if we were every boyfriend/girlfriend. They were pissed if we didn't call until they learned that we were planning the trip to Cedar Point. Then they were thrilled to go on the excursion. Cedar Point was an amusement park with world famous roller coasters.

Diane Smith. She was a waitress who asked me to help clean the stable where her horse was. I never thought of it then, but what waitress has a horse in a stable? Anyhow, she "let me fuck her" afterwards. I chose that wording because I had a crush on her. I wanted an emotional connection. When she invited me into her bedroom, I was thrilled. But afterwards, it was like quid pro quo. She was done.

Another waitress… I think her name was Linda. She dated Chuck Beck. She ended up in Real Estate and I met her again around 1999 when I was married to Patti Glaser.

Two more mother and daughter waitresses were Marie and Anne Marie. Anne Marie had never been to a rock concert. She was the mom. I said if you let me, I'd like to take you to a rock concert so you can see what it's like. The band Cheap Trick had a show at the Cleveland Coliseum and I told her I would buy the tickets. Her daughter could not believe I wanted to take her mom to a rock concert. I said Marie, it's not a date.

The day of the concert came and Anne Marie backed out. I took Bill DeGidio. We left during the encore song "Surrender."

There was a waitress named Joanne. Willoughby High School student. I really liked her (as a friend) and she liked me. One time she invited me to a party. I didn't know it but she was setting me up with her friend.

This is where I reveal what a shit I am. I fucked her friend and her friend was delighted. But two days later, Joanne brought her friend to the Bob Evans where we both worked and I hid.

WTF, over? Why did I hide? I can't tell you why. Joanne told me how very ashamed she was of me and how could I do that? I could not answer her question.

I'm sorry. I can't say that Bunny fucked me up. I have no idea why I did that.

To this day, I don't know.

She was pretty, smart. I have no answer. I should have been flattered and humbled. And grateful.

Chuck Beck was the manager I respected most, admired, and practically loved. No, I didn't want to have sex with him. He was my first teacher and mentor. Chuck busted me *every single time* I tried to get away with some stupid shit... like sticking my empty cigarette pack out the window in the Bob Evans parking lot. He was there handing it back to me saying you know better than that.

He also loved David Bowie and Jazz. We went to see live performances of Jean Luc Ponty and Ian Hunter together.

One night we closed. We had to do biscuits. In the manager's office there was a ladder to the roof where we opened the hatch and smoked a joint. I sang "Folks you got trouble" from the Music Man and Vincent Price's intro to the Alice Coopers song, "the Black Widow." Then we went down and opened the book and made biscuits according the recipe. The next day, the waitresses said we made the best biscuits ever.

I remember one time giving blood at Mentor High, then walking from Mentor high on 615 to Bob Evans on 306. It was a long walk. I think I prepared myself for the Army by walking so much. I couldn't tell you how many miles it was from Mentor High to Reynolds road. But I took a route that would start at Phoebe's home on Texas avenue. Phoebe had a garden in her back yard. I think we pulled weeds.

I spent two hours on Texas Avenue working in Phoebe's garden. I loved Phoebe.

One day she came to Bob Evans in a Gray pin stripe suit. She had red hair. I told her she looked like David Bowie in his 1976 tour outfit. She was not amused. Phoebe did not like being compared to David Bowie.

When I arrived at Bob Evans, someone had called in sick. I filled in and closed.

I gave blood and then worked until closing.

There was a waitress... God forgive me how many names of important people have left my memory... probably due to alcohol.

This waitress, she had dark brown hair and "olive skin"... that's the complexion when it's not white and not black or latino. Why do they say olive skin? She wasn't green? As Doug would say, "But I digress..."

She had a close friend die in a car accident. It devastated her. I tried to comfort her. For all of the suspicious serpents out there I was not trying to get laid.

I went with her to the funeral and we would take drives into Concord to talk and grieve... well, she would grieve. I would listen.

The funeral was strange to me. It was my first funeral since Grandma Ross died. We went there... 1967?... children were not allowed to see the body.

My waitress friend's friend was open casket. We walked up to view the body. What I saw was not a person. The shell was a mannequin. A wax figure. The essence was gone. What ever had been there when she was alive was gone.

Every funeral since then, that I'd gone to, I saw the same thing. Karl – my French professor at Cleveland State. His last name spelled with no vowels.

So where does the life essence go?

Some say Heaven. I ask where does what animated the shell go?

The shell was animated. Alive. That substance was gone. After death, the life essence leaves. Where does it go? Newton said you can't destroy energy.

I never told her. I saw a casket with a mannequin.

More on Bob Evans -- Phoebe and Mark

Phoebe was a great woman. I remember working in her garden off Texas avenue.

She came in one evening and wore a grey pin-stripe pants suit. Pink blouse. She looked like David Bowie. I told her so. She did not consider it a compliment. Okay I had a crush. She was red headed.

Mark was a manager. Phoebe and Mark started "dating" in secret and fell in love. Phoebe told me they had passion. That was the same thing Lynn said about me. Phoebe told me her husband was a good man, a good father, and a good provider. But she felt no passion for him.

I helped them move to Canton (?). Mark was taking over a restaurant as the new manager. This was where they would start a new life. I took a bag of pot and papers for rolling joints. Phoebe's kids weren't with us. So the three of us got high. After the truck was unloaded.

Fishing trips to Canada

Every summer, the bunny took trips to Canada with a group of doctors and lawyers. My father considered it his right to go on trips without his family. But he would leave and we were relieved. We had two or three weeks with him gone. That meant no one got tortured. Not one got beat. No dog was killed.

When he returned the hate and violence came with him. That is the idiom that captures it. Hate and Violence.

What I will never grasp is why he hated us. The consequence was hate. Why else punish us? But what prompted the hate? Did we not live up to his expectations? How did we disappoint?

The Bunny returned with a cooler full of frozen fish. It was my job to clean them and make them filets. They were mostly walleye and large-mouth bass.

Packed on ice, they stank. They secreted a gel that reeked. I fileted them and had to dash to the back yard to gag. And usually throw up.

The smart, sexy, successful, intelligent and kind ladies of Ridge Junior High

There was something in the water at Mentor. All the smart girls were also the most gorgeous. Teri Pealer, Bonnie Booth, Michelle Jaczesko, Bravina Travato, Helen Pelacanos, Connie Turpak, Allison Farone, Mickey Maleski, Michelle Kean, and Shari Wakely. I'd add the names of the others. Each one had brains and beauty. I might be biased. I valued and still value intelligence over the physical or the popular.

I remember a day at Fairport harbor and meeting several classmates at the beach. They were in bikinis. They were prettier than ANY Playboy playmate model.

Why did the douche bags guys call Allison, "Fifi"? Back then if a girl was deemed ugly, they called her a "dog." How ironic, that that term now means close friend. In 1969, Iggy Pop had a song called, "I wanna be your dog."

Bravina Trovatro

When I worked at BP, 1991 to 1999, Bravina Trovato had her barber shop in the Euclid Arcade. Third floor. Bravina and I were at Ridge together. Bravina would use her massager and give back rubs after your hair cut.

That had not been done since Frank's barber shop on Lakeshore Blvd in 1970.

At some point in time, Bravina moved her operation to Vine Street.

Comic Books in the 1990s

In the 1990s I still bought comic books. Jim Williams had a store in the Euclid Arcade downtown. All he knew about me was that I was a customer in a suit and tie. That was the uniform at BP.

Little by little Jim and I had conversations about comics and I think he realized I knew writers, artists and comics – mostly 1960s and 1970s. I told him that the 1980s were a void due to the army.

Jim introduced me to the part time employee who was also a bike courier. His name was Brian Michael Bendis.

Brian told me he went to CIA – Cleveland Institute of Art. Brian was a beautiful artist when it came to cityscapes and characters. His professor at CIA told him that comic art was not a legitimate form of artwork. I said that fans of Jack Kirby, John Buscema, Johnny Romita and John Byrne would disagree.

Brian published his independent graphic novels. One was called "Quills" about vigilante women who used bows and arrows. I liked Brian and liked his artwork. But I was a dedicated Marvel fan and DC only when Jack Kirby did the story and art. Until Frank Miller came around.

In 2003, the "DareDevil" movie came out. In one scene, there is a movie theater style marquis. It was for a boxing arena. The name Bendis was shown on the marquis.

I hit the libraries for graphic novels. Brian had become a very successful writer of DareDevil and many other titles. His film noir style was a really popular motif among the fans.

Good for you, Brian. I knew you were smart, creative, talented and had a future. I never had the artistic skill and couldn't plot a comic story. Though I tried with the MCA back in the 1970s.

DareDevil 2003

Matt Zolnay and I were at Tower City in downtown Cleveland when the poster for the upcoming DareDevil movie would premier on February 14, 2003. Matt said, "we're there."

Doug Enkler

I met Doug in kindergarten. We were in the same class. I didn't know Doug in Kindergarten. I didn't know him at Ridge. We actually met or re-met at Mentor High. As I recall, I had class photos from Kindergarten to fifth grade. After that they did year books.

My kindergarten photo showed Doug and me on the same bleachers. I just didn't know or didn't remember him.

In the late 1970s, Doug said his Dad, Carl, would ask him when he got home from Kindergarten, "So… how was Clem-Clam today?"

Doug didn't say if he answered the question, or if he did, what his answer was.

Mark Vocca told me that Doug once said, "Clem would take a little detail and make it grand."

I miss Doug. He disappeared in 1999. Mark called it getting "Enked." He did it to me first then to Mark. Come back, Doug – all is forgiven.

Doug and I had a disagreement. Remember the milk cartons in Elementary school? Each of the four sides had a president. They showed his face, years of service and nickname – there may have been other facts. I don't recall.

I recalled one milk carton had a President whose nickname was "Old Kinder Foot." I insisted it was president McKinley.

Doug said I was wrong. He said it was Martin Van Buren and it was Old Kinderhook.

Google proved Doug right and me wrong.

Sometime in the future, perhaps 1997, Doug sent me a post card. It read: "A toast to my big brother George, the richest man in town." Frank Capra allusion.

No greater compliment has anyone ever paid me.

<u>13 years old – 1974 – 8th grade</u>

In Painesville there was a bookstore. It was really a magazine store. I went to the Orthodontist there across the street. I met Lauren Coyne there. The bookstore had Travel magazines, cooking, politics. It also had an adult section. I went there while waiting for mom to pick me up after the appointment with Doctor Vosmic. He was the orthodontist. The adult section was restricted to 18 and over. I did not venture there.

Back then, Orthodontists pounded braces into place with a hammer and a chisel.

It hurt like hell and I waited for him to break a tooth.

At the book store, the clerk would have conversations with me. He asked me if I was AC/DC. I didn't know what that meant. He said it meant "both ways." I still didn't know what that meant. I said I don't even have my driver's license yet. He was 40 something and saw a child as a sexual object. Was I a target?

The system of education in the 1960s and 1970s did not teach kids anything more than "don't talk to strangers" and "Don't get into a stranger's car."

They never said, if a pervert wants a liaison with a 13-year old child --- IT'S WRONG. I eventually figured out what the clerk wanted. My naivete. That made me slow to catch on.

Once I went back to the book store after an appointment. Angry or curious? There was a different manager or clerk – whatever his title was. The new guy said, we let him go. The pervert got fired.

<u>Father Kline and Becoming Catholic</u>

In 1973, My sister Cyndy and I took classes with Father Kline from Saint John Vianney parish in Mentor, Ohio. It was a slide show with artists' renditions of various scenes of the Biblical history.

The slide show with a carousel displayer of slides like the old days projected on a movie screen... it covered Adam & Eve, Cain & Abel, Abraham and Isaac, Moses like the "The Ten Commandments" movie, Jesus, the crucifixion, resurrection, the forgiveness of our sins.

Ask any thirteen-year-old, what is your favorite question? The answer is, "Why?"

So "God" -- who is a god? Explain that to a 13 year old. Anselm said, "that than which nothing greater can be conceived." No 13-year old gets that.

Try Aquinas. The first mover. Compare it to a pool table. Who takes the first shot – that sets the universe in motion. That means the universe already existed? Like the pool table?

Designer made sense. I could accept that. Robert Frost taught me design.

But science steps in and calls it instinct. Yeah tell that to bees who dance to tell the others where the flowers are.

Instinct sez, my bladder is full, I have to pee.

Instinct doesn't say, the flower orchard is 300 meters on a 90 degree angle and then 250 meters on a 120 degree angle. But that's what bees do with their dance. Not instinct – design. Hence a Designer.

They – His followers -- call him "He." Males deliver seed. Woman gives birth. Who is the creator?

Why isn't it She?

And He had sex with the virgin Mary. Not a virgin anymore. But's it's the immaculate conception. Define the two words and that's a hard definition to explain. But she was a human being. Different species. How is that possible?

I had a jewish friend who was a Jews for jesus say to me, "that's why it's a miracle." I dismissed his answer. I hope I did not dismiss him with condescension like Lise. She was proud to be an elitist snob. I didn't understand that and neither did Bill.

Karl Strmn taught me that "snob" came from the time when the British Royals would sign in for French University... they had to sign in without royal title of duke, duchess, prince, princess...

Written it was "Sans Nobilité." That meant without the official royal title. Abbreviated it was "s.nob."

Two thousand years ago, in a time of war and commerce, there was this son of a carpenter who said, "Love." That was cool. He was a rebel. Forget wearing t-shirt or hanging posters of Che Guevara. Jesus Christ was one helluva rebel and revolutionary.

But I didn't get the Old or New Testament. It was presented as historic fact. If they would have said metaphors, allegories, parables, I would have possibly accepted it. Leviticus though causes me headaches. Unclean and abomination? The text is bullshit.

But Job is the classic. God and Satan are arguing? Satan said let's "test" Job? And God agreed and Job became the poster child for every shitty thing imaginable. Murphy's law would be a walk in the park for Job.

This defies the All-Good concept. Job suffered horribly. I don't care if he won publishers' clearing house in the end.

Philosophy courses in college said: God by definition is and must be – all knowing, all-powerful, all-good.

Enter into the scenario... Evil.

Evil exists. Hitler. Pol Pot. Idi Amin. Ku Klux Klan. Read "Bury my heart at Wounded Knee." The native American rapper called it genocide against native Americans. That is accurate. Bertrand Russell and Jean-Paul Sartre brought up America on crimes against humanity for Vietnam. My lai was only one massacre. My lai was a drop in the bucket compared to what the Cavalry did to native americans. Blankets donated to tribes – blankets infected with Polio.

I've had discussions with friends... which was worse? African Slaves or Native Americans slaughtered? I don't have an answer. I just ask questions.

Back to the point I was trying to make...

God is all-powerful (omnipotent) – God can stop Evil... All-powerful. Evil exists. Therefore, God isn't all-powerful. He is impotent.

Evil exists.

God is omniscient – God knows about Evil... God is all-knowing. Evil exists. Therefore, God isn't all-knowing. He is ignorant.

Evil exists.

God is all-good – God could intervene and stop evil – God cares about Evil... but God is not all-good. He is apathetic.

These are the theoretical that philosophers practice. If this, than this.

With God we only have theories. Souls are different. We have ghosts.

Ghosts must serve a higher purpose. Therefore there is God.

The Bible is a chronicle of years of intervention. Sodom and Gomorrah. Why not Auschwitz? Buchenwald? Dachau? Why not when the Trail of Tears occurred? Or when George Floyd said, "I can't breathe." Why is there no intervention now? Do not dismiss that question. I have not heard an acceptable answer. I would welcome a visit from an Arch Angel or anyone from that realm to explain to me the absence of "Divine Intervention." Why the flood and not now?

The "idea" of Jesus was cool. But I could not accept immaculate conception. I had a dear friend in college who said she challenged racists by saying according to the rules of biology, if I fuck a black man and produce an off-spring, that proves we are the same species. I loved her. We were English department geeks.

Scholars and historians have located temples and geographic locations that are referenced in the Bible. Old and new. Some aspects are supported by fact.

Keep in mind, that I grew up a heathen and an infidel. AKA an ignoramus.

Father Klein tried to teach us – Cyndy and me – about the Bible. This was a big book with rice paper-thin pages.

What else is religion other than a means of comfort for those about to die. Because it offers hope that death is not final – that death is a doorway into an afterlife. Does that mean it preys upon the terrified and frightened who are willing to accept any explanation that "it ain't over"?

I like Edgar Lee Masters. He wrote a poem called, "Silence." The last stanza says what I prefer as an explanation.

> And there is the silence of the dead.
> If we who are in life cannot speak
> Of profound experiences,
> Why do you marvel that the dead
> Do not tell you of death?
> Their silence shall be interpreted
> As we approach them.

And proof? Don't ask. The answer is you gotta have faith. At age thirteen, I was certainly not a pragmatist. I listened and asked questions. I always asked more questions.

I grew up loving and studying dinosaurs. I had plastic replicas of all my favorites. Stegosaurus, ankylosaurus (who I called clubby), and my favorite, cynognatheus. I asked Father Kline, "Was Adam homo sapiens, homo erectus, homo habilis, neanderthal, or cro-magnon?"

He said, "well, we just don't know." Yeah, ask a creationist about Darwin. I did not have those words back then.

All kids have a bullshit detector. It protects us from adults who think we're stupid. Mine rang three times. KRANG, KRANG, KRANG.

My parents wanted this, so I went through the rite and became a Catholic. The whole shebang. Baptism, first communion, and the other part where you profess your faith and dedicate yourself to the Church. Confirmation? They didn't take it seriously, so why should I?

The evening after the ceremony, there was a celebration party at Nelson and Tony Murrin's home. Nelson and Tony were our godparents. Tony was Italian. Antoinette. .

The adults had alcoholic libations. I remember a conversation between Father Klein's second in command and the Bunny. He was an irish priest. He said, "you look familiar to me."

The Bunny said, "I don't know... where you been hanging out, Father?" He loved telling that story over and over.

The irish priest was disappointed. I saw his face.

The weird part is that he intended it as humor but the truth was that the Bunny and Jack Kernodle used to frequent adult book stores and adult movie theaters. Of the latter, the closest was West 25th street or Brookpark road. Quite a hike from Mentor. And suburbanites went there to meet tricks.

I had no clue what Catholics were all about. But I was going to their school.

Cyndy and I went through the rites together. I didn't believe a word of it. Some would say that's blasphemy. I can accept that. I wanted to hear the facts.

Cyndy tells me now she's an atheist. Go figure. She's a scientist. Computer engineer. She doesn't follow Isaac Newton. Maybe Stephen Hawking.

Isaac Newton said the more he studies nature, the more proof of God's existence he discovers. I agree with Newton.

Keep in mind, I was 13. Imagine a 13-year-old child in ancient Greece being told about Zeus. Now we call it "mythology." I was told the same thing and told to call it truth and religion as if both are simultaneously synonymous.

I wrote poems about God, religion, the soul and published them. My first book was called, "Always asking more questions."

God

In nature, I find more proof of a God than anywhere else. Robert Frost wrote of design. Paul Simon wrote of the same. St. Thomas Aquinas wrote of the first mover and of the governance. It can't be without.

I never thought existence was dependent on a superior being. Until I wrote poetry about it. I won't reiterate the narrative here. But I concluded that God and souls do exist.

I experienced proof of souls. Supernatural means "above the rules of nature" so, therefore, there must be other rules above natural law. Natural law governs our world and our science – including their limitations in our world. We lack the tools to measure the supernatural. None have been invented. The purpose of souls must have something to do with God. One cannot exist without the other. Or the one necessitates the existence.

Once I speculated, you carry the spark until you die and then you dissipate out into the universe into nothingness. Jean-Paul Sartre probably said that first.

But I changed my mind. Granted I base it on something I cannot prove. Ghosts. No, I haven't seen Casper. But I've experienced ghosts to the extent that I know they are real and exist.

A ghost is a supernatural entity. A spirit. Every culture (I'm going out on a limb here – every culture? I don't know that for a fact... But I'd bet it's true). Has stories about ghosts. Some are fabricated to scare. But the source material. Accounts from those who had first-hand knowledge. I do and I have. So allow me this – I believe and I know that ghosts exist.

Contact me and I'll be happy to share the stories. Each encounter.

But given the fact... Why would ghosts exist unless it has something to do with God. Not a question. It's rhetorical. Ghosts would not exist unless they served a purpose. Otherwise – dissipate.

So my conclusions are God is real. Ghosts are real. Why? I don't know. I rely on Edgar Lee Masters. And his poem "Silence."

But nature shows me out of necessity, there needs to be a Great Spirit. Science wants to say "instinct." Robert Frost said how can design exist in a thing so small? In that does he equates design to instinct – not a designer?

God to me is like a scientist who designs then engineers a planet – then the life on that planet.

Jesus however... God and Mary... same species? The rules of biology state.: same species, then an offspring; different species – no offspring.

I think Jesus was a great person. Perhaps he called God, "father" because God was father to us all.

Why must it be male? Females create life. Males deliver sperm. God's gender should be female.

I used to use an argument when Lynn's father, Charlie would say, "a black man and a white woman were kissing in the bar"... he'd say, "it's like dogs and cats." I'd say, Charlie, they can mate and produce a child. Dogs and cats cannot produce a puppy nor a kitten. Black or white? Same species." He likely tolerated my counter argument but chose not to agree.

In another time, another place, I'd be burned at the stake. Or lynched.

My moral philosophy came from: do no harm and protect from harm (those were the precepts – was I born with them or did I learn them?); and Marvel Comic books. I think mostly Marvel Comic. Not the example of the Bunny.

I must make a concerted effort to restrain duplication and redundancy... This entire book has been written either during scotch #3 or after getting up at 5:00 ayem. During the day, I cannot write. I have pain in my lower back and my neck and my hands tremble from essential tremor.

Mark Vocca, my best friend, he once said, if asked, "who he would invite to a party, if he could invite ten persons from any time in history." He said his first answer would be, "Jesus." He said, "think about it. At that point, you'd know without a doubt if He were real or not."

I'd invite Jesus and I'd invite Adolph Hitler. And I'd say, "Jesus, you beat the shit out of the nazi scum or I will. The choice is yours." Dare I add, "and why didn't you do it the first time around?"

Saint Joseph High School, fall of 1975, age 14

My mom took me in to sign up for classes in August of 1975. I knew I wanted to continue French. But I also wanted to sign up for the football team.

The counselor said that a letter had been sent out to parents in July and that enrollment for football was closed. I was pissed.

When I lived in Mentor, I wasn't allowed to try out for football. And varsity players told me how good I was. They called me DareDevil and Suicide man.

Caveat... St. Joes was on East 185th in Cleveland. I lived in Mentor. That was 30 minutes away in good traffic. I forgave mom for many things, things I never forgave the Bunny for.

I knew what Father Klein wanted me to learn. You Catholics, hold back your pitch forks and torches.

Jesus is the Son of God. Mary is the mother of Jesus. The Holy Spirit is Groucho Marx? Come on, he had to be jewish.

It was mostly bullshit. Or at least he could not show me anything worth learning. But now I was going to be enrolled in a school, the very foundation was Rome's Vatican and the Catholic Church. Kicking and screaming. Most of the way, but not all the way.

Catholic High School… I missed my friends and teachers at Ridge Junior high. Catholics had a lot of holidays… when I was off from school, I went to Ridge to visit my friends and teachers. Parents? Did you get that? Sheesh!

As I write this, there is a soap box adjacent to my chair. Is that metaphor still in use?

Saint Joe's. In my sophomore year, I met Bob Sablack. Brandon Zart. Jimmy Damm. Luke Powers. Dave Sukys. And Bumbles. We became friends.

Bob remains a true close friend to this day. The others have fallen to the wayside. Sadly because I really liked Luke. I'm fairly certain that I saw Luke in a play at Andrews school for girls. I was dating and in love with (infatuated with) Lauren Coyne – now Podolak. I think it was the Samuel Beckett play, "Waiting for Godot." Because the first time we went out with Brandon, Luke would hang his head out of the window and call out, "Godot…? Godot…?"

Luke wanted to be an actor. Besides that, he introduced me to the Ramones (1st LP) and Iggy and the Stooges' "Raw Power." He loaned me those two albums when he didn't know me from any other stranger other than as a friend of Brandon's from Mentor.

Turned out, I loved those two albums. As soon as I could afford them, I went out and bought my own copies. To this day, I have them on CD. Parents and siblings? Not fans at all. I embraced punk rock music.

In the 1950s the musical rebels were Link Wray, Eddie Cochran, Gene Vincent, and Duane Eddy. The rebellion is on a twenty-year cycle. In the 1970s it was punk rock. In the 1990s, it was grunge. That said, the 2010s should have its own rebels. I'm just not sure who they are or were.

I was class of 1979. One year younger than my friends who were class of 1978.

My freshman year, I was alone. I met Brandon during the summer before my sophomore year at a party at Janine Feeney's house.

Lauren Coyne

My very first girlfriend was Lauren Coyne. She went to Andrews school for girls. She stood her own ground. That says a lot for a 13-year-old. She had guts and courage and she backed down for no one.

Lauren was a comic book hero without a costume.

We both liked Science Fiction. Lauren was smart as hell. Smarter than me.

I don't remember why. Lauren and I broke up. She was hotter and hotter with age (I saw that from her facebook pages years later).

Doctor Vosmic, our orthodontist told me never put "it" in writing. He was chastising me. I did not know what "it" was. He was alluding to a letter I wrote to Lauren that I did not recall. Back in those days, I wrote volumes. Mostly at night. I would stay awake and write poems, stories and letters. Self analysis. Expressions of feelings.

Always asking more questions

I had questions. Who was the self? What are feelings? What class ever taught this?

Wouldn't it be nice if there was a class called "Discover your self"? Who you are. Or let's talk about feelings."

Connect happy to when and why. Connect sad to when and why.

When and why are critical. When specifies the time – what led up to the impact? The context? Why becomes the meaning according to Victor Frankl.

I suppose it was because I was a neurotic teenager with no clue. Lauren would have been a great catch. That's cliché. I need to describe her better.

We met at the orthodontist office. Yeah, that's sexy. Two teens with braces and zits. Well, I had zits. Lauren had great hygiene. I did not.

But we talked. Really talked. Substance. Lauren would say, "And…?" I'm at a loss. Was it too early? I have shame. Lauren was better than me. Perhaps I could not admit it.

I do not remember why we broke up. I could be flippant and say "chalk it up to teenage immaturity." I think it was more like she was the better. Who was I to bring her down? I knew how damaged I was. Lauren did not deserve damaged goods. She was a prize. Her respect was to be earned. Her love, sacred if ever offered. Not a trophy. The man who won her heart had to be a genius, a scholar, and a prince. And treat her like a queen.

1976

Marvel Comics had a whole Captain America celebration of the bi-centennial.

That year, "Marathon man" came out. The Bunny took me to it. Dustin Hoffman played the main character. The Nazi dentist tortured him in the chair. "Is it safe" and he would drill into the nerve. Relief meant oil of clove.

Bunny never offered oil of clove. He offered "Is it safe? Tell me about those bad grades…"

He also took me to see "One flew over the cuckoo's nest." About a nuthouse. The message was clear. He wanted to send me to one. Or maybe he wanted to see my reaction to people living in an asylum. He often threatened to send me to one.

Art Class at Saint Joe's

Early on, I excelled at Art. Every art teacher I ever had saw my talent and praised me for it. In ninth grade at Saint Joe's, I got jaded. There was student who copied the artwork of Klaus Voormann and submitted it as his own work.

Saint Joe's had – like most high schools – a "literary journal" which they called the Carpenter (after the father of Jesus… But God was his father so was Joseph the step-father?).

Anyhow, this student copied a piece of art from Klaus Voormann.

Ringo Starr had an album with "Sixteen" and "Photograph" – I loved Photograph so I bought the album. The liner notes had artwork for each song by Klaus Vorrmann.

This student copied an exact replica of one of Klaus Voormann's pieces of art and submitted it as his own. I think it was for the song "Six O'Clock" written by Paul McCartney. I sent the CD to Morgan, my niece.

Now this student who copied the art was the teacher's pet. I didn't know that term back then. Because there were no teacher's pets back then. It was 1976.

I approached the Art teacher and offered to bring in the Ringo album to show the copy.

I learned the word, "Hurumph" that day. After the hurumph, he dismissed me as a jealous classmate. He made me feel small. Metaphorical back hand to dismiss.

I stopped taking art classes in 1976.

When I got expelled from Saint Joe's and tried to take art at Lake Catholic, I signed up for the last semester of my senior year.

I would not practice art again until 1992 – I took a class at Lakewood Adult education. Pastel Drawing 101.

Many works were framed and sold.

<u>Cutting</u>

There are pictures of me in the water in Canada. Cathy is nearby. On my forearms and biceps were scars. After remodeling the home at 7398 Lake shore Blvd, we got brand new, freshly-cut house keys. They were perfect for carving deep groves in my flesh.

Was it the proverbial "cry for help"? Probably. But it went unanswered.

The closest that the Bunny ever came to that realization was when I came back to the mentor house with Jimmy King from skateboarding and I had abrasions on my legs and arms. On a skateboard, if you hit one little rock and skid, you got tossed. Bunny thought I collected scars on purpose.

That meant, the scars I got accidentally – he thought those were on purpose. But the scars I created **deliberately**, he ignored.

I learned "What's the use?" And I learned "he never cared." I know. That sounds like, "Oh woe is me."

I realized very young, that I tolerated physical pain. A high threshold. Would that be a conditioned response?

Pain. When I became James Kennedy, pain was all about sex. Danger and Risk. And I always had Bunny's voice in my ear saying, "you are worthless. You deserve pain. You are worthless." It was always twice.

It was never "oh, woe is me." It was I deserve this.

Certain movies

"Billy Jack." When Billy goes berserk in the ice cream shop. "The Exterminator." Blow-torching the pedophile. "The Cross of Iron." I was Rolf Steiner.

Punishment and revenge. I could take the punishment. But I wanted revenge.

I questioned would the punishment and need for pain end if I ever got revenge?

I had dreams of being in jail for killing the Bunny. Hailed as a hero.

Rolled Joint

This happened too many times.

You took a toke off a joint and passed it. And if the next receiver complained about excessive saliva on the joint, he would say, "You nigger – lipped it."

Where the fuck did that come from? Once again – heard too often. Racist scumbags.

Back to Saint Joseph

Ninth grade English class. We were told to read four books during the summer before class. That summer, the Bunny demanded that I read for four hours every day. He had great hopes that Saint Joes would straighten me out.

Some times my narrative says that the Bunny cared about education of his offspring. He really didn't. He actually sought new reasons to punish. We kids were punished so often, we got clever in hiding "misdeeds" to avoid his wrath.

When we started in the fall, the teacher, Jerry Intorcio had us read them on every Friday. I already read them during the summer before, so I did other homework. I should have re-read them.

The book selection was mostly strange. Ray Bradbury's "The Martian Chronicles" was a good choice. Beautiful prose, excellent narrative. THAT Book was literature. But the others?

Next was Piers Paul Read's "Alive" about the Andes survivors of the plane crash who ate human flesh to survive. It was a non-fiction tome of about 300 more pages than it needed. He could have told the story in 150 words, but he stretched it out. Verbosity.

Next was Bill Russell's "Go up for Glory." I was not a sports fan. I would have rather had "the Invisible Man" by Ralph Ellison or "Native Son" by Richard Wright. Nothing against Bill Russell. But Toni Morrison does better prose than his ghost writer.

The last one was just weird. "A Separate Peace" by John Knowles. It's a novel about an all-boys school. The two main characters were gay. The more popular one imagined himself with his head on a female body. The other character pushed him down a stairwell and killed him.

Now I have to say that being gay is not an issue with me. I went to the Rocky Horror Picture Show in Drag. But for an all-boys Catholic school? Leviticus says abomination! Yes sir, three bags full. Leviticus is an asshole.

I support gay men and lesbians. I support Bi and Trans people.

My uncle Barry was gay and died from AIDS. I saw him last in 2004 when I was separated. I gave him a pastel drawing of a fox. He picked it out from my portfolio.

When the Names Project Quilt came to Cleveland State University, I was active and participated. The Cleveland Contact rewarded me with four tickets to the Cleveland Playhouse production of "As Is." We saw it with Todd and Kurt.

The Bus to Villa Angela (VA) and St. Joes.

Two buses were needed to arrive at St. Joes. Some rides were semi-bad, and some were really bad.

I picked up a bus for Willoughby South with kids along lakeshore boulevard just across the Mentor/Willoughby border. I think it was at Tioga Trail. Winters were cold. Bunny bought me a jean jacket and said that it would be warm enough. It was not. Bunny offered no hat.

Cleveland Winters had "Lake Effect." That described the Canadian winds that swept off Lake Erie and hit our northern shores of the lake with bitter cold. Mentor and the east side had the cold front. In Cleveland that meant Mentor got three feet and Lakewood got a dusting.

On the cold days, mom sat in the van with me until the bus showed up. When the Willoughby south kids boarded the bus, they always gave me shit.

Assholes would have been welcomed into the van. Any one who asked would have been invited in. There was plenty of room. Instead, there were comments, "Oh, baby girl waits in the van with mommy. Is it too cold for baby girl?"

At Willoughby South, I picked up a bus that went to Villa Angela and then to Saint Joe's.

Mostly I slept. The bus ride was along the shore-way, route 2, to East 185ᵗʰ and then side streets to VA first and St. Joe's second.

I used to have the driver drop me off at the south end of East 185ᵗʰ. I'd get a slurpy with a Marvel comics cup from the 7-11 and then a bagel from the bakery closer to Saint Joe's.

But there was this girl. VA (Villa Angela) was an all-girls school just like Joe's was all boys. The older boys – seniors - from Joe's decided she would be their target. She was a sophmore or junior at Villa Angela. The juniors and seniors from Saint Joe's would torment her. I think she was a target because she was pretty. I don't know. I thought she was pretty.

What inspires bullies to pick a target and then torment? Is it "because they can"? Somehow, they get their "jollies" – that word downplays the degradation. The act was never "Jollies." It was cruelty. But that's how I viewed it. That's what they displayed.

These superior and holier than thou assholes… they called her slut and whore and asked her if she would suck cock. She cried. Sobbed is a better term. No one deserved that torment.

As a ninth grader, I knew my next act was self-destruction. Ninth graders were called "Frosh." Short for freshman. What's the cliché? Evil occurs when good people do nothing.

I stood up and told them leave her alone. If they need to pick on someone, make me their target.

They were delighted. "Whoa we caught another fish!!" They said gladly. Ooh, you're in for it now!

They spat on me and punched me. That lasted the entire freshman year. Even after she was gone. My dilemma. I never fought back. Six to one?

Despite all the comic books I read where the hero wins. I was afraid. So I tolerated it. I convinced myself that I would lose painfully if I stood up as a defiant David to six Goliaths. Technically I did already when I told them to stop picking on her.

My father beat me into submission. He broke my mom's spirit and he broke mine.

Yes, I stood up to the bullies. But I lacked the courage to face the consequences. I did not fight them. I just gave them another target.

They would take turns punching the back of my head. And laugh and cackle after each punch. I was alone. No one stood up for me.

But I told myself, I asked for this. Because I would not let it continue with her. She was no longer their victim.

Was she a surrogate for mom? Probably.

The day after I volunteered to be the target, she handed me a note and thanked me. She left Villa Angela. Her note described a bad relationship with her father and how she took drugs to quell the pain and distract her mind. But she emphasized how much she appreciated my intervention.

Another female student on the bus, Mary Beth – after the boys had all left, she thanked me for what I did and told me how brave I was. I told her I wasn't brave. I was scared. But I couldn't watch and do nothing. I said I can take the consequences.

I don't have her name anymore. She left Villa Angela. I never saw her again. I kept her note and many others in a cedar box with momentoes. But Lise pitched them. They are gone. She picked jealous fights. Like she did with Carolyn Cola from Lake Catholic.

Were there good memories of Bunny?

Roasting marshmallows on the fire. The outer shell gets charcoal black. It pulls off easily. Then you roast the inner part slowly to just brown it lightly.

No one is completely evil. That's what Lynn tells me.

He bought me a 1976 Mercury Comet. That was in 1980. Before I joined the Army. In retrospect, I should have asked Uncle Lee Haywood. "What do I do to maintain a car?" Uncle Lee would have said, "Oil change and tire rotation after 3,000. Tune up every 25,000." Bunny never taught me how to change a flat.

Brandon taught me about the three electrical components when his VW bus broke down on East 6th street. I came to his rescue. 1986 or 1987? I don't recall. Bunny was shocked that I would go to his rescue. The teen who refused to shake his hand.

In 1983 in Savannah, the engine of the mercury comet from 1976 caught fire. Piece of shit car. My fault. I didn't know how to maintain it.

I try and try to think of good memories. Some of his sisters would probably like that. Temple loved the Bunny. "And flowers never bend with the rainfall"… continue to continue… [intentional allusion to Paul Simon and Art Garfunkel… please google it.].

Why would anyone "love" the cretin bully who beat the shit out of the Pennsylvania farm girl?

Shhhh… Because no one stood up to him and said STOP. I didn't. I was a coward. I was also a child. I blame myself.

I read or heard this years ago… "my innermost consciousness screams at me, 'I am a failure.'"

No one made his crimes public. Oh, and crimes they were. Is there a club for fans of bullies who get drunk and beat wives and children? I'm not a member of that club.

Halloween

Halloween in the 1960s. Bunny was a dentist. Instead of candy, Bunny gave out tooth brushes and tooth paste. The box raised with a cartoon illustration. A man's top hat and arm raised with the raising of the box. Cheers for the Bunny.

Paul Endres and the Chucklehead

Paul Endres needed a letter of recommendation to "Brown" for ninth grade. Bunny as a dentist was asked to write it. I was a sophomore. In high school. I wrote it.

Bunny was a doctor of dentistry. I was a 10th Grade student with a C average.

Paul was the son of an eye doctor.

Bunny was illiterate.

How did he pass ENG 101?

So I wrote a letter of recommendation as a sophomore in high school, to an elite high school of education. Because my dentist father could not compose a sentence. Does this make sense to anyone?

Off the subject, I suspect that Paul stole records from me. I think. Well it was either Paul or Chuck while I was in the Army. The Rotters, "Sit on my face, Steve Nicks" was the first one I discovered missing when I got home after the Army. It seemed my collectibles were available to any hands that grabbed. It sells now for $50 to $100. That record got banned and pulled from the shelves immediately.

I had Japanese imports of Bowie albums that were under the sheets of Chuck's bed covered in beach sand. Chuck was a slob and had no respect for anyone else's property. Sand and record albums did not mix.

Lynn sez...

Lynn tells me there has to be good. She is my wife and my best half. I listen.

1974. I was 13 in 8th grade. Scott Smyers was my friend from Ridge Junior High School. I did not know it then, but his father or step-dad was a member of Cloverdale. The Bunny's fishing club.

Bunny gave us a six pack of Stroh's beer to share.

Scott would eventually become a member of Cloverdale. Bunny had a plan for me to become a member of Cloverdale.

Scott and I each drank three and didn't think anything of it. Was that good or bad? Why do I suspect an ulterior motive?

If I become a drunk like him, then is all forgiven? I would then forget all his sins just like he did.

He won. I am a drunk. But I only have three scotches a night. But I wear depends and sleep in the den at the office chair because I pass out and piss where ever I am. I think part of that is I'm in pain for most of the day. My back and neck pain have woken me at 3:00 am or 4:00 am and I stay awake and read or study Spanish. I think once saturation occurs and the alcohol numbs the pain, then the urine is like a fire drill to evacuate the building.

I used to brag about my high tolerance to pain. It has reached a new level. I do not tolerate any more. It starts as discomfort. I can't put on underwear or socks without the "Uhhh" – what is that? Involuntary response. A groan. Fuck it. It hurts.

Neck is weird. Mornings are usually okay. But afternoons and evenings? I slowly turn to look left or right – and the knife stabs. That's a metaphor. But it feels like a knife – a quick and sharp jab. In-out like Alex would say. But he was talking about fucking.

Bunny and a movie in 1975

He took me to East 185th Street and the LaSalle movie theater and we watched "One flew over the cuckoo's nest."

Why did we go to the LaSalle theatre on East 185th Street? That was at least an hour on 306 and the freeway. We lived in Mentor. I did not question it back then.

In walking distance from the LaSalle there was an adult video arcade. I learned about that when I went to Saint Joe's.

I don't recall if Bunny left during the movie. But he and Jack Kernoodle used to frequent where porn was shown.

During the 1970s, most of the time, he would take me to the Great Lakes Mall or the Mentor Mall and drop me off with $20. And say, "go see a couple of movies and buy yourself some lunch. I'll pick you up at eight or nine." I don't know where he went. But I was his alibi.

One time, I watched Mel Brooke's "Silent Movie" (1976) and something else. He never said, "Don't say I dropped you off." But I was never asked, "Did he drop you off?" Mom assumed I spent the day with him.

This is an interesting... what? A paradox? A dichotime? Why would I keep his secrets? He was the asshole. The abuser. Because he did a good deed and gave me twenty and dropped me off so he could go and do what exactly?

There are so many foggy and gray areas.

I'm really trying to honor Lynn's request and think about good things he did. But so many started as supposedly a good thing and then. Fill in the blank.

In 1977, he took me to lunch at Fairport Harbor. I had scallops. I had never had scallops before. I thought they were really good sea food.

Then we went to the Mentor Mall and he took me to a Charles Bronson movie called "Telefon." Twenty minutes into the movie. I told Bunny I have to go to the bathroom. It turned out that the scallops were bad. Dead. Poison. And the idiots in the kitchen didn't check them.

I spent the entire time in the movie theater in the bathroom on the floor of a toilet stall puking mustard-colored yellow bile. I'll never forget the smell. Worse than the taste or smell of vomit. The bile was like a sewer system backed up.

After the movie was over. Two hours later. Bunny came into the bathroom and called out my name.

He drove me home.

Movies have always been important to me. There are scripted scenes where a parent comes to a child who was missing or distressed and says, "Are you okay? Are you hurt?" It was more like, "Come on, let's go."

My only conclusion was that I was convinced that I was allergic to scallops. How the Bunny reacted? That was par for the course. "Normal." Define normal?

Matt Zolnay

In 1988, my friend Matt Zolnay said, "You eat crab and shrimp, yes?" I said yes. He said you're either allergic to all shellfish or none. He said, "I'm going to make you scallops tonight." We had a feast. And I did not get sick.

Matt and I have an expression… S.A.B. It stands for separated at birth. One day we were driving on the shoreway (the freeway that belts Cleveland along Lake Erie) and I said, we're travelling at 65 miles per hour and we are literally inches away from the car in the next lane…" Matt said, "S.A.B."

In 1996 when I moved to Ohio City to Franklin Blvd., Matt and Darla lived across the street. Matt had clam bakes every autumn, September or October. He worked for C.E. Foods. He did the fresh seafood and his boss, Codino, did frozen.

Matt was one funny comedian. Matt would tell stories of his alter ego, "Dick E. Lee." Okay on one hand, he was mocking Chinese people. On the other hand he was mocking the ignorant Americans who had stereotypes about Chinese people.

Matt would answer the phone and say, "Dick E. Lee here. How you go?" If the other person cracked up, Matt would you say, "Ohhh you no like Chinese people. Fluck you buddy." And hang up.

Dick E. Lee was the "manager" [aka personae] in charge of supplies and reordering… Dick E. Lee was Matt. He was fiction.

One time Dick E. Lee ran into (perhaps under) a fork lift. Dick E. Lee got flowers and gift baskets and care packages sent to the hospital. Matt would narrate every scenario. He was brilliant and so creative.

Matt was also a gourmet cook. One night he offered to cook me dinner. I never heard of grouper. Matt blended ground peanuts (like butter) and sriracha sauce in my little food processor. He may have added garlic and other spices. I wasn't sure. I was on beer three or four. He spread the concoction on the grouper and then broiled it. I was treated to a feast.

At his clam bakes I was taught, you take the clams one at a time. If it's open, you tap its shell. If it closes, it's alive. If it stays open, it's dead. Throw it out. It's that simple. The same practice works on mussels and clams.

That's the reason why I had food poisoning.

"That's so Mentor"

Lise created a metaphor.

One day I made her a sandwich of grilled bologna with Dijon mustard and sharp cheddar.

She laughed and dismissed it as low white trash.

Sans Nobilité.

Karl Strmn was a brilliant professor. When he died I attended his funeral. I respected him.

He took a sabbatical to Japan to study ancient Japanese poetry. He went to Lapland to document their oral traditions because they had no written language. He translated Dante's inferno into polish. They said he knew 17 languages.

At CSU, First day of French 101, Professor Strmn walked in and said, "Hello Human Beings."

Professor Strmn wrote on the black board the following:

"S. Nob." It was French and stood for sans nobilité

Sans means without. Nobilite means without your official title.

He told us the British lords and ladies had to sign in without royal title. They resented that. And that is the origin of "snob."

Lise was an elitist snob. Her father said, "it's okay to be an elitist, but don't be a snob." Lise ignored him and chose to be a snob. She defended it. Arrogantly. I knew that was the end. Sadly it took eight years. It should have ended after two. If that.

Mumsy

Anne Stevens, Lise's mom, decided I was a "smooth operator." She was so quick to judge. Perhaps to be protective of her baby of the family, the fifth and last child. The spoiled brat.

Bill Stevens sold the movie rights to his novel, "The Gunner," and took his family to Martha's Vineyard. Lise tells the tale of sitting on the lap of Thorton Wilder who wrote "Our Town." Holly said that James Taylor gave her girlfriend in high school the crabs.

I liked and respected Bill. He taught me about Jazz. I never had a teacher about music until Mark Vocca. Bill was second but he was great.

Martha's Vineyard was where they lived until Bill took the family to Barcelona. Bill loved Ernest Hemingway. Hemingway and George Orwell joined the Spanish Revolution in the late 1930s in Spain.

Lise and I met at Cleveland State University. Fall 1987, I enrolled. We met in the fall and became beer buddies. Sadie Hawkins day, she proposed to me. I thought it was a joke so I said yes.

When I realized that she was serious, I considered it. Fucking her was fun, but it wasn't making love. She gave lousy head. Tried anal once without success. Her bush was hairy like 70s porn. When I trimmed it short, her mumsy asked if I liked children. [No, I like shaved adult women... not children. Sensuality is beautiful.] Priorities in my 20s would evolve.

We went to Manfield on the weekend. Annie (Mumsy) had a game she wanted to play.

"When will you die and under what circumstances." That's fucking morbid.

I remembered seeing a film about Chariots of the Gods and how the Space gods would return on 12/24/2012. So that was my answer.

The one called Anne -- they lovingly called Mumsy – became something.

Later, when Anne came down from Mansfield and we had dinner, Lise and I had said we'd plan a fall wedding.

I said fall [because I needed time to see if "this" would work]. We were together less than six months. "This" referred to Lise and me. Annie said why do you need to wait IF you're sure?

[I wasn't sure. That's why wanted to wait. Lise was psycho. I just didn't know yet.]

I answered Annie saying "Fine, I'm sure." I lied

God, Lise was psycho.

After she was raped in Barcelona, she said -- ONLY her mom and Holly saved her. Years later in 1986, she made her mom and Holly cry.

She screamed a total reversal – she said, "You (mom and holly) never supported me. You were never there for me."

Saint Joe's, Cleveland Ohio

Religion class scared the bejesus out of me. I have no idea what "bejesus" means, but I like the sound of it.

I never opened a bible let alone read one. In 2019, I started reading the Glorious Qur'an because I wanted to know.

Ninth through Twelve grade, religion class was required. The instructors were merciful to a heathen like me. They said, "you've had the Bible pounded into you from all the nuns at your schooling from K through 8... so now we're going to focus on morality." They didn't say that to me personally. They announced it to all the ninth graders in the class. I had never opened the Bible. What a relief.

On a personal note... I should be really fucked up. Perhaps I am.

In my 30s or 40s I read Leviticus... What a fucking asshole. Go back and read his rules... he's all across the board. And who was he? Just a name. Not a prophet, not a saint.

Leviticus, I stand with Gay, Lesbian, Trans and all of them.

It became like taking Philosophy courses that I would later do at Cleveland State. This heathen got straight A's in Religion. How was that possible?

I got straight A's in French. Grades in English were decent... not the foreshadowing of a future poet. Algebra and biology were each an easy A.

But come junior year... Brandon and I would get high on the way to school (once he started picking me up) – (it must have been the fall of my junior year, 1977)… Chemistry was my first class. Getting high first thing in the morning? I was doomed to fail. Some classes – you can fake it. Sociology, Communications, those were common sense based and easy. Chemistry? I needed loads of remedial. From what source?

Not from a father who majored in chemistry for his Bachelor's degree.

Freshman year "History" was taught by Mario – last name escapes me… he told his classes how he sunk a German submarine in WWII with a 45 (M1911) that he shot down the periscope. One might suppose that it was like the telephone game where a story is told and passed along until it completes the circle and when retold at the end of the circle, the final version is altered dramatically. Except that Mario was the circle.

Sophomore year, English. Was taught by Mr. Teurosy? Something like that. He spent the entire year on poetry. I loved it. I credit him for inspiring me to write poetry. The two major poets that I remember from his class were Robert Frost and e. e. cummings. W. H. Auden and Emily Dickinson were also there. And Walt Whitman. Two of the aforementioned poets were gay. I broach that subject, not because I banished them as abominations like Leviticus said. I broach it because of Mr. Hroblewski.

The Mouse and the Rat

Saint Joe's had two brothers who were teachers. Students called them the mouse and the rat. The rat taught chemistry. I can't say if that was fair or not because I was always high as a kite. I would like to buy a high school chemistry book and see if I can figure it out. Now that I'm 59, I'd like to see if it was as difficult as I perceived it in my Junior year.

The other Hroblewski taught anthropology. The Mouse. It must have been my sophomore year because I finished the class. He was no mouse. He had brass balls because in a Catholic high school, he taught evolution. He was a scientist.

I should preface this by saying, he would introduce the course with the caveat, "this could get me fired." I also recall him saying, I'm teaching this as a theory, not fact. The truth was that it was historical fact and not theory at all. Empirically proven fact. Fossil records, carbon dating.

He then taught us about paleontology and the dinosaurs. Evolution beginning with Lucy (Australopithecus), Neanderthal, Cro-Magnon, Homo habilis, Homo erectus and home sapien. Not one student asked about Adam and Eve.

My take-away was teach catholic boys about gay poets, give reading assignments about gay students in an all-boys school (a separate peace, John Knowles), but walk on thin ice if you try to suggest Darwin and evolution in lieu of creationism.

I remembered my conversation with Father Kline when I was being brain washed – well attempted, not successful. "Well, we just don't know." KRANG.

I never understood Mr. Hroblewski's paranoia until I saw the Spencer Tracy movie, "Inherit the Wind," about the 1925 Scopes Monkey Trial. But this was 1977, fifty years later.

Black human beings

As a white boy from Mentor, I'd never met or interacted with anyone who was black. It was not a choice. It was the demographic. The closest we had to a person of color was Teri Pealer who was native American and Jeff Ficke who was Hawaiian.

But derogatory jokes that mocked or insulted blacks (actually referred to with the n-word) were common among parents, their friends, neighbor kids and the school yard.

In elementary school, my mother took me to Uncle Bill's (like a Wal Mart or Target now). She said I could pick out any G.I. Joe I wanted. I forget if it was a birthday or something else. I picked out the black G.I. Joe which I wanted because I didn't have a black G.I. Joe. Hogan's Heroes had Sergeant Kinchloe and Baker. He would be my Sergeant Baker.

Mom said, "Okay, but you have to keep it hidden from your father." What did that mean? I didn't understand racism. I was a tabula rasa. Or just incredible naïve. Most likely the latter.

At Saint Joe's, ninth grade algebra was with Mr. Farrell. I sat next to Clark Kellogg. Clark was a varsity basketball player in his freshman year of high school. We sat next to one another and worked out the various math problems together. He helped me as much as I helped him. I saw us as equals. I could care less that he was black. Clark signed my yearbook "Special K" which was a brand of Kellogg's cereal. He chose it as a nickname. Clark was special. He was gifted as an athlete. He was intelligent. He was kind. He was polite and gracious. He had manners. He respected others. And how to say this without sounding gay? Clark was one handsome dude. He could have acted in movies. Leading man. Like Sidney Poitier.

Perhaps I was just weird. In elementary school I used to comb garage sales for books, comic books, and 45s. Comic books – anything by Marvel. DC – only if drawn by Jack Kirby. 45s – Beatles or Motown. Books… chariots of the gods and anything related; science fiction especially Edgar Rice Burroughs who wrote more than just Tarzan. Like John Carter of Mars or Carson of Venus, the Moon Maid and Pelucider.

Then other books would catch my attention and interest. "Black like me" by John Howard Griffin. I read it in fifth grade.

He changed his pigment with a doctor. So that he could tour the south and write about how black people were treated. He was white and wanted to know.

I remember the most moving line. The author was talking to a black man who said to him, "But you can always go back." Which he did.

In college at Cleveland State, there was a student newspaper called the Cauldron. I contributed cartoons under the title, "The Guru atop Fenn" featuring a guru on the roof of the Fenn building on campus who gave smart alecky answers to student questions. I borrowed the idea from Ambrose Bierce who wrote the "Devil's Dictionary." He played devil's advocate and gave sarcastic answers to definitions. Grandpa Ross had the published book of the "Devil's Dictionary." I inherited it from him. I read it from cover to cover. And I loved the humor in it. I emulated his humor. I made up my own definitions. But it was Ambrose Bierce's idea that sparked the flame.

I also wrote five essays about racism called, "Notes from the Zebra Monastery." One argument addressed whites with sun tans and blacks who were light skinned and how each gained status by more closely resembling the other race.

A black woman who was Cauldron staff came up to me and said, "Did you know 'Zebra' is a derogatory term for a biracial child?" I said no. I was doing a modification of Dostoevsky. I thought Zebra was a metaphor that represented both races. Obviously, I was not the first to think of that. I never meant it derogatorily. I thought it meant a joining of both. Striped but grey, blended.

Back at Saint Joe's, Clark Kellogg became my friend. We only had algebra together. I read that the Lakers recruited him. Mark Vocca said he met him in Texas and that he was a really good guy. I second that emotion.

First Dance

1975 at Saint Joe's. School dances were held in the Gym. Mom agreed to take me to one. I remember the band name as "Back Seat Romance." It was the only time I went to a dance at St. Joe's.

Villa Angela was the school for all-girls. So they were invited. I suppose the Catholics opposed boys dancing with boys. Damn that Leviticus. Spoiler of fun.

I came to the dance. For the most part I stood on the side lines. I didn't know anyone. I listened to the music and wallflowered.

A girl from our bus ride home approached me. She was from Willowick. The seniors teased her because she had envious breasts.

In my mind, she was kind, polite, respectful. Pretty? Of course. I was an insecure boy. My father tortured me. Mom turned her back. I did not deserve… anything. That's not pity party. Or woe is me. It was what I knew as truth.

Everyone is damaged. Some of us just take longer to realize it.

She came over and asked me to dance. It was a slow song. A cover of "Nights in White Satin" by the Moody Blues. While we slow danced she pressed her breasts against my chest close enough that I felt her nipples and they were warm. I did not know how to take that. A sign? An invite? I backed off and told her my mom was there to pick me up. Late night for her. Saint Joe's was 30 minutes from Mentor. 30 minutes back.

The next day or someday thereafter on the bus, I gave her a present -- the Queen album, "A night at the opera," with Bohemian Rhapsody. She danced with me in ninth grade to a song with a chorus that sang, I love you. I did not know how to interpret that. *She* asked *me* to dance to that song.

I've always been confused about sexuality. And sex in general. She just wanted to dance with a boy who showed her respect. That's all it was.

Later Janine made me ask that question.

Mom told me sex was penis enters vagina. Wait – what is the element of love? Parents tell kids birds and the bees. They tell mechanics. Here's the part that left out.

LOVE. Sex is great. What does love mean? I never knew. Until Lynn.

In High School and Junior High – Teeny bopper Lingo

"Necking" was called making out. That meant hugging and kissing. Some kids included "groping." That meant massaging a breast or nipple. Or both. Serious groping like under the belt – that only happened in movie theatres. And only when mutual.

"French Kissing." That meant the tongue was included. Probably because Soixante-Neuf meant "69" – the French word for simultaneous fellatio and cunnilingus.

"Going Steady." It meant you were committed to one another. But the guy had to have an "ID Bracelet" engraved with his name to give to the girl that she could wear it. The ID bracelet was only in junior high, 12 year olds to 14 year olds.

In high school, your parents bought you a class ring. Girls going steady would wrap colorful yarn around the ring to reduce the size to make it fit more snugly.

These were the norms at school. Back then.

Saint Joe's and books

Along with my textbooks and English Lit, I always had a book that I was reading. One day it was "Serpico" by Peter Maas. A classmate touched the cover and said, "what are you trying to do? Impress us with the books you're reading?"

I thought about the question. I was never pretentious. I read the books I carried. I got them from garage sales. I didn't care who knew what I was reading. If they cared that much and wanted to borrow it to read, I would have let him.

About thirty-five or forty years later, I learned that my friend Rod Schaffter read Ken Kesey's "One flew over the cuckoo's nest" because he saw me reading it. I wrote to him that he honored me with that revelation. I never knew I influenced anyone.

I read Victor Hugo's tale of Quasimodo in elementary school. Edgar Allen Poe had me looking up words in the dictionary. I bought many used paperback books at garage sales. As to the student at St. Joe's, I answered his question asking, "what impression does it give you?"

I read garage sale books. Books other people had read and didn't want any more.

The Science Fiction Book Club

Jimmy King encouraged me to join the Science fiction book club. Then he told me which four books to buy with the membership order. He said buy Isaac Azimov's Foundation, and the Hugo Winners volume one and two, Frank Herbert's Dune and one other. I did. The Hugo winners was a great two volume set. I read Isaac Asmov's "I, Robot" but never the Foundation. Or Frank Herbert's Dune. "Soul Catcher" appealed to me more.

"Strangely Enough"

Aside from books I found at garage sales, I felt at heart certain books that were introduced by English teachers. Rice

Elementary never had books assigned. We had the option to buy books from the scholastic book service. Mom would approve. In fourth grade, I was allowed to order "Strangely Enough," by C. B. Colby.

Mrs. Heisner had a competition going. She was our fourth-grade teacher. The first competition was to design the head of the "Bookworm." I won.

Next Tim Deegan and I were racing to see who would finish reading "Strangely Enough" first. It was a collection of Urban Legends. Globally. Reportedly true.

"Invisible Fangs" scared the shit out of me. When I ordered it on amazon in 2018, that story was not included.

As I recall, a woman in Manilla, was being attacked. Police held her as fang marks appeared on her arms. In the court room before the judge, fang marks appeared.

Change of subject…

<u>1977 - Age 16 – the summer before I went into 11th Grade</u>

I bought Changes One Bowie and Alice Cooper's Greatest Hits. I really liked Alice… but I loved Bowie.

I played that album over and over until I memorized all the lyrics. I loved David Bowie and could not wait to get more.

Marty O'Leary and were friend because of comic books. His sister gave him Ziggy Stardust. Full title: the rise and fall of Ziggy Stardust and the spiders from mars.

He played the album once for me and I was committed. I traded comics for the album. I played it until I wore it out. And had to buy a new one.

I joined the RCA record club. That was years before BMG music club that dealt with CDs. RCA had a deal of x-number of albums to join. I got Young Americans, Station to Station and Low.

I was already a Bowie fan.

Mark Vocca and Brandon Zart were working at Sambo's restaurant – across the street from Bob Evans where I worked on route 306 (aka Reynolds Road) in Mentor.

Teenagers in the 1970s had limited employment opportunities. Restaurants or retail. Mark eventually got hired by a record store. His love and knowledge of music earned his position. Mark wasn't a specialist of just one genre. His knowledge base included all genres. He also was a musician. I'm sure that helped. He proudly showed me his ovation acoustic guitar.

Brandon started in food service. But he eventually learned flooring from his father Paul. He could do tile and linoleum.

Brandon Zart

Brandon and I met at Janine Feeney's party summer of 1976. Friends told me that Brandon said, "He's a freshman? I don't want to meet him. He'll be asking me for a ride to school."

I was leaning over Janine's record collection asking, "does she have any Bowie?" Brandon said, "you're into Bowie?" Brandon asked me if I was into Roxy Music. I said, "Roxy Roller?" He said, no that's Sweeney Todd.

Brandon said that he made it a habit of buying a live album from bands he'd heard about. He said, if the Live album rocks, then the band probably rocks. He bought "Viva! Roxy Music Live" from a cut-out bin. I suppose cut outs were like remaindered books. With cut outs, a corner of the album cover was clipped off. About an inch of a triangle. It was then sold at a discounted price. In the age of CDs and digital music, there are terms we took for granted as common that now have to be explained.

I bought "Viva" and loved it. Especially "If there is Something" with Eddie Jobson on electric violin. Oh my God, it was and remains so beautiful. Bryan Ferry's lyrics were poetry and his vocals added a musical instrument to the composition.

I took Brandon's advice and listened to Roxy Music. Bryan Ferry's lyrics revealed his knowledge base of literature and philosophy. He added references to Dorothy Parker and Friedrich Nietzsche in his songs.

Okay so those are so obscure... Dorothy Parker – "you might as well live" from her poem "Resume" and Friedrich Nietzsche – "thus even Zarathustra..."

Mark Vocca had never heard "Station to Station" or "Resurrection on 84th." The latter was the bootleg from the 1976 tour. Mark told me he wrote off bowie after "Young Americans." "David Live" foreshadowed that Bowie was moving toward soul. Like Motown Soul. "Knock on wood" paved the way.

Brandon told Mark about this guy "Clem" from Mentor. Brandon played my two post-Young American albums for Mark. He gave Bowie another shot.

Clem vs. Clement

Allow me to interrupt. According to the Oxford English Dictionary (OED), "Clem" has two definitions.

My father was Clem. He was an asshole. But I digress...

According to the OED, the verb meant to whither and die from starvation. And the noun was a brawl between the "townies" and the carnival people. Neither one is very appealing.

But in Latin, clement means calm and merciful. I'll stick with the Latin.

Somewhere I read that in Bohemia, Saint Clement was martyred by being tied to an anchor and thrown into the sea. Why do I have an irrational fear of drowning? No that's not sarcasm.

Clement --- Not Clem

It was during the Army that I decided that my name was "Clement" to differentiate me from the Bunny. It started in Berlin. I defined the OED source of clem and clement.

1978 – Mark Vocca worked at this record store off 615 (Andrews Road)

Mark knew music. How to describe him. He was a dichotomy. Mark was THE kind soul juxtaposed with a "defiant wolf" (I wrote a poem about him with that same title). He was "I'll carry your groceries to your car for you." Juxtaposed with "You just crossed the wrong guy." And wicked smart. Mark loved education and knowledge. Some people study to prepare for a test. Mark had a thirst for knowledge like no one else. He sponged it all and grokked it. And he loved history.

Digression: When I first read Albert Camus and his essay about Sisyphus, I mocked it. I compared it to the pleasant valley Sunday suburbanite mowing his lawn. Mark would say, "no, man. I get it. He just did the right thing." It needed no further explanation.

At the record store I asked Mark about classical... we both loved punk. But I wanted to know more. Mark McAdams worked there and he always wanted to interject. McAdams wanted to impress with his knowledge because he was studying music in college. Mark McAdams (God love him) loved a soapbox. Mark Vocca would just say, "this is cool." That's all I needed to hear.

I told Mark Vocca, if you get the tickets to Blondie at Music Hall and I'll pay for us to go. November 11, 1978 was the show. Stiv Bators was there in the audience and so was Crocus Behemoth from Pere Ubu.

At the record store, I told Mark I loved Hayden's trumpet concerto (looked it up... it was in E flat). I wanted to explore other classical pieces. But I did not know where to start. I knew stuff I'd heard but I didn't know names: composers, titles or conductors and all three mattered.

Mark smiled. He had this smile that said, "just relax. And trust brother Mark." I always did... with one exception. Regrettably with shame. More on that later.

Mark played the Egmont overture from Ludwig van Beethovan. I loved it from the first time I heard it. He told me that George Szell conducted the Cleveland Orchestra better than anybody else. Years later, at Cleveland State, the novel, "Egmont" by Goethe was the reading assignment. It was about duty. Goethe never impressed me. I always thought he was overrated. When I signed up for a creative writing class, I wrote short story to mock Goethe and praise Schiller. The professor who had studied German said I had more allusions than even he recognized...

One of the English majors in the class announced, "I read through the entire manuscript and did not find one error grammar or syntax." Perhaps he expected thank you. I wanted to say, you condescending prick, if you study foreign language, you cannot learn foreign language grammar unless your English grammar is perfect.

Studying German at Cleveland State, I fell in love with Franz Kafka (fiction) and Rainer Maria Rilke (poetry). Georg Trakl was in second yet, I don't understand all of his poetry. He moved into abstract the way many German artists did in that time.

Franz Marc began painting animals. He was part of the Blue Rider with Kandinsky. He painted Fighting Forms which was his first step into Abstract. Then he answered the call of World War One and died in 1914. How much great art was lost due to war? Franz Marc was my personal favorite. How much more art would he have created had he not died fighting in WWI? The question is rhetorical. We will never know.

I served in the U.S. Army when 52 were hostages in Iran. I volunteered. I sacrificed for my country. I was lucky I did not die doing so.

Mark Vocca does not like that I'm writing about our history. Nothing was secret. But maybe there was an unspoken rule that it should have been. If anyone should be angry it should be Brandon Zart because he was a Nazi devotee and by his own admission, hated Jews.

Despise an individual – hate is too strong a verb --- perhaps that person was an asshole. I can accept that. "Hate a group"? Any group. Not one redeeming quality in the entire batch?

Let's remove groups based on hate for others… nazis, KKK, white supremacists…haters of "abominations" – because gays and lesbians are such horrible people. Let me say this: Leviticus was an asshole.

He wrote stupid rules. His rules were sexist and homophobe. A child determines the duration of the "unclean" session of a mom whether a boy or a girl?

Leviticus should have been left with the dead sea scrolls. His opinions smell like assholes. Lick away.

The first star wars movie in 1977 had a great line. "Who is more foolish? The fool or the fool who follows?"

Seventh Son

Idiots who follow Leviticus are morons. It's bad enough that they're hypocrites. Sadly, Cyndy comes to mind because she became a trumpster... rhymes with?

Further about classical music...

I knew Tchaichovsky's "Waltz of the Flowers" from a 1960s cartoon about mice in a meadow who would disguise themselves as flowers to avoid capture and being eaten by a cat. They crossed the meadow dancing with flowers around their waists. I learned years later that it was part of the Nutcracker.

Mark Vocca turned me on to the 1812 Overture. The canons. The Philadelphia Philharmonic. Digression: is that why Paul Simon used them in the Boxer?

Definition: "Turned me on to"... I think that's a phrase from the 1960s. Sounds like it, doesn't it? It means "introduced me to." Turned me on because "turn me on" meant previously stagnant or unplugged on the shelf. You hit the power button to turn a device "on." "Turn on" also had a sexual nature. Turn on meant made you aroused. Straight guys never said that turned me on in that way unless revealing bi.

I suppose that was weird about Mark and Brandon. There were occasions in Mark's car. One or the other would drop trousers. Now was that the competition to measure who had the bigger dick? I saw each and saw no difference in length or girth. Of course that was flaccid. I never saw either pumped up. I write this to make light of a situation when I was in the back seat watching two teenage boys argue some point – a point that was never made – about male sexual organ.

Further about classical music.

I eventually loved Vivaldi's Four Seasons and Marin Marais' the bells of saint Genevieve. Guild hall string ensemble does the best version.

149

Mark included others like Stravinsky's The Firebird and Schoenberg's 12-tonal classic, "Pierrot Lunaire" which Mitzi hated and could not listen to at all.

Then there was Bill and Jazz...

In the 1990s, I found a love for jazz that was inspired by and influenced by William Frank Stevens, an extraordinary writer and novelist. When I last knew him, he was working on his fourth novel called, "In Barcelona." I was lucky enough to be privy to read his draft manuscript.

I have to say, Bill Stevens raised the bar. His prose was so beautiful and masterful. I gave up fiction as a pursuit. My short stories sit on a shelf and will never be revealed. I loved Bill's narrative and prose. It was the most beautiful writing I've ever read.

The metaphor of the brass ring. If you can reach it, it's the highest you'll acquire. Bill Stevens – his prose was the Brass Ring. I have a mastery of poetry and non-fiction narrative. Fiction is his element. I have read the master and I step aside.

Harlan Ellison motivated me to write fiction. And I tried. Compared to Bill, I was an amateur. My fiction is shelved. Permanently.

Bill also taught me about jazz. We listened to "Bag's groove" and "Time out." He motivated me to explore others of that gathering: Coltrane, Monk, Getz, Rollins, Parker, Gilllespie, Mingus, and Desmond. They are the jazz greats of the 1950s. To me that is the greatest era of jazz.

Color boundaries blurred. It was jazz. They didn't care if you were white or black. It was the music. That's the shizznit.

Years later, I was advised to check out Chet Baker. Not yet.

"Shizznit" came out of the jazz scene. For those who don't know… "that's some shit, isn't it?" evolved into "shizznit." I'm too young to know that. But I love it.

Why did I ever do drugs?

I think it started as defiance of the Bunny. "We're sending you to Catholic school where there are no drugs. Yup, yup, yup, yup." That was an intentional allusion to Mortimer Snerd. That's how he ended his dumb comments.

Bunny might as well have ended his sentences with "Yup, yup, yup, yup…"

In fairness, he was not an idiot. But he had this dichotomy going. Dichotomy is probably wrong because that's two.

His archetypes were deviations from Karl Jung. The Bunny was the pensive philosopher. Sometimes he was. Those were rare moments.

He was the angry punisher without inhibitions. Or restraints. The Sadist.

He was the jovial bastard entertaining company like the perfect host.

He was the white trash racist misogynist. With one "Nigger" joke after another. Why… don't nigger jokes just pile up like dung on a compost pile?

He was the wife beater. Child abuser. And dog killer (family pet). Alcoholic.

He died in 2006. I did not feel a thing. He did not exist.

His sisters (some not all) do not accept me any more. The Christmas cards stopped. The emails stopped.

[But not Uncle Bob… thank you.]

I hope this book reunites.

Back to the original question… if initially as defiance, maybe. But the bottom line was I liked doing drugs. In the beginning. That must be emphasized.

Pot was fun. Get high, go to a movie. Or listen to music with friends.

D.I.D.

Childhood abuse – sexual, physical, and emotional – causes **dissociative identity disorder**… also called multiple personality disorder.

- Fear of Abandonment
- Depersonalization
- Derealization
- Amnesia
- Identity confusion or Identity alteration.
- Distortions in time, place or situation.
- I do things at night. Why? I don't understand.

Digression… but then marijuana became "Monkey Paw" (in 1987) whatever the hell that was – at least one of its new strains. In the 1970s we had Mexican, Colombian, Panama and Sensimilia. In order each of those was stronger than the other.

Brandon got "Monkey Paw." I smoked it. The effect was drooling zombie in the corner non-communicado.

I liked acid. Or what we called microdot. You laughed for eight hours and your ribs ached.

Hash. A few times. Very mellow compared to pot. Old school pot – not the monkey paw shit.

Opium – Kathy Blumers and me at the Rush Concert. I hope that wasn't why we crashed.

Oh that's another story... Rush at the coliseum in Richfield in 1979. Kathy and I were in a band called Black Diamond. I wanted to call the band Blumers after Kathy's last name. It meant bluming flowers in German.

Kathy was still dating Tom Kunst our drummer as far as I knew. I asked her to go see Rush with me. It may have been the 2000 tour. Kathy liked Rush; I did not.

Kathy and I smoked opium at the Rush concert. On the way home we had an accident. As Kathy was leaving the cloverleaf ramp to enter the freeway way, up ahead all cars were stopped. It was winter. Kathy hit the brakes and slid into the car in front of her. I reached my arm across but she still hit her nose on the steering wheel.

Kathy and I spent the night in a motel. A tow truck came to take her vehicle which was totalled.

When the tow truck came, the lady at the motel was sweet. She opened the door to the room and saw Kathy asleep in the bed fully clothed and me in the chair. She said, "I expected hanky panky but not with you two."

David Bowie died on January 10, 2016

I was devastated. No celebrity's death moved me like Bowie's. Mark and I did not discuss this beforehand, but we each played his entire catalog. Every album in order. From Space Oddity to Black Star.

I heard that some reacted that way to Elvis's death. Mark Vocca, Bob Sablack and I reacted that way to Bowie's death.

Jaded Me -- How in the fuck did Keith Richards and Iggy Pop outlive David Bowie? Perhaps the fifty cigarettes a day was a factor. I don't know.

Once upon a time, music changed me. David Bowie opened my eyes. Imagine being born blind and suddenly having sight. That's how significant.

<u>1977 – Bowie was on Bing Crosby's Christmas Special</u>

Bowie and Bing did a special version of the Little Drummer Boy. Then Bowie did a version of "Heroes" that had to be seen. He combined mime and theatre of two crossing the Berlin Wall. Brian Eno and Robert Fripp were involved.

Andy Williams also had a Christmas special that year. It would be his last one. Claudine Longet had shot Spider Sabich. Years later O.J. Simpson murdered Nicole Brown and Ron Goldman. Doesn't leather soaked in any liquid – water or blood – shrink in storage?

Claudine Longet got away with murder because Andy Williams had enough money. No one cared that they were no longer married.

But there never was another Andy Williams Christmas Special.

<u>Kirtland, Ohio</u>

All of us explored Kirtland. This was years before the story of the cult and the Avery family.

Kirtland was a place of Weird Ohio. Supernatural and things that defied explanation.

Kirtland had this place we called Gravity hill. You would put your car in neutral and it would coast uphill. It must have been an optical illusion. Something about the angle of the trees and the road itself.

Then there was the Haunted Hedge. I wish I recalled which road it was on. It was a huge open field. Rectangular shaped, well-mowed area. Perhaps 200 meters in length and 150 meters deep. Centered along the road was a hedge. It formed a box around a head stone for a grave. Rod Schaffter told me it was Hart Road.

The rumor or legend was that if you stood at the head stone, you would hear the sounds of children's voices coming closer and closer.

I never heard them. But I heard that Brandon got dropped off and those in the car sped off and he was scared shitless.

Then there were the Melon Heads. One version says they were hydrocephalic children. What I heard was that they were vicious killers.

The story goes, a young couple were making out in their car. When they go to leave, the car doesn't start. The boyfriend says you stay here, lock the doors, and I'll be back with help. She waits one hour, two hours, then she hears the sound of something scraping across the roof of the car. Back and forth like something swinging. She opens the door and sees her boyfriend, his throat cut and he is hung by the ankles to a tree above the car. The scraping was from his fingernails. The Melonheads did it.

In the Army, I heard this exact same story from a guy from Tennessee who said "No, that happened in my neighborhood." In college at Cleveland State, Marianne Schiebli said, "No, that happened in Willoughby."

Ken Templin

One day in the late fall, early winter of my junior year at Saint Joseph High School, Brandon and Luke were drinking a beer in the student parking lot before class. It was a left over from the night before. Not meant to intoxicate. If it had been a cola or 7-up, it would have served the same purpose. They had cotton mouth from smoking a joint.

Marianist Brother Ken Templin busted them. They got an "in-school suspension." They were working in the library.

I felt compelled. Why? I don't know. I had to do something. I took it upon myself. That "something" would get me expelled.

Earlier, I had done the same with a letter from the school nurse. She wrote a letter to the parents about German measles. I wrote a joke about the bubonic plague. I used the nurse's signature and she allowed it. She gave her permission. I showed her before I copied it.

I took this letter that Brother Templin had sent home to the parents. I cut out the school logo header and cut out his signature and taped the two to a sheet of typing paper and wrote my own narrative. The narrative was basically an invite to the student body of St. Joe's to join him in his private chambers to smoke a joint while he sucked you off. I took the assembled copy to the school library and made fifty copies on the library copier. I then gave batches to my friends to pass out. The Librarian said, "you know this is going to get you into trouble." Statement, not a question.

It became a scandal, a sensation, and oh my God! Weeks went by and I didn't give it a second thought…

Then Joey Luptak got caught passing out copies. Joey bragged that his friend wrote this. Joey lived in Mentor and rode the bus with me.

I got called out of class. Father Reichert was the assistant principal. He took me to the office. I had never been in trouble before. It was a test. Would I lie to a priest? It wasn't confessional.

The school administrators gathered guys from my bus and guys from my classes. They lined them up. One at a time each asked me, "Why did you write the letter." It was staged. They were couched. One at a time. "Why did you write the letter?"

They brought in Ray Golic… father of Bob Golic who played for the Browns. Ray made football players cry. Intimidation was my father's most successful strategy. He was the master intimidator. These people did not hold a candle.

I made one royal fuck up. I left the original in my wall locker and they found it.

They called my mom to come and pick me up. I was expelled.

Now jump ahead… I was married to my second wife. Patti Sue Glasser. Circa 1999-2000. We were moving her Cousin's son or something like that into his new home. He had a friend helping him. Now I left St. Joe's in December 1977. But he looked so familiar. We each asked one another about high school. He also went to Saint Joe's. Then he said, "you wrote that letter." Yes, about Brother Ken Templin. He said, "My parents never believed me. He sexually abused me for years. You were my hero."

I was nobody's hero. Never will be. I felt bad for him.

I can believe his parents didn't believe him. My parents thought I was the villain in the story. I did expose a pedophile. I just didn't know I did. Except I did. At the time, I didn't know I was exposing a pedophile. Imagine that.

Vectors

In Mentor on the Lake, there was this house on Salida road. A basement was all that was left. The house overhead was leveled, gone. Trees grew on top. The basement though for the most part was intact. I don't recall who introduced me to its location. You walked down a stairway. There was a small room to the right and a huge bay area. Then two or three rooms on the north side.

Now this was on the shore of lake erie. Directly opposite the basement on the coast, was a U-shaped walkway leading to two doors that were bricked over. The U-shape had a stem that went out like a jetty into the water.

Back in the basement, where there should have been passageways to the water was cemented over.

My imagination had a field day. I created the urban myth of the vectors. My theory was that during the underground railroad, the whites who were helping runaway slaves got caught. My Lie which was probably inspired by the 1970s made for TV movie, "Don't be afraid of the dark," said that some runaway slaves and their white helpers got caught by southern redneck bounty hunters. They trapped them in the passage between basement and shore. Brick or cement to entomb them.

But they survived and became the vectors.

Three-foot tall cannibals. Who lived like moles underground.

The story scared the girls we would take to the beach. Drink beers and then go visit the vectors. The structure of the basement was perfect to lend credibility to the story and the people at the beach, they saw the bricked up doorways.

Brandon Zart & Janine Feeney

Jump back to the summer of 1976. I finished my freshman year at St. Joe's. Sophomore year would start in the fall. Cyndy and I were very active in the church.

The irony is she became an aetheist and I became a deist (following the French philosopher Voltaire. Voltaire wrote that common sense is not so common.

We were in the Catholic Youth Organization (CYO) with Saint John Vianney parish. I met Debbie McNickle there. We were a couple for a while.

Debbie invited me to a party where I met Brandon Zart. The party was at Janine Feeney's house. Janine became my first love and sexual partner.

I was 14 or 15 and she was 16. The proverbial "they" say you never forget your first.

I think I remember Janine mostly because of how we broke up. I was a child (and this is the older me speaking). I wanted to convey that we were focused more on sex than on love and I wanted Love to the primary reason we were together. I'm sure it didn't come out that way because she slapped and left the room crying. I heard from friends that she and Patty Aranavage wore black every day to school in mourning.

Brandon was a "wanna-be" Nazi. WTF? Why would anyone want to be a Nazi? He had this idolization of Hitler and openly said he hated Jewish people. Yet, Iggy Pop Lou Reed and Joey Ramone were all Jewish... and many others in the punk scene.

St. Joes showed us Holocaust movies like "Night and Fog." Bulldozing bodies. Emaciated humans. Gassed and burned. Actual film footage of the concentration camps.

Brandon, I never asked you then. I ask you now... "Why?"

Every thing is a grey area in life. I hate that Brandon hated Jews. Back then I didn't personally know any Jews -- There were not Jews in Catholic high schools. If there were jewish kids in elementary school at Rice and during my first two years at Ridge Junior High, they never let me know.

But I knew the jewish deli in Shaker Heights. Corky and Lennie's. 27091 Chagrin Blvd, Woodmere Ohio, 44122.

It is the best Jewish deli in Cleveland. And fuck you Brandon, you Nazi prick.

One "good" thing I must say about Brandon. I suppose the only thing. Brandon hated Bunny and Bunny never liked him. Brandon refused to shake his hand.

Guess what? Brandon heard the stories from me... mostly the things I've detailed in the preceding pages. Why would he *want* to shake the Bunny's hand?

I never understood Brandon's Nazi obsession. I think it may have been a means to acquire his father's acceptance. Brandon's older brother Ryan was gay. Perhaps Brandon wanted first place with Paul.

Paul was German. Paul probably hated that his first son was gay. I don't know if Darla was the oldest or if Ryan was.

Darla loved that I wore a t-shirt of "Heart" to their house. She said, "See? Look at that." Darla was married and had two boys. But was home with the family. Brandon treated the younger nephews like brothers.

Darla was such a crush.

Brandon used to be an older brother to me. I mimicked him and idolized him. Change of subject...

If Brandon ever reads this., I want him to read, Elie Wiesel's "Night."

Then tell me about what you feel about Jews and the Nazis.

Recently – 2021 – Proud boys and other scum are chanting Six and a half million was only a good start. I blame the Donald and tell the proud boys, your likeness to Mortimer Snerd is not an accident. Repeat after me, "Ah-yup-yup-yup."

Suzanne Stiffler pleaded with me. She said, "Don't become Brandon. We love Clem." I was copying him in every way.

Brandon exemplified the person I wanted to be. The broken shell wanted a re-boot. A model to copy. Because Brandon was cool.

Define "cool." It meant confident. Laid back. And knowledgeable about things that were cool...

1977? It meant:

Star Wars, Fleetwood Mac released "Rumours."

EMI dropped the rock group "the Sex Pistols."

Suzanne Lacy's performance piece about rape, "Three weeks in May."

Anita Bryant had fruit Smashed into her face. Homophobe.

Gary Gilmore is executed by firing squad .

Gerald Ford pardons Tokyo Rose.

Jimmy Carter is the 39th President. Jimmy Carter pardons draft dodgers. And pardoned Richard Nixon. Are you kidding?

I was a failure. I failed my mom. I did not protect her. Brandon was a champion. I was a loser.

I realized that Clem failed.

If I copied his mannerism, became him. I could save my mom. I could correct past mistakes. Past failings. I believed that.

But Suzanne was right. I was wrong. Brandon was a nazi. I would never be like him.

Bunny was a Clem. I evolved. I became Clement.

The #metoo movement featured a 17-year-old boy who said an older Italian actress sexually abused him when he was a minor. That is utter non-sense. If there was a hot, older woman, when I was 17? And she initiated sex with fellatio? I'm a willing participant 110% and then some. That moron is all about greed and an easy payout. He should be ashamed. And he was never assaulted, raped or abused.

I agree -- the women that Harvey Weinstein raped, they *were* raped. No question. But it's different if you're male. Now if it had been a male who raped the ass of a minor? That's totally different.

Consider N.A.M.B.L.A. I saw them on Tom Snyder's "Tomorrow" show around 1981 in Savannah. NAMBLA is the

North American Man-Boy Love Association. They believe "Sex before Eight or it's too late."

When I worked at Bob Evans in the 1970s, there was a waitress. I was 17 and she was perhaps 21. We had sex. It later turned out she thought she was returning the favor – quid pro quo – because I cleaned her stable and brushed her horse. I thought she liked me. It was the barter system. I was technically underage. But it was never rape.

Under the legal definition it probably was… but I'll be damned if I ever state her name. Actually she could say I was a bad lay. I was 17. I pulled out before she came. I probably lasted five strokes.

Bunny and his racism

Bunny did not hide his racism until he realized that I was not okay with "nigger jokes." Until then kitchen table with beer buddies meant jokes and guffahs that denigrated women and minorities. Children want to bond with parents. Bunny and his co-horts alienated me. It was a constant internal struggle. One part was the love of a father was dire, important. The other side was he's a racist, sexist asshole.

As a teenager and then as an adult, I acquired an affinity toward or a propensity to gravitate to movies that dealt with race. Billy Jack was the first. For years it remained my favorite movie.

Recently, Selma, Blackkklansman, Green Book, Queen and Slim, Just mercy, Django unchained and Malcolm X. We need a movie about Emmett Till. Google his name.

"All in the Family" was written to ridicule the racist, Archie Bunker. They wrote it so the obvious was the first thing the watcher noticed. The viewers laughed because Archie was an idiot who had no shame revealing his racism.

In homes in Mentor, it was different. Mike and Gloria could slam Archie. I was not allowed to speak out against the Bunny. Mom made me conform to abiding by the "standards" of a son of a dentist. Somehow that was an established image in his and her mind. Which I defied every chance I got. Never defy the Bunny. Mom said so.

Fuck that noise

Ridge Junior High School in Mentor

I was there for seventh and eighth grades.

I used to have horrible sinuses. My nose ran like a sieve in the Winter and Spring. At some point I discovered Halls cough drops. They were a god send. They cleared my sinuses and allowed me to breath.

No adult taught me to blow my nose. Isn't that basic?

What role is family supposed to play?

Scott Smyers

Scott and I became friends at Ridge Junior High. He lived off a side street off Mentor Avenue, aka route 20 just east of the Great Lakes Mall.

Scott's back yard had a – not a fort, not a club house. It was like a little house. It had electricity. He had a record player. We played Foreigner and Leonard Skinner. His records, not mine.

Neil Young

I was a fan of Neil Young. Matt Zolnay and I saw him in concert in Akron. His critique of the south and its hypocrisy in his song,

"Southern Man" was accurate, intelligent, and eloquent. I would have thought the impact was undeniable. Neil Young criticized the South. It's hypocrisy. Google the lyrics. They say it all.

Neil Young said the South was racist – which it was -- and Skinnard protested back. Displaying their ignorance. I lived in Georgia from 1980 to 1983. The south was racist. Not every southerner. But far too many. Those in their 20s seemed to reject the parents' prejudices. But the older generation, just like Bunny, more examples of Archie Bunker. God bless Carroll O'Connor for typifying the stereotype.

Leonard Skinnard releases "Sweet Home Alabama." It said "I hope Neil Young will remember – Southern man don't need him around anyhow." Wow, what a retort. That sure put Neil in his place, now didn't it?

Idiotas. I love the Spanish pronunciation. It drives the fork into the groin so much more… enthusiastically.

Further on Scott

Scott spent the night in Mentor when we were in 8th grade at Ridge Junior High. The Bunny gave us a six pack of beer. I was shocked. Scott and I each had three. And were asleep soon after.

Years later, I met Scott at Cloverdale where both he and his dad were members. We reconnected on the work-day that all members participated in. I forfeited my membership soon after that. It had nothing to do with Scott. It had more to do with disassociation from an establishment of white redneck racists. To their credit, there was a lesbian member who they tolerated. She probably got approved before they were aware of her orientation.

Janine Feeney

I joined the Army on May 14, 1980.

One time, when I was home on leave, I called Janine and asked if I could see her. 1981 or 1982? She still lived in Mentor in her mom's home on Dahlia Drive. She said "sure" and sounded drunk. She was. And she was now with Michael. Michael was an older hippy who had a car. When I lost my virginity, Michael drove us around with his then-girlfriend. Janine and I were in the back seat. Drinking a concoction of mixed alcohol from my father's liquor cabinet.

Janine and I had sex for the first time in her mom's house, downstairs. Split level home so it was like the basement or family room. Her mom worked nights and wasn't home. Her brother was a football player and out with his buds.

Janine had passion. Enthusiasm. Gusto. Desire. Lust. Unlike anyone I'd ever known. Or knew since then. Sex made her lose her mind. She didn't care who was around or might be watching.

I can not describe what it felt like. You can say, warm wet and slippery. That does not come close. There is an intimacy beyond. It is a physical, emotional, mental and sexual connection to another human being. Can a fourteen-year-old know what love means? I did not think so then and I do not think so now. To me, it was spiritual.

Love was a concept. A noun and a verb. As a child, I could not define it or grasp it. But what I felt, overpowered me. I wanted to relish in it and I wanted to comprehend what it meant.

Freud said all human motives are "a will to pleasure." Adler said all motives were "a will to power." Frankl said motives are "a will to meaning." I wanted to know the meaning. I follow Frankl.

After we had coitus, I passed out in the bathroom after throwing up in the toilet that night.

Janine and Michael were now drinking buddies and lovers. She laughed when she saw my hair cut. Third wheels cut out early. I was gone after 15 minutes.

The Cover of the Viking Newsletter

I got on the cover of the school newsletter at Saint Joe's. Mark Temple was my friend and probably has become a journalist for the Washington Post. I wouldn't know. We lost touch when I left St. Joe's.

Back then he was writing for the Viking. He heard about a stunt I pulled and asked me to demonstrate so he could take photos and interview me for the paper.

The stunt was this: I put my feet on one column of the entry to the auditorium and my hands on the adjacent column, and then proceeded to "walk" up to the top. I believe the secret was my shoes had polyurethane soles that kept me from slipping.

It made the front page of the Viking. Mark's interview included a question "who is your competition?" I said Spider-man because he can spin webs. When he printed it, it said Superman. That was really dumb. Completely different set of super powers.

The photographer was lame. He kept saying, "keep holding… keep holding…" while he adjusted the focus.

I eventually had to drop. He kept me up there too long.

I dropped and man, it stung. I was about 30 feet up and had to land without a roll. Jumping off telephone poles, you hit and rolled. This was concrete.

My sister Cyndy

She worked for the Bunny in the office during high school. She took my mom's place as the receptionist. She did that job until she left for Hiram college. Bunny's alma mater. Jungle Book Disney film and the song, 'you-woo-woo, I wanna be like you-woo-woo." Louis Prima did the vocals. Phil Harris jumped in toward the end of the song.

As receptionist, she was no longer his daughter. She was his subservient. Cyndy became the new abuse of target.

I can't say what or how much abuse she suffered. Cyndy loved her father. She tolerated it all.

Sometimes, I think I'm writing this to document objectivity. So many instances easily become subjective rants.

Lake Catholic High School

After St. Joe's expelled me… and the Bunny and mom were so ashamed of me.

I wanted to go to Mentor High School and re-join my friends. My parents wanted to keep me in the Catholic school system. Reluctantly, I went to Lake Catholic. Actually, reluctant isn't the correct choice of words. I abided when they said I had no choice. The implication was I had to abide for penance for the shame.

Right away, I was the enemy because I came from the rival school. Guys wanted to pick fights with me because I came from St. Joes. I'd meet them after class and tell them, this is stupid. The opponent would say, come on… hit me. I refused.

I cited the American Revolution and talked about how the rebels had a cause. Fighting because I came from Joe's was stupid. No cause.

Go figure. They were stupid jocks.

The jocks all wanted to kick my ass.

I didn't see it at Joe's. We were all freshmen and then sophmores. Juniors were interrupted with expulsion.

At Lake Catholic for me, my Junior year was December of 1977 to June 1978. Distinctions of all the cliques were well defined. Academic students were brains, nerds or geeks. I think that's where I re-met Rod Schaffter. I qualified but I didn't. I had been a nerd, but now I failed academically. I lived in a house with a Bunny. My bad grades excluded from the Brains, nerds and geeks.

The jocks were bullies with too much testosterone.

Cyndy was a brain. But how she excelled amazed me. I could not focus or concentrate. My brain became locked down. On hold? Like a computer frozen up? Like Bunny hit the "off switch."

There were the popular students. "Popular" – that meant, they walked the halls and appreciated the oohs and ahhs of the fan club. That's hyperbole. They walked the halls and acted like they appreciated the adulations of the fans. For the most part they were hypocrites. But loved and adored!

There were "Pot heads." High every day. At Lake Catholic, I did not get high. I smoked Marlboro and did valium. The latter, thanks to Slick. Valium shut out the outside world. Slick brought me 30 roche from his mom's prescription. One-A-Day. I then tolerated Lake Catholic.

There was a clique called the weirdoes. Not part of any group. I qualified. Or to borrow from Ken Kesey's "One flew over the cuckoo's nest," I was the bull goose loonie.

Chris Was

Was was her last name. All that anyone knew was she was the girlfriend of the Bob Segar Band fan. She was quiet in Honors Religion. She was Marion the Librarian from the Music Man.

Her Bob Segar fan boyfriend attacked me. He blind-sided me. Attacked me from behind with no warning. It was in the room for auditions for the LC Singers. I was under a pile of desks that toppled with me when he sucker punched me from behind.

Teek intervened. Teek calmed the attacker down. The Bob Segar fan thought I was hitting on Chris. Hitting on does not mean punching. Back then, hitting on meant flirting with. Or suggesting romantic or sexual intimacy.

Those of us in Honors religion called her "Wassers." I think she gave herself that name and we just followed suit.

"We" was Teek, Harold Norsic, Kay Miller, me and that guy whose name I have to look up.

Further on Lake Catholic

There were some good things that came out of it. I became friends (again) with Rod Schaffter. We knew each other at Ridge and got re-acquainted at LC. We are friends to this day. Same with Tom Rosplock and Neil Allen.

Sister Roberta liked me enough to place me in honors religion for my senior year. If only she'd been the teacher.

For English, Mrs. Schaeffer was my teacher and my favorite and an inspiration. We read Ken Kesey's "One flew over the cuckoo's nest" and David Morrell's "First Blood." A Frank Herbert novel called "Soul Catcher." There was one more, but memory fails me. The course was American Literature.

Because we were reading "First Blood," she told the class that during Vietnam, she was a war protestor. She also brought another faculty member in to talk who was a veteran of the Vietnam war. He presented his side.

Mrs. Schaeffer was also quite cool, on certain days, she would pass out copies of lyrics of songs. Then she'd play the song and have us analyze the lyrics like poetry. The two I remember most distinctly were Bruce Springsteen's "Thunder Road" and Jackson Brown's "The Pretender."

She inspired me -- it was then that I started reading song lyrics as poetry. My first exploration was David Bowie. I remember asking her if I could bring in a David Bowie lyric and music and she thanked me for the offer but said let's wait until the course is British Literature.

Later I would read and study Bob Dylan (thanks, Mark Vocca). Billy Joel (Tom Rosplock) and Paul Simon.

Why Paul Simon? One day my first wife and I were on the way out. I was at BP with two admin women. I think they held me off with a ten-foot pole. They knew my married life was a goner. I just hadn't pulled the trigger yet. I told them that I was going to do the hippie thing this weekend. I bought the greatest hits of Bob Dylan and Janis Joplin. I also bought Simon and Garfunkel's GH but did not admit that.

They nodded a lot which is what people do when they humor you. Catch phrases like "Oh, that's nice."

This must have been 1994. Summer in Mentor with Bunny and mom. Lise and I were separated.

Bob Dylan reminded me of the summers in Ashtabula with Veronica Overbaugh and her family. When she played guitar around the campfire and we would sing songs. "Blowing in the Wind" was one of them. She brought sheet music with lyrics. And we would sing along.

Jump ahead… Road trip to the retreat with the CYO. I rode out to it with the cop and his wife and he played Simon and Garfunkel the entire trip. I asked for Iggy Pop and the Stooges. He laughed.

But forced to listen, I listened. There should have been a photo of me as the dog turning his head for "his master's voice."

"The Boxer." "Bridge." "I am a Rock." And all the others. The songs burned -- they branded my heart. They would remain with me. Still to this day. Paul Simon is a poet.

God's Juke Box

When I get to heaven, I'm going to become God's juke box. I have so many catalogs in my head. Beatles, Rolling Stones, David Bowie, Mott the Hoople, Iggy Pop, Roxy Music, Lou Reed... And stupid songs that will make Him laugh... "Playground in my mind." Cyndy loved that song. "Guitarzan." Mike Hall loved that song.

Back to Lake Catholic...

Slick used to provide me with 30 Roche Valiums to get through the day. His mom had an endless supply. But... there was one day... I had a cold. That meant the valiums created a zombie. Guys were dragging me by my scarf to classes.

Mrs. Schaeffer intervened. That was the only time I ever felt guilty for doing drugs. She told me her sister did drugs. I never wanted to feel shame in front of Mrs. Schaeffer. I got off downers and switched to speed.

What ever happened to my cashmere scarf? And how did I get a cashmere scarf?

More importantly, I tried to contact Mrs. Schaeffer and Mrs. Miller (Kay's mom) numerous times after the Army. The school administration ignored my letters and phone calls. Those bastards!

<u>Lake Catholic Literary Journal
for Fiction, Poetry and Art</u>

There was a cubicle in the library. It was set apart for those who worked on the literary journal.

Inside the cubical were graffitied lyrics from 1977. The song by Billy Joel. Ironic to have them in a Catholic School Library.

"Well they say there's a heaven for those who wait.

Some say it's better but I say it ain't.

I'd rather laugh with the sinners than cry with the saints.

The sinners have much more fun

And only the good die young."

It cracked me up seeing it as graffiti in the Library of a catholic high school.

The editor was walking out of the library. She did a chicka-chicka-chicka-swing of her hips and wet a finger tip and touched her buttock and went "Swishhhhhh…"

Cyndy was there as went, "Oh my God?" Cyndy could be a prude.

I loved it. The editor was hot.

<u>Army dates</u>

I found some records in my files. The army dates from my calendars. So ex-wife did not dispose of all of the evidence. That's a good thing. I'll add the dates to events.

<u>Untitled, 1978-1979</u>

The caste system in India classifies the lowest as "untouchables." I wore that branded on my back.

At Lake Catholic, the hypocrisy drove me crazy. Most blatantly in the "honors" religion course. I hated hypocrites.

Spring of my junior year in 1978, just before summer vacation, they gave out awards. The "Christian Life Award" for the most holier-than-thou went to the biggest drug dealer in the school. I do not criticize the recipient because he dealt drugs. I was a user. I criticize the school for hypocrisy.

I hated Lake Catholic. I could not wait to get the hell out of there. I was sixteen, then seventeen during my penance. But I have always been the black sheep of the family.

Here's irony for you. My two sisters, Cyndy and Cathy, and my brother, Chuck all graduated from Lake Catholic. I know Cyndy was successful there. Cathy dominated the school musicals. Chuck aced at Art. Baa baa black sheep.

One day at lake Catholic -- being picked up by mom...

We were arguing... I complained about the superficiality... she said, "You are the son of a dentist —" It meant, I was supposed to respect that. It meant that I was to abide by a code of conduct. It meant that whatever He did, was okay. As long as we did not embarrass him. The argument abrupted because she threw out my jeans. My favorite jeans. My most comfortable jeans. Because they were frayed.

She said they were tattered and torn. I opened the car door and started to jump out. She slammed on the brakes and I stayed in my seat. She never apologized.

Arguments like that always went unresolved. The talking stopped. No apologies; and no forgiveness. Everything went into limbo. The silence remained. The words drifted off to an unknown destination.

1978 – Brandon introduced me to Mark Vocca

I had left Saint Joe's. The literary publication was out. That's the annual paperbound book of students' poetry, fiction, art and et cetera. Brandon picked me up in the parking lot at Mark's record store on Route 615 aka Andrews road in mentor.

That was the first and only time that Mark was in the back seat.

Brandon was wearing a brand spanking new black leather jacket. He declared, "I'm a PUNK now!" [Back when Luke Powers loaned me his copies of the Ramones and Iggy's raw power. It didn't transform me into a new identity.] I looked at Mark. Perhaps he had an explanation. He looked at me because I didn't ask a question.

I was wearing olive drab brittannia jeans that were made popular by the brits that joined the CYO youth group. I had a button-down grey shirt. Brandon accused me of being disco. I was definitely NOT disco.

The irony of that is how the last time I was in Brandon's home where he lived with his parents, the soundtrack to "Saturday Night Fever" was on the floor of the White Carpet room. Brandon told me about going to a disco called "Tracks" and fucking catholic girls who just graduated.

Apparently catholic girls loved to fornicate after graduation. Mentor had a bar under the bridge of 615 where the Lake Catholic girls would prey for sex. I learned that in 1987.

I was never a conqueror or a conquest. I was in Georgia.

The good news is that Mark Vocca and I became friends.

Someone once told me that "Tracks" was a gay bar. I've googled it. Not found.

Brandon had an older brother named Ryan who was gay. One day in 1997 I was at the West side market on West 25th with Karen Cuiskelly. The vegetable stand had a seller who looked so much like Brandon that I asked if his name was Ryan. He said no. I didn't believe him.

Long John Silver Parking Lot – Eckley Corner

Tim Freeman was the manager. Brandon would park his VW van behind it. Tim was Janine's ex.

Brandon and I would smoke pot behind the restaurant. This was 1978 and 1979. Maybe 1977 also.

One day Jimmy King joined us. It was years after he moved to Florida. His family came back to Mentor for a visit. Jimmy insisted that he was not high.

Suzanne Stiffler and her objection

I loved Suzanne. Suzanne thought that I was becoming a replica. I admired Brandon so much, I was becoming just like him. I mimicked his mannerism. My own identity was based on insecurity. Bunny telling me I was a worthless piece of shit and mom saying, "You're handsome, you're intelligent, you're perfect." I had no clue where the middle was. I thought the middle must be where the truth was hiding. I replicated Brandon and Suzanne didn't like it.

Suzanne said she liked "Clem" – She said "this new you is not you."

I talked like him, I did so much like him that Suzanne said I forfeited my identity.

Suzanne eventually introduced me to Kathy Blumers – Suzanne and Kathy worked together at the Perkins on route 615. My first rock band, Black Diamond was formed. Kathy played guitar -- and flute for our rendition of Jethro Tull's song, "Locomotive Breath."

Mark Vocca

I spent a lot of time in Mark's bedroom. Mark was a natural teacher. He reminded me of Mrs. Schaeffer from Lake Catholic. He used music and watched you. If you "got" it, he smiled.

Mark loved Bob Dylan. I had "Blonde on Blonde" from Phoebe (Bob Evans). Mark said I should get "Blood on the Tracks." He said "Idiot Wind" is the best "Fuck-You-Song" ever written. I bought, "Blood on the Tracks."

That same day, he played Hurricane for me. Wrongfully imprisoned for a murder he did not commit. It was not a one-time event. Watch the movie, "Just Mercy." Hurricane was just one example. Black outcry of injustice fell on deaf ears.

[In part, I'm documenting Mark's history along with my own. Mark plays an important part in my life from High School to post 50s life.]

Mark had an Ovation acoustic guitar. He was so proud of that instrument.

His brother Scott played the banjo.

Tom Miller and I came to get some record

I don't remember when I first met Tom. He was (I assumed) a rich kid of Mentor. My father was a dentist and I didn't have half the crap that Tom had.

Tom unfortunately had a bag of pot in his tube sock and it fell out and guess who found it? The bunny.

Sometimes I capitalize the first letter of Bunny and sometimes it's all lower case. Don't attribute meaning to that.

Upstairs, we had a large bedroom referred to as the Family room. My room was to the left. I noticed on television, the siblings and their friends were watching "The Exorcist." It must have been 1978 or 1979. Why do some details

– superficial at best – get retained in memory? I never said, I'm going to make a concerted effort to remember that the Exorcist was on TV.

I heard my father's voice calling me to come down stairs. He showed me the bag of pot and demanded "what's this?"

"It's Tom's. It's not mine." Well he has to leave. I said okay and went upstairs to tell Tom he had to leave. When I came back down I asked him, "What did you do with it?"

What do you mean what did I do with it – I flushed it down the toilet.

Oh, man, that was twenty or thirty bucks worth of weed.

Bunny was an asshole. Pot was not addictive. You could drive a car. Alcohol is, was and always will be addictive. And you cannot drive drunk. (A) it's against the law and (B), you can kill yourself or others or both. Bunny was a hypocrite. How many times he got inebriated and drove home drunk? Mom says so often with the kids in the back seat. How did he not get ten DUIs?

Tom Miller and the "Hitler Game"

Once Mark and Dennis were pissed at Tom and wanted him out of the Seneca house. I played this "Hitler game" (I learned it from Brandon) of uniting allies against a common enemy and made myself the fall guy. I call it that because Hitler united Germany against a common enemy – the jewish people.

I took some of Tom's records home with me one night. Stupid shit like the Rasberries and Alice Cooper. No impact at all. I returned the records and told Tom that I took them home by mistake. Really? He believed that crap? "Oh, I accidentally took home your Alice Cooper and Rasberries albums? And they say that I'm gullible?

So I returned them and took more valuable records… ones that Tom would notice. I kept a journal noting each step. It was a school notebook really. I wanted to document passages so I could say, "See? I really had a plan."

The day my mom said, Mark and Tom came over and went into your room and took a bunch of records. They said they were Tom's records. I said they were.

Maybe two days later, I took my journal to Mark's record store at the Great Lakes mall and asked him to read.

Turns out, Mark and Jay kicked Tom out anyways and I moved in. Efforts were in vain. My plan did not work. The saving grace is that Mark and I are still friends. Best friends.

In Berlin, I learned from letters that Tom became "Tommy Hawk" and shaved his head to join the punk skinheads as a leader. That's likely hearsay. But so ironic. He DID have a bird's nose.

In 1997, Karen Cuiskelly and I went to see Tom's band "Swank Motel" at the Edison in Tremont. They were good. They even did a cover of "Spider-Man" from the 1967 cartoon. I would have gladly bought a CD of their set.

Kay Miller and the "Prayer for the Fool"

I met Kay in Honors Theology. Her mom was a History teacher at Lake Catholic. I never had a class with her, but Teek called her Madame Rasputin.

I wrote a poem called "the Prayer for the Fool." Kay swiped it. Swiped sounds like theft. I probably gave it to her. But I wanted it back. It was my only copy.

Her mom read it to her history class. Her mom became my strongest ally. I respected and admired her for her loyalty and devotion based on a poem that I wrote.

Honors Religion

Sister Roberta. I loved her. She was intelligent, strict, fair, and unfortunately, after my junior year was getting a promotion to become a principal.

She recommended me for Honors religion at Lake Catholic High school for my senior year. A little secret – I've never read the bible. Well, that was true then, but I did read parts of it in college at Cleveland State University (CSU).

Honors religion bothered me. It wasn't about scholars.

I sat with Tim "Teek" Kenneley, Harold Norsic, Chris Was and Kay Miller. There was one other guy who should have been with us. I'll pull my yearbook and get his name. {Update 2021 – I can't find the year book.]

The rest of the class were the pretentious, holier-than-thou hypocrites.

Miss Larkin was the teacher. She was the most asexual person I've ever met. I don't think she favored men or women. I could be totally wrong, but I thought her destiny was to be a spinster with thirty cats.

Truth could be that she had a husband and four kids. Or she was a bull dyke with a strap-on and a lesbian wife. I just don't know.

Alienation

We had to do a paper. She gave us a variety of topics. I picked "Alienation." I personally related to the topic. I belonged at Ridge Junior High School. I grew up with these kids.

I think she expected a history paper on how early followers of Jesus were alienated from society and martyred. I wrote it on alienation that I felt. I quoted Iggy Pop and his song lyrics from "Dirt" off the Funhouse album and "I got nothin'" from Kill City.

I also invented a Canadian book that the title and author could not be verified and cited passages... I may have named the author, Iguana Stone or Paradox which was my band name. Miss Larkin brought up the topic of reference material in class and said some papers were written with reference material that could not be confirmed. She looked at me. I would have been busted if she could proof it. Why didn't she say, "show me the book"?

I hope she reads this 50 years later and sez, "I knew it!!"

More on the summer of 1978 when I met Mark Vocca

Brandon picked me up in his car. Off 615 where Mark worked at the record store. The Saint Joe's Literary book had just come out. "The Carpenter." Named for Saint Joseph. Remind me why he was a saint? He escorted a pregnant wife and he was not the father... to a barn where she would give birth to the son of god. If my wife told me, "I'm pregnant, but you're not the father." I think I'd be pretty rejected.

Brandon decided to embarrass me in front of Mark. He read a poem I had published. It was for Janine Feeney. I called it fulfillment and submitted it anonymously. How did Brandon know it was my work?

Lake Catholic and the party in someone's basement

There was a juke box. Someone played Aerosmith, "Dream on." I sang the song. I sing as if I'm performing the song. As if I'm on stage and I'm the lead singer of the band playing the song. It's almost as if I go into a trance and not just sing the song, I perform the song.

Afterwards, Teek came up to me and said, "Fuck. That was amazing. Can you do that again? The dancing and the song. The singing." I said no, I can't. The song takes me over. I don't plan that. It just happens.

Brian from the apartments on Mentor avenue just west of the Great Lakes Mall

Once upon a time, there was She.

She was the girlfriend of a marine. I respected her intelligence.

Here was my dilemma. I thought, if I loved her, she would respect me.

Okay so which was supposed to come first?

I don't know. One night we spent a whole night. Sitting on the steps of her front porch, talking until dawn

Part of me said, he was in the marines now. The other part said, he was gone.

I can't remember her name.

The apartment complex was adjacent to and east of the Great Lakes Mall. The movie theater was just over the fence. I met her friends. One big girl had two kids. And there was Brian. Brian reminded me of Jimmy Damm. Long blondish brown hair parted in the middle.

Brian asked me to drive him to Eastlake for a score. I thought he'd share so I agreed. We left Mentor and drove to a suburban home off Vine Street.

Brian and I went to visit his buddy. He cut three lines and we each snorted one. He had a three inch piece of straw which we each used. When it was my turn, I felt the rush. I didn't know what it was. But it was strong stuff.

I remember thinking, okay, this is cool. I don't have to drive. We can just hang out here and listen to music or watch TV.

Abruptly, Brian's friend is ushering us out. He had a place to go and couldn't leave us alone in his home. I thought, dude, you just gave me a line of something for free. That was generous. But now you want to kick me out and make me drive? That's crazy.

Brian and I climbed into the ford Econoline van. While backing out of the driveway, I backed into the hedge row that flanked the right side of the driveway.

What drug did we take? I drove us back to Mentor. Eventually I had to get on Route 20 / Mentor avenue.

I had the where with all, to travel side streets. Brian had this paranoia that kicked in. He turned around in the bucket seat. His back was on the horizontal seat and his thighs were along the back. Knees bent across the top. Feet dangled over the back. Brian was almost crying. I remember him muttering, "Do the cops know where we are? Oh, God, does my mom know what we did?"

I had to reassure him. That probably gave me the concentration to arrive at his apartment complex safely.

When we arrived I just wanted to sit and calm myself down.

I was never sure about what drug we did. But I think it was angel dust. Or PCP. I am so lucky to make it back safe without getting pulled over and arrested.

Attitudes about drugs. In the 1970s, it was anything goes.

We had for lack of better words, prudes. They were usually girls who under no circumstances would ever do any drugs.

Some were scholars. I compliment them. But some were just prudes.

Drugs came in all sizes back then.

Pot was a dried plant that you took a double live album and separated the stems and seeds. Rolling paper made the "joint." It was very thin paper with an edge with adhesive. My friends said that I rolled a joint like a mummy's leg.

It was thick.

Pills. We took white cross. That was speed or black beauties. Other pills. I took valium. I explained this at Lake Catholic. Then with Mark, we took microdot. I loved microdot.

Bill introduced me to crank. Injected into a vein. I did not know until "Breaking Bad" that it was crystal meth. I think we did it three times.

Dennis Terry (aka Jay) said it was a chemical reaction of aluminum foil with hydrochloric acid.

Yes, and I wanted it injected into my veins.

Idaho deployment

Idaho. Years later, I was on deployment. Stacy Nowak and I were at a rock club with a live band. I asked them if they did any Bowie and if so, could I sing. They said no. A girl agreed to dance with me. It happened again. The song possessed me and I went into that same trance. The guitar player said we were the best dancers that night.

Years later, the Defnics played a show, and I danced with Chrissie Hill and she said the same thing. The music moved me. It took me over. I had no control.

I later learned Brandon was jealous. She was his girl. His woman. He played bass in the Defnics. I was on leave and danced with Chris. I knew her from Ridge Junior high. He did not need to be jealous. Rangers don't fuck with wives or girlfriends of fellow rangers. Some call that the seventh stanza of the Ranger Creed.

Some need a barrier about other people's wives or girlfriends to say they are off limits. Rangers don't need a barrier. It simply is not an option.

Regarding the trance, I don't have an explanation. My description doesn't capture the experience.

In Tremont, I did the same thing, naked on the roof top. People probably saw me. I didn't care. I sang and danced with abandon. It's the only way to enjoy life and music to the fullest. I sang Bridge over troubled waters and matched Art Garfunkel note for note. I sang Melanie "Ring the Living Bell" and matched her note for note. I sang Janis Joplin "Me and my Bobbie McGee" and matched her note for note. Years later, I sang the Cranberries' song, "Zombie" and matched the vocalist note for note.

Brief bragging rights… until in my fifties when acid reflux destroyed my voice. Some people with acid reflux, just clear their throats repeatedly. I did that until it sent me running for a toilet or a sink. I'd gag and puke like dry heaves, shaking, convulsing to get it out.

Bad scene. And Lynn hates bodily functions. She has to shut it out.

Lake Catholic Honors Religion: The Chain

Each of us had to conduct a "something." Forgive me. I forget what you call it. A chapel gathering for readings and prayers and some function. A service? A retreat? I don't recall. No matter.

When it was my turn, I puzzled about the "Function" part. Most of my class mates were phonies. Ego-centric. I wanted to take them out of their place of comfort and make them feel "something" about another person. Shift the weight of balance from self to another. Ego was overboard.

I thought about it. My concept was a Chain. Fleetwood Mac had a song called "the Chain." I wore a dog collar choker chain most of the time. I turned that metaphor into "my function."

What I wanted the class to do was announce a name of someone in the class and describe his or her talents, skills, personality then take his or her hand to start the chain. Praise someone else. No self promotion. No praise of self.

I started with the introvert. I'll name him. But I didn't want to be suspected of being gay, so I did not take his hand. In the background I played the David Bowie song, Cygnet Committee. It had the line in the lyrics of "I slit the Catholic Throat with slogans like…"

Each student participated and it went around. I expected to be last to complete the chain, but someone named me early. It was Kay Miller.

My "something" got me an A for the class.

In the Army I wrote to Kay often. She wrote back. Her health was poor and eventually it took over.

Somewhere along the chain, a student named Miss Larkin as the next link. She in turn named a student and the chain continued. The chain eventually included every student.

Miss Larkin was funny. When I cheated, she knew. I never cheated on tests. I cheated like the fabricated references to my paper on alienation. But then she would praise me for stunts like the Chain. Pretty good for a deist or an atheist – at that time, I didn't know which.

Sometime in 1977 or 1978

I asked my brother Chuck to come to the woods behind our house. I pulled out a joint and said this is marijuana. Would you like to smoke it to find out what it's like?

He said why. I said because the FBI is spraying crops that they know about with a drug called paraquat. Back then we users pronounced it Pear-Quat.

Paraquat was a disease that attacked the lungs. Those who smoked the infested pot got a horrible lung infection. I never heard of any deaths. But it was the wrong approach.

I told Chuck, if you want pot, ask me and I'll get it for you. I don't want you getting pot from the street when it could be infected with paraquat.

I don't recall if he tried the joint. THEN.

Years later he had a bong and hookah collection in my mother's house in Raleigh.

Lori Terry and Char Vocca

Mark Vocca introduced me the Terry Family. Mitzi was the eldest daughter and his woman.

Jay aka Dennis was the older brother. He told this weird story about selling his plasma in New Orleans to buy drugs. Jay always reminded me of Eugene Reynolds from the Rezillos. Later the Revillos.

Tracy Terry was a tall big girl dressed in denim with a cowgirl hat ready to line dance.

Lori was the baby of the family. Lori loved Rod Stewart and...

Her brother and her two sisters, Tracy and Mitzi, called her "Weiner." It was based on her obsession with the penis. Lori expressed enthusiasm. But I always thought that it was feigned. Like going along with the fascination but never really subscribing to it. I never called her "Weiner." I always called her "Lori."

Lori loved Rod Stewart.

Mark got her a cardboard stand up of Rod from the "Do ya think I'm Sexy" tour.

Lori also loved Charles Manson. Now this I did not get. She made it a study.

I think Lori had a crush on me. I thought of Lori as my little sister. If I even suggested a sexual relationship, I imagine she would have been an enthusiastic participant; however, it would have been too incestuous to ever amount to fruition.

Fred and Boo were dad and mom. Mark told me that Fred was a "snake handler." Appalachia Christians would let poisonous snakes bite them – the idea was that if your faith in Christ was strong enough the venom would not kill you. I heard they also drank arsenic. Boo was called Boo because she had big boobs. Fred and Boo were decent, kind, loving people. They accepted me "into the fold" and loved me from the time they met me. That was who they were.

Char Vocca was Mark's little sister. Lori and Char were best buds and always together.

Leave it to a member of the Vocca family to introduce me to some new music that I never heard before and suddenly would love for life.

That's what Char did. The album was Willie Alexander and the Boom Boom Band. The hit that got the most airplay was "Radio Heart."

In 2003, I used the internet and got an address for Willie Alexander and sent him a fan letter. He wrote back. He was still doing live shows in Boston.

Lori Terry

After her parents moved the family out to Perry or wherever it was… I drove out to spend the evening with Lori.

What I most clearly recall is the drive back home.

I made her laugh. That is what felt great. I did an ad lib of a southern hypocrite preacher. It was forty years ago. But Lori loved it.

I loved Lori Terry -- and her family, was my family.

Mark Vocca told me yesterday that Fred is still around. This is 4/23/2020.

Charleen called me when Lori died. Her heart. Lori was my Goth queen. Char wanted me to drive to Texas with her to comfort Mitzi. I couldn't. I was unemployed at that time.

1978 or 1979 – Octagon board games

Mark Vocca, Brandon Zart, and Mark McAddams played board games. If Tobruk was involved, Brandon was Rommel. He loved playing the WehrMacht General.

Mark Vocca once said to me, "here we were pretending to be generals and soldiers, and you – the least interested – you go and become a Ranger. We were pretending. You became the real thing,"

I hate the term "Real Deal."

2003 in Raleigh on-line

SOC COM – Special Operations Command has this group. The on-line group are a bunch of he-man chest thumpers. "Who is the real deal more than you?" Real Deal became this metaphor. You went to ranger school. But did you serve in a ranger battalion? No? You're not the real deal. You served in battalion, but did you see combat? No? You're not the real deal. You saw combat but you don't uniformly hate all muslims? You're not the real deal.

I will not participate in Quatch. That's German. Look it up.

The name Clem

My father, the bunny was called "Clem" – in junior high and high school, I was also called "Clem." I was not and never will be a carbon copy of that misogynist and racist sadist.

In seventh grade, I tried to change my name to James. Randy Pietilla took his middle name. I could say that I was sick and tired of the teasing of "oh my darlin, oh my darlin..." but that was already old in 1965. No, I loathed being "Junior" to the bunny. I wanted to disassociate my identity and name from him.

In seventh grade I was introduced at Ridge Junior High School as Jim Ross.

The bunny was totally disgusted that I would prefer James. He cornered me and slapped me around. His anger and disgust made me question his sanity.

His father changed his name from Edward to James.

He said, "You haven't earned the right or the privilege to be named 'Clem.' You have to earn it first."

In the Army, I became "Clement." Once and for all.

As the years pressed on, I told people that my father was Clem. So I choose to be named Clement. The bunny could be "Clem."

The OED (Oxford English Dictionary) has two definitions of "Clem. The noun is a brawl with the townies (local people of a village) and the carnies (the workers at a travelling carnival). The verb means to wither away and die from starvation. I used those in my defense to not be called "clem."

The word Clement comes from latin and means calm and merciful. I think I prefer that.

Tom Miller's Movie

One day, Doug Enkler and I were at Fred and Boo's place and I had my skateboard. Somehow, Doug and I managed to sit on it together and ride down the hill. With two of us on it together, steering was difficult and so we would eventually crash into the drainage ditch on the side of the road. Tom Miller happened to be there with his movie camera. He filmed us.

Tom had a movie camera. Who had a movie camera back then?

He then filmed Chris Hill – I knew her at Ridge Junior High – she was Mark McAdams' girlfriend and then Brandon Zart's girlfriend.

Eventually, Tom and I then completed the footage of the film -- with this mad scientist skit who tries a formula – test tubes and food coloring. After showing disgust that it didn't work, pours the chemical down the toilet. We then added angry eyes and fangs to the toilet. And had it now anthropomorphized into a living object. And it threw a knife and killed the mad scientist.

Mark and Mitzi and Dennis aka Jay were already living at the Seneca house when Tom and I presented the final product. It couldn't be a movie without sound. Tom and I measured each scene and noted the duration. We then dubbed a cassette with the appropriate music for the visual.

For the section with Doug and me going down the hill and crashing, it had Jan and Dean "sideboard surfing." When Chris Hill was filmed, we had the Dickies' song, "You're so hideous." For the record, Chris was naturally gorgeous.

And we ended the film with the toilet that became a living thing and the soundtrack was taken from the Nutcracker.

It wasn't until 1997 when I saw Tom again. He was at the Edison Pub in Tremont and played guitar in a band called Swank Motel.

Runaway in the Ford Econoline Van – 1979/1980

I took the family van in 1979. Fall out with Bunny. It was winter. I slept in the van in Winter Cleveland Weather. Some times I slept in Harold Norsic's Driveway. Some nights he invited me in. I slept on the living room floor.

I remember mom and Cyndy passing me in the Volvo and saying "come home."

Eventually I came home. Bunny doesn't matter now. He's dead.

Until I joined the Army in May of 1980, I did as many drugs as I could. Home life sucked. Define HATE. I think hate causes cancer. I had every reason to hate Bunny. I never hated him. I pitied him. He was a pathetic wretch.

Junior

I should hate Junior. He was the uncle – her brother -- who tried to rape my mom when she was 13.

When I last saw Junior at the bar in Eighty-Four, he was a pathetic drunk drooling on himself telling me that MY father was a great man. A great man? Are you kidding me?

Junior was a pathetic wretch just like the bunny. Sorry Britt. Sorry Brian.

But you didn't know he wanted to rape your Aunt Audrey. And tried.

She told me he failed. But what the fuck. It was bad enough that he tried.

The good new is… He's dead. Fuck him.

If I had known that post-Army, I'd be in jail for premeditated.

Do you know how easy it is to break a neck? Too easy. Movies show that all the time. The skill isn't a talented trick. It takes two seconds.

Rock 'n' Roll High School and the Ramones

It was the Lake or the Shore cinema on lake shore blvd in Euclid in 1979. The double feature was "Rock 'n' Roll High School" featuring the Ramones and "The Kids are All Right" featuring the Who. Doug Enkler and I were there to see the Ramones.

I remember Doug mocking the Who. And the hippies getting pissed off.

We stayed for at least two showings of Rock 'N' Roll high school. The hippies were probably glad to see us go-go goodbye. Glad to see us go-go goodbye.

I think John Tozzi and I were at that theater earlier to see Phantasm. We smoked a joint in the theater. Back then, smoking cigarettes and joints in movie theaters was normal and the staff did not approach you. Why didn't they?

JoAnne's Friend

Bob Evans restaurant... What is it about food service that everyone is fucking one another? I had sex with a hostess, a waitress and a friend of a waitress.

The last of those three, I should have handled better. Joanne and her friend. I met her at a party. She initiated taking me to an upstairs bedroom and there we had sex. I knew nothing about this girl. I did not have preconceived notions like "slut" because she gave it up... I was no different. I was not seduced. I was a willing participant.

Joanne's friend? I'm sorry. So sorry. I should have pursued a relationship with her. She was smart. Pretty. Fun to be with. And sex was great. She had a great laugh and a great smile. So why can't I remember her name?

I think my problem was that I understood male and female relationships based on the bunny and mom.

What the fuck was normal?

I was too immature to understand the meaning of physical intimacy. We had sex and it scared the hell out of me. Was I supposed to feel "Love" for her? Was I supposed to want to "go steady"? That was the term used back then for exclusive dating… no one else. All I felt was fear. We had sex and I had no idea what it meant or what it was supposed to mean. It was pleasurable. I enjoyed it. But what did the emotions mean? I don't think I could even identify them, let alone explain or define them.

I would apologize, but I don't know her name.

Why was she so willing to have sex right off the bat? Was I an easy target? Sure. Tell me you want to have sex with me and I'm like Mortimer Snerd, "Uh, yup, yup, yup, yup."

Intimacy. This is a topic that everyone avoids. Sex should be about exposure of one's self to another in a manner that is vulnerable. The jocks in high school viewed sex as a conquest – "I got laid." And "bravo for me." How did the girl feel? Used? Patti (wife #2) used the term Sperm Bucket.

As the adult (dare I call myself that?), looking back. I should have said, "I'm not ready for the emotional aspects of sex. I'm sure it will feel great. But I'm too immature to understand the emotions that are significantly linked."

Maybe this was an unfair imposition of nature. By nature, teenage boys are… Lynn would say, "Horn Doggies." Yeah, horny all the time. Jerking off at least once a day. When someone is that focused on the orgasm of hisself, how can he have any concept of intimacy or what it could feel like for the girl?

To all the young women in the 1970s and 1980s, if I had sex with you, I apologize. I did not have the emotional or mental capacity to understand what intimacy meant. Girls mature sooner than boys. You most likely understood that and that was your goal or objective. Intimacy. Perhaps that's why very young girls sleep with older men… Carol and Suzanne with "Dad" – John's father. He was mature enough to know what intimacy meant. Just not old enough to know what morality meant. Or rape.

I think Mark Vocca said it best when he met Sarah. Back in 2006, he told me I've been fucking for years and called it making love. For the first time in my life, I'm making love to a woman who has my heart and I'm vulnerable and brave. It's worth it.

I'm paraphrasing Mark. But that was essentially what he told me. It put a new perspective on the sex act for me. Here we were, forty years later since when we met and Mark was still my best teacher about emotions and intimacy. And there is nothing wrong with that.

… JoAnn's friend… I'm sorry. I should have sought intimacy. I should have wanted intimacy. Sadly, what was your name? Shame on me for asking that now.

She gave herself to me. Freely and eagerly. I feel guilty because I took advantage of that. I was wrong.

Again, Mentor High School

I transferred to Mentor High by choice.

Let me back up… when I was getting expelled from Saint Joe's, the principal, Joe Radigan tried talking to me.

[Context: I'm a kid. First semester of my junior year. I have piss poor grades in most of my classes which I should be acing. My father is tormenting me nightly, especially on Saturday and Sunday nights when he's free to inebriate. This has been going on for years. My only respite is smoking pot with Brandon Zart or Mark Vocca and music. Music salvaged me and healed me.]

Joe Radigan was talking to me about the Ken Templin letter. He said, "You strike me as cold and emotionless." I write this account of the facts deliberately devoid of emotion. I do not want this collection of recollections to be sprouted with the weeds of "Woe is me." But back then I wrote sophomoric poetry about every detail I felt. Like Enkler said, I took a minutia and made it grand. I took details and studied them. Elevated them. The platform enabled me to examine.

I heard Radigan's comment and I was thinking, I write poetry. I feel emotions exquisitely, painfully. When I love, I love with all my heart. Where was this coming from?

Lake Catholic versus Sant Joe's.

Joe Radigan and Joe Simones traded roles as Principals at Lake Catholic and St. Joes. That had nothing to do with me. But it raised a red flag. An alert. It said pay attention.

At Lake Catholic, I was taking an exam from the math instructor for "Analysis" – like a pre-calculus course. I was unprepared. I did not understand the material and the instructor was horrible. Caveat --- I was always good at math. Great – pardon my conceit. My only handicap was I could not do math in my head. Bunny created that damage. Torment. Starting in the elementary grade when multiplication tables were memorized. He would quiz without time allowed to think. To this day, I cannot do math in my head. I have to write it on paper or in excel.

Back to the analysis class and the test. I did not write one answer to the math questions. I wrote a poem on the back of the exam criticizing the instructor. I insulted him physically because of his nose and I implied that he might be gay. I was 16 and immature.

What was weird was they reprimanded me by making me take counseling sessions with Mr. Koenig. Mr. Koenig announced he was seeking to get certified in counseling... does that mean he was not qualified at this point?

As an alternative to expulsion, I agreed.

Initially, I went in with an open mind. Mr. Koenig was my teacher for a course in criminology. I thought he was good. He asked questions about my mother and father. What home life was like. I was opening up.

Newsweek published an article in the 1990s called the Secret Shame. How a family member does not share information like about an abusive father or mother. Index finger to the lips and "Shhhh…"

<u>T.V. Eye, 1970</u>

Koenig taught that in 1970 there was a bill before congress to allow a "TV Eye" to be installed in television sets.

I tilted my head to the side.

The Stooges' album "Funhouse" came out in 1970. There was a song called TV Eye. It became one of Iggy's most famous songs with the Stooges and he would perform it as a solo artist.

The lyrics are vague. But I always wondered if there was a connection to the bill.

<u>Mr. Koenig</u>

One day, Mr. Koenig said in a counseling session, "You know you strike me as cold and emotionless."

Click. I got up and left and never went back. Coincidence? Paranoia? I don't care. I know what I am and I know what I am not. I knew it then and I know it now.

My decision was made that moment to never spend one more day at Lake Catholic.

I was never cold and emotionless. I sent hurt to a deep strange place. I still felt it. But there, it didn't surface. Not it's raw form. It did surface in the manifestation of allowing others to hurt and punish me. Pain became my release. If others hurt me, it was good. Because I chose to let it occur.

Bunny didn't give me the choice.

James Kennedy did. Pain was pleasure. The more degrading the better.

But I loved fully and whole-heartedly. My devotion was never questioned by anyone. My passion. My caring. How dare they ever insinuate such. What manipulations were they planning? I did not know. I did now care. I had to get out.

Therapy

The previous passage reminded me of something I'd forgotten. My parents sent me to a therapist to learn why I was not excelling grade-wise in school. Really? That was so hard to figure out? The previously cited examples of terror were never limited occasions. It was a constant. My constant was an existence in a state of fear. Not calm and certainly not safe. Why did Marvel's DareDevil appeal to me so much? He was the Man without Fear.

We drove to Mayfield road. I wish I could remember the name of the Jewish therapist. He was on the right track. But I was too afraid to give him all of the clues. Consequences from the Bunny. What would he inflict if I was honest? The therapist did not offer a haven.

He gave me a sheet of paper and asked me to write answers.

The first question was: "My father, I _____ (fill in the verbs)."

I wrote: "Love, fear and respect."

You're *supposed* to <u>love</u> your father. I was told to <u>respect</u> him as a dentist. But I <u>feared</u> him and was so afraid it shook me to my core. He damaged all those I loved.

Chris Rock comes to mind here. He talked about men being proud of stupid shit. "I've never been to jail" – and he'd counter with "you're not supposed to go to Jail." "I don't beat my wife." You're not supposed to beat your wife.

I used to think I'm going to go to jail. Because I'm going to kill the bunny.

The therapist never touched on the fear aspect. After that session, I said I'm not going back.

The therapist was also trying to say that everything was someone else's fault. Everything. That I had no accountability for any part. Bullshit. I played a role.

I had dreams that I was in prison for murdering my father. It was inevitable. But as fate would have it, it never happened. I was in Florida and he was in Cleveland.

Punishment

Why did I deserve punishment? I wondered if I was a masochist. Bunny episodes continued. I have to say that The most memorable are here in this book. The ones that damaged the most. But sorry... there were more.

If Bunny went to drink, he came home and punished.

Mom would tell me I was perfect, intelligent, handsome, and the adjectives slid off my back as superfluous. "And flowers never bend with the rain fall." [Intentional allusion to a song by Simon and Garfunkel].

In my mind, I deserved punishment. Mom was getting beaten. Bunny was the victor. And I did nothing to prevent it. Who was right? Who was wrong?

Secret Shame

Mom never said to lie. She never said, "Don't tell the truth." But we all knew. Don't say nothin.' Why?

All the years, and all the abuse. She had my silence. I abided.

Reputation. The Bunny had a reputation as a great dentist. He gave presentations at Rice Elementary on dental health. I borrowed the metaphor from Robert Louis Stevenson. Doctor Jekyll was a great man. Just don't mix with alcohol.

Mentor High School

Mark Vocca saved me. The funny thing is... Mark thought after I became a Ranger, I would kick his ass. Mark told me that and I shook my head. No way. Mark Vocca – you saved me. Mark was and is my hero.

Doug would say, "...but I digress..." Here is a Doug Digression. Doug Enkler's sister gave him a DEVO costume for his birthday. It was the original yellow plastic suit from 1977. I told Doug he should wear it to school.

Doug was the creative mind behind the t-shirts printed in the graffic arts department at Mentor High. "Three mile island – hate to say I told you so." And "52 dead in Iran – hate to say I told you so." This the Spring of 1979. The last semester of our senior year of high school.

Sam Petrella was also in there... he found a Beatles-mania screaming fan who became the emblem for his Pagans t-shirt and the Pagans' pink album cover.

Back to the DEVO suit... Doug said no way, I'm not wearing it. I said if you let me, I'll wear it. And I did. I even had the 1950s-style wrap-around shades. In the cafeteria, they pelted me with garbage and milk cartons. And there were shouts of "Devo sucks."

Back to Mark Vocca. He overheard a bunch of thugs planning to beat me up. Mark told them they would have to go through him first.

Mark was a menacing dude. He was tall, strong, long brown hair and soap opera star unshaven look. He wore a WWII waist-length Army jacket. His image commanded respect or fear. Or reverence or all three.

Only those who knew him understood that he was a young, honest man with a heart of gold. I'm sure he could hold his own in any combat situation. But he was also a strategist and would use brains over brawn first and foremost.

The thugs never approached me and I never knew of Mark's intervention until years later. Post-army years, so after 1986.

The thing about Mark… that should have been bragging rights. "Yeah, dude, I saved your ass from a beating." Mark never said shit. I went on thinking I wore a DEVO suit to school and my gravest offense was the objects tossed.

I crack up at this. A year or two, I went to visit Joann Southwick on her street in Mentor. She either lived on Firwood or Thunderbird. At the south east corner where it turned north, a voice called out, "DEVO Sucks!!!" I cracked up laughing. I wasn't even wearing the suit and someone from that day recognized me.

Joann Southwick was a sad story. She was a crush in high school. But she wouldn't have anything to do with me. I used to tell Suzanne Stiffler that she reminded me of Cheryl Tiegs.

Jump ahead. I'm home on leave and Suzanne asked me to meet her and some friends at the brass rail bar in Painesville. That was the bar I used to take Mitzi to, so she could meet her Florida construction worker. My memories of that bar were jaded.

Suzanne met me and said, "Remember her? That's Joann. Go tell her she still looks like Cheryl Tiegs." Joann was at the end of the bar – alone. She had gained weight.

Here is what's sad. She still to me looked like Cheryl Tiegs. I remembered my affinity. My endearment toward her. I wanted to date her and I wanted to fall in love with her. That was very ambitious for a nineteen year old Ranger.

I walked up to her and she was crying.

I looked to the left and the right. There was no one.

My dream girl of high school. Alone at a pick up bar in Painesville, Ohio. Crying. And nobody wanted her. That was sad.

Joann – in high school, she was the Farah Fawcett. After high school, she thickened. At the Paineville Bar, Joann was not Farrah. She was thick. I still thought she was pretty.

In High School, Joann would not have anything to do with me. I was dismissable.

What happened to Joanie? She broke up with me during the song, "Angie."

Okay, women get to choose. "You can fuck me or not. My choice."

Men have to go along with that choice. Men do not choose. Men comply.

A woman sez, "I want you to fuck me." A man will comply. If a man says, I want to fuck you -- the woman has the option to say, "I want to think about it."

Women have an orifice – nature said it's for a vessel to deliver seed.

The question of who plants the seed is always with the woman.

Men are willing planters of seed. But the women open or close the door.

Men have the appendage that delivers the seed.

It just so happens to enter that orifice.

I wish women were instigators of sex. I wish God made all women horny and men were the ones who would say, "Let me think about it" or "I have a headache." Is that misogynistic?

High School Diploma

I would have graduated class of 1979 from Mentor. I had 26 credit hours and only 17 were required. But I never got point 50 in American Government. The teacher tested with essays. And she failed me. I suspected bias against punk rockers. All I remember was writing an essay about anarchy and quoting Thomas Jefferson.

I tried going to summer school to complete the class. But I missed too many classes. I was cutting classes to play junior shrink. Two of my friends were getting raped by the father of a kid I went to kindergarten with. He had them so brain washed, they called him "Dad" affectionately.

I've come to understand that victims of sexual abuse by family justify the experience by focusing on praising the abuser… "he was a saint who helped so many people" – interpret that as he committed no sin. And shift the focus immediately off the deed, the action against, the rape. Deflect it away. Because reality is too stark. If it even scrapes the surface, it screals.

Poetry Class, 1979

Back to senior year at Mentor High School. It was my last semester. Spring of 1979. Mark Vocca and I had poetry and history class together. Mark loved the history class. Mark and I would get high as kites from smoking pot and then we'd go into that history class and I'd put my head down and sleep. Meanwhile, Mark – just as high as me – was interacting with the teacher, answering questions. Mark was the superstar of history class. I half heard it in my stupor and didn't bother to pay it much attention because I was lost or unprepared.

Poetry class was with Miss Scott. Miss Scott read one of her poems. I recall it was about sex with a man and made reference to her womb, it revered her womb as sacred. It was free form and the imagery was intense.

Mark wrote a brilliant poem about taking a WASP into the night and letting it crawl out an asp (snake).

There was a black student. Bob Hackney. I wrote a poem for him. I titled it "the invisible man" – honestly, I knew nothing of Ralph Ellison Not back then. I learned about Ralph Ellison for the first time at Cleveland State University in 1988.

I also wrote a poem for Vicki Gardner. She was another classmate. A gorgeous blonde like a modern Jean Harlow.

We kind of dated… we went out. Nothing would happen. No kissing, no petting, no groping. "Petting"… does anyone even use that term anymore?

But afterwards, we'd talk on the phone. I would be in the dental office downstairs. She must have been in her bedroom with a phone because, I'm convinced, she would masturbate while on the phone with me. She would stop talking and then I'd hear her breathing. The tempo would increase. If I called her name softly saying Vicki? The breathing would sharpen. Sometimes with a squeak. And eventually the crescendo. Then heavy sighs. Until recovery. And it happened every time we "talked" after our "date."

Then the conversation would pick up as if nothing happened in between. As far as I knew, she was the fragile daughter of a rich father. She had a lot of secrets. And a lot of demons.

The Rocky Horror Picture Show

At Bob Evans, we used to go to the midnight movies at Coventry in Cleveland Heights. First, I would do my own make up. Then I would do Chuck's make up. Chuck, not Beck, would allow me to paint his eyes. This Chuck was another busboy.

Chuck Beck – the manager I respected -- would send me out to deliver a dinner order to one of his friends while I was in make-up.

I wasn't a transvestite. I wasn't gay. But like Bowie, I wore make up. What did that make me?

Behind the scenes, I certainly questioned who I was. What I was.

One evening I got dressed up for the Rocky Horrow Picture Show. I wore a leotard and army fatigue pants. The former represented the essential feminine, like for a ballerina. The latter represented the essential masculine, the army infantry soldier. The two were juxtaposed together. A paradox.

In the early days, I called myself Iguana Stone. Charles Laughton portraying Quasimodo said at the end while looking at a gargoyle, "I wish I was made of stone." His heart was breaking because of Esmeralda.

At some point, I renamed myself, Iguana Paradox. I was no longer stone or wishing to be. Stone was my self who wanted to stop hurting and feeling. Paradox didn't care any more. Iguana Paradox could be anything. I talked myself into thriving on pain. As if to say, "hey bunny give me more."

Just ask Harold Norsic when I asked him to beat me with a dog chain during a live show of my band, Black Diamond. The song was Mott the Hoople's "Violence."

Or Tom Rosplock when he put out the cigar on my palm during "Fiorello" at Lake Catholic.

Years later, I just became Ranger Iguana. My book of poetry was by Clement Ross (Ranger Iguana). I dropped Stone and Paradox. Perhaps too pretentious.

Ohio Sweet Corn

Those of us who grew up in Ohio or the states adjacent, we were pampered and spoiled. We grew up on Ohio sweet corn. Those who haven't had it, can't appreciate it. The Cramps did a song called, "Corn Fed Dames."

Move out of Ohio, and buy "sweet corn." It's not the same.

I have been in Florida since 2004. I love Publix, the local supermarket. But when they sell "sweet corn" – it's not Ohio sweet corn.

My buddy Mark Vocca. He's in Southwick, Mass now. When he goes back to Ohio, he returns with Ohio sweet corn.

Matias Ernesto Zolnay. His fall clam bake. Every fall had Ohio sweet corn.

Should I call him Matias Grave? That's his Chilean Name.

Scrambled eggs

Perhaps that would be a better title for this book. I go from page one to the last page and along the way, I insert – "oh, yeah, that occurred to me."

That was Paul McCartney's first name for "Yesterday."

Mentor High School summer school

I did not graduate from Mentor with class 1979. I lacked American Government for a half credit. I mentioned that already.

I tried to make it up during summer school. But Carol Nieman. I can't blame her for my absences. I chose to wait in her car until she came out of class.

I had no business being in her glove compartment, but I went there out of boredom. I found a letter – it didn't say to whom. What it did say was she and her friend had sex with the father of John. John and I were in the same kindergarten class. Carol and her friend were 16. That technically was rape. I didn't know how to deal with that. Have you ever been between betraying a friend and a legal obligation?

How were two friends of mine seduced. Raped. And smiled about it?

Suzanne laid next to me and stroked my face while Janine grinded, groud… Scott Smyers wanted more than anything to fuck Suzanne. She said no– Janine did not pay any attention.

Scott did not notice or if he did he did not say.

Janine came at least three times.

Mark & Mitzi in Painesville

Their apartment in Painesville off route 20. Many nights, we spent with laughter and kinship. And comraderie.

Yes we smoked pot. I should say we smoked a lot of pot.

But we also did acid (microdot). I've always been curious if L.S.D., acid and microdot are supposedly different. I'd love to know the difference.

I've been told L.S.D. makes you hallucinate. That would be so cool.

At the apartment, we only took microdot.

I can tell you that we laughed for eight hours. At the acme, we called it peaking, my ribs ached. I laughed so hard that my sides were in agony. I saw what we called "tracers." It was like if you passed your hand laterally, horizontally across your field of vision. And it looked like it was doing a freeze frame every second. That's what you saw. And the freeze image would linger so the images of your hand ahead, would still be there as the trailing image lingered.

But I never saw crazy shit. And I wanted to. I thought, hey, I've got a vivid imagination. What kind of hallucinations would my crazy brain create? I never got an answer.

Jay aka Dennis Terry said, "If you drop acid and make love to a woman, I guarantee, YOU WILL fall in love with her."

<u>Acid in Berlin</u>

1985 or 1986 -- one time in Berlin, Michaela and I took microdot. I wanted to put Dennis's (Jay's) theory to the test. So we had sex. I could never call it making love. It was sex. It was reflex action, like a sneeze or a fart. Her vagina was a receptacle. But never acted as a source of pleasure. True, she conceived and birthed a child, Julian. But that seemed its sole function. I never knew Michaela to have an orgasm. Something was in her history.

Like a prostitute who never enjoys sex but gets paid.

Other woman, they seem to view it as a duty. An obligation. Perhaps out of love. They don't orgasm and that's okay with them. Rosa was like that. She was a Hungarian prostitute looking for an American boyfriend to take her to America.

Leda was another and she was different – I bring up later. She loved sex and had multiple orgasms. I wanted a relationship with her. She was horny and gave her all with total abandon. But she moved on. She had one night with me and was eager for the next. Perhaps she was a collector. Collectors are running away from something. They enjoy the thrill of the current experience then move on. Because if they stay, they have to feel. They have to remember. The present is all that matters because the past hides a secret pain. Collectors have no future.

There was one woman in 1998. A mom with two kids. She said her torso was ugly. I told her it was not. We made love and it was spiritual. At least to me. I loved her but I didn't fully realize, she was fucking away the mourning pain. A stalker killed her sister in the Bad Lands. If we fucked missionary or doggie style, there would come a point when she said, "I want to cum." That meant, I performed cunnilingus until she came. Honestly, I have to say, I love that act. I never minded and would do it at any suggestion. I never asked why she could only cum with oral.

I had been with many damaged women. Many were more damaged than those who weren't. Why? Isn't that the question? I don't pity them. I'm just sad because I know why.

Back to Michaela… and taking microdot aka acid…

At one point, during coitus, Michaela panicked. She said there were spiders on the ceiling. She wanted to stop having sex and allow me time to take care of the spiders. I wanted to cum to see if Dennis was right.

Bottom line: Dennis was wrong. And my conclusion was that the smarter the mind, the less hallucinogenic activity. The weaker the mind, the more hallucinogenic activity. Hence, the spiders. I didn't see any spiders. I would have liked to.

More on acid…

When Mark, Mitzi and I did acid, we played two albums every time: Brian Eno's "Here come the warm jets" and "Taking Tiger Mountain (by strategy)." Those two were primary for microdot.

Mark also introduced me to Gil Scott-Heron. We listened to the H2O gate and The Ghetto Code. As I recall, there was a Bob Newhart album called the Butten Down Mind and an album with the Slow talkers of America. Bob and Ray.

Prior to that there was a passage about Dennis Terry saying if you do acid and have sex, you'll fall in love with her and then doing acid with Michaela. And in case you were wondering, the spiders won. I have yet to have an orgasm on acid.

Painesville Harvey, 1979

I registered for night school at Painesville Harvey in the fall of 1979. I had a great teacher who was Mormon and passed me with an A.

His son and I would smoke pot in my parent's van. We talked for hours. About what, I can't say now. Music and movies. Just not about being a Mormon.

His Dad told me about being a Mormon.

Joseph Smith, he got from the angel the gold tablets with new words from God -- delivered -- then taken back -- by the angel. But during the time he had the tablets, he wrote down the words of God – by rote. Three days of transcribing became the word of Mormon.

He also told me that during the three days when Jesus was buried in the cave behind the rock, he visited South America. He said the Mayans adopted his rite for the mass. But the Aztecs corrupted it. They turned it into human sacrifice with the removal of the heart.

I listened. I liked my teacher. But I did not buy into any religion. Father Kline jaded me when he said, "Well we just don't know."

What determines Jewishness?

I did not know what or who Jews were. Funny thing is that I'm part jewish. Two events. The first event: Seventh grade English and Miss Cippolla had us read, "The diary of Anne Frank." Anne Frank was an innocent girl. Hitler and Goebbels demanded her arrest and execution. She was white, brown haired, literate, and cared about family. What was her crime? Being a jew. That's like saying I was born on Thursday in 1961. Thursday's child has far to go. Punish him and her.

Historians say, the German people needed a common enemy. Hitler gave them an enemy and he called that enemy, "the Jew." To me, that's like saying left-handed people are the enemy. Round them up and gas them! Sarcasm means How Friggin Absurd.

[Catholics probably tried something like that because "left" was considered "sinister" – evil – and left-handed students would be punished by nuns so that they would write with the right hand. But I digress...]

The second event was Brandon Zart telling me about his boss, Shelly. Brandon hated him because he was Jewish – because of the label. The Word. The Title. Wait. Brandon was hired by Shelly to do flooring jobs. Shelly paid Brandon for work. Here is the disconnect that I don't get. Let's take a group and for whatever reason, some schmuck sez I hate them. Then let's ask why. They don't have a reason. Because there is no reason. Just like, "I don't like Mondays."

Brandon was a punk rocker. Iggy Pop, Joey Ramone, Lou Reed and Richard Hell. All Jewish rockers.

I would not know who muslims are until 9-11-2001. Yet in 1988, my neighbor was Faribe who was engaged to Georgio. She was Persian and he was Greek. She told me that when she told her father that she was going to become a Christian to marry Georgio, her father told her, "Then you become the best Christian you can be."

Decency is not limited to any race or religion or sexual orientation. Decency has followers everywhere. Ellen says be kind to one another. Be Kind. Does that need to be taught?

1976 Punk Single and bashing Gays.

Here is Forest Gump's classic line, "Stupid is as stupid does." Pagans first song, "Six and Change." It starts off with the vocal, "Freddie, you didn't have to hit the Fag, Freddie... I hate queers..." And the band started the song. Tim Allee the bass player was and is gay. What the fuck was up with that?

In junior high school, high school and after… If a guy insulted a guy, it was to call him a fag, faggot, queer, homo, or cock sucker. And what if he was? He could say, so what? I am. But no one did.

In elementary school, Terry Jenkins was in our class. He was my friend. Perhaps he might have been gay. I don't know, I never cared.

Tim Deegan used Terry Jenkins as a metaphor. When I dated a girl who liked the bay city rollers, Tim said they are so Terry Jenkins.

Mentor High and High School Diploma

When I talked to the staff at Mentor High, they said they could not accept the night school credit from Painesville Harvey. I would need to repeat senior year. That was bullshit.

My next move was unavailable. I did not know what came next.

I continued working my job at Bob Evans in Mentor.

These excel inserts are from a spreadsheet I did to record concerts. Date, location, and whom I went with.

Concerts 1970s

1977	19-Oct	Iggy Pop, Ramones	CLE Music Hall	Brandon Zart
1978	4-Nov	Jean-Luc Ponty	CLE Music Hall	Chuck Beck & Mike Taylor
1978	6-Nov	J. Geils Band	CLE Coliseum	Teek, Slick, & Turk
1978	11-Nov	Blondie	CLE Music Hall	Mark Vocca & Doug Enkler
1979	8-Jan	Rush	CLE Coliseum	Kathy Blumers

1979	24-Jan	Alice Cooper	CLE Coliseum	Mike Taylor
1979	4-Apr	Roxy Music	CLE Coliseum	Doug Enkler
1979	21-Apr	Tubes	CLE Coliseum	Mike Taylor
1979	21-May	Ian Hunter	CLE The Palace	Chuck Beck & Mike Taylor
1979	2-Oct	U.K.	Painesville Agora	Denise Dugger
1979	9-Nov	David Jo Hansen	Painesville Agora	Dennis Terry
1979	12-Nov	Iggy Pop	Cleveland Agora	Bill DeGidio, Mark Vocca, Doug Enkler and Dennis Terry

Bob Evans Restaurant in Mentor off Route 306

I was a busboy, then assigned to dishtank, then grill cook.

Chuck Beck. He was the best manager. His music taste and mine were identical.

I bragged that I knew every Bowie song and when I was on dish tank, he'd come in and say, "Watch that man." I'd start singing and as soon as I forgot a line, he'd be there to say "Gotcha."

I loved Bowie and knew by heart "most" of his canon. Chuck was a clever boss. He might as well have picked "Wild eyed boy from free cloud." Most obscure. I didn't know all the lyrics. I knew most of them.

One night we had to close the restaurant and Chuck had to make biscuits. I said let me stay and help.

We climbed the ladder in the manager's office that led to the roof and while we smoked a joint, I sang, "Oh, you've got trouble, right here in river city" from the Music Man soundtrack and the intro to "Black widow" by Vincent Price on Alice Cooper's album "Welcome to my Nightmare."

Chuck laughed. We then went down and made biscuits. By the book. According to the recipe. Everyone said they were they best biscuits ever.

Chuck Beck, Mike Taylor and I went to several concerts. Jean Luc Ponty who played on Frank Zappa's "Overnight Sensation" album. We went to the Ian Hunter / Mick Ronson show at the Music Hall. Chuck was a huge Bowie fan, hence his interest in Mick Ronson.

Mike Taylor and I went to see Alice Cooper. The "From the Inside" Tour after his release from the mental hospital when he checked himself in to detox from alcohol. Now they call it rehab and there's no stigma. Alice borrowed Bernie Taupin from Elton John for the lyrics to that album. It was a great show.

Iggy Pop did the same (re-hab) in the 1970s for heroin. He recorded "Kill City" with James Williamson while out on visits. One of his best albums second only to "Raw Power."

Bad Acne

In the 1970s, I had bad acne. Mom took me to a dermatologist for tetracycline and ultra-violet treatments. The truth was – I just didn't maintain good hygiene. I didn't shower. When I was depressed, hygiene went out the window. My zits were my fault.

Black Diamond

My first band was a cover band. That meant we did covers of popular songs of other musicians. Black Diamond was Kathy Blumers on guitar and flute, Joe Zbaznic on guitar, Tom Kunst on drums and me on vocals. We had no bass player.

Our set started with Ian Hunter's Once bitten twice shy and ended with Mott the Hoople's Violence. In between was My Best friend's girl (the Cars), Two tickets to paradise (Eddie

Money), Locomotive breath (Jethro Tull), Cat Scratch fever (Ted Nugent), Honky Tonk Woman (Rolling Stones), Sweet Jane (Lou Reed)… Kathy did a great solo on flute with the Jethro Tull song.

Joe told me don't smoke pot before we perform. He said it adds bass to your voice. I never had a hard time hitting the high notes. Not until my 50s and acid reflux killed my voice. Once upon a time, I could match Art Garfunkel on Bridge over troubled waters and Janis Joplin on Me and my Bobby McGee.

I sang Bobby McGee in gay bar in 1999. Rudy's on west 25th. They wanted me to do it again.

Black Diamond did a live show at Perkins on 615 in Mentor. Kathy was a waitress there.

We did a second live show in someone's basement. I asked Harold Norsic to become part of the act. I said when we do the song Violence, I want you to beat me with this dog chain.

I was into Iggy and the Stooges and self-destruction was part of his act.

I mentioned this earlier… Harold was a theatre guy. He had the lead in a play at Lake Catholic about a murder mystery. Half-way through "Violence," Harold came out and commenced to beat my back with the chain. Harold understood. He beat me with gusto.

Some good Samaritan in the audience decided the song motivated the act, not the theater of the performance and decided to intervene. I had to tell him that it was okay. It was part of the show. He did not understand.

I said Black Diamond was my first band. Unfortunately, it was also my last band. I tried to form new bands with various musicians. Never got off the ground and then I joined the army and was gone.

Bill DeGidio

Mark Vocca introduced me to Bill when Bill was the lead singer of the AK-47s playing a concert on Mentor Avenue (AKA route 20). He wore a Schott's black leather jacket with an American Flag attached with safety pins. That got him arrested in Eastlake.

Bill did the lead vocals on the Pagans' first single, "Six and Change."

Punk and Pot

I had not yet wrapped my head around this concept of punk. Luke had introduced me to the Ramones and Iggy and the Stooges. But to me, it was music. Great music. But music.

Bill and I would become great friends. Until I left the Army in 1980. What changed? I still loved punk rock. But I stopped smoking pot and switched to scotch.

Brandon was still smoking pot and introduced me to "monkey paw." In the 1970s, there was Mexican, Columbian, and Sensimillia. The third was the top choice and or but, the most expensive.

Getting high was like an out of body experience. Alcohol freed inhibitions. Pot did that and more. Pot made visuals – art and movies – more stimulating. Pot made music more sensual, erotic, more like an experience of love making.

"Monkey Paw" meant getting stoned. That meant zombie staring and drooling. High was fun. Stoned was not.

Bill wanted his pot-smoking buddy to be in his life again. I didn't like the zombie effect.

Us versus Them

There became a growing "us versus them." If you were punk, you held contempt and disdain for the stadium bands like Electric Light Orchestra and Fleetwood Mac. I should say, one was "supposed" to...

John Lydon (aka Johnny Rotten) walked into the SEX shop of Malcolm McLaren wearing a t-shirt with Pink Floyd that said, "Pink Floyd Sucks." He became the lead singer of the Sex Pistols.

I don't know why it became us versus them.

Truth was I had ELO's new world record album. I also had records from Fleetwood Mac and Thin Lizzy and Alice Cooper. But my primary play list was the Damned, the Sex Pistols, L.A.M.F., and the Ramones.

Mark Vocca again became an exception to the rule. He liked or loved the songs, "Candy-O" by the Cars and "Kings and Queens and Guillotines" by Aerosmith.

Pink Floyd had two great albums – "Wish you were Here" and "Dark side of the Moon." If John Lydon (aka Johnny Rotten) really hated those two albums. Would he have feigned it? Pretended? His "image" demanded it. But was it true?

I suppose the "fun" of punk, was you could. My album collection had records from Melanie Safka, Donovan Leitch, Focus, and many other "un-cool bands" of the punk scene.

Remember that Mark Vocca taught me about Beethovan, Stravinsky and Tchaichovsky.

Summer of 1979 – Doug Enkler and I went to Ohio University

Doug was accepted to enroll as an undergrad for his freshman year in the fall of 1979. He asked me to go with him. We drove to Athens, Ohio in his Volks Wagon Beetle.

VW Beetles back then – there were two symptoms. The floor boards fell out and the heaters stopped working. As Doug would say, "But I digress…"

Along the trek to Athens, we smoked joints and listened to John Valby and made up our own Yeah-Yeahs. Dirty Doctor John sang ragtime piano. "Yeah, yeah, yeah-yeah… your mother goes down on Egyptians. So sing me another verse, worse than the other verse and waltz me around by my willie…" Then he'd recite a dirty limerick. After the limerick, the chorus of Yeah yeah would come again.

He had many other tunes. The point was to push the envelope to the point that you'd laugh out of discomfort. No topic was off limits.

When Doug and I arrived in Athens, we dropped our overnight bags at the house where Carol Enkler was with her friends. There was one young hottie, I called her Debby Harry. She was one of Carol's roommates. Doug later confessed he had sex with her in the cemetery. If he did or not, it certainly made me jealous.

Doug and I went through his orientation as two new students. He introduced me as someone "undecided" who was considering OU.

Later he teased me because Professor Wolf was hoping I would enroll. And he was sad that I had not made up my mind. My naivete was bubbling. Professor Wolf was gay and wanted to have sex with me. Doug learned that after I was back in Cleveland.

The Seneca House in Mentor

Tom Miller moved out. And I moved in. I was working at Bob Evans and could afford the rent. It was Mark Vocca, Mitzi Terry and her brother Dennis -- everyone called him Jay -- and me.

Dennis was the embodiment of Eugene Reynolds from the Rezilloes.

There is no comparison of Mark or Mitzi. They were beautiful people. No one was like them.

When Mark and I were moving my stuff from Mentor to Seneca, the Bunny stopped us. He refused to let me take my stereo with me. Mark and I were carrying down the speakers. We put them back. The Bunny was an asshole to the end. I was allowed to take my albums. My clothes. My bed and dresser. Nothing more. Why did he care about the stereo? My comics were worth more.

Home on Seneca

Seneca was drug -filled bliss. We smoked pot every night. Carol Nieman visited as often as she could. After she left, Mitzi loved to tease me. "Carol Nieman who loved Semen."

I never told Mitzi about John's father. They called him "Dad." He raped them both. Somehow, managed to make it so romantic and so affectionate that they both believed it was okay. Not just okay. They spoke of it as a wonderful experience.

I never knew how to approach either of them about it.

Sometimes Thai would visit. Mark and Mitzi called him Thai Tchaichovsky.

Thai would scan the house. Looking out our windows. Muttering, "where are the cops? Do the cops know we're here?" His paranoia was unsettling. But that was *his* normal.

Mark said that Thai did a lot of acid on the beach of lake erie. Consecutively one after another with no break in between. We did microdot in moderation.

Mark, Mitzi and I did a lot of microdot. That was a form of acid. Presumably not as powerful as LSD or maybe it was… I never did pure LSD. I wanted to. I wanted to see things. Hallucinations. The funny thing is that at age 58, I see hallucinations. In the bathroom. Patterns in the wall-paper. Faces form and move. Is that age or was it drugs?

Mark Vocca influenced my thought process like no one else ever did. Here is the cool thing about Mark. Mark Vocca never said, "I want you to think about this and make up your own mind."

No. He would play Bob Dylan's song "Hurricane" about the boxer Hurricane Carter. And then he would watch. When he saw my eyes light up, he realized that I got it. He didn't tell me the background story. He let Dylan tell the tale.

When he played "Idiot Wind" off Dylan's "Blood on the Tracks" -- all he said was "this is the best 'fuck-you' song I know." It was.

Mark gave me an appreciation of Bob Dylan. I knew "Blowin in the Wind" from Aunt Veronica. That song had profound lyrics. But not like the ones that Mark introduced me to (and many more). And Phoebe from Bob Evans gave me "Blonde on Blonde."

I take that back. "Blowin' in the wind" was profound.

New Salem Witch Hunters – early days.

One day Mark and I visited Tom Fallon. He lived in Mentor. Somewhere off Salida Road. Dave Atkins was there along with Sam Petrella. Sam was in the graphic arts department at Mentor and designed the Pagans t-shirt based on a Beatles' mania fan screaming.

Tom played a Bowie bootleg called Bump and Grind.

We laughed when Bowie messed up the lyrics to Suffragette City.

In 2009, Jones/Tintorreto Entertainment company LLC released "Bump and Grind" on CD and called it "Live Santa Monica '72." I wish they'd do the same for "Dollars in Drag, the 1980 Floor Show" and "Soft in the Middle." I had them on album. Brandon borrowed them in 1986 and never returned them.

Robbie Ferrar

Suzanne Stiffler introduced me to Robbie Ferrar. Suzanne worked at Perkins with Robbie and Kathy Blumers.

Robbie loved Steely Dan and David Bowie. I loved David Bowie. Robbie said I would probably also love Steely Dan. The songs of Steely Dan are certainly etched into my memory and when I hear them I know almost all the lyrics by heart. Not because I tried. It's just what I do. I memorize. And I memorize some of the stupidest shit.

No, that is not calling Steely Dan lyrics stupid. Here's a good example. The cast of Hogan's Heroes. Bob Crane as Hogan. So on and so forth. It's still in my head. Bunny imprinted it there. And for the life of me I can't delete it.

Back to Robbie.

He always wanted real cream for his coffee. He said I hate chemicals.

Suzanne introduced me to Robbie because we loved David Bowie. It was years later that I had an Oscar Mike Golf moment and thought... Robbie may have been gay.

If Suzanne thought I might also be – was she trying to be matchmaker matchmaker?

In retrospect, I think Robbie was. I still love him as a brother. We Bowie fans must stick together.

It's September 13, 2021, and tomorrow I become sixty years old…

Over the years I've tried to find Robbie on social media like facebook. I fear the worst.

CVS Pharmacy

I jump around a lot from month and year.

It's June 2021 and I work at CVS Pharmacy on Fort Myers Beach. Our music that's piped in is like smooth or soft jazz versions of songs from the 1950s to the 1980s. Some are almost dead-on renditions like Dave Brubeck and Stan Kenton doing "Take Five" from the album Time Out.

The station plays a lot of Stevie Wonder, Beatles, Carol King, and Seals & Croft (Where did they go after 1975?). But also Bobbie Darin and Dean Martin.

Back to Robbie Ferrar. He was intelligent. Educated. Loved great music. Suzanne knew Robbie and I would be friends. And we were.

Robbie said when he ordered coffee, "I don't like chemicals." He insisted on real cream or half-n-half.

Robbie was a kind, loving soul. I think Robbie was gay but back then you didn't tell anyone. Or ask anyone.

If Suzanne knew, she didn't say. Did she know?

Bottom Line: I loved Robbie like a brother.

Gay or straight was never an issue.

<u>1977 – Bowie was on Bing Crosby</u>

Bing and Bowie sang the Little Drummer Boy and then Bowie sang "Heroes." I knew I would go to Berlin. Eventually.

Which pull pulled me stronger? Cabaret or Bowie?

Tim Deegan used to believe I had an obsession with Hitler. In seventh grade we watched the Last Days of Adolph Hitler at the Mentor Mall. It was a film about his final days in the bunker in Berlin until he shot himself. Seventh Grade English we read the Diary of Anne Frank. I was never obsessed with Hitler. I was intrigued with Evil. Hitler was Evil. Bunny was Evil. My question was – what made men Evil and made them commit evil acts.

In my reading and Berlin experience, Berliners hated Hitler. They thought he was the nutjob from Munich. The failed corporal who never made it as an artist.

Brandon adored nazis and Hitler. God forgive him.

I hate Nazis, Hitler, anti-semites, and elitist snobs.

<u>Scott Summers</u>

I met Scott through Sue Heeter. Scott had this amazing light show in his basement. He played Queen, "Now I'm Here" and the lights followed the music.

One weekend, he had a concert in his basement. Dave Adkins was there and sang an Iggy Pop song and did a 180 arc through the crowd while the band jammed.

Scott let me sing "Rebel Rebel" with his band. They jammed longer than the song and so I adlibbed verses not in the original.

Then he had Sue sing "Ziggy Stardust." Sue thought she could sing. Scott loved her so he encouraged her. Sue could not sing. She was a gesticulator.

Scott gave me three albums. The Velvet Underground, "White Light, White Heat." And the New York Dolls, "Too Much too Soon" and their first album. They all remain my favorite albums to this day. Thank you, Scott.

[Update 2021: due to Facebook, Scott revealed to me that he is now (perhaps always has been?) a republican. I do not hold that against him. I have many friends from the olden days who are now republican… conservative I get. I do not get followers of Donald Trump.]

Donald Trump

This will have to be done in parts. Where do I begin?

He married Melania. Was the promise to bring her family here? Who cares? Less than a year later, he fucks Stormy Daniels the porn star.

Pays her $140,000 to cover it up.

Then the playboy model.

Look up the cost of the Ken Starr report that proved Bill Clinton got fellatio from Monica Lewinsky.

The Donald really pissed me off when he mocked the cripple saying "Uh, Uh, UH," with his hands gnarled.

The Donald needs to crawl back into his hole.

Donald Trump is the worst example of American ever. He is greed, ego, narcissistic, vain, condescending, conceited, and stupid. Really, really stupid.

Everyone has a bad gin story…

Dennis Terry was a hoot. One night we drove to Lakewood from Mentor… that's a haul… The Wild Giraffes were playing a live show. Most likely at the Phantasy night club. We went there a lot for Pagans concerts.

Tom Miller had a van and he drove. I put on make up and my dog collar. Dennis attached a leash.

We drank Gin and mixed it with Squirt. By the time we reached Lakewood, my inhibitions were gone.

Iggy did a song called, "I wanna be your dog." I acted the part. I lunged at passersby and growled or barked. Some comedian on NPR said to make the sound of a dog barking, you bark while breathing in, not out. I don't know if that's how dogs do it, but it sounds more genuine. Dennis would pull the leash and say heal, and whoa. It was 1979 okay? All across the USA. Another year for me and you. Another year with nothing to do.

We scared the local citizens of Lakewood, Ohio.

I do not recall the rock show. I know I paid the admission fee and we sat at a table and then then I asked Tom for keys to his van. I had bed spins and needed to lay down before I puked.

I spent the rest of the evening groaning and trying not to puke in my friend's van. I never puked. Eventually I passed out. I don't remember the drive back to mentor or getting out of the van once we arrived at Seneca.

Wild Giraffes were popular with Clevo locals. Like the Savage Tractors were popular. "We" and we is italicized... we liked Pagans, Pere Ubu, Dead Boys and the Lepers. Especially Pie Tin. A female punk rocker was our goddess.

The Freak, 1979

On Seneca, there was also this other guy. He told me how he and Brandon were rivals playing chess and he wanted to play me.

His dad was involved in the CYO. His dad took me to a production of Fiddler on the Roof with an interracial cast around 1977. We went to a cast party. I was 15 or so. Nothing inappropriate happened. I loved meeting the cast. They paid so much attention to me. They were thrilled a young person was sparked by theater.

His son, Steve? Perhaps -- I don't recall his name... Would come to visit and want to play chess.

I had one opening move. Just one. Who taught me that? Anyhow, it involved a pawn, a bishop and a knight and took either the queen or check mate.

I used that move on Steve. I'll call him that since I can't recall his real name. He didn't catch it and I took his queen and won. He never came back. Mitzi said that was good because he gave her the heebee Jeebees. He looked like Benedict Cumberbatch with really bad acne sores.

Ramones and Muppets

At the Seneca home, Mark had this cardboard cut out of the Ramones from album cover of "Rocket to Russia." Somewhere he also found these color cut outs of the muppets – Cookie Monster, Grover, Oscar the Grouch and Bert or Ernie. We added them to the Ramones and they became the Ramuppets.

The Defnics

After the AK-47s, the Defnics came into being. Bill De Gedio was the lead singer of the AK-47s with Larry Lewis on guitar. Mark Vocca took me to see a show of the AK-47s. Great punk music on Mentor avenue. Guitar was great from Larry. Lyrics from Bill were mediocre.

Bill DeGido teamed up with Bob Sablack, Brandon Zart (both from Saint Joe's) and Johnny on drums. Sorry Johnny – I keep forgetting your last name.

With the Defnics, Bill's writing of music and lyrics excelled.

After 1980, I helped with lyrics in the army. I sent Bill letters with lyrics. I wrote "Governor's Daughter," "Life's So Fast," and "Suck my breath away." Bill wrote the music.

Brandon Zart wrote "Hello from Berlin." He started the recording with a Hitler Speech. What a joke. Why was Hitler elevated?

I met Mike Hudson through Bill. Mike started out as a drummer. Bill also introduced me to his brother Russell.

Bill told me that if I ever wanted to join the Cleveland Mafia, his uncle had the connections. But once you joined, there was only one way out and that was dead. I said no thanks.

I think I would have made an excellent hit man. They could have tested me by letting me kill bunny as my first target and then take it from there. But I'm an Airborne Ranger and have never fired a weapon at a live human being.

Bill and I went to many concerts together. Iggy, Ramones, Dickies, Public Image… classic punk rock.

The Defnics

After May 1980, when I was in Basic Training at Fort Benning and at Hunter with the Rangers, I used to send Bill DeGidio song lyrics. Sometimes he kept them intact and sometimes he changed them.

So I was the unofficial fifth Defnic. Behind the scenes.

I'll take that badge of honor.

Racism and assumptions of Whites

I loved Bill like a brother. And here's the "But..." Most of the men, when I saw I loved them as a brother, there were no conditions.

My brother Chuck (by blood) was an asshole and a moron. He would never be my brother.

Now Bill had a sawed-off shot gun and etched into the wooden stock, it read "Nigger killer." When he showed me that he laughed. I didn't get the joke. It was wrong and not funny. Bill was proud to show me. Sorry. I don't get "Nigger Killer."

Bill also told me about Freddy. Freddy was a black man in Cleveland that if you wanted someone murdered, you paid Freddy $50.00 and it was done.

Time and time again. Caucasions assumed. Skin pigmentation if shared or closely similar implied that bigotry was a shared belief. Arrogance assumed it. In all chapters of my life, I have been the stand alone.

Not quite. Mark Vocca stands with me. Just not about Trump.

In ENG 101 in 1988 at CSU, I read Doctor Martin Luther King's "Letter from Birmingham Jail." Assigned by Professor Daniel Melnick. Dr. King's prose moved me.

Especially "Lukewarm acceptance." Dr. King said it was much more bewildering than outright rejection.

Passive turn-the-other-cheek? Or wearing blinders while injustice is committed and you just look away. And flowers never bend with the rainfall.

I want a Black Lives Matter protest in Naples or Fort Myers, because I am there. I write this in November of 2020.

Ridge Junior High School

I entered Junior High School at Ridge Junior High in 1973. It would be fifteen years before any writing of Dr. King would be presented to me by any teacher.

Why? "History" in seventh grade said the Civil War was all about States' rights. History was taught by White Teachers. That's how it was taught. It was never about slavery. 1973 we had not come far enough away from 1968 Selma, Alabama.

No history class I ever took taught of the massacre in Tulsa, Oklahoma in 1921. Greenwood neighborhood called the Black Wall Street. Look it up. Google the name "Dick Rowland." 10,000 black people were left homeless. Over 300 black men and women were murdered.

Donald Trump called the Confederate Flag a symbol of Southern Pride. He is a dangerous idiot and an asshole. During the civil rights protests…

- Whites passively tolerated dogs, fire hoses, and billy clubs used against black marchers and protestors.

- Whites passively tolerated baseball bats wrapped with barbed wire used against black marchers and protestors.

- Whites passively tolerated the Nightly News with reports of beatings. As black persons attempted to register to vote – their legal right.

How did anyone "passively" tolerate this? Not one iota was "taught" by white teachers. This outrage condemns the white education system.

I won't ever practice "lukewarm acceptance."

Late Winter 1979 and early Spring 1980

Mark joined the Airforce. Doug was at Ohio University in Athens. I was working at Bob Evans and spending my free time with Mitzi Terry or Bill DeGedio and Barb, or Russ.

Mitzi told me that Mark used to beat her. Based on my experience with the Bunny, that did not settle well. I was too quick to judge. And shame on me for not asking Mark for his side of the story. No, I instantly put Mark and Bunny on the same shelf. Mitzi was guilty of hyperbole and fabrication. Okay let's call it lying.

Mark told me later that Mitzi told Fred, her dad, that Mark hit her. Fred told Mark what Mitzi said. Fred told Mitzi, "that's bull shit. That's not what he does, that's not him."

I should have reacted the way Fred did. Fred trusted his instincts and what he knew. I relied on my personal history with mom and the Bunny.

Why? Did my caring for Mitzi outweigh my caring for Mark? Mitzi was my sister. Mark was my brother. They should have been equal. At least equal. Cancelled each other out.

Back then, I had access to my parent's van and some nights, Mitzi would ask me to take her to the Brass Rail in Painesville. There was a construction worker from Florida whom she met and would repeatedly have sex with. I don't know why Mitzi wanted me to know this. Did she think I would tell Mark? Perhaps to make Mark jealous? Sometime there after, Mark married her and took her to Texas with the AirForce.

Additionally, according to their confessions, Doug Enkler and Russell DeGidio admitted that they slept with (aka had sex with) Mitzi. Mitzi didn't tell me. Doug and Russ did.

<u>Joining the Army in 1980</u>

One day, Russ came home [I think in all honesty, he came over to Bill and Barb's home] and said he joined the army. Later, I was sweeping the foyer at Bob Evans on Route 306 in Mentor. I said out loud: "This is not for me."

After work, I went and talked to Russ and said how can I go with you?

He said tell them that you want the 1st ranger battalion 75th infantry and that you want to leave in six days. Russ came with me and that's exactly what we did.

Forty years later, I have to ask… why and how did Russ know anything about the rangers? I read a lot and I never heard of the rangers. But I was willing to join the army and become one.

I scored 125 on my GT test. They told me that that would get me into West Point. I'd heard about West Point. Nothing I heard was good.

Martha Alexy was my girlfriend at the time. She used to be Russell's girl. He introduced me and said we would hit it off. We did.

The day before we left for the airport, Bill had a party for us. I think we did microdot. We may have also done crank.

Bill's uncle took us to the downtown federal building. I don't recall getting the plane tickets. Someone was appointed to get the plane tickets for the group. I think. I don't recall. We took the overground subway to Cleveland Hopkins Airport.

At Cleveland Hopkins airport, there was a USO person with doughnuts. He was a black guy who asked us where we were going. Russ and I said the Rangers. He looked at Russ and said, "You're not going to make it." Then he looked at me and said, "You. You're crazy. You'll do just fine."

I didn't know what to make of his comments. But why did people meet me and decide I was crazy?

In the 1980s, I missed a lot of concerts. Punk shows I know I would have loved. Plasmatics for one. They played the Agora when I was in Berlin. Doug sent me a clipping from the Cleveland Plain Dealer. He was in the audience.

But I also saw a lot of great shows.

I remember that Mike Hall – eventually my platoon sergeant in the rangers – told someone, "I don't know what iggy will do after the army, but I'm sure it will have something to do with music and singing." I wish that had become true. Acid reflux destroyed my singing voice.

Mike used to say, "Fuck around, fuck around, ain't gonna be around."

I knew what it meant. I always hoped it didn't apply to me.

Concerts 1980s

1980	17-Mar	Jimmy Buffett	CLE Coliseum	Mitzi Terry
1980	18-Mar	Iggy Pop	Cleveland Agora	Mitzi Terry, Russ DeGidio
1980	24-Mar	Ramones	Cleveland Agora	Mitzi Terry, Russ DeGidio, Doug Enkler
1980	1-Apr	The Dickies	Cleveland Agora	Russ, Bill, Barb, Jay, Bob Sablack and Mark Vocca
1980	30-Apr	Public Image Ltd	Cleveland Agora	Russ, Bill and Bob Sablack
1980	April	Cheap Trick	CLE Coliseum	Bill DeGidio
1982	June	X	Pirate's Cove	Doug Enkler & Joe Kronick

1983	May or June	Ramones/Pagans	Cleveland Agora	Bill DeGidio & Mike Hudson
1984		Barclay James Harvest	Berlin	Birgit Pauels
1985		Super Tramp	Berlin	Michaela Becker
1986	14-Apr	The Cramps	Berlin Metropol	
1987	Nov	Iggy Pop	Phantasy	Beth
1988	14-Sep	Iggy Pop	Phantasy	Lise and Mike
1989		Anita Baker	Front Row	Lise

Music was important

In the 1970s, music was different than in the 1960. Granted in the 60s you had motown, rock, folk and country. But in the 1970s, it split even more and walls were erected. The fans of Led Zeppelin and Pink Floyd hated disco. The fans of disco hated punk. The fans of punk hated, well, everyone.

As immature as that may have been, I formed the greatest friendships out of that bond and love of music. Mark Vocca and I loved punk rock. With us were Bob Sablack, Brandon Zart and Doug Enkler. Time would test our bonds.

Mark Vocca and Bob Sablack are still my friends. Most others from high school are fallen to the wayside.

Mentor was/is a white racist town

There were no black families in Mentor until I went to Mentor High School in my senior year and Bob Hackney was there. If his family was the first, God bless them.

Mark Vocca tells me a different story of Mentor because he was an athlete and spent his time with other athletes who were both black and white. There was no divide among athletes. You were good, mediocre, or you didn't play.

The Bunny took me to Cloverdale – a fisherman's club in Concord. Concord was east of Cleveland, south of Painesville. AKA the boonies.

Some good memories came of it.

Matt Skoff made home-made Slivovitz. All the adult men got FUBAR. For those who don't know the Army jargon, that's "fucked up beyond all recognition." Matt Skoff was a pig farmer. Slivovitz was plum brandy. I'd say fuck that noise, it was moon shine. But if you buy it at the local liquor store, they will call it and label it plum brandy.

The men sat around and told racist jokes. As a teenager, I had to listen and keep my mouth shut. "How do you babysit a bunch of nigger kids? Wet their lips like suction cups and stick them to the wall."

We live in the world of Rodney King, Trayvon Martin and George Floyd. Here's the problem… the list goes on and on… how do names so easily get forgotten?

Black unarmed men being killed by white cops. The most recent one, the racists asshole had his knee on George Floyd's neck. Mr. Floyd repeated said, "I can't breathe." Thank God the cop was charged with and convicted of murder. Why was it a question?

Or Jacob Blake. Shot seven times in the back. Paralyzed. How does any American defend that?

"To Serve and Protect."

For the moment, tell me I'm the chief of police… without hesitation, you're not just fired, asshole, you're all under arrest. Murder and conspiracy to commit murder. But in 2020 and 2021 -- there was this "reluctance." I'm not sure that anyone can explain that to me.

So if you're black, do you get used to it? Do you resign yourself that this is the norm? Does Selma become the norm and George Wallace what we can expect? 1968 and Bloody Sunday was a year on the books. Historians document, protestors suffer. Let's pause a moment… 1968. This is 2020. Selma was Fifty-Five years ago. Whiskey Tango Foxtrot, over?

Geneva Foster

Non Sequitor. Geneva Foster and I worked at the New Student Center at Cleveland State University (in 1988 or 1989?). I was married and should not have been. I never cheated on Lise. Could have, would have, didn't. I ask myself… often… Should have? Always will be a question. Eight years, I was miserable. Pretender. Of something I was not. I performed as the husband. But I didn't want to be there.

When we were beer buddies, she was sweet, kind, intuitive. But later was arrogant, egomaniac, elitist snob. Better than everyone else. But oh, also the victim.

Trump card was suicide or divorce. That held me hostage. So many, many occasions. Back to Geneva…

I had a ring so most just assumed I was off limits. Geneva tested that boundary.

There was one day, she threw my head back and planted a kiss on my lips that was the most sensual experience I ever had. Geneva was a proud African American woman, and I have never forgotten that kiss.

I've had sex with women whose names are in limbo. But not Geneva. All we shared was a kiss. But it's a kiss that I have never forgotten.

There was one evening, I drove her home from CSU. We sat in her driveway. I wanted to say to her, please invite me in and let us become life-long lovers.

I think Geneva knew that as long as I was still married to that wife, I would never do that. She left the car and went inside. We talked about it years later. She agreed with why I thought she went inside. Alone.

Lise, "how do you compete with that?"

One day Lise told me, if a guy sez to you he's gay, how do you compete with that? I remembered that and tried to use it to my advantage.

I told her in front of my parent, "I'm gay." No I am not. But Lise always pulled the divorce card first – that was an acceptable term. But then the suicide card. How do you counter that? She pulled the suicide card on me so many times I was paranoid and had so much anxiety, it's not even funny.

I was always looking for a way out. I wanted nothing to do with her. She was psycho. Sadly. But psycho.

When we divorced, she pleaded, said she'd go to "anger management." She almost admitted it was her fault.

I talked to her attorney when I met with her when she was representing a new client and I was the QDRO person for the former BP employee.

She told me, Lise wanted blood. She asked me to do things that were illegal.

I've been with Lynn for 19 years so far and love her with all my heart.

More on Cloverdale

Bunny had a cloverdale buddy who worked at the Lakeland community college on route 306 south of Mentor. After my ETS from the Army, he'd come over to have beers with the bunny.

Some might call this obnoxious.

If his buddy told a nigger joke, I'd say, "oh, I got the next one…" And I would feign the most degrading southern redneck accent. "Didja hear about the ignorant redneck dumbfuck who entered a spelling bee? He said bees can't spell…" I did not have to continue… I was told to leave. Not asked. Nor was it polite.

I imagine the bunny tried to compensate

He never admitted to what he had done. The damage when he got drunk and punished his wife and children.

Perhaps somewhere in the dark reaches of his mind, he knew. Not willing to accept it, he took the family to Cedar Point, Geauga Lake, Sea World and Conneaut. These were amusement parks within driving distance from Mentor.

They represented the sober Bunny. Somewhere in his mind, he had to know. He damaged innocents, and he damaged mom. Guilt is a strong motivator. But saying, "I'm sorry" would have healed wounds. Some but not all.

Bunny never said, "I'm sorry." Perhaps that should be the title of this book.

Martha Alexy

Russ introduced me to her in 1979 or 80. She lived in her parents' home off lake shore close to Eastlake. Martha worked in a factory. The factory that eventually took her fingers tips.

Martha and I became intimate. I can't remember if she ever told me she had protection. I loved Martha and if I got her pregnant so be it. I wanted to marry her.

If we weren't at Bill and Barb's home, we would drive to Concord where my parents owned a lot. The only structure was a garage and a man-made lake. I would pull up to the garage and we'd make love on my field jacket. Martha and I never had sex. We always made love. As much as I understood the concept back then.

1976 Mercury Comet

Spring of 1980, the Bunny bought me a car for $1,000. He drove me to the dealership and handed me the keys.

I never knew why he did that. He treated me like I was the failure of the family. Perhaps he thought I 'd runaway with the car and he'd be done with me.

My poetry grew darker – prior to that time but during this time frame, it grew even darker.

None of those written then appear in my book. But I was convinced I was evil. Ironically, I never did evil deeds. I just thought my heart and soul were evil. Bunny taught me that. Because I deserved to be. Punished. Bunny taught that the Good punished the Evil. And evil deserved punishment,.

So why buy me a car?

Joining the Army with Russ DeGidio

I was visiting or sleeping over with Bill and Barb which I did a lot of back in those days. I don't think I ever showered at their house which meant I probably stank most of the time. When I'm depressed, personal hygiene goes out the window.

Russ came and announced that he was joining the Army. He was going to be in a Ranger unit.

Shortly thereafter, I was sweeping the foyer at Bob Evans Restaurant and realized, I have no high school diploma. I'm in a dead-end job. Why not go with Russ and see what happens.

I talked it over with Russ. He said go the recruiter in downtown Willoughby. Tell them you want Rangers, 1st Battalion of the 75th Infantry and you want to leave in six days.

I did exactly that.

My GT Score was 125. I have no idea what that means. All I know is that for the first two years, I got letters inviting me to the West Point preparatory school. CPL Craig Riley told me, "if you wanna become an officer, fine. But come up through the ranks and become an NCO first. Then if you wanna go, more power to ya.

My experiences with West Point Officers was not good. They were loyal to one another and had no loyalty to their unit or their troops."

Reading books educated me about the WPPA (West Point Protective Association). More on the WPPA later. But it gave me more ammo to hate them.

At some point in my future, I was again in contact with Craig Riley. Now he was an officer, a major in Special Forces.

Prior to leaving for the Army, the Bunny learned that I would be stationed in Georgia. His parting words to me were, "Just don't bring home no Kizzie girl."

His racist fucking attitude was like George Wallace and Archie Bunker combined. But I have to give him credit... I had no idea he even knew any of the people from Alex Haley's "Roots."

Bill had a going away party for me and Russ at his sister's apartment off Lost Nation Road in Willoughby.

Bill's uncle was going to pick us up in the morning to take us to the federal building downtown Cleveland.

Martha Alexy was there. Aside: Martha, I'm sorry. I wanted to marry you. Russ fucked that up. I don't know what he wrote to you. But I can only guess he lied. You conveyed to me based on Russell's letter that I was using you as a means to an end. That was not true. I got the unicorn tattoo for you in 1981. That was the first step. The ring was next. Barb told me she knew that.

Best laid plans of mice and men... desperation. To this day, I have not forgiven myself for believing Mitzi carte blanche and not even asking Mark for his side of the story.

My next act perhaps gave Russ the ammo he needed to sabotage my relation with Martha.

In basic training, I proposed to Mitzi because she told me Mark was beating her which was not true. I only proposed to get her away from Mark. I told her I would pay for her college. I'd pay for the apartment. And I would not ask for sex in return.

Wouldn't you think that for one instance, I'd say, isn't this your mom you're trying to save from the abusive Bunny?

I've said this before, but shame on me for not asking Mark for his side of the story. Bunny jaded me. I was so quick to conclude that the male was at fault.

And I would not blame Martha for doubting me if she considered how quickly I proposed to Mitzi when we were supposed to be in love. I didn't love Mitzi. Well, I did. But love like family which she was. I did not love her like to be her husband. I loved Martha like that.

I wrote to Martha asking her to tell me what Russell had said. Four or five letters sent and she wrote back to say "I'm done with both you and Russell. I have no idea who I can trust."

I still have the unicorn tattoo. That was for you, Martha. The protector of innocence.

PART TWO: THE RANGERS

The Rangers are the Army's Elite. Spearhead operations like Normandy in World War II. Special Operations like Grenada in1983. Behind enemy lines combat patrols like in Vietnam, first as "Lerps" – the acronym for LRRPs (long-range recon patrols) then as rangers. LRRPs were 51st then redesignated at 75th rangers.

Rangers also included Merrill's Marauders in the pacific theater of WWII in Berma.

Read the "Ranger Creed" that I post at the beginning. Those are words taken to heart by each and every ranger.

What do I want to document about my life that merits a record? This isn't retaliation. It is a record of facts. Perhaps some parts are retaliation... Berlin and the chain of command who backed Kavecki – to all of those who supported him, I have to ask, a platoon sergeant who starts a squad leader meeting by asking, "Who has got any good 'nigger jokes'?" – those who backed Kavecki accepted that. Condoned it. And supported his leadership decisions. 1LT Andrew Burris, CPT Donald Cox, 1LT Rogers, and (acting) LTC (actually major) Keirn C. Brown. They all backed the field grade article 15. Each of you in your actions justified a redneck SFC conducting a squad leader meeting, by telling "nigger jokes." Oh, but you didn't ask that question? Why the fuck not?

Burris, Rogers, and Brown were all tab wearers. Hypocrites. They took the word of a leg and testified against a ranger. A leg who told "nigger' jokes in his squad leader meetings. Does anything need to make this clearer?

Do I need to say, "Nigger" jokes are wrong?

"Duh."

I quote Billie Eilish.

Rangers were and remain the Army's Elite. Berlin Brigade was the Army's most superficial, lame, dog and pony show, pathetic, bunch of sad sacks. Not everyone. Mind you. I had some great friends there who were totally squared away. NCOs, privates and one – only one – fucking ossifer. Christopher Reddish. I will never forget him. He was the best.

If I were to retaliate against anyone, it would be against Shinseki when he was in charge of head gear in the Regular Army and later of the VA. Shinseki gave the Rangers' Black Beret to all active duty personnel. The Rangers led a campaign called "Earned, not issued" about the Black Beret. There is a website (the last time I checked) that still has the letters – mine included – that were sent to Shinseki to protest.

Degenerative tissue between C3 and C7

In 2009, I was at my desk and suddenly it felt like someone had taken a sledge-hammer to my left arm. I had a headache and I was having a hard time putting together a coherent sentence. I assumed heart attack or stroke.

I drove to my doctor. He did an EKG and said the heart is not the issue. He sent me to get an x-ray. They discovered degeneration of the tissue between the vertebrae C6 and C7. Since 2009 it has spread to where now it's between each vertebrae from C3 to C7.

Sports medicine documents hundreds of cases of injuries that remain dormant until later on in life when they surface. I am such a case. I had a neurosurgeon from Naples sign a document stating that my neck issues are a direct result from parachuting. Dr. Nick Bhasin.

I'm getting ahead of myself.

May 14, 1980

That date. That's when Russ DeGedio and I left for Basic Training. The start of our enlistment in the US Army.

Russ and I made a bet – whoever went further paid the other $50.

Remember that.

BASIC TRAINING AND ADVANCED INFANTRY TRAINING

May 1980 to September 1980. Fort Benning, Georgia.

During that summer during Basic and AIT (advanced infantry training) my Mom sent me photos of Cyndy's graduation from Lake Catholic. One photo featured Cyndy's friend Tina – I liked her a lot. She was smart and funny.

Cyndy went to Hiram college. That's where Bunny went to college. Mom said he got his degree in Chemistry and had a

"C" average. Cyndy spent one year there and then transferred to Northwestern where Kathy Endres was. Kathy was Cyndy's best friend from Lake Catholic. Cyndy and Kathy would become computer engineers and get recruited by IBM for the research triangle park in North Carolina.

The nonsensical part is that Chuck and Cathy who remained at home – they blamed Cyndy and me for "abandoning them." I could not wait to leave home. I went to the Army. Cyndy, she got great grades. She earned her tuition paid for. She was a straight A student.

Chuck and Cathy developed this burning resentment and never let it go. We did not abandon them. We escaped.

I didn't know it then. Neither did I care. I was going to the Rangers and I didn't know if I should be scared or elated. There were 52 hostages in Iran.

At least let my leadership be the best. Rangers were the best.

Basic Training: Fort Jackson then Fort Benning

14 May 1980. The plane from Cleveland landed in Charleston and then a bus to Fort Jackson, South Carolina. They called this reception. They issued us $50.00 and gave a shopping list for the PX. Toiletries and extras were cigarettes and candy bars.

Chow line came around and we were all in line for lunch. Army has a hackneyed cliché. "Hurry up and wait." Everywhere you go and everything you do. Hustle to get there and then wait in a long line. One caveat needs to be stated here. This was forty years ago. Okay?

While waiting in the chow line for lunch, outside there was a platoon of female basic training recruits. The female drill sergeant was trying to teach them a lesson. Humility, discipline or humiliation?

She said, "One more time, Ladies, and when I call you to attention, I want to hear all those pussies slap together in unison." The drill sergeant knew we were close enough to hear. That was the point.

"Platoon, Attention!"

I thought how humiliating. Here we are – fresh recruits. Still in civilian clothes. I imagined red faces but I could not see them. And in South Carolina, didn't everyone have red faces?

Reception Center, Fort Jackson, South Carolina.

We were issued our fatigues, dress uniforms, head gear and TA-50 and sent to Fort Benning. TA-50 was the nomenclature they used for field equipment -- LBE (Load bearing equipment), your pistol belt and shoulder straps, canteens, magazine pouches, compass. Field gear like your ruck sack, sleeping bag, poncho and poncho liner. There was also a dangly device they called GP Straps or spaghetti straps. GP meant general purpose. Not in basic, but in the rangers I figured out a way to attach the GP strap to the ruck sack frame in order to have the fart sack (sleeping bag) secure and attached in a tight and taught manner. CPT Wiles asked me to teach him how. He was the tab wearer in Berlin.

Poncho Liner is essential. To this day, I have two.

We also got our haircuts. You see that in movies. Buzz cuts for guys with long hair. Rangers called it "high and tight." We called it "a dick with ears."

Fort Benning

From South Carolina to Georgia, we bussed. To Fort Benning, Sand Hill, Columbus, Georgia.

Bravo-Three-One Bushmasters. That was us. Bravo company, third battalion, 1st division.

SSG Malley was our drill sergeant and CPL Carr was the drill corporal. Corporal Carr was a Vietnam vet who'd been in the Marines in Vietnam and re-enlisted Army.

Lots of guys did that back then. Maybe they were drafted. Maybe they volunteered. They cycled to Vietnam and did one or two tours. "Tours" sounds like they had a tour bus. But they would ETS – leave the military – and find that civilian life sucks. Stranger in a strange land. Learned that lesson later.

Early one morning, we were on the PT field. That's "Physical Training." The instructor was a Drill who was Latino and his English was kind of funny.

In 1977, the lyrics to the Devo song went like this... "Are we not men? We are DEVO." It was lifted from "the Island of Doctor Moreau" by H. G. Wells who borrowed literally from scripts of satanic rites from Germany. I came across that by accident. I wasn't looking for it. But I found it. The German satanic rite even included the reference to the House of Pain.

Next thing we know, the drill instructor is shouting: "who you are? Are you not men?" We were supposed to say, "We are Bushmasters." And we're laughing. Russ and I are saying "We are devo."

Jim Darden knew the band and was with us. Also cracking up.

Nut Job #1

This one guy was an eager beaver. That's putting it nicely. He said he was going to Special Forces to become a Green Beret.

We didn't know the process so we said, "okay" with an ellipsis. Years later, I would express that reaction with the phrase, "All righty then…" meaning that's done and now let's move on.

For Special Forces, I later learned that to qualify, you first need to obtain the rank of Sergeant E-05 and only then can you apply. No guarantee. But you can apply. A basic training private was not going special forces right off the bat. He was a private E-01. The E meant enlisted grade. Officers started at O-01 for second lieutenant. And there were Warrant Officers. These were helicopter pilots and medical Physicians Assistants.

This Green Beret Wannabe approached me and Jim Darden one day and said, "Do you know what this is?" He was holding a P-38 C-Ration can opener. I think Jim answered first and said, "Yeah it's a can opener for C-rations"

He defiantly said, "no, you're wrong. It's a weapon. I can use this to cut throats." You judge that how you want to. To me, he was a nut job.

Mess Hall and rations

Note to clarify. A-rations are meals served in the mess hall. B-rations are prepared in the mess hall but trucked out the field to be served. C-rations were the box meals of four cans and cellophane wrapped spoon, salt, pepper, napkin, instant coffee, powdered cream and sugar.

For the B-rations, they packed everything in Mermite cans. By the time they reached us in the field, the scrambled eggs were green. Large cylinders dispensed coffee in the morning and grape Kool-aid at lunch or dinner. I'm sure that most will agree… the silver bullet containers were never cleaned to eliminate residue. So the coffee was blended with grape

Kool-aid and the grape Kool-aid was blended with coffee. I understood why the Brits preferred tea.

Physical Training

Basic Training was easy for me when it came to road marching. Hard when it came to running. I sprinted fine. Short distance. But two or five miles? That killed me. I also smoked cigarettes. This would have been the perfect time to quit. It was 1980. I was nineteen. Sadly, I wouldn't quit until 2006. Twenty-six years later.

Sit ups were also hard. Not because of stomach muscles. But because Patrice Nerone in eighth grade at Ridge Junior high stabbed me with a thread puller into my coccyx, tailbone. That was in Science class with Mister Gooding. That was vicious. Her motivation was surprise. I never understood it.

M16A1

Qualifying with the M16A1 was a challenge for me. I was right-handed, so I used my right eye. At the M16 range there were three levels that one would qualify for: Expert, Sharpshooter and Marksman. Below Marksman, you didn't qualify. The M16 had a maximum effective range of 460 meters. The qualification range had targets that popped up starting at 50 meters out to 300 meters. At 300 meters, the target was tiny. I could not imagine what a target at 460 meters would look like.

In Basic training, I qualified sharp-shooter with the M16.

Later in the Rangers, they taught me to figure out which eye was stronger, dominant... in my case, it was my left eye. That was strange because I fired the weapon with my right hand, but I used my left eye for the target. The next time I went to qualify,

I used my left eye. I scored expert every time. As I recall, expert meant a minimum of 38 hits out of 40.

Our first Day Pass – limited to the post

Limited to the post meant not off post. We could not leave fort Benning. No adventures in Columbus, Georgia.

Russ and I went to the movie theatre and watched a movie of warner brothers' cartoons. A Bugs Bunny and Road Runner marathon. Then we went to the NCO club and got drunk. The juke box was lame. We were starving for music. No punk, no glam. The closest we got was a tom petty song called "Refugee."

I wrote to my sister Cyndy and asked her to record a cassette of three albums and mail it to me. Iggy and the Stooges, "Raw Power." Roxy Music's debut and the Pretenders' debut. She gratefully complied.

On our pass, I should have stuck with beer. That's what I knew. Instead I sampled drinks that I had heard the name but had not tried. Black Russian, white Russian, Manhattan, and God knows what else. I should have been sick as a dog. Perhaps I got bored and went back to beer. I don't recall.

Russ liked things like Galiano and especially Yukon Jack. Bill introduced me to Yukon Jack. Syrupy Canadian whisky flavored with honey that was intended to fuck you up quickly. It was 100 proof which meant 50% pure alcohol. Go Canada! You folks love to party! My adopted son would testify to that.

Chris O'Connor. I'm not his father, but I am his father. Chris should explain that one. Biology sez, I'm not. Our love, respect, caring, those things say we are.

When we got back to the barracks, we had to polish our boots for the next day of training. Russ got so drunk, he was on his back, rolling back and forth and moaning about how sick he felt. I polished his boots for him. In the early days I used

Lincoln polish because it seemed to shine better than Kiwi. But eventually I realized that Kiwi was the best. I never turned my back on Kiwi ever again.

In 2002, Chris O'Connor joined the army. I started a letter to him the day he left for Basic Training. I told his family, letters are so meaningful. Mail call comes and if you don't get a letter, it says to you nobody cares about you.

Chris was / is the son of Bernie Yamane – her last name came from her second husband, the father of Briana and Michael. Chris and I shared a love for punk rock. Unmatched by anyone else. Well let me qualify that – Chris could hold his own with Bob Sablack or Mark Vocca. Chris is the son I never had.

I met Chris when I was married to Patti Glaser. Chris never liked Patti but his mom and Patti were friends.

Now is when I should talk bad about Patti. But I won't. Out of respect for her mother and her daughter, Megan. Her mom once said to me, "Todd was a schmuck, but you are a mensch." I once made potato pancakes for her, but she said these aren't latkas. I made up the recipe. It was my own. Todd was Megan's father.

Back to writing to Chris --- I had to wait until we got an address for Chris. By the time we got the address my "letter" was 75 pages long (or thereabouts). That is not hyperbole. I write long letters. Just ask Chris. And I date every passage. Like a journal. Yeah, Lise would challenge that because no one ever read her journal to say, "that's bullshit."

Oh, and by the way, I wrote to Chris every night and he got a ton of letters from me. Okay so "ton" is hyperbolic.

Back to Chris…

The first mail call, they called his name. His drill sergeant held this package and said we had to check this for contraband.

It was thick. Like I said it was 75 pages long. I wrote on one side. The return address came from Ranger Iguana.

Chris wrote back to me before he wrote to his mom or Babci. They were not happy with that. Chris said the platoon sergeant said, "who is writing you this many pages and who the fuck is Ranger Iguana?" Chris said he told the drill sergeant that he's my step-father. In his letter, he wrote that that was how he felt. Since then I refer to Chris as my adopted son.

Before he got out, he got an assignment of recruiting duty. This goes back to the Kiwi story. As I recall (and recollection is fuzzy), his office was on Mentor avenue aka Route 20. He had jump boots that needed to be spit shined.

Chris had some new product for spit shining boots. He was happy to brag that this stuff worked great. I did not ask the name of the product. I just said that I still had my boot shining kit with Kiwi boot polish.

I worked on one boot while Chris worked on the other. He had a good base built up on the one I was doing. So it didn't take me long.

We compared. Mine looked like a black mirror. His needed a lot of work.

Chris said, "Fuck you, Iggy. Fuck you."

I said, "Old school. Can't beat it."

Frank in 1980

In Basic Training, we – Jim Darden, Russ De Gidio and me – we had a friend named Frank. Frank was gay. Tim Alee was gay and he was the bass player in the Pagans, our favorite punk band in Cleveland. We did not have a problem with those who were gay.

Frank was our friend and we convened every time we had a cigarette break. It would be Jim Darden, Russ, Frank and me.

We worried about Frank because it was obvious to us that Frank was gay and although we didn't care, the Army would care. This wasn't the era of "Don't ask, don't tell."

Frank used to look over his shoulder to examine his calves and announce how the running was going to make his calves look great when he got back to Phoenix.

Now I have to ask... we were in basic training and AIT – Advanced Infantry Training. Why would a gay man, especially an obviously gay man, enlist for infantry?

All three of us said, "Frank you have to be careful so you don't get caught."

Frank bragged about the guys he had sex with. Some one named Wolf.

In the barracks, every night, we had fire watch. That meant rotating shifts. You got woken up to pull your shift and for an hour, you roamed the bay in the barracks. Back and forth. Looking for a fire. I don't know... like if someone threw a lit cigarette into a garbage can or on an adjacent bunk. Well, it never happened.

Every night I had fire watch, as I passed by Frank, he slept in the nude. His wool blanket and sheets pulled off. I looked to see if he was awake. He looked asleep. But he had an erection. Was he awake and inviting anyone?

I've had gay friends who proudly say they have "gay-dar" – radar to detect other gay men. I don't know what the secret is. We all knew Frank was gay and we did not need a secret weapon like gay-dar. Lynn told me the same thing about her best friend Glenn Olson. She also knew without him saying so. That made him paranoid that he was giving off some signal.

I think it's like when you meet a trans person, it's no surprise that she identifies with female because you see the facial features. So sad the junk got switched in utero. I've had many trans friends who are ladies and look like ladies. I'm not sure I "get" the ones who look like Jackie Gleason and wear women's clothes and make up. Except the comedians. Oh, they are a riot.

Second Pass – off post

Jim Darden, Russ DeGigidio and I went to the main drag. Columbus Street. Decadence waited. We never asked Frank where he went.

We probably found some strip club and libations that intoxicated.

No, that's not true. A black prostitute named Chocolate approached us and offered us a fuck for $50 each. She provided the rubbers. I was third.

Strip clubs came next. They were all about pay money for a cocktail for your date.

Later in the Rangers, SGT Howard Mullen told me that in Korea, up around the DMZ, villages sent their daughters to have sex with soldiers. They brought in income to the family. It was a tradition. He said that any soldier with a Korean wife, married a prostitute. Unless she was a student in Soeul. I heard the same about the Philippines. The same about Thailand. The same about too many countries. The nickname is the world's oldest profession.

So I have to ask, why is there shame? Drop the legal argument. America has been cloaked in puritanical hypocrisy for too many years.

I knew I did something illegal. But was it morally wrong? Chocolate was a kind woman. I suppose I have to revisit this... she didn't do anything wrong. But did we by having sex with her? Yes -- because we used her as a means to an end. But I didn't learn that moral precept until I studied Immanuel Kant at CSU.

She was willing. That did not make it okay. It only meant that she complied for money.

Ranger Tab T-shirts

Russ and I bought Ranger Tab T-shirts and wore them. We were heading to the 1st Ranger battalion so we thought that was okay. **It was not.**

You don't wear credentials you have not earned. The Ranger Tab is more than a symbol. It represents an accomplishment that few achieve. It is earned, not issued. Shinsecki, are you listening? You are and remain a disgrace. The Ranger Black Beret was earned. Not issued. Marlin Maynard died for the right to wear it. You took it away. PFC Maynard died in Grenada in October, 1983.

Shinsecki was relieved of his command post of the VA. Thank God. So much has improved since then.

Wearing ranger tab t-shirts -- someone could have and should have kicked our asses. We were basic trainees and dumbasses.

After Ranger School class 10-81 a year later, I could say that I had orders that confirmed I was awarded the Ranger Tab and that I became a graduate of Ranger School. But that was a year later. Not in summer 1980.

I eventually had orders that confirmed I had the right to legally wear a ranger tab. That was August of 1981.

Grenade Range

Here's the thing... Qualification range. I wanted to do an overhand hook and wing it. Like a basketball.

The army wanted me to a forward thrust from the shoulder --- I think like a shot put. It was stupid. No one ever explained why the shot put was better than an overhand sling. But that was required to qualify with a grenade.

Tennis ball. Do you do an overhand swing or do you shot-put push it?

Is that so hard to figure out?

Cow Killer Ants

One day we were digging foxholes. These ants were everywhere. Black and orange. Like something that emerged from hell. They were Red Velvet Cow killer ants.

These things were scary.

First of all they were large. Hairy. Orange and Black. Google sez they are wasps.

Mitzi Terry

During Basic Training or AIT (advanced infantry training) Mitzi sent me two photos of herself. They were like photos from a modelling portfolio.

She wore black, which suited her. But one showed her skin of her torso down to just before her bosom.

Russell De Gidio said, "I get the one that shows more skin, because I slept with her." I don't know why. I gave that one to Russell.

The one I kept, I placed in a photo album. One of those peal the clear plastic and stick it to the surface. I kept it until 1985 or 1986. Michaela Becker was jealous. You will read about this in Berlin (unless I forgot it by then). She made me prove that she was my first priority by burning that photo. I torched my photo of Mitzi.

If I still had that photo today, I would frame it and hang it on my wall, because Mitzi was first and foremost, my friend.

Not my lover or my crush. Well, maybe a potential crush. Mark, Char and Lori would understand and agree.

Cedar Box & Carolyn Cola

I had a cedar box. I still have it. I used it for momentoes. Things that meant something. There was a page in my cedar box. When I was at Lake Catholic in the fall of 1978, Carolyn Cola was a freshman. I don't know why, but Carolyn thought enough of me to write a poem. The bunny taught me how worthless I was. Carolyn spoke otherwise. She handed me a note one day. My name was written in green ink (my favorite color). Vertically. She then wrote adjectives for each letter and followed it with why. Lise Stevens burned that note. She was jealous of a sentimental token.

Carolyn was a dear and a sweetheart. I would welcome her friendship any time.

Carolyn Cola… I wish I had looked at you differently. By the time you were eighteen, I was in West Berlin.

The Bet

Back to Basic Training and A.I.T. Russ and I made a bet. One would go further. The loser paid the other $50. Remember that. At the time, I considered it a sucker's bet. I knew Russ would go further, faster. But it was a gentlemen's agreement. We shook on it. That meant, I would uphold the agreement.

Transition from Basic Training to AIT in 1980

When you join the Army, you have reception. That means haircuts, getting uniforms and field equipment and cash to buy toiletries and cigarettes.

Then you have Basic Training. I think back then that basic was the same for all recruits that joined the Army. Physical Training (P.T.), running, road marching, drill and ceremony, bivouac and the M16.

AIT was advanced infantry training. We learned about mines, the gas chamber, grenade qualification range, qualifying with the M16 and automatic fire, digging a foxhole.

The first time SSG Malley brought out a box of C-rations, he tossed the box into the center of the group in our assembly area. There was enough for one box per person. They were "C-rations." But the boxes were labelled B-1, B-2, and B-3.

I don't recall which one I had. The box was labelled with the name of the main can. Beef with spiced sauce, Beans and meatballs, Ham and Egg. There were four cans and a condiment pack.

You got that "can one" was your main meal. Can two was your fruit (peaches, pears, fruit cocktail, apricots). Can three had candy and crackers. We loved "John Wayne bars." Two discs of chocolate and toffee. There were others but those were the only ones worth remembering.

Can four had cheese or peanut butter. For the crackers. Some cheese with caraway seeds which I loved because we ate sauer kraut growing up. Some c-rations had cake. Less fruit, more cake. Cake meant Pound Cake which was a rarity and the best. The others were chocolate nut roll, cinnamon nut roll and fruit cake.

Later on in Battalion (that means 1st Battalion Ranger), Stacy Nowak said he hated Beef with spiced sauce because he found a vein in it. I personally loved it because I would mix the canned peanut butter and add Tabasco and it tasted Thai.

That day in A.I.T., after we finished our c-rations, I thought, "okay, so that's what we'll survive on in combat. Now let's go to the mess hall and have a real lunch."

THAT was lunch. No mess hall today. The funny thing is that SSG Malley didn't tell us, that was lunch. He tossed the box and let us wonder in mystery. WTF? Are we getting lunch today? Are they going to starve us? What's this boxed c-rat crap?

Tear gas was called CS gas. We wore our protective masks in the chamber. Once the mask came off, you had to say your name, rank and social security number before the drill sergeant would let you leave.

I had a high tolerance for CS gas. I did not choke. I did compress my chest after reciting. It burned.

Outside the chamber, and I saw this after I was dismissed – guys were puking, guys were plugging one nostril and snorting out snot on one side, and then on the other side.

Sand Hill Barracks

The barracks were kept at 68 degrees Fahrenheit. Outside it was 110.

I caught pneumonia or something. When I woke up. I thought someone had dumped a bucket of water on me. My bunk was saturated. I woke up in a puddle. I was angry and accused those around me of dumping a bucket of water on me. It soon turned out, those befuddled looks were genuine. No one dumped water on me.

I sweated it out. I was in disbelief mode. That much water came out of me while I slept? It was a lot – the mattress was soaked.

Sick Call

In basic training and AIT, you did not go on sick call.

If you woke up and had a belly ache or a broken bone or a fractured skull, you were supposed to go on sick call. That meant, go see the medics. They would treat you or send you higher up the chain of command.

In Basic, it was made to be humiliating. The sick call troops would march passed the company.

The leader would do cadence, "Your left, right..." And the group would reply in high-pitched Mickey Mouse voices, responding, "Sick Call." How is that labelled, falsetto voices?

Basic training conditioned you... morning running cadence... "I wanna be an Airborne Ranger..." That was the goal. And I was scheduled to do just that. Become an Airborne Ranger. Who the fuck was I to think that I could reach that brass rail? Bunny taught me how worthless I was.

I don't know. Did I think I would coast on Russell's coat tails? He was the stud and I was the wannabe.

Private Fox

Fox. That was his last name. He gave me a sob-story about his family on a farm in Kansas.

I gave him $100. He promised to pay it back. He gave me his address in Kansas.

How naïve was I? I wrote to him. Said, "Hey remember me?" I don't want interest. I just want my $100 back. One day, I will find him and I will get it back.

Hear that, Fox?

Lynn tells me that I'm naïve. No question. She's right.

Graduation – five mile road march

I was fine with road marches. Running killed me. Partially because I smoked. But road marches were easy for me. So I would try to help other soldiers.

On the last qualifying road march, C. J. Jones was a very short black man. I marched by him and constantly encouraged him to keep up and hang in there.

I think I pissed him off because I was white and none of the other black soldiers were there to encourage him.

I was thinking, "Fuck that I'm white. That doesn't matter." In the end, C.J. made it. He may not ever give me credit for helping him complete the five-miler. I don't care. It wasn't about credit. It was about completing it together.

September 1980 -- Airborne School

Russell DeGidio, Richard Allen, Juan Espinosa and I were the ones who completed Basic and A.I.T. and were heading to the 1st Ranger Battalion after Airborne school. No leave until done.

Every morning of Airborne school, you had to pass inspection of your uniform. Clean and pressed fatigues and boots that were spit shined or acceptable. "Acceptable" meant that the boot blacks did them for you.

The boot blacks were these guys close to the barracks. You signed up and paid -- I think $20 a week -- and they did your boots. They always passed inspection. My roster number was written with a sharpie on the inside. I was 55. I think they used edge dressing from Kiwi and some combination of shoe polish. They were shiny, black like edge dressing. But it didn't crack off.

We all went to the boot blacks and turned in our leather boots to have them prepare the boots for inspection. When you turned in your boots the guys who were part of the crew were outside, shining boots.

They numbered your boots and we would drop them off and pick them up Friday night. Woe be to him who forgot to drop them off or pick them up on Friday. Monday was going to be torture… It was called the "Gig Pit." Relentless PT until most quit.

City Week – week 1

Airborne School -- City week had no training. Privates got sent around Benning for clean up. I was at the HQ for some group. Vacuuming. In Georgia, they call them palmetto bugs. They are huge-ass three-or- four-inch long cockroaches. Yeah we have them in Florida too.

We would have company formations before PT. We ran in fatigues and leather boots and white t-shirts. They called it the "Airborne Shuffle." Perhaps 15-minute miles. I could go all day doing those.

In front of the barracks, 1SG Laurendine would come out and swiggle a glass full of liquid and ice. And he'd say, "Gin is no sin." Probably ice water. We never knew. His job was the barracks and motivation. I thought he did both really well.

He was a great guy. I would later have audience with him during pathfinder. I was surprised that he was still there. Cherie Begnaud loved to call him "Top" and flirt with him. Airborne for me was September 1980. Pathfinder was May 1982.

Ground Week – week 2

Week two was Ground Week. Ground week, you were in the harness. Yes, aka the "Nut Crusher." It taught you to tighten the thigh straps as tight as you could. Otherwise, when the chute opened, you were going to experience a squeeze that would prevent any future children.

Part of ground week also included the 30-foot towers. The black caps would judge how you jumped out of the aircraft. There was a structure 30-feet high. They connected you to cables that used gravity to coast you to a berm about 200 meters away.

You jumped out and dangled along cables that carried you to a mound. There fellow classmate "caught you." That meant stopped you from swinging out and in reverse, coasting back out.

For the female officers (back then there were no female enlisted), we were required to say, "Spread 'em, Maam." About the legs – so we could halt the swing.

Tower week week 3

The first time I went through tower week, they recycled me. I don't know why and can't tell you what I did wrong.

Tower week was supposed to involve the 250-foot towers. I never got hoisted.

Perhaps they had quotas. Dart board selection. I was recycled and had to repeat Tower week.

Tower Week second time

I was Tango Niner. Tango stood for Tower.

The James Woods character was my new roommate. He looked like James Woods. But wasn't the same.

He was the one having sex with a male lieutenant and huffing edge dressing.

I washed my fatigues by hand at night and hung them out the window to dry before morning inspection. Inevitably, one night we had strong winds. My uniform that HAD to pass inspection was on the ground three floors down. I got it before someone swiped it.

Tower week step #2 and Jump week, I had a new room-mate. He was opportunistic. I did not agree with his moral code. He told me about going out with a male lieutenant. My roommate was enlisted. He looked like James Woods with acne scars on his face. He huffed edge dressing and bragged about getting fucked by a 1LT. He said, "Come on... He buys me things."

I didn't have an issue with him having sex with a guy. My initial reaction was you need to be more careful who you tell this to. Most would not be okay. But huffing? He had no future nor caution. He might as well have said, "I want brain damage."

Tower week was with the 250-foot towers.

In 1999 we were told that they were retired.

The towers had huge rings. An open parachute hooked in. The jumper was attached.

There were chants of "Hit the hole, Pole man, stick it in." That referred to a pole that attached the chute from a central point to the center of the drop ring.

The ring would raise up and snap and the dangler would be released. The idea was to steer to the ground. Without steering into the tower...

One guy steered into the tower. The chute collapsed against the tower, he clung to it for dear life. Black caps were in a panic mode. The student was an idiot.

I really wanted to do the 250 – foot towers. They looked like fun.

Instead, I did not pass Tower week. I don't know why. Maybe they had a quota of how many had to fail. I became Tango-Niner. That meant that I was a "recycle of Tower week" – hence the Tango for Tower.

Jump week

I had a bandage on my arm that never got noticed. I was lucky.

Russ went on to Jump week along with Richard Allen and Juan Espinosa. We four were supposed to go from Basic to the Rangers. I became the stag along.

1980 -- Airborne Wings Tattoo

Friday night after successfully completing Tower week, I went to Sailor Bill's tattoo and got my first. Right arm just below the shoulder. Airborne Wings with "AIRBORNE" written below it. My paternal grandfather had a military tattoo. Therefore, so would I. It was just under the right sleeve of my t-shirt.

Monday morning of Jump week... here's the rub. You don't get an Airborne tattoo until you're qualified. You're not qualified until you've completed five jumps.

I was not qualified.

And for PT during jump week, men ran bare chested. I did not know this.

I thought, I'm screwed. If they tear off the bandage, and see the tattoo, I'm seriously fucked. They will dog me until I quit. Then I'll have this badge of shame forever.

Somehow, thank God, I went through Jump week and no one questioned the bandage, no one lifted the bandage and saw. I completed my five jumps and graduated.

11 SEPT 1980 – Graduation from Airborne School.

1SG Laurendine came out and did the blood wings for me.

Here is what that means... the metal Airborne insignia that attaches to your uniform, it has these little spikes like a thumb tack. Once it pierces your uniform, you secure it with what we called "Dammits." They were called that because you lost them too often. Without attaching the dammits, the little spikes were over your heart. To get blood wings, the person who pinned the wings on your uniform would then punch you hard to drive the spikes into your chest. 1SG Laurendine gave me my Jump Wings.

Interestingly enough, he was still the 1SG when I went back in 1982 for Pathfinder school, because Cheri Begnaud sat on his desk and called him "Top."

Cheri comes into this story later. She was a private bound to Kansas as a medic. She was in Airborne School when I was going through Pathfinder School.

Taxi to Atlanta Airport

I should have studied.

I graduated Airborne school on a Friday. I had already made my plane reservation for Delta.

This was fucked up. Years before the internet. I reserved a flight over the phone. I would pay cash on arrival.

I was in Columbus. One hundred and eight miles to Atlanta.

I offered the taxi driver all the cash I had except what I needed for the plane ticket. He said it wasn't enough. I offered my boom box. It was worth about $100. He accepted that.

He said look me up when you're back.

I said I would. I never did.

Bill De Gedio picked me up at Clevo Hopkins

Things worked out. I had enough for the plane ticket and flew to Cleveland.

Bill picked me up.

We sat at his kitchen table and drank black tower white wine. Bill's uncle was making calamari.

Martha Alexy

Martha Alexy... I wanted to marry her.

Russ De Gedio fucked it all up. His lies led to our break up.

I still have the unicorn tattoo.

There was this Dancer in Savannah...

Savannah had dancers and strippers. The strippers took off their clothes. The dancers would dance. Horney soldiers knew not a difference. I appreciated art. I was still a horney soldier. Make no mistakes about that.

Some years later, I was talking to a stripper in Savannah. In fairness, she was a dancer. She could dance. Yes, it was without her clothes. Panties stayed. But she was a great dancer.

Her body had stretch marks on her belly and thighs and her breasts were small and hung to the sides. But I liked her because she was smart and sassy and funny.

Strippers knew that if any one of them would have hinted, do you want to have sex with me? The ranger like a puppy would have followed her all over. But there was never that hint. It was a game of waiting in anticipation that the hint may follow. It never followed.

In the Rangers, strippers were the friends of the rangers... Savannah had yuppies who would not give us the time of day. And strippers who appreciated our generosity and our time. And our dollar bills. Let's be honest. Pay me five bucks for a three minute song and I'll entertain your story.

Back to the dancer -- we talked about blood wings because in her realm, it meant performing cunnilingus on a woman during her period. She was very bi. She proudly bragged about having black blood wings, gold blood wings, white blood wings, red blood wings and brown blood wings. She beat me five to two.

For the record, I never had a sex with a stripper. That was not an unwillingness. There were just no offers.

Stupid me... I always thought the best of people. I met a stripper at a club in Savannah and she told me she was cold. I put my Schott's leather jacket on her. After she said, "I'll be right back," I never saw her again. She stole a $150 leather jacket.

Naïve asshole.

Back in Cleveland, 1980

Just after Airborne school in September of 1980, I had 30 days of leave in Cleveland. Most of it I spent with Bill DeGidio and Martha Alexy. But initially I was stranded at Fort Benning. I needed to get to the Atlanta Airport.

To get there, I did not know where to go. I needed a plane ticket. I had just enough cash for a plane ticket. But what was left over was not enough for a cab to take me to Atlanta.

I went to the cab station and asked the driver if he would take me and another graduate to the Atlanta airport. It was a two-hour trip for about 110 miles.

I offered the cabbie my boom box as part of the barter. He asked me to look him up next time in Columbus. I only had enough cash remaining for the plane ticket. After that I was broke.

Bill De Gidio picked me up at Hopkins airport.

September Leave, 1980

I do not recall that leave. Was that when Russ ruined everything between Martha and me? He did eventually.

22 SEPT 1980 -- Back to Fort Stewart, Georgia

I had orders reporting to Fort Stewart in Hinesville, Georgia. Fort Stewart still had WWII barracks up on stilts. It was home to the 24th Infantry Division (which we called the Two by Four). Mechanized infantry. They rolled around in APCs, armored personnel carriers. Rolling coffins. We called them that because we trained to kill them. "We" meaning "A.T." – Anti Tank. The section I would join in the Rangers.

Upon arrival at Fort Stewart, I had CQ duty which was an all-night shift (charge of quarters) answering the phones and watching television. Back then there was only one station that ran all night. You were stuck with whatever they offered.

There was one night, a warrant officer was on duty. When he came in, I stood at attention and saluted him. I did not call the others to attention which I should have done, but I did not know better. I learned that night that warrant officers are cool. He raised his index finger and waived it back and forth and said don't wake them.

He and I had a great conversation about all the helicopter pilots I was going to meet.

Hinesville was as red neck as you could get. I did luckily find a bookstore and bought several of Robert E Howard's Conan the Barbarian books. I would later share them with the platoon. We did that. Books in the field. Our cargo pants had pockets on the side. Books fit in easily.

Eric Van Lustbader's "the Ninja." That was the first I recall.

Eventually Fort Stewart bussed me to Savannah and Hunter Army Airfield.

R. I.P. – Then Aco 1/75 RGR

RIP was Ranger Indoctrination Program. All privates from E-01 to Specialist class four (E-04) went through RIP. Were you tough enough to make it? That was the question.

Aco 1/75 RGR -- that's Alpha Company, First Battalion, 75th Infantry, Rangers.

Russ had graduated from Airborne a week earlier than me and so he was already at RIP (Ranger Indoctrination Program). At 2nd platoon.

RIP was for the purpose of attrition. Weed out those who would fall to the way side. It could last three weeks. It could last six months. Those who failed were sent to the two by four. 24th Infantry Division of Fort Stewart, Georgia.

29 OCTOBER 1980 -- Ranger Indoctrination Program (R.I.P.)

The NCOIC was called the Commandant. I learned pretty quickly that all or most NCOs were Vietnam vets and officers ranked Captain and above were also Vietnam vets. They found a safe haven in the rangers. They could train men "old school" and no consequences. That meant, if you fucked up, it was simple. You got your ass beat. But you never made that same mistake twice. It was highly effective.

In RIP, we built an obstacle course and a rappel tower. Perhaps you've seen photos of military personal carrying telephone poles on their shoulders? It's not limited to Navy SEALs. We did that. Or I should say, those of us who could, did.

In RIP, we did PT in the morning. But eventually, we did PT twice a day. Morning and before dinner.

Sometimes we had the evening free to explore the base. Not Savannah. Just Hunter Army Airfield. That meant the PX and the Post theater. Russ and I went to the post theatre and watched "From Here to Eternity" with Montgomery Clift and Burt Lancaster. The post theater played the national anthem before each movie. All audience members would rise and place the right hand over your heart. The theater in Fort Benning didn't play the national anthem and I wondered why.

I don't remember the guy's name. He'd been in RIP for six months trying to get to battalion. The cadre announced he was going to the two by four. They apologized and said in six months, you can apply to come back. He was sad but not without hope. I never saw him again.

Mid-October 1980, they called our names to be transferred to Battalion. Russ and I and Juan Espinosa were assigned to Alpha Company. Richie Allen who was with us in Basic, AIT, Airborne and RIP was going to Bravo. Richie would later become a Captain in the Brooklyn NYPD.

Russell told me that Richie joined the rangers to learn to kill so he could take vengeance on the guy who killed his brother. Russell told a lot of hyperboles. I never asked Richie if that was true. After all, the source was Russell.

Non-Sequitor

The cavitron emits sound when used. It's the dental instrument used to clean teeth of plaque and tartar. It sounds like high pitched whining. It sounds like pulsing frequency.

In Mentor, growing up with the dental office inside the home, the cavitron's sound became feared like the buzzing of bees in a hive. The sound triggered fear that pain was coming.

It took me several years to realize the sound of the cavitron was nearly identical to the tinnitus that I acquired from the M67 ninety millimeter recoilless rifle. My beloved bazooka. That sound would remain with me permanently. It's with me now as I write this.

Graduation from RIP

When we arrived at Alpha company, they lined us up. I was the tallest. They looked at me and said, "You're going to be a ninety gunner." They laughed. Like it were a punishment. And I was sent to Weapons platoon.

This is told about "they." It occurred to me I never knew who "they" were. They wore the ranger tab and they made decisions. I was an insignificant private newbie.

Russ De Gidio went to second platoon. Juan Espinosa was eleven Charlie -- that meant mortars. He also went to Weapons Platoon.

Richie Allen was sent to Bravo Company.

Was Pogenpohl with our RIP class then? Perhaps. He went to second platoon, Alpha Company.

We rarely knew first names. Your first name was Private, or Specialist or Sergeant. No Ralphs or Giddy or Toms. That's from some song.

After R.I.P.

In October of 1981, arriving at Battalion, my uniforms were all sterile. That meant, no patches. No last name, no US Army, no ranger scroll, no airborne. They were supposed to be turned in during RIP to have the patches sewn on. I suppose my three weeks at RIP were too short to get that memo.

SGT Randall H. "Andy" Anderson volunteered to sew the patches on... he had a sewing machine. Who has a sewing machine in the Army?

I was grateful. I stayed up very late attempting to spit shine my jungle boots. Tomorrow was supposed to be spit shines and starches. Andy brought me one piece with patches sewn. I starched. Who had starch, an iron and an ironing board?

Starches meant a uniform that was starched. Army standard was extreme. They would starch your uniform and it would come back like cardboard. That's how the post dry cleaners did them. I think S-4 (Supply) issued each of us six sets of camouflage fatigues. Two were dedicated to being starches. Four were field uniforms. All had patches sewn on. Field uniforms could have tears (tears in fabric, not lacrymose tears) that were sown back together with zigzag stitching from a sewing machine. That strengthened the already durable rip-stop cammies. The field fatigues eventually looked like Frankenstein. At that point, you could "DX" them at S-4. "DX" meant direct exchange. Turn in an old piece of TA50 and get a brand new one. TA-50 was the generic term we used to describe field gear. The LCE (load carrying equipment – pistol belt, Shoulder straps, and two ammo pouches and two Canteen connections. In the rangers we had an extra ammo pouch. It held the signal mirror and tabasco sauce. We also had the sterile dressing pouch and a pouch for your compass and another for your flashlight.

Weapons Platoon was AT (anti-tank), Mortars, and those other guys who talked to satellites.

AT trained with the M67 90 millimeter recoilless rifle ("my ninety"). It was a bazooka that fired an anti-tank round with a shape charge. Point initiated, base detonated missile that bore a hole in the hull of a tank and released its blast inside. It also fired an anti-personnel round with 2400 flachettes. Little inch-long arrows. Ninety gunners wore them in our patrol caps in the back where the name tag was sewed on. One in each corner.

We also trained with the M67 Dragon. This was a wire-guided missile system. My first attempt on a "live" moving target, I got a direct hit. It was hard because you're looking through the scope and meanwhile you've got this projectile bouncing left and right and up and down in front of you. But you have to stay locked in on the target.

In 1980, AT had SGT Childers, SGT Andy Anderson, CPL Craig Riley, PFC David Bazemore, PFC Ronnie Carle, PFC Rick Knight (aka Knightro), PFC Ross McVey, PVT Bryant (who would go AWOL) and me.

Mortars had SGT Dale Kennedy, SGT Tony Lewis, Danny Doyle, Scott Owen, Doug Droesch, Juan Espinosa, Mike Passmore, Michael Gonzales, Paul Teigland, Huck Anderson and Tiny Adkins.

The other group... SGT Howard "Song Jong Moe" Mullen, Eric Stahl and Stacy Nowak.

Our training was broken down like this: qualify for the Expert Infantryman's Badge (which I got as a private, E-02), patrolling – I was assigned as the 90 gunner for second platoon, and special operations aka special ops.

Patrolling meant conducting raids and ambushes behind enemy lines. My Ninety (M67) initiated the attack.

Special Ops meant we'd roll off the C-130 in a gun jeep and secure a location around the airport. We didn't know it then, but this was all prep for Grenada in October 1983.

Perhaps the first night or the second night in the platoon, Rick Knight and Craig Riley were in charge of instructing me to prepare my field gear.

Rangers call tie-down 550 cord. It's the same that's used for parachutes. I think 550 meant tensil strength. How much weight before it snapped.

The pistol belt was attached to the straps that hung off your shoulders. How it was attached was with metal clips. We removed the metal clips and replaced the clips with 550 cord. The pistol belt had two ammo pouches, two canteens, a compass pouch, and a pouch for the sterile dressing. They were attached with clips. But the clips were reinforced with sections of 550 cord tied with a square knot. Long ends were burned short with a lighter.

The flashlight, one D size battery was always turned upside down. It saved on the life span and ensured it would not accidentally come on during a jump. Ranger flashlights had a white filter (never used), a red filter for signaling, a blue filter for checking eyes at night for scratches (the scratch would appear purple), and an IR filter for use when night observation devises (NODs) were being used.

We bought (at our own expense) brand new TA50 that was kept clean and new in the storage closet. Before an inspection, we used edge dressing – normally for our starched boots – on all the metal parts of the pistol belt.

The rooms were two bunks, two storage lockers, a book shelf. Two rooms shared a bathroom with a shower and toilet and a door leading to the storage closet for TA50.

The brand new TA50 was for the Inspector General. The "IG."

The IG was a joke. We saw that the first time, when my gun team was tasked with building a defensive fighting position on the right hand side of the road for a head on attack of a Russian tank. First off, the strongest armor was on the front. Secondly if we were to attack from the front, it would be on the left side of the road. Lastly, a flank shot or rear shot would be the most effective. The evaluator took off points because we were on the right side of the road where they told us to dig.

We told the idiot. He ignored us. Army. Worse in Berlin I would learn.

Preparations for the IG were ludicrous. We polished, buffed and shined the tile hallways with Johnson's Turtle Wax. The sink in the bedroom had to pass the q-tip inspection. Swab up and around and no black debris could be attached to the q-tip. It was that intense.

Rangers felt invaded by Legs who would judge us. We stifled anger, disdain, contempt and rage. I kept hearing, "Fucking Legs… who the fuck are they to judge us?" But I digress…

SGT Hall

In charge of Weapons platoon was SGT Michael Hall.

Context. All the other platoon sergeants in the rangers were SFC (sergeant first class, E-07) and Vietnam vets. SGT Hall was an E-05. But he was so squared away. If someone said he saw him walking on water, I'd believe it.

We did most of our training at Fort Stewart aka Camp Swampy from the Beetle Bailey comics. Fort Stewart was brutal. Monday, you got eaten alive by mosquitoes. Tuesday, you were so coated with sweat and dirt, you didn't feel or notice the mosquitoes.

It was nothing to do a ten-mile road march and then spend all night patrolling.

Ruck sack run - 1980

One day, perhaps in November of 1980, PT uniform was cammies, jungle boots, ruck sacks. We were going on a ruck sack run. We turned around at the 2-1/2 mile mark (I think?). On the way back, at about a mile from the barracks, Juan Espinosa started to fall out. His NCOs were brutal, screaming at him. "Is this what you would do if we were in combat?" I wanted to fall back. But I didn't dare. Not hearing what they said to Juan.

Once we reached the company AO (area of operation), SGT Hall called us to quick time and we marched to the barracks. When he said "Fall out," I collapsed. I don't recall if I feinted or passed out. All I remember was Tony Lewis carrying me in his arms to the barracks. When I opened my eyes, he said, "Welcome to the Ranger Battalion."

Winters in Fort Stewart were cold dropping to 17 degrees. We wore the field jacket liner underneath the cammy jacket. Somehow it sufficed. We had black leather gloves. Most rangers cut off the finger tips. Tolerated the cold for manual dexterity.

My comrade and friend Russell De Gidio

Everything came easy to Russell De Gidio. He was a natural. I thought he would be the better ranger. He ran better than me. As I recall he qualified expert the first time with the M-16. I only got sharpshooter in Basic because they told us – if you were right -handed, you use the right eye. If you were left-handed, use the left eye. I was right -handed, or maybe ambidextrous... The rangers taught me that I needed to use which ever eye was my stronger eye. That was my left. And I scored expert every time after that.

Perhaps Russ would win the bet. If either one of us quit, the victory went to the other. That was clear.

Aco 1/75th

Training in the Rangers was just as hard as what I would learn in Ranger School. The difference is that in the Ranger Battalion, you got breaks, you got more sleep and more food.

1st Ranger Battalion had "celebrities" (as far as Rangers are concerned).

Sergeant E-05 Mike Hall would eventually rise up the ranks and become the Command Sergeant Major of the Ranger Regiment. He was the Alpha Company Weapons Platoon Sergeant.

Don Lamica was "allegedly" a Rhodesian Merc, Don Purdy was a Vietnam Vet, Gary Carpenter served in Aco/75th Rangers, Bill Acebes, Gil Berg (Aka General Greb, the OPFOR Commander) and CSM Schalavin.

CSM Shalavin would approach you and say, "Ohh Ah Ranger – You my hero."

In 1980, CPT Rice was the Aco commanding officer. The troops called him "The Fly" because morning PT was smoking. Rangers said, smoked to describe if you got pushed past your limit during training or PT. Or they said, someone can't bring no "P" on me. I'm not sure what the capital P represented. Mark Ross taught me that with his Ranger School story of SSG Stuckey and Ranger Urine and Ranger Nate from Aco/75th at Fort Hood, Texas.

Our First Sergeant was 1SG Stanley Fox. Everyone loved 1SG Fox. In Panama, he told me that the jungle reminded him of Vietnam. I only had brief encounters with him like for the Soldier of the Quarter board. SGT Hall sent me to those. SGT Hall thought more highly of me than I thought of myself. I think I realized that due to writing this book.

November 15, 1980

My first promotion was to Private E-02. They called it mosquito wings.

Schott's Black Leather Jacket

Some point in the fall of 1980, I went to the Oglethorpe mall and bought a Schott's Black Leather jacket. It was so punk.

Back in Cleveland in winter leave 1980, Bill DeGedio said it was great. His wife Barb said, he thought it was great because it was the same leather that he has. You flattered him. I didn't know that. It was just the most punk jacket in the store.

Christmas 1980

I was briefly home on leave. Family had not seen me since May. Christmas morning, I actually had presents which I was not expecting. I remember the whiskey bottle shaped like a canteen.

I went to see a former waitress from Bob Evans and her husband. I gave it to them as a present. I told Bunny I slipped on the ice in their driveway and dropped it and it broke on the asphalt.

The other present I remember was a polaroid camera.

Martha Alexy and I took nude photos of each other wearing my black leather jacket. Martha kept all the photos.

Further on that Leave – December 1980

Doug Enkler and I would depart Mentor and head downtown. I drove my parents' Dodge Econoline brown van. It had removable seats in the back. On this night, the seats were gone.

I think it may have been New Year's Eve. The ranger battalions rotated that.

Doug and I stopped for a six pack. I recall it was Michelob. Doug bought a National Enquirer that had John Lennon's photo – he had been recently murdered. I had a goofy photo of Doug making a face with the tabloid next to his head. Empty michelob bottles were thrown out. A sin to litter but Ohio had the open container law.

Doug and I visited a bar called the "Top Hat." I had forgotten the name but Doug remembered it when we spent the night talking when I worked for BP in the 1990s.

There was a white woman in the bar. Average looks. I assumed she was for rent. I asked what it would cost to spend the night with her. She said $500. I wanted to wake up with a woman in my arms. But I did not have that kind of money.

I know I was supposedly with Martha Alexy, but I didn't know if she was committed. Russell had been filling her head with lies.

I realized after so many years in the Army, that the Army taught me loneliness like I'd never known before.

But at age 59, I realize, I experienced that loneliness in the Army but it wasn't the Army's fault. The Army did not create the condition of loneliness. I was simply lonely because I was alone. But so were the other guys. That fact bonded us. We didn't have a woman who loved us and gave us sex, but we had each other as comrades. Perhaps that's why the bond is so strong.

My Army brothers helped. They gave me comraderie. But with women, I did not have sex (that's first) and I did not have intimacy. Reverse that.

I longed for intimacy that would have included sex as a result or bi product.

Then again, the white woman at the Top Hat may not have even been a prostitute and was just providing a hyperbolic astronomical figure to indicate that she wasn't available to rent. I'll never know.

And if I had $500? Well I didn't so it's not an option.

Made me think of something else...

You might think your buddy's girl friend is hot and sexy. But when they break up, he talks about how the sex was. When he says, she laid there enduring it while staring at the ceiling until it was over. My best buddy in Cleveland in 1997 told me that. That's so sad. How does a woman in love with you do that? I think Michaela did that.

Unless, "Love" is a word and not an emotion.

Two sides to every coin? I suppose I have to tell her side next.

Doug wrote in a letter, "you know in your heart you will fuck her." He meant Darla – Matt's ex.

Never occurred to me but oh how that pissed Karen off when she read all the letters from Doug.

Details... Karen found all my letters from Doug Enkler and read them.

Karen, you had no right and I am convinced you stole my grandfathers's civil war bayonet. Oh, and you're the screamer by the way. Of anger, not passion.

Lisa was the cheater, with her so-called stalker boyfriend. Ashley was collateral damage.

Monica was the moaner. Tim Funjar gave us the seal of approval. Her tats and piercings made her fully divine.

I called her Moanica. She had so many piercings on her labia and clitoral hood that it hurt my teeth. The rings were constantly banging around.

Women who pierce everything around there, I want to know what is the goal?

Bolts in the nipples, and bolts in the hood that protects the clitoris. Do they enhance or hinder pleasure? I'm asking because I don't know. I'd like to know. More I'd like to know why.

She told me I was good because I gave her three orgasms when she was drunk.

Ranger List Server

This part jumps ahead to the 1990s.

Stephen "Peter" Parker aka Spiderman started the list server in the 1990s. It brought rangers together from Darby's rangers to Vietnam to what became known at the "Batt Boys" to the regiment.

List server. I learned in reverse order. A ranger committed suicide. He had no connections.

Ranger Parker was an IT guy and said that's not okay with me. He created a listserver. This was in the 1990s. I subscribed. I started getting emails from rangers from 2nd battalion, from Vietnam ranger companies, and even from Earl who was a Darby Ranger in World War II.

If I sent an email, it was replicated to all who subscribed. Anyone who sent an email, it went out to all.

This was cool. It brought rangers together who may not have ever met.

It also gave scumbags an avenue in.

He called himself, Fred "Boom Boom" Jackson. At first he was a hero. He told me he trained Mike Hall a newbie in his platoon. He claimed all kinds of merits… RAF, Green Berets,…

He once told us that he pulled a woman and her child from a burning car and handed her a ranger coin.

We all went, "Aww, shit – that is so cool."

Years later, we learned that Fred Jackson was a fake, a fraud.

He made it all up.

He got DX-ed from the first batt when he was a private and sent to the two by four.

A second batt ranger told me a great story about then 1SG Shalavin through the list server. I expect an email to say, "Iggy, that was me! How can you say you forgot my name?"

1SG Shalavin was the "prisoner" (in the exercise) to be extracted. The NCO telling the story said he cleared the room and said, "First sergeant, get up – we have to get out of here."

Shalavin said, "But mah feet are tired."

"I don't give a damn about your tired feet. We gotta get out of here."

He had a strong accent. Hungarian as I recall.

He said, "No. You don't understand me. My feet are tied." His feet were bound, roped up and tied together.

Anyone who knew 1SG or CSM Shalavin, knew his accent. And knew why this would be funny.

Shalavin went through Malaysian tracking school. He went out deer hunting with two rangers from Aco. At one point he said, turn around, the deer is behind us.

Back to 1980…

Citizens and Southern Bank

All the Rangers had their accounts with this bank. There was this one teller. She was very pretty. A normal girl or young woman. She knew I was a ranger. I came to the bank wearing a t-shirt that said, "What's on a man's mind." The illustration was of Sigmund Freud, but over his head was a nude woman. She didn't like that.

What made me laugh is this: When I went back in 2014 for the 40th Anniversary of the 1st Ranger Battalion, she was still in

Savannah, she approached me and made me realize that she was the same teller. I thought that she thought I was a scoundrel. But she remembered me in terms of endearment. She actually liked me but never let on.

Imagine that… A Savannah woman who deemed a ranger a human being. I would have asked her on a date.

Barber Shop 1981

Not far from post there was this barber shop. We were expected to get hair-cuts every week. And this barber shop was the "favorite" among rangers. I questioned why after my first visit.

I have to ask -- why did / do Georgia southern folk in the 1980s and beyond view Black folk as beneath them? I saw Georgia Black folks in shacks of corrugated steel in Macon. It depressed me. No human should live like that.

Barber shop… I was there this one day. A Saturday. I think Marcus Brown was in the chair at the time. But it could have been any Ranger – who happened to be black.

I'm from the generation of calling black men and woman, "Black." African American came out in the 1990s. I use that identifier. My mom used "coloreds" and "negroes." My father – the Bunny -- used the N-word. So did many racist assholes.

After Marcus left, the barber turned to the rest of us (who happened to be all white) and said, "When will y'all get those colored boys out of your unit.?"

This was not Selma Alabama in 1968. This was Savannah Georgia n 1981. All rangers got up and left that barber shop and never returned. Rangers were not racists. Southern Georgians were. Not all but most. Tony Lewis was from Georgia. I heard that the barber had to declare bankruptcy. Aww shucks.

I hope so. Savannah was filled with rednecks, poor black families and yuppies. That was a new term in 1980. Young Urban Professionals. Good company for West Pointers.

On Sunday nights, I ended up as the "barber" who could do ranger haircuts without them looking like barracks cuts. Every Sunday night, in the laundry room. HHC – second floor.

Privates were sent to supply or otherwise fucked with

In Weapons platoon, we called the troops in first, second, and third platoon the Line doggies.

"It" didn't happen in Weapons platoon. But we heard about it.

"It" was when squad leaders would send privates to S-4 (supply) for bull shit items. "A box of grid squares." "A can of Squelch." "Riser grease."

The NCOs in the line companies also tested the new privates. To be Koala-fied and inch-worm tested. Koala-fied meant being grabbed and forced to be attached to a tree upside down. Like a koala bear. Inch-worm meant being in your sleeping bag with the zipper pulled all the way up and only your head showing and you had to crawl like an inch worm across the hall of the barracks.

I thought the supply runs were funny and a good prank to pull. I did not agree with Koala or inchworm.

Luckily, my platoon never sent me on such an errand.

IV Training by our platoon medic

One day we were doing IV training with Doc Carmody. He was our medic. SGT Mike Hall called for a volunteer to receive the IV. Before I responded he said, "Ross, come up here." Lots of guys were fearful of needles. Not me.

I forget how he phrased it, but he basically told Doc Carmody to find an old hole in my veins.

Punk Rockers from Cleveland were ALL suspected of being junkies. I only mainlined three times with what we called crank. No junkie here. Had I stayed in Cleveland, I could have become one sooner or later. Crank was later called crystal meth. A huge hit on the show, "Breaking Bad."

Back in Basic or AIT, there were so many innoculations. Some of them used an "air gun" – that's what they called it. If the private flinched, it dug a gash horizontally across the bicep. Some guys behind the line waiting their turn would faint after seeing the bloody gash. I saw them feint. That was sad. But it was also funny.

Ranger Training

We were stationed at Hunter Army Airforce Base in Savannah. Most of our training took place at Fort Stewart around Hinesville, GA. Fort Stewart swamps were nasty. Biting Bug infested. Avon's "skin so soft" was the best bug juice.

We did patrolling which was either training to conduct raids or ambushes. They were squad, platoon or company size. We did live fire and demo training.

During live fire, we wore patrol caps – not steel pots. "Because that's how it would be in real combat." SGT Mike Hall said that. Years later we switched to steel pots because the Army said so.

I saw gradual recessions taken out of Mike Hall's hands, because some Army or DOD official said so. Mike was and always will be a professional.

I liked demo training. SGT Hall taught us we could heat our c-rations with C-4. SGT Hall said, it will heat at high intensity. Just don't step on it. It's the compression that will cause it to explode.

Demo training taught me about det cord and time fuse. Blasting caps could be replaced with det cord – six wraps.

We also did special operations training. That meant securing an airfield. I have to ask Mike how much of this -- 40 years later -– is still classified.

We had a term called OPSEC – Operations Security. Loose lips sink ships.

We trained for Grenada for years before it happened.

SGT "Name escapes me" – not in the 1982-1983 yearbook -- we were out in a gun jeep -- ¼ ton jeep -- and Specialist class four (SP4) Sean Kelly was in the driver's seat. He said, "put it in 2nd gear and release the clutch and take us over this hill." We were on a berm. Six feet tall. Pretty steep incline.

Sean tried three times and stalled each time. The NCO said, "Ross, you get in the driver's seat." I climbed in and then he said, "start it in 1st gear."

Sean shouted "What? That's not fair. What the fuck?"

I put it in first and travelled over the berm. The NCO was fucking with Sean. Sean invited being fucked with. Not because anyone wanted to be mean to Sean. We all loved the guy. It was because his reactions to being fucked with were so damn funny. Perhaps reading it does not do it justice. Hearing it made it hilarious.

Saturday morning cartoons. 1968-1970, there was a show called the Banana Splits Adventure Hour. It featured these guys in costume who were a rock band. Fleegle (a dog), Drooper (a lion), Bingo (a gorilla) and Snorky (an elephant). Fleegle was Paul Winchell. He was a famous ventriloquist. He followed in the footsteps of Edgar Bergman. It was directed by Richard Donner who would later do the Lethal Weapon movies with

Mel Gibson and Danny Glover. Sid and Marty Kroft were involved. The four characters would move to King's Island in Cincinnati.

They did slap stick and played songs. The opening song was Tra-la-la. There was another called "when my beautiful calliopa saxophia tromba rhythma clara basa trombo phone plays." Fleegle the dog character had this huge machine.

The banana splits featured live action and cartoons. "Danger Island" – Uh-oh Chongo, it's danger island!" was live action. Then they had the Arabian Knights. A cartoon by Hanna-Barbera. Shari Lewis was one of the voices (I love google). She was princess Nida.

They were Prince Turhan, Princess Nida, Farik the magician, Raseem the Strong, Zazuum, the donkey who could turn into a mini-tornado, and Bez the shape-shifter.

Sean Kelly would copy Bez's line and say, "Size of a –" which initiated the change to the animal named. It was a great series but sadly only lasted for eighteen episodes. Ironically, it was a show that featured muslim heroes. As kids, we never cared nor questioned. I can't imagine a cartoon appealing today with muslim heroes. Isn't that sad? Back then, we knew what Arabian or Persian described, but no one would connect the adjective with muslim or islam. We knew Aladdin and Ali Baba. But not Allah. Or Al-Queada or Taliban or hezbollah or Isis. I have ranger friends today who hate all Islamic muslims. I don't get that. In Cleveland I have friends. They happen to be muslim. It was never an issue. We met in college at Cleveland State or as neighbors at CSU.

Sean Kelly became my good, really good friend. He was a friggin riot. Some would call him nuts. I didn't.

When we had company formations – starch if in garrison, field fatigues if going out to Fort Stewart. Sean would come and scream or yell – however you classified it - "BAWK – BE – BAWK Bawk-Bawk,… it's Chicken Man!"

It was Sean. No one ever questioned what the fuck.

Other times he would come out and say, "Let's talk about… ANAL SEX!"

It seemed like the more shocking the better.

One day he came out and said, "Size of a YAK" and clapped his hands together. I got the reference. Perhaps the others did too. Or perhaps they wrote it off as another Sean Kellyism. It was a reference to Bez from the Arabian Knights.

Expert Infantryman's Badge (E.I.B.)

By this time in 1980, it was five years since the Vietnam war ended. There were no wars. No combat ribbons or awards to earn. The E.I.B. was a big deal. There were two levels. EIB and CIB. CIB was Combat Infantryman's badge and you only got that if you were in combat.

All rangers aspired to earn the EIB only because the CIB was not an option.

One part of qualifying was the land navigation test. Day and Night.

I failed the day land nav and passed the night.

Here's why. You follow an azimuth for 500 meters. Your pace count is 55 (that was mine – every 55 steps with my left foot was 100 meters). During the day… one time I looked up and there was a snake dangling from a tree branch at eye level. The serpent was staring me right into my eyes.

Next stop, there was a spider as big as my hand. In a web right in front of me.

Mind you… Spiders and snakes do not bother me. Unless they "surprise" me.

I retook the land day portion and passed.

During the test, you're required to follow the compass azimuth, but also to turn toward a new azimuth after so many meters. The method of determining how far you've gone is based on your pace count. Mine was fifty-five. It's different for each person because it's based on the length of your leg. When my left boot hit the ground 55 times, that was 100 meters.

To qualify for the E.I.B., the hardest part was supposedly call for fire. I found that to be the easiest. I earned my EIB as a Private E-02. Sean Kelly was so pissed off at me.

I really did not want to piss off Sean. He was my friend. Sean had to wait until the next time around and then he got it.

Fort Stewart Nights

Beetle Bailey comics in the newspapers took place in "Camp Swampy." That was Fort Stewart, Georgia.

The first night at Fort Stewart, in the swamps, you could count on being eaten alive by mosquitoes. Bug juice did not help... some guys said skin-so-soft from Avon did the trick. Until you sweated it off. Once sweated off it did no good. Only day two made you mosquito proof from the sweat and dirt.

But nothing ever prepared us for the "Wait-A-Minute Vines." Perhaps it snagged your arm. Perhaps it snagged your LCE. Something got snagged.

We trained to do patrolling to conduct raids and ambushes. And we did special operations. The latter was airfield seizure and security. We used gun jeeps for that.

We also did NBC training. NBC was "Nuclear, Biological, Chemical" Warfare.

One time, we spent one whole week in MOPP gear. That was the suit that was supposed to protect you from chemical, blood, nerve and mustard gas. Not Nuclear. Nukes fried you. No protection.

We did a ten-mile road march in full MOPP gear. The shoes kept coming untied. You were dehydrated and had to stop to pull a canteen and hook it up to a connection to your mask.

I have never heard so much bitching about being uncomfortable. Me included. I hated it too.

R.I.P. Rappel towers at Hunter

We built them during RIP. Aco trained on them. Bravo and Charlie most likely also did.

In 1980, when we arrived at the rappel towers, Corporal Riley told me to pull out my rappel gloves. They were still cream white.

I had not used the leather dye to turn them black as he had instructed. He said to me, "You will never again embarrass me in front of Sergeant Hall, do you hear me Private?" Yes, Corporal, I said. He said, "when we get back to the barracks, your ass is mine."

Craig Riley and I eventually became friends. But that day… he slammed me up against my wall locker many times. Ranting the whole time about Sergeant Hall and never to embarrass him again. It worked. That was the point. Old school. He never again had to tell me twice.

Some other time back at the rappel towers…

PVT Cordero was going over the edge. I told him, you have a 1/3 stretch factor. Cordero was afraid. I told him – listen, anticipate the stretch factor.

Cordero hyperventilated.

I said "Cordero, just breathe and slowly release the brake hand and step down the incline." He got there. As soon as he was "L-shaped," he calmed down. The stretch factor can be unnerving.

Mike Passmore came next. He was a daredevil like Spider-Man. Mike was doing Australian. That meant face first. Mike ran off the platform and screamed, "YEAAAAHHHH" – he dove and halfway down, he hit the brake and landed halfway down on the surface of the tower. He made it.

Next was Mark Rademacher. He was doing Australian rappelling, face down. Rademacher looked and noticed he had no rappel gloves on.

He went any way. Why? Oh God I saw his hands. When he used his brake hand, he ripped the flesh off. I understood. He could not disgrace himself. He had to jump. It wasn't worth it.

Ronnie Carle

Ronnie Carle came back from Ranger School in the early winter of 1980. He was Weapons, AT section like me.

He told me he had *the Ranger School Blues*.

I didn't know what that was. He said, "when you're done, you've proved yourself so many goddamn times, you're done proving yourself and just want a little break."

Ronnie had a "live to ride, ride to live" tattoo. He lifted weights all the time. So that would suggest he was a biker and gym nut. But he was so much more.

Ronnie was in Weapons platoon... this book "real men don't eat quiche" was out and popular in the early 1980s. Ronnie made up his own version... "Okay Cherries, let's see if you're ranger material..." He developed his own real men test. What's most ironic is the basis was observation of mannerisms of men and women. When we weren't even around women.

He'd bark, "Put your hands on your hips." The newbies would put hands on hips fingers forward, thumbs to the rear. Ronnie would say, "Good. You passed that one. It occurred to me then that women did the opposite. But so did David Bowie.

Now look at your finger nails." Newbies would curl the fingers and hold the palm forward toward their faces. Ronnie would say, Good. Then he'd hold his arm outstretched, back of the hand raised, palm out and fingers pointing up… demonstrating how women look at their finger nails. Never saw Bowie do that gesture.

Next he'd say, "look at your heel." Guys would raise the right foot in front of the left leg… Ronnie would say "Good." Then he would demonstrate how women raise the foot behind the other leg and look over the shoulder. I was fascinated because these were all observations of actual behavior that Ronnie made. He just noticed and made a mental note to remember. He was like that.

I made mental notes of things that were important to me. Things that I deemed worth remembering to me. Like elements of this book. Granted that there were a ton of details that I've forgotten – because I choose not to commit them to memory.

What we memorize – is what we choose to memorize, or what we have to memorize like for a test of American history. Like how I remember the Gadsden Purchase. I had to remember that for a test. Why do I still know it?

I've told Lynn that I wish I had a selective delete button. To rid my mind, and my memory of not most, but much. The hate, the anger, the violence. Did some of it serve a purpose in developing who I became?

Back to Ronnie Carle.

The clincher came when he would say, "now here's the final test... look at the sky." And he'd say, "look at the sky" with dramatic effect. The youngsters would look up, confused, not sure if this were part of the test.

Ronnie, would shout, "WRONG –" he would then strike this pose; easier to demonstrate than to describe. Left arm extended out, palm down, fingers straight, body leaning back in the opposite direction, right arm in a V shape with the hand flat pointing the same as the left, head almost cradled at the right arm elbow... and Ronnie would say, "Real rangers GAZE at the horizon..."

The first time he did that, I had tears from laughing.

I want to honor these men

Those who deserve it. When I praise someone, there might not even be a recorded document giving testament to what they have done. What they meant.

They deserve a record of the history that they contributed to. I volunteer as their historian.

There are also those who deserve to have light shed on the deeds that warrant being taken out behind the woodshed and whalloped. Taken out of the shadows.

We called them shit-birds or shit-stains or dick-weeds. They expected respect that they never earned. One would say to me, "Looky here. You see that? I'm an E-07." And how many times did a southern drawl accompany the quote? I had to constantly remind myself that Tennessee Williams, Carson McCullers, and William Faulkner were brilliant writers. Otherwise it would have become easy to mock and despise southerners.

Add to that list, James Mercer Langston Hughes from Joplin, Missouri. I hope one day, his poetry is required reading. "What becomes a dream deferred?" is my favorite.

On second thought, George Wallace will always be a shit-stain.

Tough Skin

We did road marches. Minimum of 10 miles. Tests of endurance. Blisters -- the size of a silver dollar. The medics had a cure. They called it "tough skin." Some medics put mole skin on it. That didn't work. The good ones used Tough Skin.

It was tincture of benzoin. The medics would use a hypo and drain the fluid out of the blister. I learned that because I asked shortly before I left for Berlin, because I wanted to take it with me. More on that later.

Picture this: Arms room. Medics on little benches. Hypo to drain the fluid and then replace it with the same quantity of "tough skin."

After the injection, guys screamed out. "AHHHH, what the fuck did you stick in me, man?"

When I had it done, the blister was the size of a silver dollar. Our medic drained it with a hypo and then replaced the fluid with tincture of benzoin. I think my eyes bulged the size of silver dollars. The breath came out of me. It felt like a branding iron. On raw skin.

I began to laugh. That's what I do when I experience extreme pain. Perhaps cackle was more accurate. Nothing had ever hurt so much.

But in one hour, I could have and would have done another road march. The "tough skin" bonded dead skin with raw skin and formed a callous that was stronger than a regular callous.

I've seen hard-core rangers cry from the pain of tough skin. No lie. It hurt. But it worked. It was effective. I became a fan. Not for pain, but because it worked.

SGT Howard Mullen AKA Song Jong Moe

I don't know what it was about Howard Mulllen, but we hit it off. Not like a gay couple. We hit it off as brothers. He was black; I was white. He called me his blue-eyed brother from another mother.

NCOs were not supposed to fraternize with Privates. Howard took exception with me.

We each had no words to describe it. We called it "the Bond."

I'm the alleged "writer." Why can't I describe this? Howard always looked out for me. But I also connected with him.

When I got food poisoning in Camp Ripley, Howard pressed his fingers on my stomach. Dale Kennedy jumped on his ass. "Mullen, what the fuck are you doing with that private?" He said, "I'm stimulating his Chi." Kennedy said, "Get the fuck out of there now."

When I was in Berlin, he invited me to his wedding. I didn't have any leave remaining since I took thirty days before going to Berlin. I wish I had. He honored me with an invitation.

Later he told me when my PCS orders said the 197th at Benning in 1986, I should have come to Ranger School as an instructor.

Howard sent me a photo of him with Danny Trejo. I love Danny Trejo.

To this day, Howard and I refer to and value the "Bond." No one understands why... we don't question it. It's just there and we accept it.

Leave December 1980

Rangers rotated leave with 2nd Battalion. 1980, we took leave for Christmas. 2nd Batt took leave for New year's eve. In 1981, we reversed it.

Christmas Leave 1980. I spent half of my time in Mentor and half in Eastlake with Bill and Barb DeGedio. And Martha Alexy. I was seriously thinking about asking Martha to marry me. In 1981, I got my second tattoo, a unicorn, for her. Also because a unicorn is symbolic of the protector of innocents.

As the child of a mother who was beaten by an alcoholic, the unicorn was fitting. Bullies beware. I will always be the greater tyrant toward bullies. And rangers taught me how to inflict pain to eliminate an obstacle. Our goal was the objective. Nothing and no one stands in our way.

During the December Leave in 1980

I was at a party in December of 1981. It was at a house on Emery Circle next to a Schwinn bicycle dealer. That was around Eckley's corner. Lakeshore, Andrews, and Munson Road. Teri Pealer was there. Now Teri was a secret crush. I was nervous about seeing her because I was a geek. A nerd. Teri was a force to be reckoned with. Like a cheer leader but she was about causes.

And now suddenly I had the "Dick with ears" hair cut. Could I have been more embarrassed?

Teri said, "Hi. What are you doing now?"

I said, "I'm an Army Ranger."

She said, "A forest Ranger?"

The music was really loud. I said yes. I thought about saying, "Only you can prevent forest fires." But that would be mean. I really liked Teri.

Years later, she told me that she remembered that.

The night before we (Russ, Pogenpohl, and I) were to drive to Savannah, we were at a bar in Mentor along route 20 (aka Mentor avenue). Either Russ or Debbie (Russ's ex) was driving. That should have meant I was free to consume as many beers as I wanted to. It turned out that Russ and Debbie both got so hammered that I had to drive us home.

I'm sure I was weaving. A Mentor Police cruiser pulled me over. I thought I'm busted. DUI for certain. I told the officer that I was not the designated driver. Russ and Debbie were passed out in the back seat.

He handed me back my license and said, "I pulled you over because you were weaving. Here's my card. Next time you're home on leave, look me up. We'll have a beer. Be careful driving home."

No ticket. No DUI.

Some how I lost his business card. That's too bad. I would have loved to take him up on his offer to go have a beer together.

After the leave, we drove my 1976 Mercury Comet back to Savannah. It was Russ, me and Pogenpohl, who was another ranger in second platoon.

Back in Savannah, on New Year's Eve, Russ reminded me of the "bet." He said since he arrived at RIP a week ahead of me that he won the bet and I owed him $50. I paid him the $50. We drank a bottle of Galliano yellow liquor that night. Since we were at a bar, we probably *paid* for four bottles of Galliano.

We welcomed in 1981.

I also was thinking that we haven't even been to ranger school. Who would go further? That was the bet. Who would accomplish more?

If I went to Ranger school first and graduated... He would owe me the $50 I paid him – AND the $50 for winning the bet. That's $100. A gentlemen's bet. It must be honored.

Russ De Gedio left the First Ranger Battalion in January 1981

Prior to our first deployment to Camp Ripley, Minnesota, Russ made up a lie and said he got his girlfriend (Debbie) pregnant and had to leave. He and Debbie were not even a couple anymore. He went to the two by four. That was the 24th Infantry Division at Fort Stewart. Leg Land. It meant APCs and Hinesville.

Before he left, Russ introduced me to Lou Reed and Frank Sinatra. I have him to thank for that. Scott Summer had given me the Velvet Underground's "White Light/White Heat" and the two New York Dolls albums when I was in high school. But I never knew Lou Reed's solo work. It was brilliant. "Coney Island Baby" would make me cry. It brought up suppressed emotions. That was my guess. I'm not a shrink, so I can't say for sure.

Russ was my friend – I did not reveal his lie. He had no Honor. I had no obligation to keep his secret.

Russ borrowed my 1976 Mercury Comet to transport him and his belongings to the two by four. He "said" he would return my car before I came back from Minnesota. Russ kept my car for the next several months. I got it back before Ranger School.

But I had to go by bus to Hinesville and fort Stewart to retrieve it. Russ was indifferent when he turned over the keys. He acted like it was his car and how dare I ask for the keys back.

I'm sorry. I was expecting "thank you for letting me use your car and I'm sorry I kept it longer than I said I would."

In the 1990s while on the Ranger Listserver, a visitor posted that he was in bar and met Russell DeGedio who said he was an Airborne Ranger.

I said he did go through Airborne. But he did not attend Ranger School. He spent three months in the Ranger Battalion and quit.

There are many military people who want to claim credentials that they have not earned.

Fred Jackson comes instantly to mind. He told me he trained Mike Hall, my platoon sergeant. Fred was sent to the two by four like Russ. Fred Jackson was DX-ed as a private. He "trained" Mike Hall? What a douche bag Fred Jackson was. He conned us into thinking he was Fred "Boom Boom" Jackson – some hero ranger.

This list server allowed liars to spread so many lies. We took so many testimonies at face value -- as actual and factual. It was not "Peter" Parker's fault. These duche bags signed on and claimed to be who they weren't.

We trusted other rangers. Why? Major Robert Rogers. Rogers Rangers Standing Orders. 1759.

"Tell the truth about what you see and do. There is an army depending on us for correct information. You can lie all you please when you tell other folks about the Rangers, but don't never lie to a Ranger or officer."

These were rules for Rangers.

Fred said – he was an EMT. Came upon a mother and child in a burning car. He told us on the list server that he pulled them out then handed her a ranger coin. We went, "oh man... Shizznet." He lied -- it never happened.

Russell and Fred are in the same canoe. Down stream over the water fall. Good riddance.

<u>Deployments</u>

In the rangers we went on a lot of deployments. January 1981 to Camp Ripley, Minnesota. That was the first one. After that I had Pre-Ranger and then Ranger School. Ranger School was June 6, 1981 to August 6, 1981. Camp Frank Merrill was the Florida phase.

Next would be Gowan Air Force Base in Idaho, outside Boise in September of 1981. Fort Campbell, Kentucky for Anti-Armor School in November of 1981. Fort Sherman, Panama for Jungle Operations Training Center in December, 1981. Fort Bliss, Texas and Oro Grande and White Sands Missile Base in New Mexico in February of 1982. Roosevelt Roads Naval Base in San Juan, Puerto Rico in June of 1982. Yakima and Fort Louis, Washington in September of 1982. Mount Yohna, Dahlonega, Georgia for mountaineering in October, 1982. Cape Canaveral, Florida in January, 1983. Fort Bragg for MOUT Training in January 1983. Fort McCoy, Wisconsin for Arctic Training in February of 1983. Camp Ripley was much colder. Sixty below at night.

<u>Camp Ripley MN – JAN-FEB 1981</u>

At Camp Ripley we had an Ogio sled. Spelling is wrong. On it we had our 90 mm M67s, Mortars and the 10-man tent and Yukon stove. How the Russians and the nazis did it in World War II, I'll never know. You became a slow moving target. Easy to pick off.

We would drag this sled and its contents through the woods during the day. At night, we would set up the tent and stove. It was so unsafe. We could have blown up at night or caught fire. All we cared about was getting warm.

Once the tent was set up, we set up the Yukon Stove. It had a drip line into a rectangular box. Drip line provided gas and the Yukon stove provided heat. The exhaust pipe led to the top of the tent so we would not die of carbon monoxide.

In the morning we would make "yukon toast." We would sprinkle salt on the surface of the Yukon stove and place a piece of white bread on top.

For personal hygiene we would take a snow shower. Yes, that meant rubbing snow on your underarms and chest and crotch. Not a pleasant experience.

Minnesota – I got frost bite and hypothermia. Hypothermia and I would become close friends. How many times at fort stewart did I wake up in a puddle when it was thirty degrees and raining? You stand up and you can't call it "shivering" or "trembling." You vibrate close to convulsing.

At fifty-eight years old, I vibrate now, but the neurologist called that essential tremor. What Katherine Hepburn had during "On Golden Pond." It's supposed to be hereditary. But no one in my family recalls having it.

Back in Savannah after the 1980 leave.

Probably after Camp Ripley. Savannah was a lonely city. If you were a yuppie or a redneck, it was great.

I was a romantic. I never admitted that. I was also a yankee. Women in Savannah would not even treat you like a human. Some rangers went the route of banging heads against the wall. Others decided that strippers were the only company of the female persuasion that we would ever get the chance to meet. I was one of the latter. I questioned. I was smart, I was funny, I was kind. No Savannah women would even grace me with a smile. I was not the kind of guy to fuck and leave. I truly believed in romance. The lyrics from the Music Man – Shirley Jones sang "Being in Love." That was my credo. Mom introduced me to that musical early on. The lyrics went like this: "And I would like him to be, more interested in me, than he is in himself. But more interested in 'us,' than in me."

I was at a strip club close to the entrance to Hunter. Mostly rednecks and a few soldier. Bikers sat back in the bar in the dark. I tipped a stripper with one dollar. After wards she came and sat beside me. Naivete is so stupid.

She said I'm cold. I offered my Schott black leather jacket. She said thank you. Then she said, I'll be right back. It wasn't a bathroom break. I never saw her again.

I went back, described her, gave dates and times. Can you describe "Gullible"?

After Ranger school in 1981, I replaced my Schott's leather jacket with my TDY money. Money I got from Ranger school for going TDY.

Platoon Medic

When I arrived at Weapons Platoon, Doc Carmody was our medic. Medics were in a different class. Rangers called everyone by their rank. Never "Sarge." It was Sergeant First Class for E-07s. Medics were all "Doc."

Doc Carmody was from NYC and told me about seeing the Cramps in concert in the 1970s which I loved hearing about.

I don't recall if Doc Carmody, if his departure was a PCS or an ETS. PCS is a transfer to another unit while still active duty. ETS is expiration time of service meaning it's over and civilian life is the next step in the journey.

Eventually we got Doc Barber.

However, in between we had this Aid-bag that someone had to carry in the field. That would be me. Do I look like a hump-a-lot?

Funny thing was, in Cleveland "White Cross" was speed and sold hush hush. In Georgia, it was over the counter in pharmacies and made its way into the platoon aid bag. White

Cross was so named due to the plus sign etched into its side during manufacturing. It was likely a diet pill. Rangers used it to replace sleep. It was speed.

When Doc Barber took over as platoon medic, I liked to fuck with him. One night I came in from a night of strip clubs and many libations. I must have been loud because he poked his head out the door of his room in the barracks. I planted a wet sloppy kiss on his lips. I did many things for "shock value." That was the punk rocker in me.

Veterans' Administration

The VA is funny. Ruck sack runs and road marches crushed one of my lumbar vertebrae on one side. Our Battalion surgeon, Captain Chip Pettigrew kept saying it was scoliosis, curvature of the spine. My mother is a registered nurse. She said I never had scoliosis. It wasn't until years later that Captain Eaves became the battalion surgeon and he recognized it. He called it a "compressed or wedged disk." The VA gave me 10% compensation for that.

Hearing loss is documented as "service connected." They are glad to give me 10% more for tinnitus. But the hearing loss is zero percent compensable. What's ironic is that I can do a hearing test that shows 85% hearing loss. I can show bills paid for hearing aids that total more than $10,000.

Hearing loss occurs at 85 decibels. The M67 90 millimeter recoilless rifle comes in at 188 decibels. I wore hearing protection every time we did a life fire. It simply was not adequate.

Douchebag Shinseki used to be in charge of the VA. He was relieved of command. He was the same general who donated the Ranger Black Beret to all active duty troops. "To improve morale." How is the morale now, Shit Bird?

Okay, I'll be nice. Rangers are never supposed to lie to an officer or another ranger. I wrote a letter to General Shinseki before his act was implemented, an appeal that fell on deaf ears.

PFC Marlin Maynard died in Grenada in October 1983. He died to earn the right to wear the Ranger Black Beret. Shinsecki showed naught but disrespect to his memory as a fallen soldier. Marlin was on my gun team in Aco 1/75.

But tinnitus? All I have to do is say I have it and it's done. 10% for life. My tinnitus is so extreme it wakes me up at night. There are four or five different tones that pulse. Like a wave. It waxes and wanes. Move to Florida in 2004 and what a discovery. Rainy season breeds frogs. At night on the lanai, you hear the croaking of the frogs. So loud it drowns out conversations. THAT'S what tinnitus sounds exactly like.

Neck is the fun one. Fun as in ha-ha, not fun as in funny. Guess what... Rangers did not go on sick call when they attempted a stand-up landing and screwed up the timing. I'll explain. Your T10-1B parachute has an orifice in the rear and two toggles for steering in the front. The orifice gives you a 10-knot forward thrust. Remember that when I talk about Rock DZ (drop zone) at Hunter Army Airfield.

At about one hundred feet off the ground, you pull both toggles together, simultaneously. It partially closes your chute and you plummet. The tricky part is you've got a quick release to lower your ruck sack before you land.

Key words: at the right moment – you release the toggles and immediately pull the quick release for the ruck sack. The chute opens and acts as an air brake and then you land flat-footed. Hence the term, a stand-up landing.

But... until you got the timing right, you landed as if you jumped off a roof and landed flat-footed. It hurt. But I never went on sick call for it. None of us did. You simply "drove on."

That said, my lower back was different. I went on sick call. Not often. Only when it was really bad. Because I knew, something was getting seriously damaged, and continuing to get damaged worse. Turned out it was true. Age 59 as I write this. Lynn gave me a back brace. Some nights I am awake with back pain at 3:00 ayem and sometimes at 5:00 ayem. I go to our den and study Spanish with Duo Lingo. The back brace helps, but I also need the distraction. Especially when I sit awake for four hours.

The VA initially gave me 10% for the wedged disk and 10% for tinnitus.

In 2015 or thereabouts, I was appealing the denial of claim of benefits to the VA during the time when Shinsecki was in charge. He was the douche bag General who gave the Ranger Black Beret to all enlisted troops. That prompted the "Earned, not issued" campaign of many Rangers past and present, including myself.

I wrote an appeal to his sorry ass stating that Marlon Maynard gave his life in Grenada in October 1983 to earn the right to wear the Ranger Black Beret. Giving it out like M&Ms to all active duty troops was an insult to his honor.

And the honor of many other rangers who fought and died but earned the right to wear the Ranger Black Beret.

Shinsecki ignored the protests and gave it to the troops any way. He said it was to "improve morale." The Rangers now wear a tan beret. To replace the dress Khaki uniform.

Shinsecki was relieved of duty from the VA. I know this is redundant.

In July 2019, I sent a letter to the VA to re-open my claim. It got ignored. In January 2020, I hand delivered a copy in person. Further updates are coming.

The VA without Shinseki... they sent me a letter on 7/28/2020. New decisions:

- Hearing loss & Tinnitus – 10% (combined – was separate)
- Radiculopathy left lower extremity – 10%
- Radiculopathy right lower extremity – 10%
- Dextroconvex lumbar spine and degenerative arthritis – 10%

Nothing on the neck. The Doctor I saw in early July asked me to get the radiologist's report / analysis of the MRI on my neck from 2015. I received it after I received the VA's new decisions.

I sent it to the VA with a cover letter.

Back to the story...

Boxing at Camp Ripley, Minnesota - 1981

Camp Ripley was a national guard post so it was closed on the weekends. What would we do? In the stair well, rotating boxing gloves.

When I arrived at Alpha Company and was assigned to Weapons platoon, Rick Knight was my roommate. He never told me why but he did not like me. He was a PFC who just got back from Ranger School. Rick was a former UPS driver who loved delivering packages and snorting cocaine. He was the first example I knew of when the judge said, "Army or jail." Rick requested to be moved to a new room in the barracks. How much could he have detested me? I was that punk rocker from Cleveland. My initial reaction was: "*you're* judging *me?*"

At first I was an audience member. I watched Sluggo against Sluggo.

Then came my turn. I heard Rick say, "Okay, Ross... you're next." I actually didn't want a turn. I did not have a choice. The gloves were put on me. What choice did I have? I thought about the cliché… "he fell down the stairs." I think Rick volunteered me to see me get my ass beat.

Context #1 – privates did not punch NCOs. Privates without the ranger tab did not punch NCOs with the ranger tab. I took a deep breath. I thought I was fucked.

When the gloves were on my hands, they put me up against an NCO sergeant, Ranger qualified, polish-american. A big healthy human being. I think he was a squad leader in third platoon. I was the runt against the powerhouse.

But this child was not afraid of the Bunny.

To clarify, this ranger E-05 was not the Bunny. He became a friend of mine. But back then, I was a newbie and a private. And he was a tabbed Ranger NCO. And they wanted me to box him?

Context #2 - Rangers are the baddest asses around. Running cadence. "I wanna be an Airborne Ranger, I wanna lead a life of danger." A civilian enters the Army and the drill sergeant is considered hard as woodpecker lips. A Ranger is so much more above and beyond that. Words fail to describe. And now the gloves were on and we were going to box. I didn't know how to box. If only Brandon had taught me like he taught Joel and his other younger brother. I knew I had "reach" and that was my only advantage.

My only saving grace was I had SGT Mullen in my corner. He was my coach, my mentor, my brother. I heard his voice, "Keep your guard up. Look for openings and take them." I got my bell rung, but I also rang his. My stance was arms at my sides. Howard kept saying, "Ross! Guard up, man. Guard up!" I got clobbered a few times. Guard up meant, I would push each punch. Hands at my sides, I swung and had velocity. They were all left or right hooks and upper cuts, but I could feel the impact. The NCO I fought, he out did me in jabs and his guard was always up. But when he came in for a jab, he left that side of his head open and that's when I swung. Most often we connected simultaneously. Bells rung in unison.

I have to look for the NCO's name. We became friends.

Years later, Rick confessed to me… by this time we were friends. He said he had serious doubts about me until that day in Minnesota. He said he saw my spirit. The fighter in me.

Shit. I hadn't been in a fight since Eddie Jewart back when I called his dad a pretzel.

<u>Pre-Ranger</u>

The night before Pre-Ranger, Danny Doyle and Craig Riley asked me to drive Tim Hubbard to the Savannah airport. Tim had a flight out. I should have just handed them the keys and said bring it back in one piece.

At the airport we met three women who enlisted for the Marines and were on their way to Paris Island. We offered to drive them, but they wanted a hotel room for the night before. Danny Doyle and Craig Riley took two of the bedrooms. I was left with the third woman.

We made out on the couch. Then she said, before this goes any further, I do not want to have sex with you. I told her that was okay. But I was willing to go down on her. No need to reciprocate. She agreed and I went down on her.

Eventually, Craig and Danny came out of the bedrooms. I suppose they had sex. The smiles. Cliché as it may be, they are tell-tale, give-aways.

We got back to the barracks at 4:30 am and SGT Hall was already there.

He told me that if I fell out of the run for pre-ranger PT, I would not go to ranger school until a winter ranger slot became available.

I don't know what consequences Danny Doyle and Craig Riley faced.

But Spring 1981 I started Pre-Ranger. This was a class that Battalion sent you to before you would start Ranger school. Tony Lewis was now an instructor at Pre-Ranger. When he called for a volunteer to be class leader, no one volunteered. I raised my hand. I had to. SGT Lewis was from Weapons. I was already gleaning the meaning of loyalty that bonded us.

My "oh shit" moment came when I had to give the drill and ceremony commands to the group to march them from the barracks to the classroom. I knew how to *follow* the commands. I was never taught how to *give* them. The first day was a friggin disaster. The other rangers were grumbling and bitching and not trying to cover it up. At the end of the day, I was embarrassed --- but I was also pissed. Before I dismissed the group, I scolded them. I told them that I was the only one who volunteered for class leader. I've never led D&C and I could use their help. That made a world of difference. Someone came up to me and said my comments made them all see me in a different light.

The next day, one of the guys marched behind me and prompted me with commands. After that, I could do it on my own.

In the mountain phase of ranger school you get tested on tying knots. They are so precise about them that the extra rope cannot extend past your palm and thumb. Pre-Ranger taught us short cuts, especially with the double butterfly knot.

The instructor with the bad teeth (not Tony Lewis) taught us how to smoke a cigarette and not get caught. SSG Hyde. You keep the lit end inside the pistol grip of the M16.

Writing the operations order was the hard part. I was up all night. They wanted such detail. "SGT Mather turns the door-knob clockwise and clicks the safety off." That specific. But it helped.

Scott Owens and Pathfinder School

Spring of 1981, I took Scott from Mortars to Pathfinder. It was actually him and another ranger I think from HHC.

We took Route 16 to Macon and then another freeway route to Columbus. Macon was like a step back into the 1930s. Shacks with corrugated steel roofs.

But the faces. It wasn't despair. The black faces of Macon lacked hope of any kind; they had given up. Resigned. I was never so depressed.

Savannah had a black section of town. It was nothing like Macon. In Savannah, it was not equal but it was separate. I wondered how Dale Kennedy and Howard Mullen felt about it.

The three of us drove to Fort Benning and spent the night. I would leave the next day.

After we unloaded our overnight stuff in the hotel room, we went to Victory Drive. At Fort Benning, Victory Drive is the place of tattoos, vice, strippers, prostitutes and wasted money.

Scott and his friend and I went to a Korean strip club.

They were playing pool while I was with a Korean woman.

Americans in places like Korea and the Philippines, they married Asian woman and brought them home to America. Howard told me that in Korea, the families insisted that the daughters become prostitutes to bring in money for the family. He said that only the soldiers in Seoul South Korea might have met a student.

My first wife's brother was married to a woman from the Philippines. She was a former prostitute. He had been in the Navy.

At Fort Benning, the Korean woman pulled up her tube top and allowed me to fondle her breasts and nipples. She never said, "I like you, let's do something intimate." There was an indifference that I just did not get. I think she was numb. Like the Tina Turner song, "Private Dancer."

Was I trying to be a moral person? I did not want to be a loathsome scoundrel. But I liked fondling her bosom and especially her nipples while she was gyrating her butt on my crotch. It reached a point when I realized that I did not want to succumb. This was the not the direction "of my moral compass." Wait. That sounds so pretentious. I don't think I ever had a moral compass. I eventually had an ethos.

I told Scott I had to leave. I think back then I talked about decadence like it was my middle name. Or maybe it was only okay to be deviant when nobody was looking.

Scott asked me to stay and drive back the next day.

I said okay. I said I was going back to the hotel room. I went back. Scott and his friend came with me but they went to the bar.

Suddenly, Scott burst into the room. I was probably reading. I assume that because I was still dressed. Civvies, but dressed. Scott shouted, "Iggy, Iggy, you gotta help us. This guy is beating the shit out of us."

I went. In the hotel restroom, Scott said the Korean guy said he was waiting for the champion. I went in and there was no one there.

Scott and the other guy were ranger qualified. I was a newbie.

The Koreans were gone. How was it that I was their champion?

What mysteries the world held... Catholics taught me about sin but not morality. They tried at Saint Joe's. But it was easy to fake it. To Pretend. We did role play. Two kids riding in a car at night. Pretending to be teenagers, and one says let's smoke a joint. And I say, "No thanks man, that's not me. I'm a Catholic."

It was most likely high when I said it. I smoked pot all the time. Hypocrite.

Ranger School

What is Ranger School? These are the basics: you lead combat patrols behind enemy lines. The Ranger Instructors (R.I.s) evaluate your performance as patrol leader or assistant patrol leader. How well you would perform behind enemy lines. Your leadership and stamina. They starve you and deprive you of sleep. That's over simplified. You got one C-ration a day and averaged two hours sleep a night. Sometimes less. We walked until dawn one day in the mountain phase and the R.I. made an admin move to lead us to the Appalachia trail to turn us over to the next shift.

That was 1981. I don't know if the standards are the same.

Ranger School -- Further

Let me qualify that. In the 1990s, I was very active on the Ranger listserver. All subscribers received every email posted. Someone posted an email about a "stress card." His description said, standard issue to basic trainees. If the drill sergeant is stressing you out, present this card for him or her to back off and give you space." The rangers on the list server reacted with expletives that were not deleted. No filters were on that day.

I was in a class dominated by ROTC Cadets. The R.I.s made it harder for the "Batt Boys." We carried more weight, more often. I learned that label from the Ranger listserver years later.

Hump the M60 then hump the AN/PRC-77 radio, then repeat... you get the message.

Mark Ross was a ranger with Aco/75th – a company ranger. Before Battalion. Mark Ross tells the best story of the "Idiot Stick" with his tale of Ranger Urine and Ranger Nate. A five-foot section of telephone pole attached to an M-60 sling. Mark was Aco, 75th at Fort Hood. We call each other Big Brothers and Little Brother out of affection. Not the huggy huggy kissy. Just brothers. Rangers.

June, July and August of 1981, I attended Ranger school class 10-81 with a guy named Heath from Bravo company.

You started at Fort Benning, then went to Dahlonega, Georgia for the Mountain phase, and lastly to Eglin Airforce base for the Florida phase.

Benning phase had the worm pit. You had to low crawl under barbed wire with your face half buried in the mud. An RI would pour a canteen at hip level with his back to you so it looked like he was urinating into the worm pit. Some said he actually did pee.

The idiot stick was reserved for extreme cases. It was a section of a telephone pole about six feet long attached to an M-60 sling. Woe be to he who had to carry it.

The Benning phase was conducted in WWII barracks at Benning. They have since been torn down which I learned in 1999 when Mark Ross and I went to a ranger rendezvous at Benning when Gil Berg was made an honorary member of the Battalion. CSM Michael Hall was there and 1SG Doug Droesch.

Many times I overheard, "Do you know who the most squared away NCO in First Battalion is? Ranger Mike Hall." They never said, sergeant E-5. They said, "Ranger Mike Hall." Hearing this I would proudly say, "I know. He's my platoon sergeant."

Back to Ranger School... Benning phase PT Pit. This is where we all got Chiggers. It was a saw dust pit to protect you during landings.

One of the instructors was notorious. SFC Skip Swackhammer. His very name means pain and destruction. SFC Swackhammer was like Schwartzeneggar when he was competing. Arms as big as my thighs.

If he saw that you were not throwing your partner in order to cause pain, he stepped in and demonstrated how it should have been done. I fucked up. Skip threw me. I hit hard.

I had chigger bites around my waist and around my ankles where my boots were tied up.

I got edema or something like it. All around my ankles. Normally, I would lace up my boots and wrap the loose ends of the laces around the boots then tie a square knot in the front. The swelling was so bad, I could not do the wraps. My feet and ankles were like they were in L-shaped boxes. I could not bend at the ankle. Benning was hilly. Not steep. But with L-shaped boxes, navigating those hills was painful.

At the eight- hour break, I called Battalion and talked to Andy. He said, eat match heads. Sulphur will stop the chiggers. He said and get clear nail polish and paint the tops. That will suffocate them below the skin.

I wish someone had told me that before the Benning phase. Then again, maybe the information was withheld deliberately so that you have to learn the hard way.

The most memorable part of the benning phase was when the RI told us all to empty a salt packet into one canteen and drink and swallow. I instantly threw up. I don't know if it was his intention to induce vomiting, but it worked.

I completed the Benning Phase and we were all given an eight-hour break. That meant, laundry first. Then pig out – calories. Mucho grande.

I had the car so a group of us jumped in with laundry bags that most likely stank of weeks of ranger field duty.

Ranger school makes you sweat. I was twenty-one. What's funny is that here in Florida, my latino friends in landscaping companies tell me that they try to hire white gringos. They pass the piss test. But day one, they are puking at lunch time from the heat. We're in Florida. Yes it's mid-90s in the summer.

In the rangers, we did road marches for 10-12 miles at Fort Stewart, Georgia in the summer heat of 110 degrees.

I admit I'd have a hard time now at 59, but at 21, I dealt with it.

Benning Phase: City Week

If in class, and you started to doze off. They made an example of you. They gave you a BFR to hold above your head. That's a Big Fucking Rock.

The instructors made jokes about the "Dreaded Z Monster." The Z Monster would leave foot prints on your page of notes.

It looked like a zig zag line going down the page as you fell asleep.

Most held the BFR successfully. Some didn't.

Victory Pond

At Victory Pond, there was a ladder. You climbed the ladder and then had to walk across a foot-wide lateral section. It was like an upside down "L" – up then across.

In the middle was a Ranger Tab you had to step across because you weren't qualified. True it was a test of balance and fear of heights. You were walking out on an upside down L. Thirty or forty feet up? Water around you. Ask me to do it at 59 with all my conditions especially vertigo? No way.

Then you grabbed two hand grips attached to a pulley attached to a steel cable. You had to put your patrol cap on backwards to blind you and then fold down the inner flaps like Elmer Fudd and turn around because you were going down backwards.

You had to wait for the R.I. to say let go to plunge into the water. If you didn't let go, you smashed into the tree.

In my class, no one fell off the platform and no one hung on and smashed the tree. Two good things.

Darby Queen

The Darby Queen was the obstacle course. Let me say this. I love obstacle courses and I do great. If American Ninja Warrior were a competition back then, hands down. Winning – no issue. I was ferocious. I was Spider-man and Dare Devil combined. And the Black Panther was my wakandan chieftan.

Eight-Hour Break

I had a car during ranger school. During the eight-hour break, we would do laundry first. Eat second. Then what?

We decided to go see "Stripes" with Bill Murray. I don't know what happened, but when the movie let out, we had 20 minutes to get back. I must have been doing 80 mph. We were so lucky not to get pulled over. Or maybe the RIs were all asleep.

Mountain Phase: Frank D. Merrill

Dahlonega came next. The mountain phase. Pre-Ranger prepared me for the knot test. I passed it with flying colors. No, that's a hackneyed cliché. I passed it positively pulsing. Okay, that's pretentious. I passed it. Leave it at that.

On Hawk Mountain, we had to do this climb. We were in two-man pairs. To do this climb. The cliff went out overhead. About a 200-foot drop if you fell. The pitons were already driven into the rock. You had these sections of rope with three knotted loops. The top or highest was attached to a snap-link. Lead ranger (me) also had a 120-foot rope that I had to loop in so my buddy could climb up behind me. So here I was dangling from one three-loop section of rope hanging from one piton and I had to hook the second one into the next highest piton four or five feet above my head, while I'm dangling from a sling rope hoping I don't fall or my combat boots slip and fall. I should have worn my jungle boots. Better tread.

Once I reached the top, I was shaking. That was a harrowing climb, but I made it. The RI at the top was merciless. Where you from, Ranger? I said Alpha company first batt, Sergeant. He said get down and lock into that cable (that ran laterally left and right) and give me fifty. My forearms were still shaking. He goes, "Does 1SG Stanley Fox know he has a pussy in his company?" I wanted to throw his ass off that mountain. I think I said something like 1SG Fox is a decent man and an outstanding Ranger. He let me recover.

Land Navigation in the mountains.

Patrolling – no azimuth. Navigate by terrain features.

In the beginning, the patrolling began up and down hills. It kicked our asses. We were following the azimuth of the compass. I think the R.I.s waited until we knew this wasn't efficient. Then one RI would say, why not navigate by terrain features? Why was that not obvious? Well, we were 19 and 20-year-old kids.

We continued our patrols. But then we navigated by terrain features. It added more klicks to the route but we were much more alert and less exhausted when we arrived.

It meant instead of going up and down hills, we skirted them.

Ghana officers

We had two offices from the country of Ghana in Africa. They did this dance and song. The song mocked our officer RI and our NCO RI. We didn't understand a word of Akan. English is widely spoken, but Akan is the official language.

We all laughed. Although we did not know a word they sang. The cues were their names. As soon as we heard their names, we cracked up.

The Ghana officers linked arms and danced in a circle. I loved it.

Off Limits areas

Our maps in Dalonaga… they had these huge sections cordoned off with diagonal lines from red magic marker. They were the moon shiners' territory and off limits because they would kill to protect their stills and kill to get an M16A1 rifle.

Bee stings

Northern Georgia also had yellow jackets that would sting for no reason. I spent the last part of our patrol with my right eye swollen shut from a bee sting and my right hand, I could not use due to a bee stings.

Florida Phase: Camp Rudder

The Florida phase at Eglin air force base. The pan handle of Florida.

RB-15 meant a rubber boat that sat 15 rangers.

We started our training in the gulf of Mexico doing capsize drills in the RB-15s. I don't think I gave a second thought to sharks.

When we patrolled, we used an RB-15 to a certain point. That point was called a cache site with a person who was friendly to our side. God, I'm embarrassed about how many terms I've lost due to time and scotch.

After we left the RB-15 with the partisan. We were then in the swamp water. Waist high was normal. Florida phase gave me either trench foot or immersion foot. I did not diagnose which one it was. My feet were swollen, wrinkled, white and spotted with black points.

Guys in my platoon warned me about Florida Phase. They said you hallucinate in the swamps. "One guy thought he was in front of a coke machine and pulled quarters out of his pocket and hit the button for a coke and when nothing came out he slammed the machine over and over again… But there was no machine in the swamps."

During the day, we saw lots of snakes. The R.I.s would ask us – during the day – when there was a snake to say, "here is a snake." At night, we were chest deep in swamp water. "We," or at least, I blocked it out.

Florida had the 12-day patrol. What I remember most about that is that I did not defecate for 12 days. Was that chemical induced?

A fellow ranger school student had a necklace made of human bones from the hand. Why he took it to ranger school was and is an interesting question. I was totally into the Cramps. Lux Interior was the lead singer. Ivy Rorschach was the lead guitar. Nick Knox on drums was Mike Metoff's cousin. If anyone knows the catalog of music of the cramps, then you'd know why a necklace of human bones appealed to me.

I told him, "if you ever decide you're hungry, I'll trade you a whole c-ration for the necklace." At some point during the Florida phase he said yes.

I gave him the c-ration and he later in the barracks gave me the necklace. We probably each had a story to tell from that.

When I was leaving Berlin in 1986, I gave the necklace to Drew Paul. He was a ranger from 3rd Battalion and loved the Cramps. So he could relate.

I bet if I had that necklace today, Lynn would say, "get it out of the house."

No shit. It was human bones.

2nd Batt 75th Rangers

The Ranger list server that Peter Parker initiated taught me that 2nd Batt rangers were really good. Parker, Coyne and Mir Bahmanyar stand at the top of the list.

1st Batt had Lindo and Cordova and tons of white trash guys who never should have graduated RIP.

Further in Florida...

But back to Florida Phase of Ranger School... we had a guy from second battalion who went crazy. One night in patrol base. I cleaned my M16, did personal hygiene, and ate my c-rat while pulling perimeter watch. It was now his turn to watch and my turn to sleep. At some point the RI woke me up. I asked is it my shift now? He said no, there was no one on watch. I said where is private... What's his name?

He fell asleep. When they woke him he went crazy. They removed him from that phase and offered him the chance to recycle.

The RI checked my weapon which was clean. He checked my socks. I pulled first watch. That meant they did maintenance and hygiene and eating before me.

Ranger School. Everyone has a point of exhaustion. Here's the deal. When you're physically exhausted, your brain can kick in and push you further. When you're mentally exhausted your body can carry you further. There will come a time when both happen at the same time.

When it happened to me, I had total amnesia of the event. The RI said I was calling him every name in the book. I had been carrying the M60 machine gun and at switch over, I then carried the AN/PRC-77 radio. RIs did that to battalion guys because we could normally handle it.

He apologized and told me he had to give me a negative spot report. I said I understood. Then he said, don't worry, you'll make it up.

Back at 1st Batt, I learned that the 2nd Batt guy who went crazy -- he climbed a flagpole and jumped off. Sorry for his family.

After Florida Phase.

Like I said I had not defecated in 12 days. I went to the latrine with my M16. Pulled my pants down and sat on the toilet. I fell asleep.

I heard someone say something like "last call for weapons…"

I ran. My M16 did not pass inspection. They said they would reinspect it at Benning.

Graduation from Ranger School

The day before graduation, all the parents were invited for a super supper. A super supper was a royal feast. A meal of BBQ, steaks, burgers, hot dogs… Heath and I sat alone.

Ranger Heath – his family was from Tennessee. They were poor. He asked me about my parents. I said my father is a dentist.

Years later when I graduated from Cleveland State University, the Bunny asked me to get the clown outfit of cap and gown so he could take pictures. I said no thank you. He offered to pay for it. I repeated no thank you.

SGT Randall H. "Andy" Anderson came to Benning to pin my RANGER Tab on my left shoulder.

I kept promising my sister to Andy. Cyndy would have loved him. He was GQ, but kind and considerate. A real gentleman, despite his bragging about how he planned to lose his virginity in Panama with a prostitute.

Years later. Mom was working as the reception and billing person for Bunny in the Dental practice. A patient came in and bragged about her son graduating from some school in the military. Mom said I graduated Ranger school. She said, "How did you like the ceremony?" She said she didn't go. The patient said, "you didn't go? Why not?"

Mom told me about this and she was obviously embarrassed that she didn't know how important it was. It was important to me. It wasn't important to her or Bunny. It's funny – ironic – not ha ha, that Bunny wanted me in a cap and gown for Cleveland State which I could not care less about. But ranger school? That mattered and was so important. It was their missed opportunity. That's combined.

Andy was there. Thank you. My section leader pinned my ranger tab on my left shoulder. Like the road less travelled, that made all the difference.

Back at First Battalion

After Ranger School, I did not feel the ranger school blues like others did. I felt great. We also went to Oro Grande and White Sands Missile Base. SSG Mike Hall had us in the bunker where they blasted the nuke. "Tested" with soldiers wearing sun glasses and sitting in Adirondack chairs. Waiting for the blast.

I ran better than I ever did in PT. I could come in and finish a run ready to run another mile. And I sang running cadence.

I introduced new songs. We did punk rock as running cadence. "Blitzkrieg Bop" by the Ramones and "Lust for Life" by Iggy Pop. The other platoons must have heard.

I didn't know… My reputation spread… they had a name for me. The other rangers called me Punk Rock Ross. That's what SFC Champaco called me in West Berlin in 1986. I think he was a 3rd platoon squad leader in Aco as a SSG.

Idaho, Sept 1981 continued

Our next deployment was somewhere in Idaho. Alpha company was conducting a live ammo raid on an objective that had bleachers for VIPs from Washington and the Pentagon. It was February 2, 1982.

We jumped in and David Bazemore and I followed the door bundle and got our 90s and ammo. We were in a security perimeter when David told me, "opsked 98." Two rangers were MIA. He said we're probably going to form a line and like a police call, search the area for the missing rangers. Baze did his best to prepare me. Missing meant they burned in and were dead. We were going to look for the corpses.

Dead Bodies

I'd only seen two dead bodies at that point.

The family attended the funerals of Grandpa and Grandma Ross. But none of the kids saw the bodies.

We sat bored not knowing why we were there. Who explains to kids a funeral?

I knew when each grandparent died. I recall nothing of the funeral except where the grave sites were. I returned in my 40s and took photos of the tombstones.

Before the Army at Bob Evans, I dated a waitress. Her friend died in a car accident. I went to the funeral with her. I held her hand. Her friend looked like a mannequin. I don't mean that in an insulting way.

I went to my Uncle Ken's funeral in 1987. I saw him in his coffin. His essence was gone. That was my first glimpse at the body once the soul left. The shell had no trace of the uncle I loved. In 1987, I was so fucked up. Army to civilian is so weird and traumatic and I felt damaged. Lost and alone. Veronica wanted me to see uncle Ken in the hospital. She said it would mean so much to him. It would mean so much to me.

I never went to the hospital. I got out of the Army in November 1986. I think I drank every night to oblivion.

Probably until I started at Cleveland State University. Fall of 1987. My alcohol intake ceased at CSU.

The Bunny died in 2006. I did not attend the service if there was one. I do not know if he was buried or creamated. I do not know the cause of death.

I do not rejoice his death. I feel nothing,

The Bunny died in 2006. I don't know why I know the date. It held no significance. I never hated the Bunny. I think hate causes cancer.

The Bunny became a non-entity. He ceased to exist. He was no longer a person. He did not matter. I felt no guilt. No remorse. No regret.

A part of me feels that I could obsess about bunny. But why?

As a child, I'm sure I hated.

As an adult, I refused to hate. A choice. Not to hate.

I hope he appreciates that.

Back to Idaho, 1981

It shocked Baze and I when we continued with the mission. A-10s prepped the objective and we conducted the raid as if nothing was askew.

Afterwards, we were in the bleachers where the VIPS from DC sat.

Captain Charles Stecker briefed us about what happened.

"Never leave a fallen comrade." That's our creed.

This is the official version: Nick Barclay was a hung jumper. He swung under the aircraft. The next ranger jumped clear and away. Nick swung out from under when Johnny Danford exited the plane. Johnny's impact with Nick broke Nick's static line. But stopped Johnny's chute from fully deploying. Johnny attempted to pull his reserve but it got entangled with his main and never fully opened.

Both rangers burned in.

We questioned what did Nick do? Were they dead on impact? If they were alive, why didn't we go find them?

Sadly the message was clear. The VIPs in the bleachers were more important than our brothers. Politics first, comrades second. A game of chess. You sacrifice pawns.

Memorial Day will always be for Johnny and Nick.

Sadly I would have to add other names.

November of 1981. Fort Campbell, KY

101st Airborne Division Anti Armor School. Dragon Trainer School.

Rick Knight had a field day with the lieutenant who taught the class. James Pritzker was the 1st Lieutenant. His joy was building model tanks. Rick Knight was a master of Tank ID. He prepped us. He said, "See those three dots? That's the T-62."

The 1LT had photos for the Tank ID portion of the class. Rick studied the photos and taught us what to look for.

Rick delighted in showing that lieutenant that he knew more than him.

I began to see that Officers were arrogant. Book smart but no common sense.

[In Berlin, I respected Christopher Reddish. He was Berlin Scouts. I would gladly meet him again. All the others were arrogant and stupid.] And some were downright cruel.

My certificate of passing Dragon Training was dated 13 November 1981.

Panama, December 1981

The instructors of JOTC (Jungle Operations Training Center) were all Special Forces guys and they were hilarious.

They told us about the vampire bats. "They don't have hollow fangs. They don't bite your neck and suck the blood out of you. They smell you. And when they do, they land close enough that they can low-crawl over to you." And then the instructor made this dramatic gesture of a bat low-crawling. "Then when they find exposed skin, they slash a small cut with their teeth and then start licking. Their saliva has an anti-coagulant. So you'll know if you've been bitten because you'll have a cut that won't stop bleeding. And. And here's the best part. We have to assume that the bat had rabies. You get the first sequence of shots in the location of the bite... until you can't stand the pain any longer. The rest of the shots go into your stomach." So to sleep in the jungle meant all exposed skin must be covered with your poncho making it really hot.

We were there in December of 1981. It was Christmas.

The radio played "Feliz Navidad" every hour. And then they played "the double dutch bus." Izzo Wizzo Kizzo Baby was the same in both English and Spanish.

Everyone got prickly heat. That doesn't sound so bad. Our medics said, it's like your pores get so overworked from sweating that they shut down. We left Georgia where it was seventeen degrees Fahrenheit. Panama was easily 100 and higher. I never took so many cold showers as I did in Panama. Prickly heat attacked you like this. You would be under the shower or anywhere for that matter and suddenly, it felt like someone whacked you with a paddle... like the paddle for swats in elementary school... But this paddle was loaded with dozens of needles. Those were the pores closing and slamming the door shut.

In the jungle, they had black palm. When you were sliding down a ravine and reached out, you caught black palm. It had rows of spikes all around its trunk. The needles broke off. What you were left with looked like some one took a sharpie and dotted your palm and fingers with black dots. Those were the broken off spike tips.

Colon, Panama

Our first pass was to Colon.

It was perhaps 1:00 or 2:00 o'clock. Eric Stahl, Doug Droesch and Stacy Nowak and I were sitting in a bar. They brought us our cervezas.

All of a sudden, there was a prostitute on my lap. She looked like the twin sister of Bernadette Peters. But this version was rubbing my crotch and pleading please take me upstairs and fuck me. I did not go upstairs. Andy said he wanted to lose his virginity in Panama. Why? The medics said they had Black Syph. The medics said if you contract black syphilis, you will show no signs. But eventually if you marry and try to conceive, your wife will simply miscarry every pregnancy.

We drank beers and talked. We watched our married brothers and made sure they were not tempted.

Non-Sequitur

This is not an account of those who fought in combat. I served in the cold war. Reagan years. Missiles in the Black Forest.

I am a life-time member of the VFW. Their rules allowed that.

We did wall patrols with live ammo and smoke grenades. Was that enough?

Back to Panama...

Meanwhile, back in the jungle... (that's my tribute to the New York Dolls)...

We were conducting an E&E (Escape and Evade). It's the scenario where you're on patrol and get compromised by a larger force and so you have to E&E to a rally point previously established. Panama is dense jungle. They call it "triple canopy." That meant three layers of overhead foliage making the night pitch black. I would have thought that we would be navigating by terrain feature; instead we were following an azimuth. That meant up and down ravines, valleys and waterfalls. Someone said it's because the maps were all from the 1950s. Now it made more sense.

Ranger School taught that in the mountain phase, you navigated by terrain features. Their maps were newer than the one in Panama.

Mike Davis and I were attached to Second platoon. I had my 90 (M67 90mm recoilless rifle) hanging from my neck with a sling rope as I scaled up this ravine. There was a tree close to the top, laterally left to right. It was too far away from the surface to go over it, so I tried to go under it. My footing gave way and I slid to the bottom of the ravine where deadfall had accumulated. A branch penetrated my ass cheek by four inches. I punched the ravine wall to keep from screaming in pain. I reached behind me and pulled it out. Yep, at least four inches.

When we reached the ORP (objective rally point) I told the platoon sergeant I'd been impaled. He had the medic look for it. He couldn't locate it under the triple canopy jungle. We continued with the E&E.

Back at Fort Sherman, the barracks, I went to see the medics. Under normal light, they said, "Holy shit, you should have been medivacced." They told me to stay in the barracks for that week and take many showers to keep the wound clean. Showers were bad enough with prickly heat. Now every time the water hit my ass, it was like getting impaled all over again.

I was awarded the Jungle Expert Patch which features Balboa's boat. This is remarkable because Balboa had his men disassemble the boat, and carry it piece by piece through the jungle of Panama and reassemble it on the Pacific side. Then sail away.

Panama City

Our second pass, we went to Panama City. Panama City made me wonder. Every woman we met – each one was a prostitute. Why do men "require" that? Need to fuck – because it's not making love. They pay for a service that involves a woman's body. Immanuel Kant said it is immoral to use any person as a mean to an end. He said that humans have intrinsic value. He was one of the first moral philosophers. I'm not some holier-than-thou. My acts as James Kennedy would make a whore blush.

While wondering the streets of Panama City, I had had a few cervezas. I came across a street vendor. He had a round BBQ grill. Skewers of meat with BBQ sauce were cooking. The sign said, "Monkey Meat – Bar-B-Que."

The medics told us, they say it's monkey… but when they can't get monkey, they get dog, or cat or rat or bat.

I bought two skewers. It was delicious.

The next day, we met a Panama cop. My Latino brothers talked to him in Spanish. One of my brothers was an E-05, Sergeant.

He said, I have three stripes just like you. How did you get your stripes?

He said, "I shoot one thief, and get one stripe. I shoot my second thief and get two stripes. I shoot my third thief and get three stripes."

Halloween 1981

Stacy Nowak and I dressed up as woman. We went to K-mart and bought woman's clothes. Stacy looked like Alice in wonderland with a blond wig. He smoked a cigar on purpose.

I got a red wig, silver metallic pants and some kind of blouse. I looked like a cross between David Bowie and Iggy Pop in 1973.

I had negatives of photos of Stacy and me. I gave them to Cyndy at Hiram. She was supposed to have them developed. She lost them. Shame on you, Cyndy.

First Aid training

Weapons platoon – we were doing first aid training with an IV. How to administer an IV correctly. So many guys were afraid of needles. I said I'll volunteer.

Our PSG, Mike Hall was from Avon Lake in Ohio. That was west of Cleveland. I was Mentor. East of Cleveland. I was a punk rocker -- that made my reputation.

For the IV, Mike said, "Just use an old hole." Everyone laughed. Me too.

That was funny because they assumed I was a junkie. In fairness, I only mainlined twice. Mainlined means you used a needle. It was crank both times. We called it crank. Now I believe they call it crystal meth.

Bill DeGidio told me that "Doctor Bill loves your veins."

For the training, I got an IV of saline solution. A partial. Not a full plastic sack.

SGT Hall

He's now Mike Hall. I am privileged to call him "Mike."

In First Batt, he was "walk on water" perfect. Back then most platoon sergeants ruled with an angry voice. Fist pounding like a teamster.

SGT Hall always had a calm voice. He didn't threaten. He was cause and effect. If this then this.

Mike used to say, "Fuck around, fuck around, ain't gonna be around."

We called it "DX-ing to the two by four." 24th Inf was fort stewart.

Mike also chewed Red Man. There was always a chaw in his cheek. I used that comically to make a comic book with Mike and all of A.T.

Eric Stahl told me once that he fell asleep in a patrol base and Mike said, "I could stab you with this pencil." That scared Eric to never forget that moment.

After CPT Rice, we had CPT Charles Stecker

Captain Stecker seemed like a decent CO. Seemed. That's the qualifier. I was in Pre-ranger and then Ranger School. Meanwhile, CPT Stecker did a witch hunt.

I did not learn this until Germany and Berlin that Ossifers get their Ossifer Evaluation with a positive grade for "Discipline" – they earn that by issuing Article 15s. For troops who were E-04, that's specialist class four or corporal. Or the ranks of E-01 (Private) to E-03 (Private First Class).

Stecker came into Alpha Company and called troops into his office. I don't know what strategy he used. I know this much… he didn't say, "So and so tattle-tailed on you… do you want to tattle-tail on him?"

No. Any Ranger would have said, Fuck that noise.

I was in Pre-Ranger and missed this. Instead he told the Ranger and pay attention --

He said, "Corporal Rudy Weeks, I have a signed statement from an NCO in your platoon that he observed you smoking pot. Do you wish to write a statement about him smoking pot.?"

He said, "Sergeant Keith, I have a signed statement from an NCO in your platoon that he observed you smoking pot. Do you wish to write a statement about him smoking pot.?"

It went on and on. Stecker got at least a dozen.

To this day, no one knows if any of them were legit.

And here is the worst thing about it. Rudy Weeks and Preacher Keith were excellent Rangers. Rudy was a former Marine and a Vietnam vet.

Charles Stecker sent Grade A Rangers to the Two by Four. I hope he had a great fucking evaluation. He was an arrogant, condescending and conceited bastard who never deserved the Ranger tab let alone take a command position in a Ranger Battalion. Probably a west pointer.

And the worst part… Ranger Battalions never did piss tests for pot. I smoked pot every time on leave to Cleveland and when Stacy Nowak and I hung out with bikers in Savannah.

And here's why. In the 1970s, everyone smoked pot unless you were a prude... Perhaps honor society afraid of your own father. Sheltered like a nun. A "good" girl or boy who could not disappoint. Or in rare cases, a young person who simply chose not to out of lack of interest. Everyone else, we all smoked pot and loved it.

I loved getting high. Brandon Zart and I got high and watched Han Solo and Luke Skywalker jump into hyperspace in the Millenium Falcon in 1977 when we were high as kites. That was one cool special effect.

After 1986

After the Army in 1986, Brandon introduced me to Monkey Paw. I loved getting high. I did not like getting stoned.

In the 1970s, we had Mexican, Columbian and Sensimilian. The latter was the best.

Monkey Paw... what the hell was it. Getting high was fun. Getting stoned? Sit in a corner and drool and vocal chords no longer functioned. How fun is that? I stopped it immediately. I switched to scotch.

I'm not a musician

I'm a singer. Or I was -- until acid reflux ruined my voice. Once upon a time, I could match David Bowie note for note and even Art Garfunkel doing bridge over troubled waters.

One night in Rudy's around 1999, Janis Joplin came on the juke box and she sang "Me and my Bobby McGee" and I matched her voice note for note to the surprise and applause of my friends there at the time.

This is a non-sequitur because Lynn and I are watching "the Crown." It's May 2020 and it's on Netflix. Whenever I hear "God Save the Queen" my mind creates the lyrics of "My country tis of Thee, sweet land of liberty, of Thee I sing..."

Mark? Bob? Am I wrong? It sounds like a match note for note.

Back to Savannah...

My friend who worked at a record store

Prince released "Controversy" in October, 1981. My friend at the record store told me to buy it. He was so much like Mark Vocca. During my years in Georgia, he replaced Mark as my best friend. Mark was in Texas and Russ was gone to Hinesville, Georgia (that's Fort Stewart).

We loved music and had many conversations about recording artists and live shows.

I brought a Blondie Boot Leg from Cleveland and all my albums of Lights Out (1934-1947) and Inner Sanctum (1941-1952). The latter two were radio show recordings of broadcasts of scary stories. I loaned them to him so he could play them during Halloween. Arch Oboler would preface his show on Lights Out with: "It's later than you think." It was October 1981.

God forgive me. I do not have record, written or by memory, of his name. I googled Savannah news to see if I could find it. It's like someone erased every record of his existence.

One day I went to the record store and the manager said he was gone. He did not quit. He was dead. Shock. It could not be true.

The Savannah police said that he shot his wife and infant daughter and jumped off the bridge to kill himself. Bullshit.

I said that was simply not possible. That was not my friend.

His parents agreed with me. His wife's family were too distraught.

PSG Hall let me attend the funeral. I was a pallbearer. I dressed in starched jungle fatigues and spit shined boots and my Ranger black beret.

I had this dark fantasy that the real killers would target me and reveal themselves. Then I could kill them. But they never showed themselves.

I tried to locate current news articles with google with no success.

To this day, I stand with my conviction. There is no way he would murder his wife and daughter and then kill himself -- That was not him.

The police never questioned me. After enough cop shows… What does that say? The cops had their answers. Case closed.

Savannah cops are pieces of shit. They never did their jobs.

Fifty years ago, he was my friend. Savannah cops covered it up. It was not murder, suicide. It was frame and murder. Were the Savannah cops in on it? I was too young to even grasp conspiracy theory.

The cops were way too nonchalant. There were no red flags as far as they were concerned. A husband was thrown off a bridge; a wife and child were shot dead. All evidence erased.

Once upon a time, I wanted to become a police officer.

Stacy Nowak

After Ranger School in 1981, Stacy and I went to Duff's Smorgasbord every Friday night (unless we were deployed). Stacy would always get mashed potatoes and corn and mix them all together. The mashed were instant so I loved them. Duff's had Bread Pudding without raisins. I pigged out. Next we had a choice. Korean Village or Showboat. Korean Village was a strip club. Showboat was a movie theater that played porn. Stacy and I were not depraved perverts. We were just lonely.

Let me reiterate: Savannah women hated Rangers. Worst is they were taught to hate. Stacy and I were respectful, kind, decent. Savannah women were conceited, stuck up, arrogant snobs. They were better than yankee soldiers. Southern Belles were by very nature, hypocrites.

1981 – Stacy and I were both 20 years old. No woman in Savannah would give us the time of day. Here is what most people don't get. Savannah women thought rangers were rapists and murderers. Murderers I understood. They had a criminal case from 1980. Before I arrived. This is where it would be easy to say "all Savannah women were foul." I refuse to use the C-Word. That's not me.

Sheila Dudley was the battalion secretary and she was such a dear.

Movie Arcade for Porn

Before I joined first battalion, there were two rangers downtown Savannah. In an adult arcade… that's one of those – deposit the token in the slot and the porno movie shows. Yes, I found them in downtown Cleveland in the filthiest parts of downtown.

Back to Savannah… some young unlucky guy offered to perform oral sex if either were a willing participant.

I won't say, he should have known better. The term, "fag bashing," was in papers in 1980. Seeing two soldiers, two Rangers in a video arcade. If it was a solo soldier, I'd say he might be looking to hook up with a sex partner. That was the nature in Cleveland in high school after closing at Bob Evans. The trolls in the arcades were creepy. I went there with the Bob Evans crew and we'd cram three or four of us into a plywood compartment and feed quarters or tokens in to watch 8 mm porn from the bygone days.

I never understood why two rangers were together in a porno video store. Unless they happened to be "don't ask don't tell"?

They -- the thugs – they beat him up. Badly. What was wrong with them?

This might be my naievity... Rangers were ultra macho. Some gay man? Not ever a target. Gay men probably avoided rangers in Savannah. I wouldn't blame them. The 1980 incident would make gay men fearful of any ranger encounter.

As I recall after one regimental ball, a bunch of drunk rangers jumped in the back of a pick up truck and drove off to go "fag bashing." A true test of masculinity and machismo. Beat the shit out of bystanders. I found a major flaw with my ranger battalion that night. I condone fag bashing like I condone child bashing. I would kick the ass of any asshole who used muscle against any one of the two. And I don't compare gay men to children. It was a simile.

The MPs and Savannah police brought the guy who got beat up on post -- that meant Hunter Army AirField – he was on crutches and walked up and down the ranks until he located the culprits. He identified the rangers who were then carried off by the Savannah police. Well, no shit. What did they expect? And they deserved what they got. I hate bullies. If I had been there, I would have defended and protected the gay man. No fag bashing on my watch. Did Rangers think "fag-bashing" was cool?

Who takes pleasure in "bashing" a man who may or may not be gay? My uncle Barry was gay and died from A.I.D.S. I'd like these idiots in a room. The bullies. Please allow me to "bash" them.

I'd never call it "Barry's revenge" because Barry had a good soul, a loving heart, and a kindness that differentiated him from my other Lindley Uncles. Barry was a good man. Barry cared. Those who knew him, loved that about him.

I could be the act of retribution. But Barry would never endorse it in his name. He would say, just be kind. Barry was kind. I knew his heart and his action toward others.

Show Boat Porno Movie House

When Stacy and I went to the Showboat, we made rude albeit funny comments about the events on screen. One might call it obnoxious. John Holmes was extremely well endowed. A mutant. No one had a member that huge. Stacy and I would utter comments like that's gotta be fake. Prosthetic. The old perverts in the audience would laugh. Probably out of discomfort.

Eventually the religious right closed the Showboat. Apparently, movies about torture that were one step away from snuff films were acceptable, while movies about horny adults engaging in consensual sex were taboo. I do not understand the logic of that. But religious preachers love to condemn sex in all its forms.

There was a feminist in the 20th century who called "pornography" misogynistic. Andrea Dworkin. Misogyny is hatred of women. Guys in the rangers, my friends. We loved women. But none would talk to us. Stacy and I went to the porno movie theater, not out of resentment. Out of fantasy of what we were missing.

If a Savannah woman would have given either of us the time of day, we would have worshipped her like a goddess. But all we had were strippers.

__Korean Village__

We, Stacy and I, also went to the Korean Village. It wasn't a village. It was a bar. That featured mostly white women – biker's girlfriends -- who would dance and strip down to just panties.

Just to see. No touch. The closest we got was a dollar bill in the garter. On the outside of the thigh. Never the inside.

Stacy met and became friends with Darnell. Stacy was not about meeting a girl. He had a girl named Karen in Detroit.

At the Korean Village, that was seeing real women's breasts. The bartenders were Korean women.

I made the mistake of developing feelings for one of those women – what I assumed were – trailer park girls. What was a "crush"? I wanted more than a one night's stand. I wanted a relationship.

I took that jean jacket that Bunny thought would be best through the winter. I cut the sleeves off. I sewed patches on it. 1st 75th Rangers, 2nd Batt 75th Rangers, Special Forces, 82nd Airborne. 101st Airborne. I wore it around my Schott's black leather jacket.

She sent me signals that I saw as an interest. At the juke box, we were talking and she was selecting her next song. Suddenly she pulled her underwear out to show me her pubic hair and crease of her vulva. Whoa, that was a big deal. No one ever did that before. Pubes were forbidden.

I made my feelings known to the KV stripper. I told her I liked her and wanted to get to know her. She introduced me to her boyfriend. She had a boyfriend? Why did she flirt with me? I gave him the denim vest.

He told me that a brother gave him – something similar. And he would treasure it. I cried in the car. Then Mick Jagger's sang "Angie" came on the radio...

Okay, loneliness. Who falls in love with a stripper?

When will those clouds all disappear?

Sad Songs

Sad songs are better than love songs. Listen to Frank Sinatra, "(over and over) the world we knew." Roxy Music, "A song for Europe." Nilsson, "Without You." And Annie Lennox, "Cold." Pain sparks more creativity than love.

I sent Anna Van der Meulen a cassette of sad songs. That was a joke. Sadly she was callous. I thought I cared. Eventually, I realized, that I didn't. It was delusional. She was cold-hearted. I'll never call her a bitch. But she was selfish ("let me orgasm first").

Korean Village again

One day, Doug Droesch and I were there – too early for the strippers so we were at the bar. The Korean women were telling us about the size of a man's penis. They measured from the lines in the wrist to the tip of the Social Finger. That's the one when you "give the finger." They said that's the length of your penis.

Doug placed his hand on the bar.

Doug's mom told me when he was born that he was 13 pounds. Doug was a huge Ohio farm boy from Germany.

The Korean women had wide eyes and expressions that conveyed shock and surprise. If they knew OMG, that would have been included.

1983 in Detroit

I was Stacy's best man when he married Karen. I drove to Detroit for that in 1983.

After Berlin in 1986, I arrived in Cleveland and called Eric and Denise Stahl. Denise told me that Stacy killed himself.

He used a shot gun under his chin.

His note said, "Mom, I hope I've finally done something you can be proud of me for."

Stacy told me his mom sexually abused him. I did not know how bad it was.

What mom sexually abuses a child?

During that time... Hare Krishna

Cleveland and Atlanta airports. WTF? Every time. They were everywhere. Orange jump suits, and bald heads. Handing out flowers. Asking for donations. Where did they go?

Tom Beechum

Tom married Temple. Her second husband. Jim Sheils was the first.

Tom was an artist of nature. At some point, I sent photos of me in uniform to Temple and Tom of my dress greens and my black beret. Temple wrote back that Caleb and Joshua loved those pictures.

Tom did black ink sketches of ground hogs and had copies reprinted. I have a collection of signed and numbered prints. Post card size. That they sent to me every ground hog day while I was in the Army. I saved each one.

When Tom died, I was married to wife #2, Patti Glasser. Living in Timberlake, Ohio. That was in 1999 or 2000. I wrote a scathing email that criticized the Bunny and threw him under the bus. Because he was driving from Mentor and didn't invite me and my family. I sent the email to Veronica, Chicky, Temple, and Kitty.

Temple took offense. In fairness, I'm sure I was obnoxious. I despised the Bunny. Has anyone read the reasons why?

We all met at a bar in Saugerties to talk about the life of the male who passed away.

I went there with Patti – wife #2 who was Jewish.

I met a writer at the bar who was also Jewish. Strange coincidence but I dismissed it.

He told me a narrative of how great the father was who sired me. How I must be proud. How he knew his emotions and expressed them with such clarity.

I said, "you've met Doctor Jekyll. You have not met Mister Hyde."

He said, "I never understood my father until I wrote a book about him."

I am writing this book. I still don't understand my father.

I'm not a psychologist. But I can say with confidence. He was narcissistic, vain, conceited, arrogant, egotistical, ignorant. Is there a term in psych, to say, you convey that you know everything in order to reject any evidence or insight that challenges those conclusions? No person knows everything. I certainly don't. Bunny – like Lise – oh, isnt' that scary? – had all the answers. So he thought.

Bunny presented himself as the one with all the answers. Go up and ask him. He loved the flattery. His ego fed on the smallest morsel.

During the stay in Wallkill, Patti and I stayed with Chicky and Lee Heywood.

Chicky and Lee are very religious. When we said grace, we held hands. We said grace before every meal.

They had three children. "Little Lee" who was Lee Junior and Amber and another son – I don't remember his name. Isn't that sad

Amber married Skye. Skye was black and very cool.

Patti insisted on taking the train to Manhattan to see F.A.O Schwartz. I just wanted to go to the jewish deli that had the caricatures on the walls of all the Broadway stars. Couldn't find it. It was either Ben's Kosher Deli, 2nd Ave Deli, or Katz's Deli. Google gave me those three names. I thought I could find it from the last time I was in Manhattan. I was wrong.

We went to F.A.O. Schwartz for Patti's peace of mind.

Before we left the state of New York, we went to a mall. Patti went into the Victoria's Secret store.

I didn't want to be in the mall at all. I just wanted to drive home.

I can do a redneck "Gomer Pyle" voice convincingly. In the middle of Victoria's Secret, I loudly said, "Is this were they sell all the extra-large dildoes?"

Patti scampered out. She hated to be mortified.

Jump back to 1996

One night, Audrey – mom -- retaliated after getting drunk, bombed, inebriated. She threw a vase at the Bunny's head but missed. He used that incident and got a restraining order. He said she was a threat to his life.

The drunken asshole who repeatedly abused and beat the farm girl got the lake country courts to agree to a restraining order. This was not a novel by Franz Kafka. And guess what? It got worse.

Leave in Coldwater, Ohio

It must have been leave in December 1981/going into 1982 when Doug Droesch and I drove my 1976 mercury comet to Coldwater, Ohio. I stayed with Doug's family and they embraced me with open arms. Doug's mom was a real treasure. I loved her immediately and she instantly called me "iggy" and wrote to me for months.

344

Doug's sister Darla and I hit it off. No sex. But a lot of kissing.

Doug's mom kept me informed of Darla's progress in the Marines.

Doug and I went to a party in Coldwater. I met a Latina exchange student. I don't recall her name, but I gave her my patrol cap from Ranger School. In hindsight, I should have given it to Darla or kept it.

December 1981. When I left Coldwater, I stopped briefly at Hiram college to visit Cyndy. She was in the dorm there. I gave her the negatives of the photos of Stacy Nowak and me when were dressed up as women for Halloween.

Cyndy lost the negatives and never developed the photos. Shame on you Cyndy! You lost them?

Some people turn off their brains. Have you ever noticed that? They are generally smart people. I've known a lot of them. Time and again, they turn off their brains. Like a light switch. I don't know how that works.

My brain works in hyper-drive. Hence writing a book during scotch number #3.

That winter in 1981 going into 1982, I was in Cleveland for my two weeks leave. I was at the Agora for a concert. There I met Bob Sablack's cousin, Colleen. We hit it off. I had to take Barb (Bill's wife) back to Eastlake. I asked Colleen to wait. After I took Barb home, the 1976 Mercury comet wouldn't start. I called the Agora and talked to a bar tender. He said he would try to locate Colleen. Yeah, right.

Colleen forgave me. I had not felt love since Martha Alexy. It took me a long time to get over Martha. My stubbornness I suppose, because I didn't want to get over Martha. Colleen tried to help me get over Martha. It had been two years. I thought I was ready. I was not.

I thought the mother of my children would have to be my partner. My equal. Janine would prove to me that she loved sex more than love. Martha showed me that an assumption of betrayal severed every connection. She believed Russ De Gedio. Not me. But I fucked a Fort Benning prostitute when I "supposedly" loved Martha ???

Now I never read the letter that Russ wrote that poisoned her. Truth is I am at fault. Or must be.

It wasn't until 2004 that I met Lynn and she revealed herself as the only choice for me. Unfortunately, I was 43 and Lynn was 50. Lynn and I both agree if we met in our 20s that we would have a platoon of kids.

My time line is "Stream of consciousness" so say my friends Mir and Rod.

1982? I'd fly back to Cleveland over the Memorial day weekend to drive my car back to Savannah after Pathfinder school. Eric and Denise Stahl would then tell me what Cherie stole from them.

G.E.D. in 1981

I don't have the exact date, but SGT Hall called Juan Espinosa and Mike Passmore to the front of the formation. And then he called me. He said you three are taking the GED test today.

I said, "Sergeant Hall, I haven't had the prep training." He said, "Iggy, you don't need it." I took the test and scored a 96% out of 100. With Juan and Mike, one passed the other had to retake it. The certificate and accompanying letter are dated November 18, 1981.

Denise Stahl, She was Eric's wife

Denise told me I had the eyes of a potential rapist. She never thought I would ever be a rapist. She used that as a metaphor, because I didn't blink.

I really do and did blink. Just back then, it was seldom.

I resented Denise for that remark for many years. Perhaps she meant it as a joke. I didn't think it was funny.

My uncle raped my mother when she was 13. Or at least he tried. She fought back and beat him off. To me, "rape" was not the subject of a joke or sarcasm.

Diversity Training

At Battalion, there was a large bay area room next to the kiosk of mailboxes and from time to time we would gather there for meetings and training. This one day, we were there for what they called diversity training.

Turned out it was an open forum to discuss race, racism, and prejudice.

I thought this was a waste of time. In Weapons platoon we had Dale Kennedy and Howard Mullen who were black. Let me rephrase that. Dale and Howard were Rangers. Oh and by the way, they just happened to be black. Race didn't matter in the Rangers. At least not to me. Mark Vocca taught me that. Rangers reinforced it.

We had one black NCO in one of the line platoons, I think he was in third platoon. Dixon? I think that was his last name. He stood up and said that the ranger battalion was a "white man's country club."

We should have laughed. Standards were not made easier if you were white or black or brown or red or yellow… that's a racist stereotype. But the cliché is the army is all green.

The PT test was total count of push ups, sit ups and time of the two-mile run. Race was never a factor.

"White man's country club"? That meant whites had privileges that blacks were not afforded. To that I say, "name one." Name one privilege that whites had that blacks did not.

Rangers hated gay men. Maybe hated is too strong. Loathed or were disgusted by... ? I suppose they were easy targets. But not blacks. Gays were a challenge to their masculinity and machismo. And God forbid that there should ever be a gay ranger.

One caveat must be mentioned. White guys from Michigan. They didn't use the n-word. They called black soldiers "Boofers." I don't know if I've spelling it correctly. I'm not sure I even know what Boofer means.

Until I met John Rellias in 2018, every white male I ever met – who came from Michigan – was a racist. John was a marine tunnel rat and Vietnam vet. Perhaps that's why he was the exception.

One fellow ranger came back to Savannah after being in Michigan on leave and had a little comic book – three inches tall, by two inches wide. He said, "hey check this out."

Why do so many white clowns assume that similar skin pigmentation translates to an assumed common sentimentality over black people?

It was published by the local chapter of the KKK and featured whitey like some super hero fighting and defeating the most nauseating and insulting caricature of a black man. I do not name him out of respect for his wife.

The weird part was these same white Michigan rangers reported to Howard Mullen and Dale Kennedy. And they openly expressed that they liked and respected both men.

Stacy Nowak was the worst. Especially when Lindo was the new private who reported to him. I never understood the name, but he called him Courtney DeLacey Chips Lindo.

I do recall one morning when we were required to be in starched fatigues and spit-shined jungle boots. Private Lindo's boots looked like crap. Nowak asked him what he used to spit shine his boots. Lindo said, "Honing Oil."

To me, Lindo could have been black, white, red, yellow, brown or purple. But man was he dumb. How in the hell did the RIP cadre allow him to be sent to Battalion?

CPT David Grange

Captain Grange was the CO of Charlie. We in Alpha heard about this. So we had to check it out.

CPT David Grange was the son of General Grange. I think he was the post commander of Fort Benning when I was going through Basic and AIT.

"This" – what we had to check out -- meant that Captain Grange bought a house on Tybee Island. The story goes his neighbors did not like rangers. Back then – NO ONE Liked us. CPT Grange told them all to fuck themselves. That's not a direct quote. Just what we heard he said.

He then asked his company for volunteers. Hardrock Charlie were more than happy to volunteer. The entire company volunteered. CPT Grange had a corner lot house on Tybee Island.

His company volunteers, they painted the house camouflage. They built a fence with concertina wire around the perimeter of the property line, they built a huge ranger tab on the roof – eight feet long and four feet wide -- and they built a sand-bag bunker around the front porch. It was likely a "deed-restricted community" and since there were no rules saying he couldn't, he did.

I would not have believed it if I hadn't seen it with my own eyes.

Defiance sits well in my heart. It stands as testimony against the Bunny and other bullies. There is a latin quote about tyrants. Perhaps I'll remember it. "Don't let the bastards drag you down." Carburundum was part of the quote. Bullies and tyrants are all the same cloth.

Tear the cloth.

February 1982 – Fort Bliss, Texas and Oro Grande, New Mexico

One of our deployments took us to Oro Grande. A desolate place. Mike Hall was still with us. We went to a nuke test site and stood in the bunker. SGT Hall said that this is where the VIPs watched while soldiers wearing sunglasses sat out in that field of sand and watched from there.

The VIPs were protected behind a special barrier.

The soldiers probably died of cancer.

At Fort Bliss, when we came in from the field, we would shake out our "fart sacks" (sleeping bags) and laugh at all the scorpions that fell out and scrambled for safety.

At Fort Bliss, in the barracks, don't ask me why he was doing this... but Roland Crawford was trying to light his posterior discharges of gas with a cigarette lighter. Rollie wanted to light his flatulence.

Joel Dewey happened to be sitting nearby, applying Kiwi black leather dye to his jungle boots.

Rollie said get ready, and before he could fart, Joel spontaneously plunged the sponged tip of the leather dye into Rollie's butt hole.

I don't think anything more needs to be said. But there were tears of laughter.

Texas skies were breathtaking. I'd never seen so many stars. Navigating at night was easy. You would shoot an azimuth, then lock on a terrain feature on the horizon. Fort Stewart by comparison was loaded with trees and wait-a-minute vines. Skies were visible on roadways. Texas had little vegetation.

In the mornings I made a fire and brewed coffee with all the C-Ration coffee and creamers I'd been saving up. I shared with my ranger brothers. Was that 1981 or 1982? I labelled this chapter 1982, but I don't remember. It's so sad when you get old. I know we were on deployment in September of 1981 after I went to Ranger school. I was in the laundry room writing poetry on my birthday when the NCO I boxed came into the laundry room. At this point we were friends. Despite I was a PFC and he was an E-05. The tab made us brothers. Divisions dissolved.

I was never a coffee drinker until after ranger school. In ranger school, when you were deprived of sleep, you relied on the caffeine of the instant coffee. We literally would dump instant coffee in the mouth. The bitter taste was the first jolt to the system. Then the caffeine would kick in as the second jolt.

I had the hardest time with the lack of sleep. I dealt with lack of food. Although I lost 25 pounds in the 58 days of the course.

Ranger are those who sacrifice. I interject it now because it occurred to me and because it's true.

I read that water in WWII for troops in the field was foul. But soldiers had to drink it. The cooks got creative. In the end, the Yanks preferred coffee and the Brits preferred tea.

There was a Bravo Company AT guy, I became friends with him. SGT Bukowski (forgive the memory lapse and poor spelling). I can see his face. He was from NYC like Richie. A 90 gunner.

We were outside and SFC Don Lamica was walking by. Bukowski says to me, "Humans generally walk with the palms turned toward the inside. Apes walk with the palms to the rear. Take a look at Lamica over there. He's somewhere in between." Sure enough – palms to the rear.

The rumour was that SFC Lamica was a Rhodesian mercenary. Another rumour that he hated his wife's dog so much that he took it on a ruck sack run around perimeter road at Hunter and ran until it killed the dog.

They gave us a pass to go to El Paso. I crossed the bridge to go to Juarez. I bought a swede jacket with Elvis style fringes for my sister and a bottle of mezcal with the worm. Every taxi that pulled up next to me since I was obviously an American and a soldier, then the driver would say, "Boys' Town? Donkey Show. Mucho girls!"

Donkey show? That can't be what I'm imagining. I later learned that it was. No, I didn't go. As a punk rocker from Cleveland, I made many overtures about my affinity with decadence. But it was a façade. An image I perpetrated. I refused to be a paying voyeur to bestial rape. I'd rather watch Dewey's plunger into Rollie's rectum. At least that was funny.

Republicans

In the elections of 1980 and 1986, I voted for Reagan. They told us he was pro-military. I was in the Army.

Republicans say that they are Conservatives. The question is "conserve" what?

Conserve means keep it the same as it is.

If that were the environment, that would be a good thing. Climate change is real. We are destroying the planet. Democrats want to *reverse* climate change. And that's doable. But not if we keep going the way we're going. Keeping it the same.

Conserve means keep it the same as it is.

When we had Jim Crow laws, "keep it the same"?

When we had segregation in schools, "keep it the same"?

When women make less than men for doing the same job, "we kept it just the same."

All Latinos from Cuba, all that I've met, are Republican. An electrician in my home to install a ceiling fan told me Richard Nixon will be remembered as a Great President. All the other Latinos and Latinas are democrats. Why do the Cubans ignore the boarder and Trump's Wall and separating children from families? Why does Washington ignore the same? I can't ignore it.

I have a friend from Bolivia. He has his own business. I worked for him. He was listing the inventory of why Republicans presented the best argument of how to govern. I asked him, who has ever done anything for minorities and immigrants and civil rights? He conceded. The conversation was dropped.

Quiero mi hermano, pero...

I have many close friends who now identify as republican. One is a math and science whiz. One introduced me to Gil-Scott Heron. One is my sister. I don't hold it against them.

Although, women's rights, minority rights, LGBTQ rights...?

I have a solution to Amy Coney Berrett. Approve Merrit Garland. Then and only then Amy can join. Too late.

April 1982 – Promotion to Specialist Class Four

I really wanted to be a corporal. Like Louie LaBeau on Hogan's Heroes. They promoted me from PFC to Specialist Class Four. No bragging rights because it was an automatic thing on your two-year mark in the service. The good news was I was no longer a Private. Army privates have three levels. E-01, E-02 and E-03 or PFC (Private First Class). E-04 is either Corporal or Specialist Class Four. I never understood why one got selected over the other. Danny Doyle was a corporal. He was mortars. Andrew Lucas was a corporal. He was A.T. Same platoon, but most of us became Specialist class four (SP/4).

1982 – Graduated May 13 -- Pathfinder School: Enlisted Honor Graduate

Spring of 1982, I went to Pathfinder school and was the enlisted honor grad as a Specialist class four. In Battalion, they called it "Badge Finder" school. In my class, the Officer honor grad was a Ranger. The NCO honor grad was a Ranger.

Pathfinder school was all about setting up drop zones and landing zones. The motto was, "first in, last out." Drop zones for either a parachute landing of troops or a delivery by door bundle of supplies. Landing zone was resupply of troops or ammo, meals, or equipment by helicopter.

You needed positive ID with the bird. Chopper or plane.

Instructors loved to fuck with students. Like mountain phase and using an azimuth.

Chopper – "tell the pilot to steer right then steer left for positive ID." Choppers are slower than planes. Chopper did so and got immediately back in the traffic pattern.

Plane – "tell the pilot to steer right." Pilot opened the throttle and headed for the horizon. Lesson learned.

We learned the correct method was dip wing left or right for positive ID.

Ranger school graded on being the patrol leader or the assistant patrol leader. Pathfinder used the same method.

In our class we had a foreign exchange officer from South America. He must have been the son of some VIP. The instructors assigned me to be his assistant leader as a graded position.

We were on the ground to set up a DZ or LZ (drop zone or landing zone).

I love my latino brothers and my Latina sisters. It had nothing to do with his background.

Suddenly, he is running in a clock wise circle and flapping his arms like a wild bird.

I approached one of the instructors and said basically, WTF? Am I to be graded on this idiot's performance?

He said, we thought you might save him. If he goes back to his country without the pathfinder badge, they will execute him. Firing squad.

I said that's insane. And so unfair. He can't help it if he's an idiot.

They passed me for my portion of the test.

They said they hoped I would save his life.

I don't think I did. Shame on me for not trying to save his ass.

Pathfinder school and the anal sex queen

I met Cherie Begnaud while attending Pathfinder. Her punk name was "Drew Blood." She herself was a medic going through Airborne school. The first time we fucked. And no, I don't say "made love" because it was strictly fornication. The first time, it was in an open field, underneath a tree on Fort Benning perhaps 200 meters from the barracks.

I slept with her one night in the barracks and we overslept passed first call. Men were not allowed in the female barracks. I dove out the window and hit the ground and rolled to a stand-up position and ran to the barracks for the students of pathfinder. In the showers, they called me Quasimodo. I didn't realize that Cherie had clawed my back while we were fucking to such an extent that it resembled lashes from a whip.

On our last Friday night, we got a hotel room in Columbus and spent the night naked. She handcuffed me with hands locked overhead. She then straddled my chest and masturbated inches from my face. She pulled out her polaroid and took a photo of me like that. A picture she later showed to Denise Stahl. Denise would tease me about that for years.

Somehow the instructors at Pathfinder school learned about Cherie. Perhaps she bragged about fucking a ranger? I don't know. During the graduation ceremony, the honor grads had to drink beer from a steel pot. While I was drinking my beers, they taunted me (in a good-natured way) about if her pubic hair was purple since she was a punk rocker.

Back in Savannah, after Pathfinder, lo and behold, Cherie showed up at the barracks. She decided to take her two weeks of leave in Savannah and located me. Eric and Denise Stahl allowed us to stay in their spare bedroom. We fucked every night.

Morning PT was suddenly a piece of cake. I attributed it to routine sexual activity.

One day we went to the Oglethorpe mall. I wore a dog collar and she held the leash. Word spread. I don't know who saw me and who reported it. But SFC Don Purdy told me that if he ever heard about me acting like a derelict again, he would rip my head off and shit in my lungs. And that's verbatim.

Cherie asked me if I wanted to fuck her in the ass. I didn't know women even liked that. She did. We used baby oil as the lube. It was the only time I came inside of her.

Memorial Day weekend of 1982, I flew to Cleveland to get my car and drive it back to Savannah. Eric and Denise took Cherie to the airport for her flight to Kansas for her duty assignment at Fort Riley

I went to Pier One and bought a wicker chair for Eric and Denise to thank them for accommodating us. But when I got back to Savannah, they were pissed at Cherie. She stole a pair of shoes from Denise and stole Eric's knife.

I never heard back from her and never tried to contact her again.

SFC Don Purdy

SFC Don Purdy was a Vietnam vet. He came over from Charlie Company and took over second platoon as platoon sergeant.

Platoon Sergeants were required to give a safety briefing before we went out to the field. Under normal circumstances, SFC Purdy would just say, "Here's your safety briefing – drink plenty of water and don't fuck with snakes."

In garrison, SFC Purdy was strange. I think Vietnam messed him up. But in the field, he had my respect and loyalty 100% and then some.

We had a young man from Vietnam in the platoon whose last name was Nguyen. In Vietnam, that's like Smith as far as last names goes. One safety briefing, Don Purdy praised Nguyen for his courage and bravery. I don't know what prompted it. But I recall that Nguyen was a skinny young man who never quit. Never gave up.

On more than one occasion, especially when he was scolding the platoon, SFC Purdy would suddenly pause. His head would tilt back and his eyes would roll up in his head until all you saw were the whites of his eyes. His squad leaders would then whisper. "Are you gonna wake him up?" "Not me, I tried that last time and he punched me." "Quiet, quiet, I think he's coming back." His head plopped down, then raised and his eyes opened and focused and midsentence or not, he picked right back up where he left off. As if no intermediate lapse ever occurred.

In the Rangers we had a newsletter and on behalf of Weapons platoon, I was the contributor. There were at that time grumblings amongst the troops about double standards. Stacy Nowak coined it best when he said, I give 100% in training, and I give 100% in my off-time to have fun. I'm not reducing one and keeping the other at less than 100%.

Captain Stecker and 1SG Abramo demoralized Alpha company with their witch hunt to ID pot smokers.

So I wrote an editorial paragraph about staying focused on the mission despite or ignoring the double standard. SFC Purdy liked it so much he cut it out of the newsletter and posted it on his platoon board.

Back then Roland Crawford and were roommates on the second platoon hallway next to the platoon sergeant's office. We shared the bathroom and storage closet with Juan Espinosa and Mike Passmore. Juan and Mike were both 11C – mortars.

11B was infantry. Me.

I had a coffee maker which I bought after ranger school in 1981.

SFC Purdy would come into our room for a cup of coffee. I was his 90 gunner and I proved myself in the field.

Years later in Germany, SFC Bill Guest and I were in the Scout platoon on a huge asphalt area and 1SG Don Purdy came over for a visit. He wore a green beret which meant he was now Special Forces in Bad Tolz. I had longer hair than in the Rangers and a mustache. SFC Purdy took one look at me and sneered. "What's that shit on your lip?" He obviously did not approve. I shaved it off the next chance I had.

SSG Michael Hall I do not recall the date...

SSG Hall gave his farewell speech. He was leaving Weapons platoon. This was where he started as a private E-01 in 1975 or 1976.

His speech was full of tears. "I know that when the mortars are called to act, they will do the job we trained them to do." He said the same about AT. He hated leaving us. He knew it was eventual. His heart was Weapons platoon.

My eyes swelled up. Mike cried. I cried.

How could one man love a platoon of rangers so much? He did. I will never forget this. Mike Hall loved us. And we loved him. How can I add significance to this? It mattered. It mattered to us. Those who heard Mike Hall.

Dale Kennedy became the Weapons Platoon PSG. Andy Anderson was in First Platoon. Rick Knight was AT section Leader and Scott Owens was in charge of Mortars. I never made note of when Chuck Childers left. He was the AT section leader when I started. The successor would have been Andrew Lucas or Andy Anderson. CPL Lucas left to go to college. Andy took over.

June 1982 – Deployment to Roosevelt Roads Naval Base in Puerto Rico.

Training was in the jungle. The rain forest. Stecker was still the C.O. He was a bastard. No one ever forgave him for his witch hunt. His actions taught me "trust no officers."

We went to el Junke. The rain forest. Climb high enough up El Toro and you're in the clouds.

Rick Knight was in charge of A.T. We affectionately called him "Knightro." Rick was Greek. Hairy. He had to shave his neck or throat area down to where the shaggy beast began.

We were doing a patrol as a platoon in the rain forest. At one point, Dale called for a leaders' recon. He called Ronnie Carle, Rick Knight, and me. I don't recall who pulled it out and lit it up… but we smoked a joint together and passed it around until it was done.

Afterwards, I went back to the platoon. Mike Davis recognized the aroma that lingered on me. He said, "You fucker. You got high. Without me."

Puerto Rico was great. I loved that the island was Latino. The music captivated me. And the gardens of San Juan were beautiful.

The navy had an NCO / Enlisted club close to the barracks. Some of the troops went there to see if they could have a one-night stand with a female navy Seabee. I did not witness this. The guys who came back said they wanted nothing to do with them. They implied with colorful language that they weren't the right gender to compete for affection.

Personal Weapons

Once we had an alert. We were on the runway at Hunter Army-Airfield with ruck sacks and weapons from the arms' room. They cancelled the alert and took us back to the barracks. Then they did an inspection of the barracks. I didn't know what they expected to find. I had Marvel comic books, Robert E. Howard's Conan novels, and Casca books.

They called it a shake down. They searched the barracks for weapons and ammo and anything else.

Rangers expected to be deployed to go into combat. No one knew when or where. There was a lot of mistrust of the M16 even after the forward assist was added to the A1. Everyone loved the M1911A1 45 calibre. Old timers would say bury it in the swamp and come back in ten years, load a magazine and it'll fire like it was yesterday.

They took the ceiling panels out and found an arsenal. The German gun maker Heckler and Koch was the most popular.

I suppose rangers thought hide it in the ceiling, that's better than a storage area.

One ranger replaced the window glazing with C-4. He was the only one who got in trouble.

Rangers didn't care if you had your own weapons and ammo. They just wanted you to store it all in the arms room. Not up in the rafters over the ceiling.

No one got busted for having weapons. They just had to register them and store them with their ammo in the arms room.

There was a rumor of a leased storage space somewhere in Savannah. A storage space full of weapons and ammo that was stolen from the legs at Fort Stewart, from the two by four, when the legs would fall asleep and leave shit unguarded at night. Guys would go in and fill a shopping cart like going to Walmart. Or back then it was likely K-Mart. The rumour also alleged that the contents of that storage unit were for sale to mercenaries and private security forces like those who protected ships from Somali pirates.

I never participated in the snatch and grab operations, but I have no doubts that they were true.

September 11, 2001. The World Trade Center

Non Sequitor. That morning I was delivering bonus packages to the managers and directors at Ohio Health – Riverside Hospital in Columbus, Ohio. I was in the office of the director of volunteers. They had the TV on. And that's when the first jet hit the first tower.

The tricky thing about disbelief, you have to turn it off. There is no switch.

I know where the term comes from… "I can't unsee that."

I went to the Army recruiting station the next day and said, "I need to go back in." The recruiter told me "All I can give you is public relations."

Airborne, Ranger, Pathfinder, Jungle Expert… And all they can offer is PR??

Beyond absurd. Beyond ridiculous. I did not re-enlist.

Drive-ins with Doug Droesch

I think it was in 1982 that Doug and I would fill a cooler with Stroh's beer and load it into my 1976 Mercury Comet and head to the savannah drive in.

Doug and I resigned ourselves that Savannah women were "Not interested" in men with ranger style hair cuts. Doug would find an exception in 1983 with a nurse who was smart and gorgeous.

The drive-in theater was usually a double feature. B-grade horror shows. We didn't care. We were there to consume alcohol and laugh.

Young men in our 20s. Goal number one was mutually agreeable willingness to participate in sexual intercourse. No rangers wanted date rape. But all young men in our 20s were "horn dogs." That meant young men who were by nature very horny. Solution was at hand. Literally. Because there was no female assistance.

Doug and I drank to forget that we would have preferred double dating.

In Savannah, we were pariahs.

Sept 1982 – Yakima and Fort Louis, Washington

Yakima was prairie like Idaho. But Fort Louis was a forest. Yakima came with a warning about badgers. The safety briefing told us a badger will take on a grizzly bear and win. They burrow so watch out for badger holes.

Re-Enlistment

19 November 1992, I had six months remaining of my three-year active duty enlistment. We still had no thought that war was coming or even remotely imminent.

SSG Nunez was the battalion recruiter. I asked what the requirements were to become an ROTC instructor. He said rank of SGT/E-05 and have an overseas tour of duty. I asked if Panama counted and he said no, you have to be permanent party. Stationed there, not just on deployment. "So I could reenlist for Berlin and then turn in a 4187 for an ROTC assignment?" He said yes. The plan according to Numbnuts (as he would later be called in Berlin when he was also stationed there) was to serve eighteen months in Berlin, then turn in the 4187 for an ROTC assignment state-side and begin my college education.

I reenlisted for four years. In May 1983, I'd get 30 days leave and then in June report to Berlin. My new ETS date was 18 November 1986. ETS stood for expiration time in service.

Second enlistment was automatic career status. That meant overseas tours of duty lasted 36 months. Numb nuts didn't know that. Or selectively forgot it.

One needed six months to be PCS qualified. That meant less than six months, you were extended to your ETS days.

I did not have 18 months in Berlin. I had 3-1/2 years. I never got to do the ROTC assignment.

Nunez aka Numbnuts (I think Tim Lindsey came up with that name) was the battalion recruiter. At 1st 75 RGR??? At 1st Batt? Let's see… do they send squared away NCOs to REMF positions? No. If you need to have REMF spelled out, you do not need to have REMF spelled out.

After the fact, it occurred to me. They didn't send NCOs who were squared away in the field to be staff pukes.

Staff positions were for "Peter Principle" people. That was the corporate America concept of rising to your level of incompetence. Reach that level and be placed in the closet. Not to be seen nor heard from.

Darnell and Thanksgiving, November 1982

Stacy Nowak became friends with Darnell. She was a stripper. Exotic dancer. She told us her "old man" was a construction worker on assignment in California. I never met him to ask. Darnell invited Stacy and me to thanksgiving with her grandmother. Stacy never hit on Darnell or suggested that he wanted to have sex with her. Darnell had long legs and was highly skilled at dancing. Stacy respected her talent. Darnell obviously appreciated Stacy's praises of her and trusted that he was not playing her for a fool just to get in her panties.

Context of this just as a reminder – Savannah people of all ages hated Rangers. Suddenly here we were invited to someone's grandmother's house for Thanksgiving.

Darnell's grandmother was a jewel. Sweet and kind. And she made a feast like I had not had since Cleveland.

Her grandma stayed with us through the meal. I would have volunteered for dishes but we were in the living room rolling joints.

We smoked many, after pigging out on turkey; and they accepted us as fellow human beings. They were bikers, strippers and one stripper's grandmother.

One of the guests was a biker nicknamed Gator who drove up from somewhere in Florida to enjoy the festivities. Gator was a comedian. Perhaps not professionally, but he could have been. His stories had us crying from laughing.

Darnell, I thank you for your kindness, your hospitality and for inviting us to your grandmother's home.

I was probably rude and forgot to tell her that at that time. Darnell was great. The bikers were mostly vets themselves and related to being treated like scum of the Earth. Stacy asked, "does it get better?" "No, but it gets easier to take once you accept that." Why should it get easier? Why do we have to accept that?

The cliché is they are free because of us. Not me personally. Me symbolically. I was a soldier then and I am a soldier now. I fight for the freedom of Americans. Everyone – black, white, yellow, red, straight, gay, old and young.

Now I have to add a qualifier. Name a black human who is black. Name a white human who is white. Name a yellow human who is yellow. Name a red human who is red. No Asian is yellow. No Native American is red. Get the picture?

Idjjit, none of us are blind.

I hope

I hope one day, some of the people I praise in this book will read it and say, "Damn, he remembered me." There are a lot of good decent people to be remembered.

SGT Tim Hubbard

Pretty sure he was 2nd Platoon, Alpha Company.

He and Danny Doyle from Mortars were close, tight. Inseparable.

I don't know how Tim figured this out. Tim found the frequency on the AN/PRC-77 radio that would broad cast on the local TV. It blocked the sound of the broadcast station (which channel, I don't recall) and replaced the sound with whatever Tim would say into the receiver. The frequency was something like 66-77.

Tim would dub the script lines of afternoon soap opera. We would watch the channel and the voice of Tim Hubbard would replace the soap opera star. Tim was genius at ad libbing and lip reading. The female soap opera starlet never said "I love you, Derrick." Tim made her say, "I fucked a carrot." For the female actresses, he made his voice high and squeaky and for the male actors, he made it deep and bass. And all so earnest.

Gotta love google. AN/PRC 77 – Army Navy Portable Radio Communication.

Tim also had a rep. They called him mule Dick. I never saw it.

Supposedly he whipped it out and beat it on the sink. When teaching a lesson to the newbies. I imagine it scared the shit out of them.

Deuce and a half rides to Fort Stewart

If we didn't parachute to a drop zone at Fort Stewart, we rode in 2-1/2 ton trucks called a "deuce and a half." They were like a big pick-up truck with the back bed covered with canvas and supports.

Stacy and I were the platoon jukebox. I think I probably had more lyrics memorized. But Stacy was the master vocalist when it came to Eagles "Witchy Woman" and the high part. Our repertoire was 1970s 45s. Brownsville station, "Smokin' in the Boys' room," Golden Earring, "Radar Love," and Doctor Hook, "Cover of the Rolling Stone." Rick Knightro asked me to memorize Tommy James and the Shondells, "I think we're alone now." Mike Hall loved my rendition of Guitarzan from Ray Stevens because we used to watch the skit by Big Chuck and Hoolihan on Cleveland television. Friday nights at 11:30. Channel Eight.

Battalion Regimental Ball.
Howard Mullen and Dale Kennedy
Chi and Allouette

I don't know the date. Again. This is redundant unless I deleted previous mentions.

I was originally asked to write a skit. I wrote the start of a skit based on a MAD magazine song parody about the Star Trek crew members who were "Expendable." The ones getting blown up or out into space. That came from MAD. My modification was about "Legs." I wrote a skit about them being expendable. Someone said no. I never completed the script.

Back to the Ball...

SGT Howard Mullen began. The demo of Chi... called Key in Korea.

Howard was a black NCO. No, his color of his skin did not matter. I only bring it up because I was a white boy and Howard connected with me. He told me that we had a bond. He should have been treating me as a cherry.

Instead he marveled at the bond we shared. And to this day it exists.

I marvel at it too. I did not know why this NCO was connecting with me.

We both accepted it and drove on. Howard will always be my brother. He called me his "blue-eyed brother from another mother."

We connected on a level that goes above and beyond being "comrades" or "brothers in arms." Allow me to address the elephant in the room, if we were gay, it would have been love at first sight. But we were not gay. Perhaps in a past life, we were soldiers fighting and watching each other's backs. Drawing fire for each other.

Regimental Ball. We were all in our dress greens.

The first thing Howard did was his "one-inch-punch." Five Rangers lined up. They braced behind one Ranger. All five backing him,. Howard bent his fingers. At the joint passed the knuckle. The forward thrusts of palm of the hand passed the joint. That scattered the five all over the floor. If they were legs, I would understand. But these were rangers. Powerful guys.

Howard had spent years in Korea. He studied Chi.

At the place where he studied Chi, they gave him a Korean name. He was "Song-Jong-Moe."

Next one involved the armorer we called Baby Hulk – Howard put him on his back. Then with bare feet he walked on broken glass. He broke wine and beer bottles. They were on a welcome mat. We heard the crunching. He was bare foot. He held up his feet and there was no blood. Glass broke. There was no blood. Howard told me with Chi, you make your feet stone.

Then he brought out a bucket of water. Two pieces of rope were attached. Howard took a piece of Bicycle spoke and pierced his neck. He pulled the soft flesh out and pierced his neck. Hung both parts of the rope on the spoke and lifted the bucket and swung it around a full circle, 360 degrees.

When he set it down and pulled the spoke out, there was no blood.

This is not – "there I was, knee deep in grenade pins..." This is a rendition that is followed by "No shit?" And the answer is, "Yes, no shit."

Howard has told me how he did these feats. But his answer is only Chi. I have to understand Chi, before I understand "How."

Dale Kennedy did Allouette.

Apologies to all women out there because this was very sexist. But it was so much degrading fun, -- this was a regimental ball. That meant "macho" rangers showing how much machismo they had.

I knew French so I knew the real version of Allouette. Allouette was a chicken. Gentile Allouette, je te plumerais. "Nice Allouette, I will pluck your feathers. Starting with the head."

Dale's version went: "Do you like her bleach blonde hair?" And the audience would reply, "Yes, we like her bleach blonde hair."

Dale would shout, "Alouette!" The audience would reply, "Alouette!"

Then all in unison, "Oh, Oh, Oh, Oh, Allouette, gentile Allouette, Allouette jauntie take a shit."

So the progression went through each body part. Big brown eyes, pudgy nose, blow-job lips, cum-stained teeth, dot dot dot. Breasts and vulva. You get the picture. It was a locker room song. Would mothers or sisters approve or condone? Hell no.

Yes, I repeated it in Berlin with my platoon. Go figure – they loved it. They were all guys. It was late 1983. We were not so sophisticated then. Doug Enkler and I used to preface a story by saying, "I'm not proud of this but..."

Don't get me wrong. I'm not innocent. I memorized all the lyrics and sang it with gusto. SSG Richard Lozano said I deserved a medal for that song. In 1983.

Live fire range and range estimation

One day we were at the live fire range. Let me see if I can explain this.

The dragon, the M47 anti-tank system was line of sight. You had a scope and as long as you kept the cross hairs on the target, moving or still, you would hit the target. It had a one-thousand meter range. But you had a limited number of rockets. Once the rockets were depleted, the missile went in the direction of the last pair of rockets. You could not over correct.

The 90, the M67 90 millimeter recoilless rifle was my primary. I loved my 90. But you had to be really good at range estimation. No laser range finders in those days. On a live fire range, you could not walk down range. There could be a dud, an unexploded mortar rounds. AT and mortars trained live fire on the same range.

I sent Mike Davis laterally to mark off 50 meters, 100 meters, 150 meters and 200 meters according to his pace count.

When he got back, I had him look to the right and then look at the Armored Personnel Carriers (APCs) down range and tell me how far it was.

He said the first one was about halfway between my 150 and my 200 mark.

I said so look in the scope and aim for 175. He said roger that.

We loaded the 90 and fired. Mike got a direct hit.

1Lt Poltorek liked my unusual approach to training and told me so. I think he coined it "unique."

That was okay. I didn't mind being called "unique." Most people called me weird.

Michael Gonzales

In December 1982, "48 Hours" came out with Eddie Murphy and Nick Nolte. In one scene, Eddie Murphy goes into a redneck bar with Nick Nolte's badge as his only defense. The line he used was memorable. But when Michael Gonzales heard it, he put his own spin on it when talking to new recruits.

He'd say, "You know what I am? I'm your worst fucking nightmare. I'm a beaner with the Tab, that means I can kick your ass anytime I want to."

God, he was funny. The Cherries had no idea if he was fucking with them or serious. By default, they took him seriously. Good choice.

Michael Gonzales was one totally squared away ranger and a damn good friend. Mi hermano. He was in Mortars.

Mike Passmore

Around this time, Mike approached me and said, "Iggy, I'm going to marry this woman." She was a 2-1/2 ton truck driver. A deuce and a half.

They were doing it for the bennies. Separate rations.

I can't believe I was this mature. I said, "Mike, never marry for benefits. Marry for love." Mike told me something that meant he liked fucking her on Roland Crawford's bunk in the barracks.

Mike married her and then they had an ugly divorce.

"I hate to say I told you so" – that came from Doug Enkler.

Tiny Adkins

I loved the mortar guys. My brothers. Michael Gonzalez, Doug Droesch, Juan Espinosa, Mike Passmore, Danny Doyle, Scott Owens, Paul Tiegland… have I forgotten anyone? Denardi? You came later.

Tiny Adkins. He was a good Ranger. In December 1981 while we were in Panama, word came down that his grandfather died. Tiny got bereavement leave and flew from Panama to Kentucky or Tennessee to attend the funeral.

THAT part did not surprise us. We were surprised when we got back to Savannah and Tiny had a wife.

Back in Appalachia, Tiny married his 14-year old girlfriend. It reminded me of Jerry Lee Lewis.

The platoon was all about saying congrats and way to go. And eventually stories creeped out of the wood work. I'd love to have a one on one with the wood work to know their secrets.

Tiny got his nick name by his football team because his penis was two or three inches long. I can't attest to that. Never saw it.

What's worse is that after 1986 when I got back to the States. I called old friends. They told me Tiny's wife decided she did not like two or three. She liked more than that and took to sampling often and willingly.

I don't know who participated with Mrs. Adkins. All I can say is they were wrong. The Ranger Creed had an unwritten seventh stanza. "Thou shalt not fuck a ranger's wife or girlfriend. Thou shalt defend her honor." Period.

JAN 1983 – "Prairie Runner" -- JSOC

JSOC was the acronym for Joint Special Operations Command. That meant missions that included Rangers, Green Berets, Force Recon Marines, Navy Seals, and Air Force guys in robin's egg blue berets who rode supped up three-wheel motor bikes.

In Jan 1983 we were at Cape Canaveral, Florida. They called the mission "prairie runner" and we were sworn to secrecy. MPs routinely patrolled the perimeter of the staging area. We did PT and read books. We knew something was up. We did not know when or where. We would have to wait until October to learn but by that time I was in the Berlin Brigade.

Like I said, we read books. "The Restaurant at the edge of the Universe" was hugely popular. Passed around.

The Ranger reading list from the early 1980s that I recall included the "Casca" series by SSG Barry Sadler, the "Conan" series by Robert E. Howard, "Ninja" by Eric Van Lustbader, "King Rat" by James Clavell, among others. These books were carried in the cargo pockets of our fatigues and traded among members of the platoon in the field.

In Berlin, a new series was added. W.E.B. Griffin's "The Brotherhood of War" starting with the Lieutenants. We read them as fast as he could write them. And we loved them and could not wait for the next one.

Later in JAN 1983 – Fort Bragg, NC

Fort Bragg was infamous. Not a good reputation. The 82nd were called "Jumpin' Junkies" in the 1980s. I never learned if the nickname applied or if it was falsely labelled.

Fayetteville – the town outside of Fort Bragg – was equally infamous. They called it "Fayette-nam" and we were told that bars had signs that read "Check your knives and guns at the door." We never had a pass to Fayette-which-ever.

For the training, it was Rangers versus 82nd Airborne. I don't recall if we were even told which company or battalion. We saw the AA patch and that was it. The "AA" stood for "All-American."

Isn't that ironic? The shoulder patch was worn by whites, blacks, Latinos, Native Americans, Asians, Eskimos, Jews and Muslims. And without hesitation, they were "All-American." I would be happy to climb aboard my soap box, but is it really necessary?

They called it MOUT training. Everyone wore a vest with sensors. The M16 had an attachment that triggered the sensors when you shot someone. The laser would activate the alarm that your target had been shot.

Mike Davis and I infiltrated the 82nd Airborne base of operations. During our E&E I jumped off a roof and did the hit and roll. Mike was supposed to follow.

He eventually showed up. I said what took you? He said, "I don't hurl myself off roofs like you do. Ranger School fucked up my knees."

Many of us were driven to complete Ranger School. You couldn't go back without the tab.

I'm proud I graduated. I'm proud to wear the Ranger Tab. Ranger school did not contribute to my Army disability.

FEB 1983 -- Fort McCoy, Wisconsin

In February 1983 we deployed to Fort McCoy Wisconsin for more arctic training. It was not as cold as Camp Ripley.

We had cross country skies. One day they took us to a place they called the "Bunny Hills" and told us to ski down. Every mound knocked me on my ass. I did not like skiing after that and I would never try it again. I was DareDevil on a skateboard. It did not translate to skis.

We had a night to go out to LaCrosse. In the bar we ended up in, a female former Marine picked me up. First and only time that ever happened. I had to borrow money from my ranger brothers for an extra hotel room. They grumbled but complied.

Back in Savannah, my Latino brothers introduced me to Xanthia

I think as I recall that I went out with Chris Pesquiera, Cordero-Torres and Saint. I was a white boy who had no prejudices. They wanted me to meet Xanthia. Xanthia was beautiful.

Xanthia only dated white men. I did not understand what that meant.

We went out. Danced. We drew eyes. Georgia was not friendly to mixed race couples. Xanthia danced like Donna Summer's "Love to love you baby" was playing in her head. Her moves were sensual. Caressing touch. With adoration.

So was I seduced? Did she seduce me? Or was I desperate and lonely? For the first time in Savannah, a beautiful woman was not only giving me the time of day, but doing so in a loving manner. How lucky was I?

One night, I remember we were on the living room couch. She said okay. She said, "if I knew it was this good I would not have waited so long."

I was falling in love with Xanthia. It was never about fucking her. I loved her. She was smart. She danced like a rock star enchantress. She was uninhibited and would dance in public at the drop of a hat. She was fun to be with. A great sense of humor. I could not help thinking, she is so perfect. What could possibly spoil this?

Then it happened...

Xanthia broke my heart when she said, "if you were black, I would not even be with you." Why? If I were black, would that make me evil? Dirty? Despicable?

With Janine, the relationship became more about sex than love. With Xanthia, it was more about white than black.

All I knew was, I had a lot to learn. I considered myself above average intelligence. But there was so much I did not know and especially about love, relationships, men and women.

Blind led by the blind? I did not know. I lost Xanthia because if I was black, she wouldn't have anything to do with me. And I was sad. She was a really good person.

In the Rangers – we mostly got drunk.

There were no relationships to be had.

Who wants to be with a Ranger? They rape women and beat up gay men.

Sorry, the latter was true. The former was a rumour. Spread by Savannah mothers. It wasn't true.

Drive In Movies with Doug Droesch

Doug and I would put a twelve pack of Stroh's beers in a cooler under ten pounds of ice and go to the drive-in in Savannah. It was usually a double feature-horror movie. I drove which was scary. It was usually Friday or Saturday night. It had to be after 1981 because it was during leave for December 1981 that I brought my 1976 mercury comet from Cleveland.

Empty beer cans landed in the backseat. I would take them out the next day.

Two movies at the drive in were two hours each, four together. Doug could drink a lot of Stroh's beer in four hours.

I drove back to the base.

That 's scary.

We probably went to Krystals – that's the south version of White Castle.

Russ De Gidio and my car

When I got out of the army in 1986, Barb DeGedio said, "You stole one hundred dollars from Russell?" I said no and explained the bet and explained that Russell kept my car and refused to return it for months.

The bet was all about who would go further. Russ quit the Rangers.

I paid him when he claimed he won. I did the honorable thing.

But he didn't win. He quit; and I won. So he owed me $100.

Now I could have said he owed a helluva lot more because he "borrowed" my car and kept it for months. Ask Herz about the daily rental.

1976 Mercury Comet

It must have been in April of 1983, I sold the mercury comet to Mike Passmore for $300. He was driving it on the freeway close to the downtown area of Savannah when the car clunked to a stop and the engine caught fire. The car was only seven years old. All I could think was what punishment did Russell put that car through?

Sorry Mike. That should not have happened. I had a brand new 2003 Toyota Corella that lasted until 2016 with 150,000 miles on it.

Non Sequitor

Jump ahead to 2003, I was in Raleigh and driving to see my BP friend Walter Jackson. He formed his own company called the Serengeti Group, Inc. Walter opened a coffee shop in the Raleigh Durham area.

A cat or a rabbit ran across the road. I hit the brakes and got rear ended. I had two scotches. That ended up as a DUI. Warning to others. Don't drink and drive. Ever. And the cops are not your allies.

<u>New Years' Eve 1982/83</u>

We were at Eric and Denise's apartment in Savannah.

Eric and Denise... did they tolerate me? Or were they entertained by me? I don't know.

Denise said that the Lou Reed Album, "Transformer" would always remind her of me. I bought it for them.

PFC Bryant was from Georgia and he brought a present from his home town brothers for us to enjoy this Christmas leave. It was some moon shine that was 180 proof. The Roger Miller song came to mind. "Moonshine in a mason jar." But it was not chug-a-lug, chug-a-lug. I only took one shot.

It frosted my throat. Like an icicle going down my neck.

The 180-proof moon shine was called everclear. Note to self... never do ever clear again.

<u>Oglethorpe Mall, Sunday breakfast.</u>

There was a group of us – we Rangers. We started having breakfast at this restaurant at the Oglethorpe Mall on Abercorn. Omelettes and sausage gravy. We became a regular table for this one waitress. I wish I could remember her name.

She was always polite and professional. Mind you, any woman who showed us the time of day, we saw that as an opening to "flirt back." But she wasn't like that. We always tipped 20%. And she treated us special.

If I remember correctly, it was Michael Gonzalez, Paul Teigland, Mike Davis, two others and me. I could have the roster completely wrong.

One day, the waitress says to us, "You know something, you guys aren't anything like my mother told me you were like."

She broached the subject. We said she had to come clean.

We said, "Please tell us. Savannah women all hate us. They think we're animals."

She paused for a moment. It was as if to say, do I dare reveal my secret?

Then she said, "my mom told me that if I ever dated a Ranger – I'd end up raped and dismembered and my body parts would be stuffed into garbage bags and left in the swamps of Fort Stewart."

We were literally writhing. "Oh, my God!"

Then she says, "I didn't really trust it so I asked my girlfriend and her mom told her the same thing. So then I supposed it had to be true."

How do you say someone hemmed and hawed. That's an ancient expression. I knew from her reaction, she didn't think it was true. She saw from our reaction that we were totally shocked and mortified.

Not one of us dated her, but we were grateful that she told the truth. It was about time.

In 2014, Lynn and I drove to Savannah for the 40th Anniversary of the 1st Ranger Battalion. At one point, Lynn needed a watch repair. We went to the Oglethorpe mall and found a jewelry shop.

I reiterated that anecdote and the woman said, "I remember that. You guys had a bad rep. It wasn't fair."

Beta Max Video Player

Joel Dewey got a VCR from his mom. Beta Max was popular on the west coast and VHS was popular on the east coast.

We would rent two war movies and one porn.

We would drink beer during the war movies. By the end, we were all good and drunk. So why play a porn movie?

We were not going to fuck each other? It did not make any sense.

But admittedly, I enjoyed the porn. This was as they call it, "Hairy pussy porn." At some point and don't ask me, actresses of porn all shaved pubic hair. And then all women did. At the end of George W. Bush's presidency, there was a campaign from women, called "No More Bush." And they were featured in poses that suggested the removal of all pubic hair.

Personally I like no bush. Both the George W. kind and the pubic kind. The latter is sexy, the former is lame.

Eventually, I bought Joel's Beta Max for $300. I took it home to Cleveland. I thought it could be used by the family for videos – even though Beta was mostly on the West Coast. There was a video store on Vine street that rented Beta Max videos. It was close to where my grandparent's home on Woodstock was.

After I left for Berlin, Bunny told Chuck he could take the Beta Max to California.

And Chuck whined that I sold a radio to my manager at Bob Evans for five dollars. He said it was his radio. Call off the grudge and let's call it even.

Promotion to Sergeant E-05

06 May 1983, the day before my flight to Cleveland for my thirty days of leave, the NCOs of Weapons platoon presented me with orders promoting me to E-05. The orders didn't have my name on them. It was someone else's name.

They said, we didn't want you to leave Battalion and go to leg land as a Spec Four. The official orders will follow and you'll get a copy when you arrive in Berlin.

They handed me orders with someone else's name on it and my name penciled in.

I have to say that the message was, if you stayed in Battalion, you weren't good enough for Sergeant/E-05. What I saw was a bunch of Ranger NCOs who never served outside of the Ranger Battalion. All they knew was the 1ˢᵗ Batt, RGR.

Leg Land was another story. I learned that in Berlin. Leg Land was all about, I'm fucking you first before you can fuck me. And they had tricks up their sleeves. Some of the shit they got away with. Wait and read.

An officer who had a connection in the piss test arena who had his piss test removed. Former biker buddies. An NCO who had a connection that must have been pretty high, to get TDY orders for an 11-Bravo grunt to take away a mechanic's slot to motor sergeant school. A slot he'd been waiting for -- for four or more years.

Wait. It gets better. Anyone who was in Berlin in the 1980s would say, "Yeah, it pretty much sucked but that's how it was."

Awards from 1st Ranger Battalion

Before I left Battalion, my platoon gave me an Army Commendation Medal, an Abrams Certificate (my second – I got my first for post soldier of the quarter), and a plaque signed by all the members of my platoon. The Abrams certificate was framed and all the platoon signed it as well – left, right, up and down – all four margins.. The AR-COMM was a big deal. I don't know how high up the chain of command it had to go to get approved. But consider that in Vietnam, it was awarded for heroism. I trained my troops. I never did anything heroic.

We had a platoon party. That meant the shell of a steel pot (helmet) was filled with five or six beers and the departing member had to drink all in one endeavor. Meanwhile the platoon sang, "Here's to Sergeant Ross, Sergeant Ross, Sergeant Ross. Here's to Sergeant Ross who's with us today... so drink muther fuckr, drink muther fuckr, drink muther fuckr... Here's to Sergeant Ross who's with us today..." And it would repeat until the steel pot was empty.

I remember doing it for Larry Allen, our mortar NCO who was full-blood native American. After reading "Bury my heart at Wounded Knee" by Dee Brown... why would any Native American serve in the Army? I never asked that question back then.

But in his defense, he was an excellent Ranger, a superior leader and a great friend. I hope his tribe honored him as much as we did.

I had not read the book (Dee Brown) until 2003. It should be required reading – for anyone born in America.

<u>Required Reading</u>

If I may interject... The following should be required reading – placement in junior high or high school should be left up to the teachers. In my humble opinion, the list is:

The Letter from Birmingham Jail, by Doctor Martin Luther King, Jr.

Something wicked this way comes, by Ray Bradbury.

Bury my heart at Wounded Knee, by Dee Brown

Night, by Elie Wiesel.

The Vagina Monologues, by Eve Ensler

Always asking more Questions, by Ranger Iguana. (Should I apologize for that?)

We did the same tradition for Rodney Alton when he left. Same party. Two great rangers.

Platoon Plaques

I liked the plaque the most. It was personal. I asked myself, do I deserve an AR-COMM? I was a troop. I liked the Abrams certificate second. Because they all signed it.

A few years, one or two earlier, someone in the platoon asked me to take over making plaques for Rangers who left. It may have even been Mike Hall? I never took shop. I skipped in in eighth grade and at Saint Joe's in ninth, they assumed I took it in eighth.

I think they (my fellow rangers) figured I could draw, so I could do plaques. When Corporal Lucas taught a class on the NOD (night observation device) he brought me a NOD and a flip chart (butcher block paper bound at the top). He asked can you draw this NOD here and he pointed. Drawing was second nature to me. I was proud to do it. I borrowed from the styles of Jack Kirby, John Romita, John Buscema and Jim Starlin. All Marvel Comics artists. (Well, Kirby did work for DC also).

But I never took shop class in Junior High. I didn't know shit about woodwork. But saying "no" in the Rangers? I never said no. I disappointed. That made me feel terrible.

When I got to Berlin, I decided I would do plaques for anyone who left the platoon I was in. I would learn how to do a plaque. And I would use the one the Weapons Platoon gave to me as the model.

And guess what? I made plaques. Decorated with shoulder patches, unit crests, and things like Jump Wings, Ranger Tabs, Pathfinder badges and Special Forces tabs.

I think my first went to Mike Roof. "Roofer" we called him and it quoted the Brotherhood of War series by W. E. B. Griffin. The Majors when Lowell was in Korea. Yes, each plaque included a brass plate. It named the soldier, his rank, dates of service and quote. I got creative with quotes. It had to be personal. Something shared. For Roofer, this was…

"Tell the bugler to sound the fucking charge."

Scroll Plaque

Look what I did!

The Army Commendation Medal

"To: Specialist Four Clement James Ross

"For: Exceptionally meritorious service while assigned to numerous positions of responsibility and trust, culminating as Anti-Tank section gunner, Company A, First Battatalion (Ranger),

75th Infantry. During the period 10 September 1980 to 8 May 1983, Specialist Ross demonstrated outstanding professionalism, initiative, and devotion to duty resulting in an impressive array of achievements. His exceptional attention to detail, willingness to assume responsibility, and comprehensive technical and tactical expertise, have contributed materially to the combat readiness of the company. Specialist Ross's exemplary performance is in keeping with the highest traditions of the military service and reflects great credit upon himself and the United States Army.

29th April 1983."

Signed by J. T. Scott, COL Inf Commanding
And John O. Marsh, Jr., secretary of the Army.

The presentation of the AR-Comm was somber, earnest. Someone read the whole thing. All I could think was yeah they said my name. Is that what I did? Fine, I was going to Berlin and leg land. I have never been about dog and pony shows and never will be. I did not know that would follow.

No disrespect. I loved my platoon. Berlin would jade me. Not their fault.

1st 75th Ranger Battalion Certificate of Achievement (aka Abrams Certificate)

We called it an "Abram's Certificate" named for General Creighton Abrams, because were "Abe's Own."

I got one when I won post soldier of the quarter in 1982.

I was awarded another in May of 1983.

It read: *"For outstanding performance in many duty positions, during the period 1 September 1980 to 23 April 1983, culminating* *in assignment as Antitank gun team leader for Company A. Your dedicated performance coupled with <u>your unusual</u> expertise has contributed significantly to the combat readiness of this battalion. Your performance is a credit to you and is in keeping with the highest of Ranger Traditions. Rangers lead the way.*

Signed by J. T. Scott, COL, Inf, commanding

Lieutenant Poltorak read it. When he said, "Unusual expertise," he paused. The platoon laughed.

I was "unusual expertise" personified. The key being "unusual."

I was exciting because my platoon framed the Abrams certificate and everyone in the platoon signed in the three-inch margin around the certificate.

Today it hangs in our den.

I consider that I have the highest of ethical and moral standards. I will intervene when spousal abuse occurs with no safeguard to my own personal safety. I can be harmed. But I will protect from harm.

I just have few sexual boundaries. No children, no animals, and no feces. All else is open.

My compass got broken.

Please don't judge me. If I ever write the story of James Kennedy, then you may shoot your arrows.

Abrams Certificate

<u>May 08, 1983</u>

I signed out of Battalion.

Most don't get. The reference to "Battalion" – it means the First Ranger Battalion, 75th Infantry.

It's understood. And needs no further explanation.

When Rangers talk about Battalion, it's either first batt or second batt. No further explanation is needed. Eventually, they added a third and a regimental unit. After my time.

<u>Paul Teigland</u>

Paul learned I re-enlisted for Berlin. We went to Ruby Tuesdays at the Oglethorpe mall and had drinks and talked.

Paul was a son of someone with rank and pull. Paul's father was an officer. Perhaps a general. His family was in Europe and Paul was fluent in German.

Paul was mortars. He went to Ranger School and came back tabbed.

Paul told me before the U.S. Army, he enlisted in the French Foreign Legion. When his dad learned about it he pulled strings and got him yanked out. He said his dad said, if you want to join the military, join the U.S. Army. Paul joined to go to the Rangers.

At Ruby Tuesdays, Paul gave me a few starters with German. He pointed to the table and said, "Der Tisch." I said I studied French so I know articles are masculine or feminine. He said, "German has three. Masculine, feminine and neuter."

I would learn der, die, das.

West Berlin

Paul said, "Berlin – that's cool. I never thought that was an option."

West Berlin was the Berlin Brigade.

David Bowie went to Berlin in 1977. He recorded Low, Heroes, and Lodger with Brian Eno from Roxy Music. He bought a nightclub he called Der Djungel. And he hired the fanstasy girls as his wait staff. The fantasy girls were pre- or post-op trans. Post-op lacked an adams apple. They were gorgeous. Run way model, sports illustrated cover girls.

His song, "Heroes" to me was about a man and a woman trying to escape East Germany by fleeing across the Berlin Wall.

She dies, and he makes it maybe. His words are to her as she dies.

David Bowie recorded it with Brian Eno, Robert Fripp and he wrote the lyrics. He performed it on the Bing Crosby Christmas special in December 1977. I watched it in our living room.

May 1983. 30-day leave in Cleveland.

I drove to Detroit to be the best man for Stacy Nowak when he married Karen. I wore my khaki uniform and black beret. Karen's maid of honor was Tina and she and I hit it off.

Tina drove me to a hotel where she had rented a room for our last night together.

I don't recall how many times we had sex, but I was chafed.

I refuse to call it "making love," because that qualifier never began until I was with Lynn. Mark Vocca taught me this clarification. He said before Sarah, it was just fucking. When he met Sarah, for the first time it was making love.

I don't mean to put down Tina. She was dear to me. But we were balling.

Balling meant "Fuck as if it were your last time EVER."

Back then, I was incapable of making love. Physically, when I wanted to I could fuck. That was never the question. I even had the audacity to ask Tina to give me oral because Stacy said she was so good at that performance. I had no right to ask that. If she wanted to – that would have been her choice.

Ladies – the message is: oral is a gift, a reward. If you like it too, that will show in your delivery. Make it cherishable. Must always be intimate. And mutual. My turn then yours. Or your turn, then mine. Equal. Remember – the one giving oral is in control.

Back to Mark Vocca

Mark was my mentor and my teacher of Emotions. I ventured into unknown territory because of Mark. He sparked my courage to take the first step.

Bunny taught me to close the shield. Like an armadillo. Mostly Mark, but also sometimes Brandon, taught me to open the shield. Mark taught me that bravery revealed vulnerability. And vulnerability was a sign of strength. Not weakness. Bunny taught the opposite.

I wrote to Tina from Germany for about the first six months. I felt love and confusion. Tina was dedicated to me. I lacked the courage to muster that conviction. James Kennedy was in charge of my actions.

Before Berlin, May 1983 Concert – Pagans opened for the Ramones

May 1983 -- The Ramones played a concert in Cleveland at the Agora and Bill DeGidio had rejoined the Pagans on bass. Tim Allee was with Larry Lewis doing their own thing. So the Pagans opened for the Ramones and I was part of the road crew with a back stage pass. Mike Metoff on guitar and Bob Ritchie on drums. They had just released the Pink Album.

Back stage, before the opening, the Ramones were hanging out back stage in an area where we were not allowed in.

Mike Hudson wrote in "Diary of a Punk" that Bill and Dee Dee were mainlining Heroin. The truth was Bill and I were peering at the Ramones through a nail hole in the plywood door.

The Pagans did a great set. Charlie on organ looked at me suspiciously. He didn't know me from Adam. But he saw that Bill approved and Mike approved so that must have meant, I was okay.

The "Pink Album"

Mike Hudson sold me a box of fifty copies of the Pink Album on vinyl for $50. And I took them to Berlin to introduce the Pagans to Europe. I traded them at a German record store and got many Cramps albums. All the ones I had missed.

My army time was 1980 to 1986. Movies, music, pop culture, and everything that came out during that time, it was a void to me.

The first Pagans CD came out called "everybody hates you" on Crypt records, from Germany. I always wondered if I had an influence on that.

PART THREE: BERLIN

<u>Berlin Brigade, 2nd Battalion 6th Infantry</u>

From the beginning, I had a feeling I would be writing this very book at some point in the future.

What made me choose Berlin? It was part "Cabaret" and part David Bowie. Sex Pistols' song "holiday in the sun" makes reference to the Berlin Wall.

In elementary school, Miss Horner had us make a paper mache historical figure. I made one of Adolph Hitler. I used to watch PBS documentaries about how he would practice in front of a mirror. It taught me people saw the mirror image. Not what was behind it.

Manipulate what people saw in the mirror and you could be anything. I wouldn't have to live in fear.

That made me a fake. Before Lynn, I was never "real." And faking it ain't making it.

Thinking back, the tyrant bully made me fear. Never grasped the concept then. Figured it out later. Bunny controlled through fear. Or so he thought. I simply became clever at avoiding capture.

Back up, that's not entirely fair. I was sincere and genuine about some parts I presented. My soap box. I hated racists. I hated liars and thieves.

How much of a liar was I? I hid James Kennedy. Were there others? Sometimes I wondered who was Sergeant Ross? Who bravely went through Ranger School?

I thought Clement Ross was the poet and the sensitive soul. Who could do no harm and protect from harm.

Rangers are hard core bad asses who killed without hesitation. I was both. And others. It occurred to me that ego might be splintered. Fragments, of the whole. Hidden from one another. I did not figure this out at the time. I went along for the ride.

June 11, 1983, I arrived in Berlin. Tegel airport.

Back in November of 1982, I had heard about this job in Berlin with the Potsdam group. You had diplomatic rights to enter East Germany.

The idea was the NCO drove a supped-up Mercedes Benz around Soviet and East German training camps and took pictures. The training involved things like spin outs on ice and fish tails to avoid getting caught.

That would be so cool!

Unfortunately, when I arrived at Tegel, the NCO who promised me the job was gone. He was stateside (aka CONUS) and no one knew of a SGT Ross.

McNair Kaserne was my new home.

I had never had jet lag before. I spent two days in the break room asleep then awake then asleep again. The others around me watched Videos of old movies.

July 1983 -- I was assigned to CSC – Combat Support Company, Recon Scout platoon. We had four gun jeeps. There were SSG George Partridge (from Bco 1st Ranger Battalion); SSG Richard Lozano (from the 82nd Airborne); and SGT Tim Lindsey (also from the 82nd). There were others. Names have faded from memory. Steve Maselli. Kelly Richbourg. Ellis from Chicago who would later ETS doing a European Out and get busted for selling tobacco and booze on the black market. Yes, this was 1983 and the black market was still alive. Forty years after WWII ended.

My first weekend with the others in the platoon at McNair Kaserne…

I was getting to know the comrades and the scene. All I knew was Rangers and Battalion. The rest of the Army was a mystery. If you know the Rangers, that's one thing. No comparison.

The rest of the Army is not – it's a disappointment. A let down.

It's a tragedy because it doesn't have to be.

We were in the barracks at McNair. It was the weekend. There was this guy from the 101st. He was a braggart. A loud mouth. We were drinking beers and I was ready to leave. He got a rope from God knows where. He made a noose.

Okay, it's known that guys fuck with each other. The classic line – you *fell* for *that*?

He tied the rope off and he put the noose around his neck. I was drinking -- I don't recall where the anchor line was. I did not think I needed to pay attention. These were Legs. Legs were not soldiers. They got the name from "straight-LEG infantry." They were army douche bags who couldn't care less.

Next thing this guy from the 101st, he's on the ledge, the window opens and he jumps out. He jumped out with his hands on the noose. So he was not trying to break his own neck.

In the fall he broke the CO's window. There went the option of pulling him back up and saying it never happened.

He asked me to lie, he said tell them I wanted to teach the newbies rappelling. That was so friggin lame. I did… but then I recanted. I could not lie about this…

His hands on the noose meant it was not a suicide attempt. But what if it was a trial run and if there was a next time, it would work.

Now, I did not know if he wanted to commit suicide. I just knew he was fucked up. And he needed a shrink. MPs took him away.

NEXT!!!!

Scout Platoon, Combat Support Company, 2nd Battalion, 6th Infantry

Morning PT was easy – calisthenics and push ups. Until the time came to run. Running on cobblestones takes time to get used to. I lost count of how many times I fell. And landing on cobblestones -- hurt.

Combat Support Company (CSC) had mortars, TOW, and Recon Scouts. Were there others?

Scouts did Wall Patrol in the American Sector. Two gun jeeps with mounted M60 machine guns and 19-year-olds with live ammo and smoke grenades.

The idea was that if someone was trying to escape, we were to provide assistance.

One might suppose that "rules of engagement" would be a crucial part of our training. Never happened. Because *that* was up to Battalion S-3. As I recall, S-2 was intelligence and S-4 was logistics and supply. Otherwise, our mission on wall patrol was to report observations.

On the American side, we had wooden platforms raised on stilts with stairs to the upper deck from where we could clearly see the no man's land. Berlin wasn't just one wall. There were technically two. The cement wall with all the graffiti was on our side. Then there was a no man's land about 200 meters deep. And on the other side was a wall, at times a fence. About 200 meters apart were pill box towers and mushroom towers with at least two east German conscripts or draftees who served for two years. Pillbox towers were rectangular cubes. Mushroom towers were a box with diagonal sides perched atop an enclosed spiral staircase.

David Bowie

My first weekend in Berlin, it was David Bowie's concert in 1983. It was sold out. Steve Maselli had tickets but sold them. That was the Serious Moonlight tour after his Let's Dance album. I'd see it on video later. I wish I could have been there.

Christiane F wrote "Wir Kinder von Bahnhof Zoo."

She was a teenage child who got hooked on heroin and became a prostitute in Berlin. Her book, "we the children of Subway station Zoo" exposed the child prostitution situation in Berlin.

Here is what bothers me. Why do adult men want to fuck children?

I hated the Jon-bonet Ramsey thing. She was a child made to look like a person older.

What makes men think that a child is a sexual being? It's a child. Predators aren't sick. Sick means they can get better. They can't get better. The best and the only cure is a bullet to the head.

I've never committed murder. But for a child. To kill the predator. Gladly.

"Fucking"

How did the gerund "fucking" become the universal adjective in every country where English is spoken?

Once I realized that my English vocabulary was being depleted and replaced with the gerund, "fucking," I began reading the dictionary. I bought an American Heritage Dictionary at the PX. I liked this one because it also gave the etymological origin of words.

I read it on the bus and subway.

Parade Season 1983

We were in parade season. That meant June 17th with the Brits, the French, the Americans. Down the boulevard.

The jeeps were painted with baby oil so that they would look shiny and new. The tires were painted with brake fluid to make them look (again) shiny and new. Although, brake fluid rotted the rubber. Everything was about appearance. And the appearance was fake. Superficiality. Russians would love this book! All the hypocrisy of the Americans and their Army.

It was weird to me. Rangers did our training as if it was for real.

My Weapons Platoon, platoon sergeant, SGT Mike Hall said, "What you do in training is what you'll do in combat." Those words stuck with me.

SGT Hall also used to say, "Fuck around, fuck around,... ain't gonna be around."

The worst was yet to come. I just didn't know it yet.

Kavecki.

Night Out

There was a first night out. I was with one of my Scout brothers, Jeff Hupp. We went to U-bahnhof Oskar-Helene Heim. Then to an Imbiss Stand. Imbiss means literally, "in the bite." It refers to a stand, meaning a grill and a cash register to make and sell food. Most had a deep frier for "pomme frites." That's the French words for French fries. The weird part is that pomme means apple. The word "pomme de terre" (apple of the earth) is potato.

Back to Imbiss… That's where you'd get Wurst or Bulleten -- with pomme frites. Some had Doner Kababs. My favorite was Bulletten with curry ketchup and pomme frites with mayo. Berliners did not put ketchup on French fries. They used mayonnaise. Bulletten were like meatballs that were partially flattened and fried in oil. I later learned that they were a Berlin specialty.

Jeff and I were at the Bahnhof – the subway station.

An MP approached us. He was a PFC and green. Did he want to see to see if we were drunk? We were not. As he was walking away, I said his jump boats looked like shit. Rangers had jump boots… Corcoran jump boots. And they shined like mirrors. MPs tried to emulate us. Close but no cigar.

Suddenly this MP is asking us for our ID cards. I said what for? But I presented my military ID card as did Jeff Hupp.

His partner came over and said come on, we're taking you in. I asked what was the charge. He refused to answer.

Jeff and I laughed at this. It was so stupid. We thought this would be dismissed. I wanted this douche bag's badge.

We were charged with disorderly conduct and refusing to hand over our military ID cards.

Our Platoon sergeant (PSG) was called to bail us out.

I told him, what's the big deal? Rangers used to fuck with MPs all the time. We'd tie them up naked in the guard house.

He said, "that's not how it works in the rest of the army… They rule. They call all the shots. My Brother's an MP in Korea. That's how I know."

I said, "we complied when asked to show our IDs. We were not disorderly. They lied."

WTF? MPs were crossing guards. Children's playground cops.

My new PSG taught me a lesson. Don't fuck with MPs. I thought to myself, one day I will pay those fuckers back. Wishful thinking. I never got the opportunity.

I think because other enemies showed their ugly faces. They were enemies worse than the MPs.

Platoon party. Friday night.

In the Rangers, we didn't have platoon parties. NCOs didn't go out to bars with Spec-4's or privates. Berlin was different. I was a stranger in a strange land and so I went with the flow.

We – and that was E-06 NCOs, E-05 NCOs, E-04 Specialists and at least a couple of PFCs (private first class)... We started the night.

We started the night at an Irish Pub. We had shots of Tullamore Dew and Pints of Guinness. Guinness in Europe is not the same as Guinness in America. Guinness stout kicks your ass. We were walking. I was drunk, but coherent. I never had Guinness that was so strong. We walked and walked. I did not know where. I suppose I did not care. We passed by a Biergarten where Germans – Berliners – were doing the chicken dance. Americans have the Hokie pokie. Germans have the chicken dance.

Mon Cherie's

We entered a night club called Mon Cherie's. The married men said this is why we get drunk first. They wanted whiskey dick.

I thought, okay it's a strip club. I've been to those in Georgia, both Columbus at Benning and Savannah. Not quite the same. This was different. All the women who worked here were prostitutes which is legal in Germany. And this was a sex show.

The first woman just did a strip show to loud music. And she stripped until completely naked.

The next was called Madame Stradivarius and she stripped with a violin bow that she used on her breasts and between her legs.

Next was Pinnochio. A stripper with a doll that had a plastic dildo for a nose and yes, she would use it like you would imagine once she was naked.

Now "mon cherie's" are also little chocolate covered cherries with liquor. For the next act, a woman got a guy from the audience to perform cunnilingus on her. And for the reward, he was given a mon Cherie chocolate.

Lastly, the stage opened into a bubble bathtub. The lid opened like a toilet lid and the tub filled with water and bubbles. Two women would pick two men from the audience and all four would get naked and splash around in the tub.

After the bathtub scene, the women were free to roam among the men to see if any were interested in venturing upstairs to fornicate. I don't remember the price in D-marks, but I didn't ask.

One cute woman with short brown hair came up to Gary DiRusso and said in perfect English, "Gary, I have cream tonight if you want to fuck me in the ass again."

Gary was a single NCO in our platoon. Gary was a regular (apparently) and knew most of the employees by name.

By the way, these were not skanky women. They were beautiful, girl next door, smiling and without shame or embarrassment. This was a job just like being a clerk, or a shoe seller, or a lawyer or a doctor. Americans are prudes. Puritanical. Pretentious. Hypocrites. I learned not to judge. They were all just people who wished to survive and some had children and some were from eastern block countries like Hungary, Czechoslovakia, and Poland. They just wanted to live.

Head Start program

I was enrolled in the Head Start program. It was an orientation to German culture and language. Two or three weeks in length. It also included a bus tour of West and East Berlin.

The instructor was a German woman who knew culture, customs, and history.

As far as East Berlin was concerned, she said please don't buy any food. If you do, some east Berliner family would go hungry. That was truth in 1983.

What I saw:

The difference between the east and the west is like Kansas in the Wizard of Oz in black and white and Oz in color. East Berlin is Kansas and West Berlin is Oz.

They also took us to a soviet war memorial. Anyone who has seen Normandy, in France, knows that there are individual graves for each American who died fighting the nazis. Not so in East Berlin. The fallen Russian soldiers were gathered in mass graves. No names. I thought, didn't they at least have dog tags to ID the bodies? So sad for the families. Russians need closure too...

At some point in Berlin, Sting (from the Police) had a solo album with a song called "I think the Russians love their children too."

I'm sure the parents did. But the military treated the soldiers who died terribly.

Now let's complicate it.

After WWII, the Russians were the first to enter Berlin. Patton was told, ordered to stay back and let the Russians enter Berlin first.

The "spoils of war, to the victor goes..."

Russian soldiers raped Berlin women. I met adult children whose mothers were raped by the Russian soldiers.

Rape is a crime. But there were no arrests. No trials. No imprisonments.

It didn't matter if they were the very young or the very old.

Leon Uris wrote how he did not understand that. Americans were different. He was right about Europe. He was wrong about Native Americans.

Kit Carson among others committed atrocities. That included slaughter and mutilation of genitals. "Bury My Heart at Wounded Knee." Remember? Required reading?

Eventually I would meet Dagmar Pauels. Russian soldiers raped her mother. I'm in my twenties and I meet this wonderful German family in Berlin who invite me in for Christmas.

How could I ever read this book sober? There are so many atrocities.

I was a victim of bullies. Was I ever raped?

That question ends in a question mark.

East Berlin

We took a tour of East Berlin. It was 1983. In East Berlin, you couldn't say, "Guten Tag" to anyone. The Stazi were everywhere. Stadts Geheimnis Polizei. State Secret Police.

If you tried, they would look over their shoulder to see who was watching. George Orwell's "1984" – Big Brother is watching you. In 1983.

In East Berlin, I bought a bottle of Russian Vodka. That Friday, my roommate and I, we opened it and poured. It tasted the same as rubbing alcohol smelled. I never got a buzz – just a splitting headache. For all we knew, we were drinking paint thinner. No repeating that mistake.

The German Language and learning Deutsch

The teacher taught us the language portion; I wrote everything down phonetically and carried my cheat sheet whenever I went off-base to practice.

"Entschuldigen Sie" meant excuse me. "Ich möchte" meant I would like. And so on.

On the tour of the west, she told us how the Olympics were held in Berlin in 1936. Hitler was in power. Jesse Owens won the Gold but Hitler left the stadium refusing to shake the hand of a black American.

She taught us about the soviet blockade of Berlin and how the American and British pilots formed the "Air Bridge" bringing coal for heat, and food, and medical supplies to Berliners. She said if you are ever invited to dinner at a Berlin household, it is rude to leave food on your plate. You wasted nothing because Berliners knew hunger. Ironically when the Olympics were last in China, the Today show presented how if you cleaned your plate, you insulted the Chinese host by indicating he or she did not give you enough food. The opposite.

The pilots also had presents for the children. They tied little parachutes to chocolate bars and dropped them out of the planes. I kept that in mind when I was the patrol leader for Wall Patrol.

The American Red Cross sent care packages during the blockade. However, the packages were marked "Gift." Berliners had to learn that this word meant "Geschenk" (present) because "Gift" in German means poison.

There was so much hatred for Germans in America. First after World War One and then again after World War Two.

I think moreso after WWII because of Hitler and the Jews.

Jewish people were major contributors to American culture: Arts, theater, film, education, politics, science, and so much more.

Jewish people were the brains of the nation. Why would Germany ever alienate them? They were the writers, the intellectuals, the scholars.

Hitler's message: Let's drive out the greatest mind of this country. And drove them out or killed them.

Marlboro addiction

The first run I did with my new platoon, was a smoking ass PT run. I had been on 30-days leave with no PT. So I made a declaration to myself, that there would be no more poison. I decided to quit smoking and drinking.

That might have lasted a week at best.

I continued smoking until 2006. I quit with laser therapy. It was the only successful therapy. To this day, I still have my three libations. Cost Co Kirkland Brand Scotch. And three means three. Not five. Only three.

U-bahnhof und eine Kniepe

I don't know why. But I learned the German language fast. U-Bahnhof meant Untergrund (underground) train station. The Subway. "Eine Kneipe" meant a bar or as brits call it a Pub (short for public house). "Imbiß" meant a little fast food grill and deep frier. Bulletten was like a meat ball, but flattened like an inch thick oval, deep fried then covered in Curry Ketchup and curry powder. All ketchup in Berlin was Curry Ketchup. I loved Curry. So I never minded. French fries were "pomme frites." French for "French fries." No ketchup. In Berlin, mayonnaise is the condiment.

In the early days in Berlin, I would pick a subway station and wander the streets until I got bored and find a bar and settle in.

I would order a beer and sit listening.

My clothing and hair cut gave me away. "There's another one." They'd call me Yank or Ami. "They never bother to learn German. They impregnate our daughters. Drink our beers and leave."

That was my cue to say, "There are exceptions to the rule," which I said in German. From that point on, they liked me. They all wanted to practice their English. I had limited German abilities. But they would not let me pay for another beer.

Several times they also gave me cab fare for the ride back to McNair Kaserne. At that point I did not argue or reject the offer.

They were a generous people. Any interest showed in the culture was repaid ten-fold.

NCO Club on McNair

Some nights, perhaps out of boredom, I went to the NCO club at McNair. As I recall, there were two. One was for enlisted and NCOs and had music, dancing and allowed German men and women in. It was in the same row of buildings. The other was just NCOs and it was close to the rear gate where the Imbiss stand was located that sold Bulletten and Wurst and pomme frites with Mayo.

At the latter, I frequented because they offered Bier and played videos of classic movies. I saw Cool Hand Luke, Rebel Without a Cause, Citizen Kane, the Sting, Butch Cassidy and the Sundance Kid, On the Waterfront, A Streetcar named Desire, Night of the Iguana, Miss Lonely hearts, From here to Eternity, and Doctor Strangelove.

And my favorite: Cat on a Hot Tin Roof. It became my favorite because of Paul Newman's line, "You can smell the mendacity."

Rangers had officers. They were book smart. And most had common sense. But in the field, they relied on the NCOs. They trusted us. We had practical application. And if there was a deficiency, we corrected it with a creative solution.

Berlin was more about Leg-land ossifers who took little if any responsibility. Everything was someone else's problem.

Chris Reddish

Chris Reddish was the sole exception. He was a Ranger first and foremost and an officer. He had and will always have my total respect, loyalty and admiration.

Chris trained rangers. Fresh recruits from Basic. But he trained them as rangers. I loved it.

Yet he paid the price. In November 1983 in Hohenfels, they fucked him over and relieved him of command of the Scouts for something that had nothing to do with him. More later. I never learned why. Just that he was the fall guy. Scape goat.

Soldiers in Berlin had an Ausdruck (expression or idiom): "Sure hate if for ya."

How would I translate that one? "Na so was. Es tut mir ganz ganz ernst ernst Leid, ABER... Du im Arsch gefickt bist. Am wenigstens ist es nicht icke diesesmal."

It makes more sense in German. The American idiom is too ambiguous. Likely deliberate so the ossifers didn't catch on.

Deployments to the West (West Germany)

November of 1983, we left Berlin for a deployment to Hohenfels, West Germany. By this time, the Rangers had been to Grenada in October but I had not heard about it. AFN was Armed Forces Network. It was radio and television. Content was screened so we only heard what they wanted us to hear.

Taking the American duty train, you left from West Berlin and travelled at night to Frankfurt. The three western allies each had their own duty train. The British duty train took you to Helmstedt and Braunschweig. Just across the border between West Germany and the DDR (Deutsche Demokratisch Republik). The French duty train took you all the way to Strasbourg in France.

The American duty train had strict rules. In your cabin and no looking out the windows. It was night so what would you see?

The British duty train travelled during the day. They gave you a map marked with times when you would pass a soviet or DDR training camp. Photographs were allowed and encouraged.

This was the first hint that Americans were petrified of pissing off the Russians. The Brits were more like, "come on – you wanna piece of me? I will fuck you up, Boris, and bring Ivan with you too."

If you travelled by jeep, you got flag orders. It was a one-page document listing the dates and times of travel to and from the West. So named because it had flags of all four Allies: the US flag, the French flag, the Union Jack and the hammer and sickle. I used to have a copy which I planned to frame... alas. Lise was Nevermind. That's a good word for her.

Check point Alpha was at the border of West Germany and the DDR in Helmstedt. Check point Bravo was where you entered East Germany from the eastern side of the West. And the famous Check point Charlie was between east and west Berlin. There was a museum there that featured photos and memorabilia of those successful escapes and the history of the Berlin Wall.

Here is a point to be made. The Berlin Wall went up in 1961, the year I was born. Twenty-two years later in 1983, no one thought it would ever come down. But it did come down in 1989.

That year, I worked down town Cleveland for British Petroleum. I was eastbound on the shoreway when NPR made the announcement. I had to pull over. I could not drive. I was crying in disbelief.

Back to 1983, when we drove the jeeps, at Check point Bravo, I had to approach the soviet sentry with my Military ID card and the flag orders. The sentry was a private in the army of the USSR (aka CCCP). He was a Russian kid freezing his ass off while the officers were in the shack with AC or Heat. The kid would look at the orders, then look at you. Then as subtly as he could, he would wiggle his belt buckle and gesture with one hand what it looks like when you take a drag from a cigarette. Without the language to communicate, he was offering his belt buckle for American cigarettes. There were stories told in the barracks that they loved American cigarettes and also American porn like Hustler and Penthouse.

However, in the briefing before we left the barracks, they told us not to be tempted. There would be a Russian major with a telescopic lens ready to take a picture of you and then turn it over to Berlin Brigade command. That meant you caused an "international incident" and would be sent to Fort Leavenworth to make little rocks out of big rocks.

Prior to my arrival in the Scout platoon there was a guy from West Virginia and before he left Berlin, he took a star cluster (it's like a signal flare in red, green or white) and shot it at a pill box or a mushroom tower in no man's land. They buzzed a lot about it but no culprit was caught. His claim to fame was an expression of dedication. He'd say, "it's West By God you better smile when you say it Virginia."

Interesting to note: We got new recruits in October 1983, fresh out of basic and AIT and some of whom presumed that Berlin was on the border of the West and the DDR. When they learned we were 103 miles into the DDR, cut off from the West, they metaphorically shat their BDUs.

We took them out on patrol just like rangers would do. I name them later.

Back to 1LT Christopher Reddish

My GT score was 125. I don't know if that's good or bad. All I know is that West Point kept trying to recruit me. CPL Craig Riley in Weapons AT said, "if you wanna be an officer, fine. But come up through the ranks. Officers don't know shit. Some are book smart but not one has common sense."

I thought Poltorak was okay. I don't mean that. "Okay" sounds like average. He wasn't average. I think I have a clear picture of 1LT Poltorak because he listened to how I trained the troops. In AT, range estimation was the hardest to teach. Troops got it or they didn't.

But Captain Stecker – he really pissed me off how he handled Johnny Danford and Nick Barclay, when they burned in. I wrote a poem about the incident called "Calling out OPSKED 98." Sean Kelly read it and said, "you're a real prick."

Poltorek? I think I was biased and prejudiced at that point. Gerald Poltorek was actually caring.

Mike Hall said he got a star at the base in Louisiana. Polk.

Christopher Reddish was different. He made me open my eyes that not all officers were douche bags. Chris – may I call you Chris? – you were human, smart, cared, and had a great sense of humor.

He was the first officer I liked and respected. As I recall, I learned he was ROTC and majored in Philosophy. I'd love to speak to him now about existentialism and if I had his address, I would send him my poetry book.

At some point and I'm sorry I don't have the date… my calendars were gone… (Lise did that)… Lieutenant Reddish took us to Bergen Belsen.

Bergen Belsen

This was the camp where Anne Frank died. There was an entry structure where they told the history. Passed that it was like a park. But it had these huge areas of a square wall encasing a mound. The wall part rose about three feet. The mound rose significantly above that. The sign would read, "700 Toten." Toten was German for Dead. Corpses. They couldn't identify the bodies so they bulldozed them and buried them together. I saw the film "Night and Fog" in high school.

It was a mass grave for 700 corpses. It must have been an approximate. Most graves had already been started with the gas chamber -- victims piled and then burned.

And there was not just one mound. There were many. I did not count how many. I did not want to know. One is a tragedy – a million is a statistic. There were so many mounds. It overwhelmed me. The memorial park for Bergen Belsen made me sad and made me despise the people who did this. The Nazis.

How does a human being digest this? Absorb this? Inhale this?

The Russians in Berlin had mass graves. But they had dog tags! The Jews had tattoos to ID the bodies. If records were kept of the numbers. Or perhaps the records were burned. Russians had dog tags. Americans cared about their dead soldiers. Mournful Germans tried to care about the dead Jews. Russian Government could give a rat's ass about their fallen soldiers. I bet Mother Russia wept.

Chris Reddish cared about why we were here and the mission. I would shake his hand today. He was the officer I respected more than any other in my six and a half years.

Bottom line is that Bergen Belsen was testament of the horror of Nazi Germany. You did not need to be Jewish to feel the impact. You walked among the graves and they reached out and touched your heart. There was no escape. You were the blank page and Bergen Belsen was the impression from the printer. It remained like a tattoo.

I started having questions about free will and self-determination. Nature versus Nurture. Trauma creates decisions. How many are voluntary and how many are involuntary?

I tell myself that my decisions are all about self-determination. But I have made many decisions that were self-destructive. These were not self-determination. Were they nurture or nature? These were the existential questions I asked.

On many occasions I chose a path of self destruction. If there ever is a book about James Kennedy, it will explain all. But I will probably say it is a book of fiction.

James Kennedy is a work of decadent art. Decay and damnation. Nothing short.

The Battle Book of Berlin

Back in Berlin, at one point, 1LT Reddish took us on the tour according to the battle book. The battle book was the top-secret document that showed our actual positions if the Russians came into Berlin with aggressive action.

We started off walking through the Tiergarten ("Animal garden" like Central Park in NYC). There were guys with shovels digging a hole. Now this was 1983 and they were unearthing unexploded dud rounds from World War II.

Reddish -- I'd rather call him Chris, because I really liked him and respected him.

He took us to where our "official" battle positions were to defend Berlin against an enemy attack. Whether it was Russia or East Germany.

Dough boy city was the training site where the Legs built defensive fighting positions with sandbags. We were on a City street with asphalt. Brick and mortar. Where would the dirt come from? Asking that question would get me in trouble.

When we trained, we used furniture. Not sandbags.

Platoon Party in 1983

Perhaps it was at Sergeant Lozano's home. I can't recall. We had pizza delivered and watched two VHS Videos. And many German beers.

Gene Hackman in "March or Die." Then James Coburn in "the Cross of Iron." Michael Quinlin had a German girlfriend who would become his wife. Her name was Birgit. When Cross of Iron started to play, she recognized the intro. "Hansen klein ging allein in der Wald mit Sohnen Schein…" She said she used to sing that song as a child.

The Sam Pekinpah film was about the German army in Russia at the end of WWII.

Rolf Steiner became my hero. I recited lines from him. "If there is a God… he's a sadist and he probably doesn't even know it." "Do you think that just because you and Colonel Brandt are more enlightened than the other officers that I hate you any less? I hate all officers." Except Chris Reddish. I was angry. I did not know who or what should be my targets. They would catch me off guard and shock me that they were my targets and I never suspected them.

Favorite Movie

Perhaps in the 1970s, it would have been "Billy Jack." The racism made me want to go berserk. I never went as far as to wear blue jeans with a black t-shirt. But I shared his philosophy.

In Berlin it became the "Cross of Iron." How can I put this? I identified with Rolf Steiner, because I was seeking to define my own identity.

I had challenges with officers and with God.

Officers should be obvious. God is different. It's explained thoroughly in my poetry.

Favorite movie now? I have to leave that blank.

Perhaps, Tom Hanks in the Mister Rogers' movie. I never knew he was so genuine.

Humboldt Bunker for Rappelling

Late 1983, Tim Lindsey, Mike Roof and I taught the privates, Jack Sax, Brian Fee, Tim Haven and Joel Kulow how to rappel off of the Humboldt bunker riddled with bullet holes from WWII.

We used snap link, sling ropes and 120 foot rope to rappel. I taught the double butterfly knot for the anchors. The same short cut that SSG Hyde taught me in Pre-Ranger.

For the rappel ropes, there were two – you always also had two anchor points. If one broke, you had a back up.

Troops who are new to rappelling had two fears. Going over the edge, you had a stretch factor of one -third. The 120-foot rope would stretch. That made it feel like falling. Until the stretch factor stopped and you became stable. The other fear was falling.

I did a falling drill to demonstrate how important the belay man is. I released my brake hand and yelled "Falling." The belay man did his job and stopped me. It was either Tim Lindsey or Mike Roof on belay. I would not have trusted anyone else.

Newbies to rappelling always want to use the left hand to brake. Most people are right-handed. As I am. The rope – two strands – go through a loop in the snap link. The right hand holds the rope from the snap link down to the ground. The left hand is typically on the rope to the anchor point for balances.

New privates don't trust the hand that goes behind the back (the right hand). So they use the left hand to grip and stop the descent. I told the privates to go down with no glove on the left hand.

I also demonstrated how you could stop completely, by taking the rope behind you and looping it around your left thigh. Once that was done, you had hands free mode. That technique is used to rescue mountain climbers.

Letters to home

One day in Berlin, I wrote a letter home stating that this would be my last letter until I received a letter from my father. Perhaps in fall of 1983 or 1984.

The Bunny wrote one letter to me in Berlin.

I then remembered why when Paul Endres asked Bunny for a letter of recommendation when I was in High School, Bunny asked me to write it. I think Paul was going to Choate. I wrote the letter for Paul to get into Choate.

Bunny was illiterate. I did not know that. His letter to me in Berlin contained superficial non-sense. Jibberish.

Once I received Bunny's letter in Berlin, I wrote back. I demanded an explanation. Each and every episode of abuse. The question was WHY. Why did you beat your wife? Why did you beat your dogs? Why did you beat and torture your sons? I never got an answer.

Mom told me after my ETS that she took every letter and put them in the trash.

Mom said my letters would have meant retaliation against those at home. Mom, Chuck and Cathy.

I would never want that. Especially not while I was not there to stop it.

She did not want the abuse that would follow. She presumed the Bunny would retaliate against her, Chuck and Cathy. I didn't think of that. I thought my letters were between the Bunny and me. I learned then that mom screened letters. How many others went into the postal carrier's attic?

In the army I wrote a lot of letters. Especially on CQ duty. That was an all night shift of charge of quarters. CQ = charge of quarters. You stayed up all night but got the next day off.

Cri Du Chat

Fall of 1983, I went to a punk rock concert. It ended late but it was the weekend so I didn't care. In the parking lot, some guys called me (in German) and said come with us (Kommst Du mit?). We're going to the "Cri du chat." French for cry of the cat.

Cri du chat opened at 2:00 am and stayed open until 11:00. It was THE after hours place. It was filled with theater people, musicians, artists, poets – my kind of people.

My first night there, I stayed until dawn.

I met a black American who was a dancer and invited me to a private party. He was shirtless and I suspected that he was gay which I didn't care about but I was Army active duty.

I met Veronica on one of my visits. She became my first Berlin lover. I can't say girlfriend because I don't know how she felt about me. We had sex the first night we met. I met her before Hohenfels in 1983. Before we left, she asked me for 500 DM for her rent and utilities. I gave her the money because I thought I was falling in love or out of some weird sense of duty to be Don Quixote. Except that Don Quixote was not a slave to lust.

After Hohenfels, Veronica "broke up with me." I use quotation marks because we never were really a couple. But she told me about a girlfriend. My German was pretty limited back then. At first I thought she was saying she wanted to move in with her to share expenses. Then it became clear that she was moving in with her because they were a couple. In love. Veronica was at least bi. After all, she had sex with me.

Love. What person in their 20s actually knows what love is? If you asked me in my teens or twenties, I would have proudly and defiantly expressed adamantly how thoroughly I knew and understood the concept. And that simply was not true. I knew love as the source of orgasm. That makes me happy. That was not love.

That doesn't mean I was obsessed with sex and only thought the connection mandated coitus. I knew romance from lyrics of musicals and Beatles' songs. Those two were my teachers.

A child loves the parents. Because you're supposed to or you need to. Even if you're invisible to one and to the other you're a target.

I did not learn love until 2004. I was 43 when I met Lynn. All I knew was that whatever she needed, that came first. It did not matter if she did not return the same. I would love her according to what she wanted or needed. Nothing less. Her needs first. That's what love is. Like the song, "Being in Love" from the Music Man. I knew that for years in theory. In 2004, I understood and lived it in practice.

Digression: In Berlin, Americans were "Scheiss Amis." Scheiss is shit and amis is French for friends. English were called "Britain Schnitten" and French were "Fransozen Hosen." But no nicknames for the Russians. At least not that I ever learned. Why did that occur to me now? That came according to Michaela. She taught me those. I would guess that she learned them in school.

I don't know why Americans were "Shit Friends." Consider the Air Bridge. Is that a "thank you"?

Tea Shops

Berlin had tea shops. Like America has Dunkin' Doughnuts and Starbucks. Yes, they have Earl Grey, but... my favorites were Jasmine and Mango. Reggie and I would make a pot of tea and talk for hours. We discussed academics. Philosophy, history, language, -- but here's what's interesting. Reggie was black and I was white. We never discussed race. Why? Was Reggie reluctant to describe issues of race? Certainly not with me. He knew me. I was not a red neck white boy who bowed to the Klan.

I dare Kavecki to know these names: Emmett Till, Rosa Parks, John Lewis, Dr. King, Malcolm X, Medgar Evans, Harriet Tubman, Sojourner Truth, and W.E.B. DuBois.

Every student should know every name and why he or she was a significant contributor to civil rights. Every student should read "the letter from Birmingham Jail." An annual event.

I think Reggie and I didn't need to discuss race because it was a given. Reggie knew.

Just like Tod and I knew. Never a jewish thing between us. We had a fun competition going... who can fill the red cross blood drive donation bag faster?

Hohenfels, October 1983

We deployed for training. Flag orders, same drill. We acquired new troops on that deployment. They arrived by train.

God knows what they went through. Arrive in Berlin and hey guess what? You're going to Hohenfels in the West?

Jack "Sammie" Sax, Dean Lavelle, Brain Fee, Tim Havens, and Joel Kulow. There is at least one name missing. Jack and Teresa now live in Maine. Tim stayed in Berlin and probably speaks better German than I do.

A Special Forces Green Beret joined our platoon. His name was Mike Roof. A transitional duty assignment before he went to Bad Tolz. I hope he met Don Purdy there. Don was insane but the best in the field. Electric Pineapple in Vietnam.

I've met so many rangers who fought in Vietnam and that war fucked them up. Henry Eggleston (aka Bonehead) had a necklace of human ears.

Tom Brizendine... another ranger... While he was active duty, Vietnam war protesters disguised themselves as military. Dress greens, the whole thing. These assholes presented his wife with an American Flag and offered condolences and said we're sorry your husband died in combat. Donna was devastated – but Tom was still alive. The cruelty. That was uncalled for. Vicious. Sadistic. They will die a coward's death. I will ask Satan if I can watch.

On the ranger listserver. Courtesy of Peter Parker, I met a ranger. He was a cop at Kent State and he partied the night before the 1970 massacre. He said the national guard troops were also war protesters. That's why they joined the national Guard. So war protesters shot war protesters at Kent State in 1970.

In Hohenfels, those new privates did not stand a chance. Ranger, Green Beret and 82nd Airborne two NCOs. We would train them to patrol the right way and LT Reddish, a Ranger himself was all in favor.

I was getting the Army Times at that point. Perhaps I thought I was a career soldier at that point. We were in Hohenfels and the Army times published the names of the dead from Grenada. My battalion, my company. Randy Cline, Marlin Maynard, Mark Yamane, and Mark Rademacher. My friends and fellow Rangers.

Prairie Runner happened. That was the mission to Grenada. They postponed it.

I was in Berlin Brigade and it happened. My company went there. Marlin Maynard was my assistant gunner.

I was sad. Our platoon had the chance to go into town, to eat, drink, be merry. I stayed in the barracks. Alone.

Something happened in town.

1LT Reddish was relieved of command. SSG Lozano was sent to Alpha company.

I kept asking and no one would say.

Some embarrassment and a cover up.

Duty train back to Berlin. SSG Lozano was transferred to Alpha Company. I never saw Lieutenant Reddish again.

When the duty train pulled in the station in West Berlin, the Army band was waiting for us. It was like that scene out of the Dirty Dozen, when the band had so many false starts. But there were no false starts now. Like a hero's welcome. Probably John Phillips Sousa. I can hear it in my head. Just never learned the name.

Wives were there to greet their husbands. It was made to feel close to a ticker tape parade in Manhattan. Where was the sailor in the white uniform kissing the girl?

Berlin dog-and-pony shows were our life. No, that's not fair. It wasn't Berlin. It was the Army. The Army in Berlin and I had to ask why.

Berlin history excited me. Captivated my mind. After World War II, there was Berlin in ruins. Toward the end of WWII, the Brits and the Americans would bomb randomly. The Soviets picked a grid square and annihilated it. A grid square is 1,000 meters by 1,000 meters. Everything inside was laid to ruin.

Russians and their allies were the first to arrive in Berlin. There is an expression I heard in movies, but never quite grasped the meaning. It went, "To the victor, the spoils of war." Americans did not get this. What it meant was Berlin women were raped by the Soviet soldiers. It did not matter how young or how old. They were the spoils of war. Women would disguise themselves to make them look ugly to avoid getting raped.

After the war, it was the "Trummel Frauen" who pushed the wheel barrels of brick and debris and started the rebuilding.

During the Soviet Blockade, the Americans and the Brits flew supplies to the city. Berliners called it "Die Luft Bruecke" – the Air Bridge.

Hitler was embraced by the Bavarian. He was despised by the Prussians. And despised by Berliners.

Hit Parade 1983

Just like American K-tel, Germany had Hitparade. I bought it in a Schall platte store. Internet has helped me find the songs. My copy of the actual album was loaned to the Jew hater, Brandon Zart. These are the songs that I recall with help from the internet: Nino D'Angelo – "Jenseits von Eden;" Nena -- "99 Luftballoons;" Geier Sturtzflug – "Brutto Sozial Produkt;" Peter Schilling -- "Major Tom;" DOF – "Kudo, Duse im Sauseshritt;" Ingrid Peters – "Afrika;" Ixi –"Knutchfleck;" and Spider Murphy Gang – "Mir san ein Bayerisher Band" and "ich schau Dich an (Peep peep)."

Brandon and his family loved Nino D'Angelo. They told Brandon "Play the German song."

The Pauels

1983, We had the opportunity to sign up for Christmas with a German Family. I signed up and was afforded the opportunity to have Christmas with the Pauels family.

Michael (Meesha-Ayl) und Dagmar (Dag-mahr) were the parents. The children were Christian, Birgit, Tanja and Diana.

They were my first tutors in German, speaking and writing. They took me in as their own. It was the first time I ever felt safe with strangers.

It was December 1983.

Birgit was the eldest daughter. There was a day she came home from school weeping. Sobbing. Distraught. They taught her – as was mandatory – about the Final Solution, the Holocaust. She said, "How could WE do such a thing?" Her rhetorical question included everyone.

Micha was the father of Birgit and Diana. Dagmar was the mother of Christian and Tanya.

I loved Diana instantly. She was the imp. The Loki.

Dagmar once told me that her mother had been raped by the Soviets when they came into Berlin. Her mother also had sex with an American who was the father of Dagmar.

It made me think of the John Lennon song, "Woman is the Nigger of the World."

This was 1984. Not George Orwell's world.

I was not prepared for this reality.

"Dinner for One"

Berlin had a tradition on New Year's Eve. Everyone watched a British comedy sketch called a "Dinner for one."

Freddie Frinton played "James" the butler and May Warden played "Miss Sophie." It was a 20-minute skit.

It was also called the 90ᵗʰ Birthday party.

It was great humor. I loved it.

The Pauels essentially adopted me

I spent weekends in their home. They bought me a suit to wear to the theatre. Pauels took me to plays. "A Midsummer Night's Dream" and "My Fair Lady."

One Opera. After a week in the field. "Der Wildeschultze." I fell asleep and snored. I embarrassed them. I was ashamed.

PFC Darryl Bryant

In 1983, Bryant reported to me in the Scouts. When we were on duty, I called him either PFC Bryant or Bryant. Apart from the military crap (and crap is what Berlin Brigade was), I called him Darryl. Yes, he was a Private First Class (PFC/E-03) and I was a Sergeant (SGT/E-05). But things were different in Berlin.

SFC Bill Guest was there a very short time and I'm sure he said, "get me the hell out of here."

I liked Darryl. He was squared away and smart as hell. Darryl would have been a great Ranger.

We had this telepathy. Not literally, but metaphorically. We would glance at one another and usually Darryl would cock his head to one side and smile and squint one eye. And that moment, we knew what each other was thinking.

It reminding me of the bond I had with Howard Mullen. Like Radar on mash.

Darryl invited me to his wedding. I attended Polter Abend (noisy evening). This is a German tradition. Those who attend shatter plates, saucers and cups and the soon to be bride and groom are required to clean up the debris.

Darryl's fiancée. I think her name was Gabi (but I could be wrong). Gabi's mom was so impressed that I was learning German, she gave me a gift. It was a book. "Die Amerikanishe Kalt Welle." An anthology of first-hand accounts of life in Berlin after the end of WWII. I still have it.

Gabi had a grandmother. Gabi told me that her oma (grandmother in German) asked her if Darryl grew a tail and horns after midnight.

I said, "Are you serious?" Bist Du Ernst?

She said yes. American soldiers. White soldiers told the French and German and probably the Italian citizens that after midnight, black people – not just Americans – all black people grew horns and tails.

Gabi's oma was suspicious enough to ask the question.

This was 1983??? Come on. People were still believing that racist crap?

When I began this book, I thought it would be about exposing the hypocrisy in the Army in Berlin. Racism continues to raise its ugly head. These details need to be documented. And exposed.

Breakfast 1983

Because of my time with the Pauels, I would take my squad on PT runs. And we would stop at a German bakery and I would buy Schrippen (breakfast rolls of bread). Schrippen had to be fresh.

As we ran I would carry the rolls.

In the barracks, in my mini fridge I had jams, and cheese and schinken (ham), and this hazelnut spread. And honey. For the rolls.

The troops loved the breakfast. But I know none of them repeated it unless I initiated it. It was a German breakfast.

Dagmar's parents

For the 50th Gold anniversary, I drew the wording on the card in old German Gothic lettering. Like calligraphy, but with an ink pen.

The Pauels loved my art work.

They kept a collection.

Primary Leadership Development Course (PLDC)

04 JAN 1984 – Mannheim, West Germany. TDY. The primary focus was on cleaning the barracks and passing the inspection. There was no teaching about leadership. Army schools were disappointing. And sad.

20-30 MARCH 1984 - Bonnland

Scouts with PSG Bill Guest. SFC Guest was a Ranger from Charlie Company. He was a marine vet from Vietman. Hard core and strictly military. I liked him as an NCO but I was getting getting a negative attitude about Leg Land and the lack of morale, the lack of spirit de corp, the lack of motivation. Troops slumped into resignation. "When is it my turn to get fucked by the chain of command?"

I don't think Bill sensed the disintegration of morale and attitude.

At Bonnland, Sax and Havens and Fee and LaVelle did a great job and showed no signs of decline in Morale.

Bonnland was a small German village that Hitler cleared out. He relocated all the families and turned the town into a training facility for the German Wehrmacht.

We practiced in city fighting. The hardest part was the road march from the train station to Bonnland and back once we finished training.

Rangers versus Legs

Rangers were better that Legs. Not all of them. Most legs were cooks, clerks, medical staff at hospitals, truck drivers. There were legs who were Infantry soldiers who were dynomite. Our new privates from basic who arrived in Hohenfels. Sax, Havens, LaVelle, Fee. There was one other. They were better because we trained them. We trained them like they were newbies in first battalion RANGER 75th Infantry. We trained them like they were new recruits in Tim Lindsey's 82nd Airborne. We trained them like they were young in Mike Roof's special forces, Green Berets.

Wish my memory was better. I see his face. There was one other.

I think the 82nd taught NCOs to be heartless pricks. They came down hard on privates. Rick Lozano and Tim Lindsey were the only two examples I had. But George Partridge was Bravo 1st RANGER Battalion and I was Alpha 1st Ranger Battalion. George and I both treated privates the same. Rick and Tim could be cold. Did George and I treat them differently because we weren't in battalion? We both showed kindness.

At Battalion, Legs were scum. "Get off the fucking grass," yelled someone when the Legs of the 24th trampled our grass.

The legs in our platoon – George and I took them "under our wing." We never did that with the Legs at Hunter. They were shit-birds. Not worth our time of day.

Rangers respected Marines. Their discipline. Hated Legs. Their lack thereof.

Christian Pauels

Christian was the oldest boy in the Pauels family. Dagmar's son. I gave him most of my American clothes. I was shedding America. Because the Army in Berlin was so deceptive and dishonest.

To me, the Army represented the best of the best of America. The examples that all should follow. Theory versus practice.

Rangers practiced well. Leg land was a joke.

Shitbird SFC Kavecki

Why should any platoon sergeant begin a squad leader meeting in a platoon that included BLACK soldiers with, "Who's got any good NIGGER JOKES"? Wait – the platoon does not need to include BLACK SOLDIERS. The platoon could be Asian, Native American, Latino, Eskimo, Sikh, and Australian. Kavecki was a racist asshole and he was wrong.

This paragraph was the result of an explosive rant from the eruption of anger from something that has not gone away. Please accept my apologies.

Christian Pauels again

Back to the clothes. The clothes included the flannel shirt that bunny gave me.

Bunny recognized that when he came to visit in 1984. His eyes conveyed resentment. I ignored him. He was still the ass.

I think Christian wore it to impress him and make him feel accepted in a German home. "I wear your shirt because I accept you."

He could have said, your son tells me you're an asshole.

Christian also wore a set of my ranger cammies to Tempelhof on open door day. I suppose I did not make it clear to Christian when I gave him the uniform, -- not to be worn on any Army or Airforce base.

Cpt Dick Head Wiles

Captain Wiles asked me if I gave my uniform to a Berlin civilian. He said someone told him… God knows he may have seen it himself. Wiles always lied to me. He was not a Ranger, though he wore the Tab. Rangers call them "Tab-Wearers." Not the same as Rangers.

He was the one who said, "Leg land is not so bad." He had no clue. I doubt he ever read my file.

While I was at Combat support company, it was CPT Donald Cox who approved sending me to LOG-213 Motor Sergeant School. Cox was Special Forces. AND Ranger qualified. Probably only went to Ranger School.

Scheiss Amis

When Americans rode the U-Bahn (Berlin subway), they stood out. They were obnoxious. Loud. Belligerent. I say they, them, I was not in the same category.

I watched them as an outsider. Disguised as a Berliner. My identity was hidden. I began to wonder, what was my identity? I clearly stepped away from being an American soldier. Yet I was committed to being in Berlin until November 1986.

The interesting thing was my accent. Berliners knew I was not native German. But they asked me, "Are you French or Scandinavian?" When I said American. They said, "das glaube ich nicht." [I don't believe that.] Dismissed as not even remotely possible.

Perhaps because I studied French? But where did Scandinavian come from?

Michael Pauels had a night job

The Pauels told me that I was invited every weekend to stay. Most weekends I took them up on the offer. They became my family. I became a big brother to the daughters. Christian was reluctant. Perhaps because he was doing drugs to escape something and I conveyed my suspicions to Dagmar and Michael. What a hypocrite I was. I did drugs. In high school, home on leave and in Berlin.

Some nights when I slept over, I was usually on the floor in Christian's room, Micha would get a call in the middle of the night. Someone had died at a hospital. We would go and get the body.

We drove to the morgue first and get the vehicle. Then we drove to the hospital.

The body was covered with a sheet. They were usually an elder person. Natural causes. Micha would show me the tragic ones. Already in the morgue.

A Turk who died from smoke inhalation when the candle caught fire to the shelter he created with a sheet. He was burned from head to toe. I had never seen a scorched body. It was horrible. He was a squatter. Squatters in Berlin occupied vacant buildings. By squatting, they established a legal right to be there.

Another corpse was a man who drowned in the Wannsee. The lake on Berlin's West side. It was – sorry. Not it… He or she was bloated. Sometimes blue and sometimes green. Bloated – swollen. Inflated. Like an obese person. But everywhere.

Micha always demanded that I sanitized my hands. He was a good man and a good friend. "Demanded" – he was protecting me. Hands touching the dead. Had to be sanitized. We know this now in the new normal of Covid-19.

While I'm thinking about 2020 and current events

The #metoo movement. Bravo to the women who came out to expose the rapists, perverts, and predators. I blame the attorneys for calling it the ambiguous term of assault. The term of the crime should accurately describe the crime. Call it rape, sodomy, groping. I don't think there is yet a term for a forced fellatio – there should be.

I have one exception. Asia Argento. Italian actress and producer.

Jimmy Bennett is an asshole.

Ms. Argento made arrangement to pay that asswipe $380K. Because he accused her of "sexual assault" when he was seventeen and she was 37. She should not have paid him a single dime.

I describe the scenario like this. I'm 17 and all 17-year-olds are dip shits and horny who cum like a rocket ship. Introduce an incredibly hot Italian actress who is drop dead gorgeous. She wants to initiate sex with fellatio then coitus? I am not a victim. I'm on top of the world.

When I was 17, I would do cunnilingus until I was fluent in Italian.

"Sexual assault"? That's a joke. Jimmy Bennett is an idiot. Worse. Opportunistic. Take advantage of. Slap in the face. Of a great thing.

She never should have even had her attorney offer the settlement of $380K. He was not worth it. He did not deserve it. He cheated her.

The Italian actress was robbed. If I ever meet Jimmy Bennett I will punch his lights out, steal his credit card and transfer $380K back to Ms. Argento.

1983 -- Ku'Damm was short for Kurfurstendamm

In that time frame, Udo Lindenburg had a song. "In funfzehn Minuten, sind die Russen auf den Kurfurstendamm." Translated to "in 15 minutes, the Russians are on the the Ku'Damm."

There was a bar on Kufurstendamm. It was like an atrium. Various floors around a center. In the middle on the basement, was a bar where a German woman, who was the bar tender, would pull out her acoustic guitar and sing songs in English and invited the bar customers to sing along.

I became a regular.

One day, I asked if I could take her to dinner. She thanked me and said she was flattered, but she has a girlfriend and that would not be okay with her.

In Berlin, gays and lesbians were accepted and respected. I should have known that from "Cabaret."

Then there was the place most Americans hung out. The Ku'Dorf. It was huge. Main dance floor played Van Halen's "Jump" and Bruce Springsteen's "Born in the U.S.A." Guys in my company, in my battalion, in my brigade all came here to get laid. German women came here to get laid. I went there and never got laid. I got my ear pierced – repeatedly. Monday morning, I'd take the thing out and let the hole close back up.

The most popular place for hooking up... neanderthal guys hooked up. I never hooked up. I must have been a leper.

Learning German

I studied French under Bea Andrews. German was completely different. For one, French was a romance language -- masculine, feminine or plural. German was masculine, feminine, neutral or plural.

It must be so hard for a person who learns German as a native language to learn English.

If I say in German, "ich gehe." It means, "I go, I do go, I am going, I walk, I do walk, I am walking."

I studied every week and weekend. And practiced with a cheat sheet every time I left the barracks.

Pagans Albums

Before I left Cleveland, Mike Hudson sold me a box of the Pagan's "Pink Album" with the Sam Petrello designed cover. The box had fifty albums. In Berlin I traded them at a record store and bought Cramps albums. Bill De Gedio was also involved. He gave me a bunch of 45s of the Defnics. "51%" backed with Brandon's "Hello from Berlin."

The guy who did the trade played "Hello from Berlin" on his record player. I should say he attempted to play it. Brandon had recordings of speeches from Adolph Hitler. Brandon would memorize the speeches phonetically. He could recite the jibberish without a clue about what he was saying. The Defnics single started out with a Hitler speech... "an dieser Stunde, Nord zu denken..." the needle lifted off the record. I didn't know that Hitler speeches were against the law in Germany. It makes sense. But once again, my naïvete reared its ugly head.

The record store clerk took them all and I got about six Cramps albums that I didn't have before.

PX albums sold

The PX had an area that sold music. No punk or glam. I found myself discovering interest in Buddy Holly and Diana Ross and the Supremes. I found myself educating myself with classics. Big Band, Billy Holiday, Bob Dylan and Janis Joplan. The closest that I got to punk was Wall of Voodoo and Adam Ant. A band called Big Country from Scotland was hugely popular.

When I couldn't discover music, I turned to movies and discovered them.

SFC Bill Guest – 30 MAR 1984

I remember him from Charlie Company in 1/75. He was Vietnam vet and former marine. He bragged about the ugly fuck contest when he won having the false teeth still on his dash-board. He followed in succession the platoon sergeant whose brother was an MP in Korea who taught me don't argue with MPs.

SFC Guest came at a time when I was searching for the friggin middle. Rangers had a standard. It was up here. Legs had a standard that was down there. I could not expect ranger standards. This was leg land. I wanted to kill leg NCOs and officers. This was irrational. I wrote a poem about the Grey Area and showed it to Mike Roof. He repeated, "where is the fucking middle?"

Bill, if you ever read this... when you met me, I hated the Army, I hated all officers, and I especially hated Leg white NCOs. They were worthless pieces of garbage.

Latino NCOs? Only Numbnuts. That was our name for SSG Wilson Nunez. He was a liar and an idiot.

He told me 18 months overseas qualifies for ROTC... "Unless you're on second enlistment – then you're on career status. That means 36 month tour.

I had many many latino brothers. None ever betrayed me. Only NumbNuts. And that stupid fuck was a ranger tab wearing E-06. Whiskey Tango Foxtrot, over?

The Pauels taught me the idiom "Kinderstube"

Kinder means children. Kinderstube means "child's room." If someone had a piss poor upbringing, then one would say, "der hat keine gute Kinderstube." [He didn't have a good children's room.] As I recall, it was mostly used in the negative, but to pay a compliment, it was also used like, "Du hast eine gute Kinderstube gehabt."

Of my own? Bunny taught me you're a worthless piece of shit, you're stupid and don't deserve my name. Mom was the other extreme – you're so intelligent, you're handsome… my middle was a gray area with no definitive boundaries. No up or down. No left or right.

And don't preach at me for not using "nor." This is my narrative.

SFC Kavecki

One day, SFC Weldon Kavecki became our platoon sergeant. I kept an open mind every time a new Leg showed up.

Kavecki was a drunk who showed up for PT at 10 or 10:30. Hung over.

Kavecki was a leg – raised by polish parents. Adopted as a native American kid.

Kavecki was raised to hate.

Kavecki would start the squad leader meeting saying, "whose turn is it to get the beers?" Squad leaders bought the beers. Kavecki was a drunk. We knew that because he would never show up for PT (physical training). He'd arrive by about 10:00 am. Reeking of some kind of bourbon.

I never got this confirmed but Tim Lindsey said Kavecki was a native American, adopted by Polish parents. Last name made sense. Larry Allen was full-blood Native American in mortars in the Rangers. He had honor, discipline and well-earned respect. Kavecki? Was more like a privileged spoiled brat.

To me, he was just another redneck leg. Even had the southern drawl.

Let me define "leg." This may not be the case today, but it was back then. "Leg" meant straight-leg infantry. I don't know where it came from but it meant non-Airborne.

My years in the Rangers, they taught me that Rangers hated "Legs." "Hate" is too strong a word. It wasn't so much hate as it was a lack of respect. Disdain, contempt, loathing. Better and more accurate adjectives than "hate." Legs were a disappointment. We were all in the same Army. But I'm supposed to be in the same category as you? No. I'm not. When "you" refers to a "Leg" – the comparison ends. I got it. Rangers and Legs were in two completely different branches of the military. And never the twain should meet.

Sadly they did with terrible consequences.

Rangers… they would say that they hated commies. Communists. Then Sting put out a song called "I think the Russians love their children, too." Back in the 1980s, no one said they hated muslims. That has probably changed now. Not for me. I will always remember my dear friend Faribe who married Georgio. My neighbor on West 110th street in Cleveland. Faribe was Persian.

Someone in Battalion once told me, "I'm in the Atlanta airport, and there's a marine in dress uniform. His military bearing was obvious. Total discipline. Two seats over, there's a leg. Drunk, slouched, drooling. I shook my head. Give me a squad of Marines and I'll wage war. Give me a platoon of legs and surrender the fight."

I should have listened. Never serve in a Leg unit if you've ever been in an elite unit like the Rangers.

By the way, references to "in Battalion" always refer to the 1st of the 75th Ranger Battalion. No other place qualifies.

Soldiers in Leg units. Sure they are jealous. They have reason to be. Running cadence screams, "I wanna be an Airborne Ranger, I wanna live a life of Danger." Then they meet a real one. Prior to that we were t-shirts.

Fellow airborne troops, most thought we were peers. We accepted that. I loved Tim Lindsey as a brother, an equal and never thought I was better than him.

But Legs... If they were my rank or above, I knew I was more qualified. I was the better trained soldier. Interestingly enough, the privates we inherited in Berlin in the fall of 1983... Jack Sax, Brian Fee, Tim Havens, Dean LaVelle and Joel Kulow – we trained them according to 1st Ranger Battalion standards. I don't care if any one of them ever went to jump school or ranger school. They performed exceptionally well. Better than most newbies in Battalion.

Leinbach, Lindsey, Partridge, Lozano and I raised them to be true soldiers. We trained them to be the best. I can say according to Ranger Standards. Lindsey and Lozano would probably say according to 82nd standards. That's okay. We had competition that was like comraderie.

These new basic trainee graduates, they arrived in Hohenfels in October 1983. The same month when I read about the dead friends in Grenada. I don't know how kindly I treated them. If I was harsh, I apologize.

But for the record, they were not Legs. True, not one was airborne. But they were willing hostages along for the ride of an infantry education from the best. And we guaranteed that. And 1LT Chris Reddish backed us 110%.

I hope I can locate Chris one day. To say thank you.

One day in Hohenfels, SSG Rick Lozano pulled me and Marc Leinbach (Bco 1st RGR 75th) aside. Well he seemed drunk, but I don't know. Maybe Marc will chime in as I write this first draft. We liked and respected SSG Lozano. He could be tyrannical. But he put all his troops first and foremost. We knew that. And so we tolerated his rant. He told Marc and me that he didn't give a fuck about our Ranger Tabs. Blah, blah, blah.

We listened and then disgarded. Useless info that didn't matter. I write about it only because I'm still puzzled, what prompted it?

Ranger Tabs never meant SHIT? I beg to differ. SSG Lozano, if you ever believed that, fuck you and the slick you rode in on.

Whatever point he was trying to make got lost in the shuffle.

Ranger tabs don't make a difference with the majority of ossifers. But they make one helluva difference with the enlisted.

One digression after another. I started this section about SFC Weldon Kavecki. But I got off track. Scouts were supposed to be the elite of the Berlin Brigade. That's why rangers – Marc Leinbach, George Partridge and me – and Green Berets – Mike Roof – got sent to the Scouts.

Bill Guest was platoon sergeant for a while. He came from Cco 1st RGR Battalion.

Kavecki? I never learned his history. He was an overweight, stupid, redneck leg. And yet somehow, he had connections. I didn't realize it then. How else could he send an 11B2V – ranger E-05 – to motor sergeant school? A slot in high demand among mechanics?

Back then, I dismissed Kavecki as just another redneck leg who posed no threat. Once again, I was so naïve.

Sure Hate it for ya

Soldiers in Berlin had an expression that you'd hear a lot. Often. "Sure hate it for ya." It was a mocking idiom. The "hate" was not genuine. It meant, you're getting screwed, but at least it's not me this time. The one uttering the phrase knew that in time it would be his turn and someone would say it to him.

Reggie Richards

Reggie Richards III became a scout. It's important to mention this now.

Reggie and I became great friends. We would sit in my room in the barracks and have amazing philosophical discussions of every ilk. I saw Reggie as an equal, mentally, intellectually. He was probably more well-read than I was back then. But he was a gentleman and never made me feel less because he had read more.

Reggie and I would sit for hours and drink jasmine tea. Berlin had the best tea shops. And to sweeten the tea, they had rock candy. White and brown. I liked brown best.

When I shared my sophomoric short stories with Reggie, he told me, "I would not to have your nightmares."

Reggie and I had this other friend in CSC. He was a young white nerd or geek. I do not mean that derogatorily, because I identify as a nerd and a geek. He often joined us in our discussions and appreciation of jasmine tea. Regrettably, I've forgotten his name. He was TOW or Mortars.

Reggie came into my room with a surprise. It was 500 mg Niacin. We were still in CSC. Reggie was still there after I got busted and sent to Alpha company.

He handed me a pill and said, "take this." I trusted Reggie so I took it and asked, what was that? He said, I hope you don't have plans for the next two hours.

Reggie explained that it was Niacin. It would now burn all the impurities from my blood. He said when it's done, you'll see colors much brighter.

I felt heat slowly working its way through veins then capillaries. The heat hit my brain and then my eyes. Reggie was right. Colors were brighter. I felt it in my hair.

Before I left Berlin, Reggie gave me his parents' private unlisted phone number. I had an address book in my student book bag at Cleveland State University (CSU). Reggie's number was in there. My book bag got stolen from the book store -- Barnes and Noble -- at CSU.

A few weeks later, Reggie was at the Cleveland Hopkins Airport. He had an overlay. He called to say come meet me if you can. His flight left two hours before I came home from work.

I want to see Reggie again before I die. He is my brother.

Kavecki again

Some point in time of 1984, Weldon Kavecki became platoon sergeant. What I know was... He rose to the rank of SFC. Kavecki would start the squad leader meeting by saying, "Who's got any good nigger jokes?" That was not okay with me.

Reggie Richards was one of my best friends. Reggie was black but that's not the point. Kavecki was wrong.

I told Kavecki that I would not stand for this. No more "nigger" jokes. He said "okay, SGT Ross, but you just wait. I'll get you." This was not the Army I joined. Fucking legs. Worthless pieces of shit.

I dismissed Kavecki's threat. I didn't give it a second thought. Afterall, he was just a douche bag leg. What could he possibly do to me?

Naivité. My downfall.

Blisters and Tough Skin

I brought tincture of benzoin with me to Berlin. I bought it in Cleveland so I could take it with me. We called that "tough skin." If you got a blister from road marches, our medics would drain the blister and replace the fluid with tough skin. In fairness, I have seen grown men cry. Tough skin was like having a branding iron applied to raw flesh. The benefit is that after an hour of healing you can do another ten-mile road march. The first time the medics did that for me, they thought I was crazy. I laughed and cackled like a lunatic or a maniac. It hurt so badly, I had to laugh. I howled with laughter. After an hour, I was convinced and a customer.

[Jump ahead to 2014… my wife and I drove to Savannah for the 40th anniversary of the 1st Ranger Battalion. I asked a medic, what do you do for blisters? He said mole skin. I said, don't you use tough skin anymore? He said what's that?]

I asked the medic at the battalion aid station for a hypo and rubbing alcohol. They asked what for. I said for blisters.

[We had a new SSG assigned to Scouts. He rotated from the 101st at Fort Campbell. He told me he was there in the 1970s when Geraldo Rivera came in with his 60 minutes camera crew and shot footage of guys in the barracks with needles in their arms. Junkies were abound. Heroin was easy.]

The medics refused.

Restaurant with the Pauels

German families would take their dogs to restaurants. The dogs had to behave and sit quietly under the table.

Once when we were leaving, Michael noticed the position of my fork and knife. He told me to place the two utensils at the three o'clock position with the pointy ends at the center. I complied but did not understand. He said that having the fork and the knife on the left and right with both pointy ends at the center communicates to the wait staff that you were unsatisfied with your dinner. If the knife and fork are pointed toward the center in the three o'clock position, it communicates that you were satisfied with your meal.

I said we don't have that in America.

But we never went through the Soviet Blockade and the hunger. There is a monument at Tempelhof Airfield called the "Hunger Kralle." Three prongs like claws. It represents respect to the allies who flew missions during the blockade when they delivered coal, food and medical supplies. And little chocolate bars attached to parachutes.

Summer 1984 – The Best Ranger Competition

"Meanwhile... Back in the States..." Yes, an unsolicited allusion to a New York Dolls' song. It was called "Back in the Jungle."

The 1984 Best Ranger Competition winners were SGT David Bazemore and SGT Gregory Georgevitch from 1st Battalion, 75th Infantry.

I never met Gregory. Didn't even know his name.

Bazemore – we called him "Baze" was my team leader in Weapons platoon. I was not surprised to see his name.

The competition was first held in 1982. Baze won in 1984. He was that driven.

In the platoon we called him "the Gazelle." Hyperbole – he could run five minute miles and not break a sweat. Caveat – most of the army runs at a 10 minute mile pace. Called the Airborne Shuffle. Piece of cake when you're 19.

Five-minute miles are a sprint. Full blast.

My PT tests included the two-mile run and I was usually between 12 and 13 minutes. And that was full throttle for me.

Back to Berlin...

TDY - PLDC (Primary Leadership Development Course) 05 January 1984

PLDC was in Mannheim, West Germany. It was mostly about cleaning the barracks. Graduated on 03 FEB 1984. What a waste of time.

13-29 APRIL 1984 -- Useldange

In 1984, The Pauels family invited me to join them for their vacation to Luxembourg. I put in a 4187 and was approved for two weeks in Luxembourg.

I took the French Duty Train from Berlin to Strausberg. That's just across the border of France. The plan was Michael and Dagmar were going to pick me up at the Train Station. They drove from Useldange, Luxembourg to Strausberg to pick me up with my suit case and drive back to Luxembourg.

Enroute, some diary farmer's fence came down and a cow wandered onto the highway. Micha and Dagi hit a cow that totaled their car.

Thank God, they were not hurt or injured during the accident. Auto insurance covered the costs. They showed up in a rental car and drove me to Luxembourg.

I met Ann (the husband) and Annie (his wife) De Jong Arend. I did artwork for them to return the favor of letting me stay in their home and eat their food. For the father, he loved his home. I drew a picture of his home. The mother loved Disney, so I did a picture of Bambi with the animal friends. I signed it, "Clement Pauels."

I was falling in love with the Pauels family. But I still had my demons. They haunted me in Berlin and afterwards in Cleveland. I never had a home until Lynn said I want you to move in with me.

Further on Useldange

During the Urlaub (leave), to Luxembourg with the Pauels family, the children of DeJong-Arend, the family of the house I was staying in… they had one of those K-tel-like albums. And there happened to be a song on it from Frank Zappa called, "Bobby Brown." The chorus or refrain started with the line, "Oh God I am the American Dream." The kids understood that part. But they asked me to translate the rest into German. I love Frank Zappa and probably know every song on Overnight Sensation, Sheik Yerbouti and Joe's Garage by heart.

"Bobby Brown" is not a kids' song. Google the lyrics. I told them in German it's too idiomatic to translate. Yeah, that's a lie, but it's also the truth. How would one translate, "I can take about an hour on the tower of power as long as I gets a little golden shower"? That's a rhetorical question. Obviously.

My artwork inspired the children. "Du malst schoen," is what they would say. It means, you paint or draw beautifully. I hope that some of them took up art. They watched me draw and were fascinated.

The children used to tell me an idiom I never quite figured out. They would say, "Ich hab' Dich Lieb." I never knew if that meant I like you or I'm fond of you. I never learned the context. I think it was like saying, "I'm fond of you." I would respond by saying, "Ich hab' Dich auch Lieb." Auch meant also or too.

Dagi and Michael would take me on tours of the country of Luxembourg. It seemed like every village had a castle. That made sense because if you were under attack, the castle was the site of protection.

Luxembourg also had Patton Square. It had a tank and a statue of General George Patton. He liberated the country from the Nazis in WWII.

The people of Luxembourg treated me – as an American – symbolically as the liberator of their country as if I had personally been there with General Patton fighting the nazis. It was a humbling experience.

I remembered Ernie Nicka. He had a farm next to the property my father bought in Concord on Breezewood lane. Ernie served in the Army in WWII under Patton. He told me that he loved Patton and would follow him to Hell and back -- but hated the cold showers and neck-tie he had to wear in combat.

As small as it is, Luxembourg has a plethora of museums, most of which document World War II. I was born in 1961, so I know WWII from the books I've read and from Museums that I've visited.

The word Museum comes from the Greek word, "Muse" in Greek mythology. Calliope represented Epic Poetry. Clio represented history. Euterpe represented flutes and lyric poetry. Thalia represented comedy in drama and pastoral poetry (or the countryside). Melpomene represented tragedy in drama. Somehow she must have been connected to Deus ex machine – God as the machine who would descend from and save the day. Terpsichore represented dance. Erato represented love poetry. Especially erotic love poetry. Hence her name. Polyhymnia represented sacred poetry (id est, think Hymns in church) and lastly Urania represented astronomy.

As a society, we have not done justice to representing all of the muses in our museums. Especially the muses who represented poetry. Or is that just my personal bias?

1945 Jazz Club

Copley Plaza

Poe Raven

<u>TDY - BNCOC (pronounced Bee Knock) 22 JUN 1984</u>

Back to Hohenfels, West Germany. I didn't record the start date. My diploma says 22 June 1984 as the date of graduation.

I attended the Basic NCO Course with three Airborne troops from the US base in Italy.

The Staff Sergeant (SSG) Randy Johnson and I became close friends. He gave me one of his maroon berets. Its crest read, "Let's Go." We had a discussion about what sets us apart from Legs. I said "Aggression." Randy agreed. Aggression might sound hostile. But it's really the assertiveness. The gusto. The fierce attitude we had.

Later, first wife Lise decided it was hers along with my red cotton Berlin coat.

International call from West Germany to Ohio

One evening in Hoehnfels, I had a pocket full of five-mark pieces. Why did I have so many? I had not planned a call to the States. But I called Mentor. Bunny answered. I don't remember why I called. And I don't remember what we spoke of.

German Jump Wings

Yeah here he was a Staff Sergeant (E-06), and I was a Sergeant (E-05) but I called him Randy. Randy and I tried to get German Jump Wings. It would have meant by jumping out of a hot air balloon. The German troops were in agreement. They were willing to make it happen. The U.S. Army said no.

More on BNCOC...

There was a young E-05 NCO, my age. From the Airborne unit in Italy. Reminded me of an ROTC cadet. He liked board games with the hexagon squares like Brandon and Mark McAdams played. The game we played was based on the Arab-Isreali war. It was a Saturday. The Arabs had Russian tanks. The Jewish army had American tanks. He pointed out that the Russian tanks had longer firing range. I said that's not fair.

He said you have to sacrifice a pawn to win. I said fuck that noise. I don't sacrifice pawns. In chess, sure. Not in a real-life scenario. I thought, is that what generals do? What does the pawn represent? A squad? A platoon? A company? A battalion? It was a learning experience.

If it meant one life, that was too much. I stopped playing the game with him. And I really did not like the lesson I learned.

I graduated BNCOC 22 JUNE 1984. It changed my perspective. I realized pawns were forfeitable, expendable. A general plays chess. He wants a rook, a bishop, a queen and ultimately the King. The pawn is the token. The lamb.

06 JULY 1984 -- 3rd Royal Regiment of Fusiliers

We were going on a deployment to Silzen, West Germany. "We" those who were left behind. The other scouts were in sniper school. And I was okay with that. Big surprise, Kavecki left me behind.

This deployment was with the 3rd Royal Regiment of Fusliers.

Being a platoon sergeant is a huge load on your shoulders. I had no idea. SGT Hall did it with gusto. I would follow in his footsteps. I'd been a squad leader. All logistical coordinations? "Oh, the platoon sergeant takes care of that." No brainer. Now suddenly, that job was up to me.

I knew our departure date, our return date. I knew our arrival location. Essentially that was it.

Lieutenant Andrew Burris would accompany us. To have an officer on board.

I arranged for logistics: food (C-rations) and water for the troops. We did not know if we would have water, so I arranged for halogen tablets. We needed weapons and blanks since it was a training exercise. These were basic standard issue for rangers. We needed gas for the jeeps and a means to pay for the gas. I don't recall how we would pay for gas if we needed it. Perhaps Burris has a credit card.

I got us a medic's aid bag in case someone got injured.

The rest of the scouts went to sniper wonderland.

Bottom line: I ran around for two weeks getting every detail ready. All we had to do was pack and move. SGT Mike Hall taught me well.

All preparations were ready. Flag orders were in hand. The only thing left was wake up and drive to the west. Day after tomorrow. We were leaving.

SGT Ziegler

1LT Andrew Burris. He was short. He had a ranger Tab. I didn't like him. He was arrogant and cocky. His shit smelled like lavender.

The morning before our departure, 1LT Burris called me to his office. He said, "SGT Ziegler stated that he has more time in grade than you and therefore, he should be the NCOIC for the Silzen deployment."

Ziegler did not lift a finger to help me prepare for this deployment. And now he wanted to take charge? As far as I knew, he was asleep on his bunk in the barracks for the past two weeks.

Burris replaced me as platoon sergeant and put Ziegler in charge. This was at about 1600 hours on the night before departure. I went to the Mini-PX on McNaire Kaserne and bought two six packs of Schultheiss beer (my favorite to this day) and got hangover drunk.

By the way that was the very last time I was hangover drunk.

The Next Morning

Mike Roof and Tim Lindsey came in and woke me up.

"Damn, you're not going to believe this shit." Mike Roof and Tim Lindsey were going on their own deployment separate from Silzen. "Ziegler went on sick call this morning. He said his feet hurt. He's got bed rest for the next two weeks."

Fuckin' Leg.

But I was one hurt puppy. I needed to sober up and quick. Music. I turned on my stereo. Tchaichovsky's 1812 overture by the Philadelphia Philharmonic. Full blast. I focused and listened. When the canons sounded, I was sober. I found a new cure for any hangover.

Deployment to West Germany

We packed and moved. Burris was a weak link in the chain. Tab-wearer but not of our ilk. I later learned that he was a short biker who had a friend that removed his piss test samples so he never got busted. It's true. He was short.

Okay that's a borrow from Ghostbusters. Dan Ackroyd talked about "Dickless here." Bill Murray said, "Yes, this man has no dick."

We linked up with the 3rd Royal Regiment of Fusiliers in Silzen.

I met with the mess hall NCO and he said if we would trade all our C-rations, then he would provide hot meals for our troops the entire deployment. Sounded like a good deal to me so we shook on it and made it happen. Some of the troops grumbled but overall accepted it. Our base was in a farmer's barn. That's where we slept each night. I never met the farmer to say thank you.

The first night was like a stuffed-shirt tuxedo and martini affair for officers and NCOs only. And I was not dressed for the occasion. NCOs and Officers mingled and discussed posh topics. Port out, starboard home. That's "posh" by the way.

I did not last long in the officer tent and my troops found me heading back to our area of operations. I planned on going to bed or relieving the weapons guard.

Jack Sax and Tim Haven told me I had to come to the tent where the brits were drinking and partying. I complied. These were the privates, the troops.

The Brits have the system right. They have career privates. They don't want a promotion to NCO. They are happy being privates their whole career.

US Army needs to get that concept. They are still hung up on the Peter Principle. They mandate if you're still an E-07 without a promotion to E-08 after X number of years, you are discharged for not being competent.

What if your highest level of competence is as an E-04? What if you were born to be a Corporal? And you were damn good at your job. The Army in the US would say, "sorry, if you haven't been promoted after X years, you are terminated." What Bullshit. Kelly Richbourg was great as a Spec-4. He could never cut it as an NCO. After he was promoted, he went downhill.

Back to the Brits in the beer tent...

Now when we do morning PT, physical training, when we go for the run, someone calls cadence. That means, I sing a line of a song and the group in formation, they repeat it.

"I wanna be an airborne ranger; (repeat)
I wanna lead a life of danger." (repeat)

Well lo and beyond, this is what the brits do in a tent. Drinking beers and singing army running cadence songs.

I'm a singer. In 1979, I sang songs as the lead singer in Black Diamond with Kathy Blumers and Tom Kunst and Joe Zbaznik. In the Army, I memorized all of our cadence songs.

I climbed up on the table and started the cadence that lasted two hours or more. By the time I ran out of lyrics, the Brits loved us. My privates were all in there yucking it up and having fun.

After I was done, a brit came up to me and said, "That was great. Have you ever done Zulu?" I said no. He said, "You roll up a newspaper and light one end, then you stick the other end up your ass and you have to chug a beer before you can pull it out."

I politely declined. Not my cup of Earl Grey.

Graham our radio connection with the 3rd RRF

The rest of the deployment, we had Graham as our liaison. He would radio with his chain of command and we did recon for them.

Any time we wanted to ditch Burris I would say "Jump" on the AN/PRC-77. "Jump" meant switch to the alternate frequency.

The only one who didn't have that code was Jack Sax because he was stuck driving Miss Daisy. I should clarify, Jack had the frequency. He just didn't tell Burris what it was. He pretended that he did not know. All Burris knew was that suddenly there was radio silence.

In "Cross of Iron," sergeant Rolf Steiner played by James Coburn is talking to James Mason and tells him in so many words, "do you think just because you are more enlightened than other officers that I hate you any less? I hate all officers." That became my mantra. It probably showed in my contempt, disdain and loathing. I was arrogant in my intelligence. But here's the gig. Rodney Norris. He wasn't the smartest guy in the room. But he had superior values. I held his values in such high esteem. That mattered most. Burris probably had a higher GT score. But he was a twit.

We called them "ossifers" because like all west point grads, they were arrogant and stupid. I wish I could say there was an exception. No there was not. They were all arrogant and stupid.

Chris Reddish was ROTC and his major was Philosophy. Love that man.

In the woods at Silzen

There was one day. We were at an assembly area. Perhaps having lunch. I don't recall. Jack Sax was driving Miss Daisy and the paved path narrowed. Left side wheels came off the paved area and the sand was so loose that it guided his jeep into a tree.

I saw it in slow motion. Jack trying to turn the wheel to get back on the paved surface. Burris sitting there clueless, probably stoned. It was only good luck that neither one was injured.

The jeep was totaled. We sent it back to Berlin via train.

At some point, it may have been after we returned to Berlin, 1LT Burris asked me to write up a SITREP (situation report) about the incident. I said, "Why? It was an accident." He said, "I want to give Sax and article 15."

I said, "that's bullshit. He didn't cause the jeep to veer off course. It was the paved road. It narrowed. If you want a SITREP, I'll write one. But it'll be about what happened. Not what you want it to say."

I made a new enemy that day. He was a disgrace to the Ranger Tab.

In the Rangers, we were all on the same side (except for Charles Stecker). In the rest of the Army, you had friends and foes.

Kavecki – attempt #1 -- TDY – Motor Sergeant School, 27 AUGUST 1984

The course was called LOG 213 conducted in Vilseck, Germany. I graduated on my birthday. 14 SEP 1984. That's what my certificate says.

Kavecki sent me TDY to Motor Sergeant School. A self-paced refresher course for NCOs E-7 and above. I was an 11B2V. Eleven Bravo is Infantry. Two meant Sergeant E-05. And Victor meant Ranger.

Motor Sergeant School was for mechanics -- NCOs who were waiting on a slot to become the NCOIC of a motor pool. You *had* to be a mechanic. You *had* to be E-6 or above. There were guys who were blocked from being promoted because they did not have that school on their Army resume. There was a long list of candidates waiting for a slot to get in. I took someone's slot who probably had been waiting for years for their turn (literally).

Kavecki got me in. What strings did he pull? I could not fathom that an E-07 had that much pull or that many favors.

The other guys in the class were nice enough, but at first they fucked with me. They were mechanics as their primary MOS and I was Infantry, Airborne and Ranger.

"Where's your tool box? You won't graduate without your tool box."

I went to the PX and bought a tool box and all the tools. I took it to class the next day and asked is this good enough?

"You took us seriously? Damn, Ranger, you *are* naïve as hell."

They were fucking with me. And I didn't know it. I think I spent seventy dollars on the box and all the tools. And that was PX prices on base in 1984.

To their credit, they helped me all through it. I had to trouble shoot a deuce and a half engine that wouldn't start. They showed me where a component of the starter was missing. Can't tell you the name of the part.

I studied every night. We went to bars on weekends and drank together.

In the end, I graduated before half the class and took my diploma back to Berlin. Kavecki expected me to "Refuse to Train."

In the Army, if you "refuse to train," those exact words, you are at the mercy of the chain of command.

Can I prove his motive? No. How did he have so much pull? I'm sure there were mechanics in grades SSG/E-06 and SFC/E-07 who were pissed that some infantry grunt took his or her slot. The waiting list was long.

The Bronx

At the Bahnhof (subway station) that was to the furthest south east corner of West Berlin, there was a street with no lights. But at night, I saw Berliners walking to somewhere. I followed. The name of the bar was spray painted on the front door. It was called "The Bronx." As soon as I walked in, I heard the DJ playing "Lust for Life" by Iggy Pop. I found a new home. I was wondering in what was called a dangerous section of Berlin.

It was a hash bar. And although I never smoked hash there, it had a great crowd and for this "Scheiss Ami," it was comfortable.

Kavecki -- attempt #2 -- the flag.

December 1984, it was Christmas eve. The Garrison flag is the biggest. It's 20' by 36' The Post flag is 20' by 20" The Storm flag is 4'2" x 8'

Kavecki gave me flag duty with two privates to take down the storm flag. It was supposed to be a storm flag because there was an ice storm. We assembled at Brigade HQ and marched to the flag-pole. The Brigade executive officer on duty accompanied us. Kavecki's spy or an officer who cared? I had no clue. Why would a brigade XO want to be on post on Christmas Eve at sundown?

When we arrived, I saw. It wasn't the storm flag. It was the Garrison flag. This was fucked up. Who raises the Garrison flag when an ice storm is coming? And on Christmas eve?

Winds were fierce. It was a black night, cold and wet, an ice storm. The wind was our enemy making the flag jump and lounge like a frenzied punk rock dancer.

Somehow we got it down without it ever touching earth. We marched back to Brigade HQ and hung the flag up to dry.

The XO complimented us on taking down the flag. He said we did not do it according to the standard, but under the circumstances that was understandable.

Can I prove it was Kavecki who set this up and put it in motion? No.

But eventually the coincidences were too tell-tale. My paranoia was not a conspiracy theory.

1984-1985 -- The Bunny and Mom flew to Berlin

They flew to Berlin after Christmas in 1984. I think they stayed until after New Years Eve. Michael and Dagmar Pauels gave them their bedroom during their stay.

The day of their arrival, I wore the grey pin striped three-piece suit I ordered through the PX on base. Micha took many pictures.

Memories are fragments of the past. Imagine a string. A kite string. It represents history. But the string is invisible. Along the way as you follow the path of the string, only the knots are visible. You can't look back and see the string that connected the knots. You only see the knots. What connected them are a mystery.

Dagmar and Michael gave their bedroom to the Bunny and mom. They insisted. It mattered that much to them. I learned later that they considered me their son. "Adopted" or what ever qualifying adjective you want to add.

Micha, Dagi, mom and I all smoked cigarettes back them. Dago played this game. "Weiter geben." Literally, "Give further." She would light four cigarettes and pass one at a time and say, "Weiter geben" until each smoker had a cigarette.

While I was on base, Micha and Bunny went to visit Micha's Dentist. Micha told me that Bunny would tell the German dentist what needed to be done and Micha would translate into German.

Mom said that one morning Diana woke up early and sprayed the bird with a water bottle. Mom asked in English, "Diana – what are you doing. You need to stop that." Diana who was maybe six, put her index finger to her lips and went "Shhh."

When we were together, we toured Berlin. Checkpoint Charlie and all the historic sites.

Once we were in a store for clothing, Bunny wanted to buy something for Cathy. He held the garment in his hands and said, "How much is this?"

The cashier, she was apologetic, she said, "Det hab ix nix verstanden. Keen English, nur Deutsch."

Bunny said louder: "Do you have this in a different size?" After I stopped laughing, I translated. Had he always been so ignorant? I guess he must have been.

Bunny once told me that he studied German to understand chemistry. His B.S. from Hiram College was in chemistry.

The weather was really bad the day they flew out from Tegel Airport. I did a trecherous journey with Diana in the car. My Opel Rekord -- I got her safely back.

Mom gave me all their Deutsch Marks before they left.

The d-Marks went to a good cause.

Michaela Becker

In early 1985, Sax or Havens had a party off base and I met Michaela there. Pronounced Meesha-Ay-lah. She was five months pregnant.

I suppose I was lonely and she was desperate. Both? Is hindsight really 20/20? No shit. She fucked a soldier from Detroit named Gary Scott and did not use any protection. He was the father. Allegedly. Who knows how many others there were?

But I was Don Quixote always searching for the damsel in distress – any surrogate substitute for my mother – to sweep in and rescue her. This should have been a red flag warning. Instead I asked her if I could take care of her. "Darf ich fuer Dich sorgen?"

The avalanche included an apartment and furniture. And eventually care for a child named Julian Detlef Becker. Detlef was her father's name. Julian came from Edgar Rice Burroughs.

I married her in Denmark: 13 JUNE 1985. Justice of the Peace. No background check for Nazi affiliations required. Yes that was still a requirement in 1985. When I first brought home the application for marriage, she was insulted, indignant. It was an application that was created in 1945 and had not been changed since.

So 1985, I had a wife. That would last 11 months. She wanted a bill payer. That meant rich or American... I wanted a romance. That meant love.

Another soldier and I drove to Helmstedt. Our brides to be rode the train. My Opel Rekord broke down. I had to leave it in Helmstedt.

It was a question of do we turn back or forge ahead?

I figured out the bus routes and we forged ahead.

We took a bus to Denmark. This was years before the internet. Based on my knowledge of German, I figured out the Danish.

I got us to our destination. We registered at City Hall. We went through the ceremony. The justice of the peace was a woman in her 40s who lit a cigar at the end of the ceremony. They delivered the documents and we headed back to the hotel.

Honeymoon? I would not call it that. There was something weird about Michaela. She never had an orgasm. Sexually abused? She tolerated sex. She never enjoyed it.

Mark Vocca pointed out that I mention sex a lot in this narrative. He said he cared more about the human details than whom I was fucking. It wasn't intentional. This is not about who I fucked. But somehow, sex played a part. I suppose that I want to understand it. I get the physical act. I do not get the emotion.

Mark told me that Sarah made him realize the first time he made love was with Sarah. I said that's the same with Lynn.

One more thing... Michaela and my friend's german fiancée -- they both stole from the hotel. Michaela stole a lamp... why steal a lamp? And my buddy – his bride stole towels. This was a fucking nightmare.

Two german tramps wed two lonely American soldiers. Eine Schlampe schwange. Die Andere nicht.

And we were stopped at the border and returned to the police station. Michaela stole a lamp as a "souvenir." My army buddy's new wife stole bathroom towels. WTF... they both got caught. Neither one was ever allowed to enter Denmark again.

I hate liars and thieves. WTF were they thinking?

Denmark did not penalize the Americans. They only penalized the two German females who thought it was their right to steal from hotels.

Denmark should have punished us both.

Julian Detlef Becker

When her son, Julian was born, I had QRP (Quick Reaction Platoon) duty. Confined to the barracks. She gave birth in the apartment. Alone and afraid.

Our neighbor and his girlfriend came in and helped. I no longer have the date.

Yeah, QRP was a bright idea... if the Russians invaded, we were first to go and fight the invaders. Russians had trucks with 20 rockets that would take out a grid square in one shot. The first launch would have taken out McNair Kaserne in its entirety and all the infantry within its fences.

We were all for show. But the entire Berlin Brigade was all for show. Dog and Pony shows.

Certainly not during die Luftbrücke. June 24, 1948 to May 12, 1949. The Soviet blockade of West Berlin. All supplies were cut off. Brits and Americans flew in coal, medical supplies and food.

Certainly not during the incident at Checkpoint Charlie in 1961. Its duration was from June 4, 1961 to November 9, 1961. American M48 tanks faced off with Russian T-55 Tanks. The crisis ended with the building of the Berlin Wall.

Michaela told me that after Julian was born, her father wanted to see her breasts.

Yes, they were bigger. But why was that his interest or concern?

Let me repeat that... "her dad wanted to see her tits."

Sax and Havens had another pair of associates I would have been better off meeting. They called them the Bumsen Sie twins. Two German sisters, identical twins who had a collection of dog tags of all the soldiers they fucked. Bumsen was the German infinitive of "to screw."

German Apartment

My good friend Tim Kenneley, aka Teek -- was an electrician. One day he told me if you ever need to check if a wire is hot, use the back of your left hand. Don't use your palm because your fingers will clamp down and hold it. Using your right hand will cause the current to pass through your heart and kill you. With your left hand, you just want to tap it with the back of your hand. Teek saved my life.

Michaela and I lived on Schmiljan Strasse in an apartment. The kitchen was small. Maybe eight feet long and four to five wide.

Over the sink in the kitchen was this rectangular cover with conduit coming in and out. We were having an electrical issue that was mysterious and Michaela asked me to trouble shoot it. I stood on a chair and studied the cover with conduit.

I remembered Teek's lesson and using the back of my left hand I tapped the conduit.

The electric jolt knocked me backwards clear out of the kitchen. I was on my back in the hallway. It stunned me for a moment. When I got to my feet I told Michaela, don't touch it and call an electrician.

Whatever the problem was, he fixed it. When Michaela told the electrician about what happened to me, he said "Sorry for your loss." The electrician assumed that jolt was fatal and killed me. Thank you, Teek. Europe is 220 by the way.

Divorce in Mentor, Ohio in 1987

When Michaela and I divorced in 1987 after my ETS from the Army, she tried to claim that Julian was mine. I testified in court that she was five months pregnant when I met her. She knew Gary Scott was the father. Gary was from Detroit. I never met him. His ETS date came before Julian was even born.

We were married on 13 JUNE 1985. And we divorced on 23 SEPT 1987. While still in Berlin, I met with JAG and asked if I could initiate the divorce in Berlin. They told me that if I did, the German courts would rule in favor of the German citizen and I'd be ordered to pay alimony and child support. They recommended that I wait until I was in the United States. I took that good advice.

Ranger, heed this warning...

NEVER go to leg land. The ossifers there who wear the sacred Tab are not of our ilk. They reek of leg land mentality. They politic and lie and hypocrite. I met NCOs who were good.

Only one officer (Chris Reddish). Chris was decent, moral, and had integrity.

To qualify this – the privates were great. I mentioned them before. The ossifers sucked.

Cyndy and Bob Alfiarie

After Cyndy graduated from Northwestern in 1985, she and Bob Alfiarie backpacked Europe.

The Pauels family gave them room and board. Time and again, the Pauels family bent over backwards to accommodate me and my family. I can't praise them enough.

There is a lie that Germans are cold and emotionless. When I learned German, I learned "Bekannter" and "Freund." Bekannter is acquaintance. Freund is friend. Germans identify a person as friend very selectively. All others are Bekannter. If you've been especially selected as a friend, it's a commitment for life.

Americans are flippant and easily call someone "My new best friend." My wife Patti used to do that at the drop of a hat. Patti was a superficial fake. She deserved an Oscar for her performance. John Lennon comes to mind. "Plasticene porters with looking glass eyes."

Cyndy and Bob showed up at the apartment that I shared with Michaela Becker. Michaela did not work. She was home all day. Cyndy and Bob showed up. Michaela insisted that they go away. I am so sorry that I agreed with her. Why did Cyndy and Bob go away? Michaela said no. She gave no explanation.

My fault. I allowed her to call the shots.

My guilt. I wasn't there when she was alone giving birth.

<u>Wall Patrol in the American Sector</u>

Close to the end of my time in Combat Support Company with the Scouts, we were on wall patrol in the Grunewald. Grunewald is like central park for Manhattan, but it covers the South western corner of West Berlin. It was a huge "park" – really a forest. The greatest danger were Wildeschweine. Wild boars. You only had to worry if you came across a mama boar who thought you were a threat to her Ferkel hoarde.

We were following our usual route through the Grunewald and in front of us was a human chain. They were blocking us in protest. Let me qualify this…

In West Germany, males had to serve two years in the Bundeswehr. That's the name of the German Army. But here's the catch… Berlin was exempt. If a West German male was against military service, he just took a train to Berlin and once he registered his address as "Berlin" then he was no longer required to serve in the Bundeswehr.

Guess what? Anti-War, Anti-Bundeswehr, and Anti-USA were in abundance in Berlin. This was a time when Reagan wanted or did install missiles in the Black Forest. Reagan was popular in America. In Germany, he was vilified. Oh, and especially after the Bitberg visit. Bitberg was the cemetery of SS Officers.

John F. Kennedy announced "Ich bin ein Berliner" back in June 1963 at Rathaus Schoeneberg. The political cartoons of the modern day showed Reagan saying "Ich bin ein Bitberger."

By the way… grammatically, "Ich bin ein Berliner" translates to "I am a jelly doughnut." The article "ein" should have been omitted. I can say, "Ich bin Berliner" and that's correct. Similarly, if I say, "Ich bin ein Amerikaner," that means I'm a cookie that is half vanilla and half chocolate. America is renown in Europe for the Race struggles. Let's not be vague about that. It's not white versus black.

Emmett Till was a 14 year old black teenager in 1955. He visited family in Mississippi. Emmett was from Chicago. The allegation was that he whistled at a white woman. A racist crew of white idiots and murderers found Emmett. He was mutilated, they cut off his penis, they lynched him and his body was thrown into the river. I read that this mother insisted on an open casket so people could view with their own eyes how brutally murdered and mutilated he was.

Europe does not have the same prejudice against blacks. Josephine Baker was a huge success in Europe. She played the cabaret circuit. The Chocolate Boys did tap.

Berliners accepted Black Americans and Black Africans. They did not accept the Turks. I don't know how serious it was. Perhaps only jokes. A plastic bag was called a Turkish suitcase.

Black lives matter. This movement was countered with "Blue lives matter." That's bullshit. It detracts from the Black Lives Matter.

Trayvon Martin, George Floyd, Breonna Taylor. That gives the names of too few.

"Blue lives matter" debases the movement. Here's why: how many jewish unarmed men were shot by white cops? How many Asian unarmed men were shot by white cops? How many native American males were shot by white cops? Do I need to add Latinos to the list?

Now let's turn the tables. How many white cops were shot by unarmed black men? Ask that question to the "Blue lives matter" supporters. Yes cops matter. But the killing of unarmed black men has got to stop.

That's why Black lives matter. I grew up with "Worse than Archie Bunker." In the Army I had Kavecki. Black lives are not disposable. Reggie Richards is not disposable. Howard Mullen is not disposable.

I implore you to read John Donne's "Meditation XVII." Google will provide a copy.

No man is an island. We are all connected.

Back to Berlin and the human chain...

Protesters were locking arms at the elbows. And blocking our passage. I halted the patrol.

I approached the protesters. Now, I'm a soldier in the army of occupation of their country. I twist my M16A1 rifles to where it's on my back and pointed down. I greet them with a smile and speak German.

I say (in German) "Good day. Would it be okay if we passed?"

He said, "Why are you invading our country?"

I said, "I beg your pardon. We patrol the Wall to protect East German people who want to escape to the West."

He said, "Wirklich? (Really)?"

I said, "Really. We have live ammo and smoke grenades. An East Berliner or East German who wants to escape – he or she has our total and complete support."

He gave me his business card and asked me to meet him for a beer.

They let us pass.

Wall Patrol made me laugh. Gary Dirusso, an Italian from NYC. This guy was so slick. So smart, he learned German on his own. On Wall Patrol, he would casually walk up to German women who were sunbathing in the nude and make conversation with them. Then he would ask them out on a date.

My first wall patrol in Germany in 1983, he did that. I didn't know what to think. I watched and he got a date with a gorgeous naked German woman. She was about 20 feet away from the two gun jeeps. Who needs Playboy? Just take a drive in Berlin.

How puritanical was my American upbringing?

Tim Havens

Tim had me design a tattoo for the "Rat Pack." The tattoo had a skull wearing a beret and with smoke coming out of its eyes. When he went to the tattoo shop the artist said I should do tattoos.

That was back in the day when tattoo artists were doing black outline and color it in. OMG – today the tatts are works of art. I've seen some amazing ones.

Filming "Gotcha"

One evening, date is gone. It had to be 1984. Because the movie premiered in 1985. Our first observation point was about two clicks south from Check point Charlie. [One click is 1,000 meters.]

As we approached, red flags went off. There was no graffiti on the Wall and there were West German Zoll Politzei walking and chatting with East German Border guards. I told Sax or whoever was driving to slow it down. The red flags were screaming.

We didn't realize it right away. But we drove onto a movie set. It was an 80s film called "Gotcha."

Anthony Edwards was the star. I later knew him in ER but back then? I didn't know him from Adam.

Sorry Anthony. I know you named shows you were in. Being in the Army, one is in a vacuum. If he had mentioned "Fast Times at Ridgemont High," I may have said, "I saw that one." He played a stoner friend of Jeff Spicoli (Sean Penn).

The Director fed my Wall patrol crew members a great dinner. He gave them a catered meal. Professional caterer from France. The troops loved it.

Anthony Edwards had photos taken with the patrol. He wore a steel pot to fit in. He might have held an M16.

During the catered dinner, Tod Ross volunteered to stay with the gun jeeps while the troops went in to have the catered meal. They brought him a plate.

I didn't eat. "Mission Mode."

Todd said it was one of his fondest memories of Wall Patrol. He said it was "Time with good friends, a great experience (the movie set), and amazing food (Damn – the French can cook!)." That's a quote. And he gave me permission to use it.

Further on Tod Ross

Tod was the first soldier I met in my Army experience who happened to be of jewish heritage.

According to interpretations, my grandmother Frances Ross was a jew from Conus, Lithuania. Rabbi Poss in Cleveland said, "your father (a jew) married a goy (non-jew); therefore, you're not a jew." God! Who the fuck cares?

If mom was white and dad was black, the rabbi would say, "you're white. Not biracial." I respect and love my jewish friends, but sometimes their rabbis make funny proclamations. I'd say I'm half jewish and leave it at that.

Back to Tod. In classes, Tod did his notes in Hebrew. For all I knew, he could have been writing a letter home to mom. All of us call Tod's mom, "Mom." And "Us" – we are the friends of Tod. I loved watching him write because it was an alphabet and a language I did not know. Written right to left.

Tod and I became blood brothers. We have a photo to prove it. I had a cherry picker knife. We sliced a cut and smeared together our blood mixture. As I recall we were on deployment to the West in a beer hall when we did that.

Now when we write, I call his mom, "Mom," and we say, "I love you," without hesitation. We tell stories of our struggles with the VA.

Veterans' Administration – Update 2020

Great news on August 7, 2020, the VA increased my disability to 40%. They documented my injuries in an official letter. I now have it in writing that my injuries were sustained while on active duty.

Look back at the description of stand-up landings. My advice? If you're active duty and you screw up the timing, go on sick call. Get it documented in your medical file.

For the decade from 2010 to 2020, I spend most days with bloodshot eyes, and I stagger. Loss of balance.

Neck and back pain result in bloodshot eyes. A neurologist told me that. My wife Lynn calls them patriotic eyes because they're red, white and blue. My hearing loss and damage to the inner ear causes vertigo and loss of balance.

The damage sometimes causes me to stammer or struggle to complete a coherent sentence.

As a community manager, owners and board members have asked me if I was drinking on duty. No. I never have and tried it once in Berlin in 1985 and it made me worthless for the rest of the day.

Digression over...

Back to Berlin...

Tod told me during a text exchange that 1SG Dawson accused him of being a racist. Tod said I scoffed. I can believe that. It's the perfect verb. Tod was a user of the perfect verb and never a racist.

Think about it. Here was a jewish man, in the army, stationed in Berlin... do you know your history? If Tod had a reason to be racist, it would have been against Germans -- some of whom were actual Nazis. But it was never against black people. I will swear to the day I die.

Tod viewed humans as human. Now if a human was an ignorant asshole, it made no difference if he or she was white, black, yellow, red, or brown. Tod and I were in total agreement.

If 1SG Dawson had said Jim Boyd, I would have said, "Sadly that's true. He drew a gorilla next to your signature on the photo that the platoon signed in 1986 when I was leaving." I blackened it out. Jim thought it was funny. I resent him to this day for revealing his racist side. I thought he and I were friends.

I question if Dawson was a racist himself or just on a witch-hunt. Perhaps both.

Nobody gets this about me, and that's really sad. Racists are not my friends. Black or white. Or otherwise. I shock white friends. I shocked Boyd. When they finally reveal that they are racists and I reject them, the attitude is like, "are you kidding me man? I thought we was friends?" No, I'm not friends with racist assholes. And I reject them.

When I stood up against SFC Kavecki – it was about "nigger jokes." It could have easily been about kike, spick, jap, chink, wop, herm, injun,… it wouldn't matter. I would have said then, "Enough. Zero toleration."

White people too often assume, shared skin color also means shared sentiment about non-whites. Wake the fuck up. It doesn't.

Kavecki assumed my pigmentation meant that I shared his evilness. Make no mistake – bigotry is evil. Just look at Selma in 1968.

Tod and I were blood brothers – literally. We slashed and smeared. We have photos to prove it.

Tod would translate notes from classes into Hebrew. He was smart. Smarter than the NCOs. Smarter than the ossifers. Smarter than me. Tod and I are friends and brothers to this day.

We spent time in Atlanta in 1992 (?). Tod, correct me here. Meanwhile, back to the story.

0630 PT formation – 06 MARCH 1985 – Kavecki got his wish

I have the date and time written down somewhere. My alarm did not go off and I overslept. I missed the 0630 PT formation.

SFC Kavecki wrote me up for "Failure to repair" and requested a field grade article 15.

This from the douche bag leg who came in at 10:00 hours still drunk and hung over. He never made a PT formation.

The statement read as follows:

"SGT Ross, Clement , did absent
Himself from the 0630 formation
At CSC 4/502 Inf without
Permission on 6 MAR 1985
End of Statement
Weldon R. Kavecki
SFC, USA
Scout PSG"

We had a meeting with acting lieutenant colonel Keirn C. Brown, Captain Donald Cox, 1LT Andrew Burris and SFC Kavecki.

Acting LTC Brown was the battalion S-3 at Fort Ord, California. The story was that he neglected to coordinate resupply of water and one-third of his battalion had to be medivacced for dehydration and heat disorders. He was relieved of duty.

Brown was a west point grad. This is where the WPPA steps in. The West Point Protective Association repairs the careers of fuck ups like Keirn C Brown.

Berlin was in the hearts of pentagon chair-warmers because of the air bridge and the stand-off at check point Charlie in 1961.

The WPPA sent Major Brown to West Berlin to be the acting LTC for 2/6 which became 4/502. Second battalion, sixth infantry disappeared in 1984. The army planned to create a brigade system and we became the 4th battalion of the 502nd. Part of Fort Campbell, Kentucky's 101st Airborne Screaming Eagles. But they weren't airborne, they were air assault. Helicopters. No parachutes.

Back to the story…

Kavecki read the article 15. Acting LTC Brown asked me if I had anything to say. I had a lot to say. Squad leader meetings and "nigger" jokes, flag duty on Christmas eve, motor sergeant school… before I could speak, LTC Brown interrupted me.

He said, "Sergeant Ross, do you know what quibbling means?"

I said, "Quibbling?"

He said, "yes, whining, complaining…"

I did not need to hear any more. I shut my mouth. This was a kangaroo court like "Breaker" Morant – just no firing squad. I was demoted to E-04 and denied any favorable action for a period of three years… during which I received my second good conduct medal, my second army achievement medal and a battalion certificate of achievement. Was anyone even paying attention?

Post Article 15 Uniform

I was so disgusted with the Army, its leadership, its NCOs and Officers, I knew I was a walking symbol. Amidst Legs, I was a Ranger. They sing running cadence about my kind.

I took every field uniform, and using a thread cutter, removed the E.I.B. (expert infantry badge), removed the Airborne Wings., removed the pathfinder torch.

I was about to remove the Ranger Tab. I couldn't.

Billy Holiday sang it. "They can't take that away from me."

Aco 4/502nd

I was now a Specialist class 4. Again. Not an NCO. They sent me to Alpha Company. My new squad leader was a black NCO with a Turkish wife. He was a handsome man who looked like Richard Pryor. His name was Paul Reed. I knew him from Combat Support Company. Now I reported to him. He was a great NCO and a good friend.

Paul told me that the Turkish women love Americans because the Turkish men want all pubic hair shaved off and they do anal sex for birth control.

13 JUN 1985 – in Danemark

Michaela Becker. The woman I met at the scouts party with Sax and Havens. She was five months pregnant from a soldier named Gary Scott. According to Michaela.

We were together for eleven months. We had an apartment on Smiljan Strasse. Our bedroom was a combo of living, dining, bedroom. Julian got the bed room.

We had two neighbors. A guy (Franz?) who was 18 or 19 and a woman (name is gone) who was somewhere between 35 and 40. The two of them hooked up and became a couple.

Less than year later, I was in the Barracks exploring divorce options.

In 1985, We did a road trip. Got the flag orders. Another soldier and I got the idea from a soldier whose fiancée who became his wife resented the Army's scrutiny about nazi past. He said, if you marry in a foreign country, you by pass the Army's requirement of scrutinizing the bride's background and if her family had ties to the nazis. Forty years after WWII? I said I'd go for it.

Our fiancees had to do the German train to Helmstedt. Me and my friend who wanted a German wife, we drove my car. One hundred and ten miles to the West German border.

My car was an Opel Rekord. It broke down as soon as we crossed the West German border and never started again. I had to abandon the car.

So there we were. Michaela was pregnant… Close to delivery.

I was about to say, we should turn around and head back. I looked at the bus schedule to get us to Denmark. I figured it out.

Across the border of Denmark, I looked at the train or bus schedule and figured it out I did not speak Danish.

I took us to the town for the justice of the peace. We got married and the next day, we took us to the bus to take us home. Back to Helmstedt for the train to West Germany.

Now that was a quick summary of getting married. Significance? It was my mission. A loophole in army regs. I never had enough time with Michaela to determine if she was the right choice. She was not.

The Danish police stopped the bus at the border. I'm thinking did we break some law that we didn't know about? No. Both our brides *stole* from the hotels.

What the fuck did I get myself into? Michaela and my buddy's wife (both German) were banned permanently from coming back to Denmark). Michaela stole towels "as souvenirs"! My buddy's wife stole a lamp. Did they think this wouldn't be discovered? This story needs to be told.

Life with Michaela was weird. I had QRP duty when Julian was born. QRP was Quick reaction platoon. She gave birth alone in the apartment we rented.

Later, when I got paid, we went to the PX. I bought enough groceries to take us to the next pay check. Kept enough money for my cartons of Marlboro and gave her the rest for the rent and utilities.

Michaela was fucked up.

Twice, she confessed she spent the rent money on clothes and we got an eviction notice.

I called mom both times. She sent the money.

I asked her what she spent the money on. She said Julian needed diapers and formula. But I started to notice the new clothes.

Pauels and Michaela comes later. So does Michaela and what Reggie told me.

In our apartment on Smiljan Strasse

I used to type my short stories in the living room. Michaela would object and rant at me.

Let me state it like this... A young German woman, without a job, with a child, was being supported financially by an American soldier. I wanted to be a writer. What I did in the apartment was type my short stories.

My skills with the German Language

Speaking German was now close to second nature to me. I found it interesting that native speakers never said, "Are you American?" They asked me if I was French or Scandinavian.

Along those lines... there is a translation of the Neil Simon play/movie "Murder By Death" and the Peter Falk character, much like his Columbo role... It was like they took the German script and handed it to a New Yorker from Brooklyn with no prior knowledge of German and said. "Read this."

That is how most Americans speak German. I cringe when I hear it. I'm not a language snob. I just believe some effort should be made to try.

Like Jack Nicholson in One flew over the cuckoo's nest, "But at least I tried goddammit, at least I tried."

German is precise. If an object sitting on the table is horizontal it is "auf den Tisch." But if it's vertical, it's "an der Tisch." Some call it nit-picky.

Adjective endings will also drive you crazy.

The Pauels taught me two clever items.

Always use the verb "machen." Because "Tuten tut nur der Nachtwachter." Machen is to do or do make. Tuten is just to do.

And this rhyme that Berliners tease themselves with:

"Icke Dicke Kicke mal

"Oogen, Fleesch, und Beene.

"Neen meen Kint so hess det nix

"Augen, Fleisch, und Beine."

The first line is ich und dich etwas anschauen. But Berliners use gucken as the verb to look at but pronounce it kicken.

The third line is "Nein, mein Kind so heist das nicht. No my child, it's not called that."

Best example is how Berliners say I don't know. High German says, "Das weiss ich nicht." Berliners say, "Det weeß ick nix."

Alpha Company

Most of our training was at a place called Doughboy City. Doughboy was the nickname for infantry soldiers in world war one also called "The Great War." Doughboy city was a cinderblock city where the infantry of West Berlin would create defensive fighting positions with sandbags.

They would put us on alert. That could mean an alarm at 0300 and we'd assemble on the asphalt parade grounds. That was a huge area on the flank of McNair Kaserne.

Flag Car. The Americans were permitted to drive around East Germany in a "Flag Car." Likewise the Russians were permitted to drive around in West Berlin in a Flag Car. The US car had the stars and stripes. The Soviet car had the hammer and sickle.

Every alert, during the assembly on the parade grounds, there sat a Soviet Flag Car with the occupants taking pictures. So we had an alert that was a surprise to us, but not to the Russians.

Pictures – do they have a file on me? FBI does. Just in case, I'm ever in a tower with a sniper rifle. They do that for all Rangers, Force Recon Marines, Special Forces, Navy Seals and Delta.

So why wouldn't the Russians?

Digression:

Once I recall, we were assembled in the parade field and the brigadier general, (Yoni Kavori?) announced over the PA system, "Where is colonel Brown? Tell that fat fuck to get his lazy ass over here." Grateful to hear that he had not fooled everyone.

My former room mate, Steve Hildebrand was a Grenada vet with the 82nd and the general asked him to be his driver. He said he learned to respect the general due to driving him.

Once assembled with ruck sacks ready, we would board Deuce and a half trucks and head to Doughboy city. Now if this were real like rangers trained, there would be two-man teams of listening posts/observation posts. They would be positioned to provide early intel of enemy activity and approach. Not in Berlin. We spent the next 48 hours filling sand-bags and building defensive fighting positions.

Realistically, if the soviets breached the wall and were invading, we would not have 48 hours to fill sand-bags.

I also recall asking one of our officers, "Where are we going to get the dirt?" I saw the actual battle plan. It would be like Manhattan without Central Park. Asphalt and concrete. No dirt.

The officer said that's all arranged with S-3 (Training) and the engineers. I said I've seen the battle plan. They would have to go outside the perimeter, dig up dirt with heavy equipment and then bring it back inside the perimeter.

He said you can't know the battle plan. That's classified. I thought tell that to 1LT Chris Reddish. There was no arguing.

Paul, 1st Squad leader in Alpha Company, Berlin

Paul was cool. I swear he could have been Richard Pryor's body double. I seem to recall that Paul was CSC and reported to me back then.

Paul hated that I had been busted and sent to his company. He told me so in confidence. I liked and respected Paul.

I think I remember his name as "Paul" because I didn't call him Sergeant X.

Paul had a girlfriend who became his wife. She was Turkish.

Paul told me, "You need to hook up with a Turkish woman. Dude, I'm telling you. Turkish women dig Americans. Know why? Turkish men make them shave all their pubic hair and their method of Birth control is anal sex." Repeat already said.

Black Vernacular

Benny Jones was my brother in Alpha company. And he had some of the coolest expressions. When a guy entered the room, he would say, "Whassup, cool breeze?" Many, not all, but many of the black soldiers were from the south. As a resident of southwest Florida since 2004, I can attest that a cool breeze feels good when it comes around. The metaphor of calling a friend, "cool breeze" was pure poetry.

Benny had another expression. Instead of saying, "okay" or "I don't object to that." He'd say, "Don't make me no never mind." I love the poetry. I regret that I had not taken notes to later use in a book (like this). That was thirty-five years ago. There were many more examples. Shame on me for not writing them down.

Whites didn't have vernacular. I tried to think of some idiom or expression that was used exclusively by white soldiers. Both black and white soldiers said "sure hate it for ya." Never heard a Latino use it. Nor Asian, nor Native American.

Another training site was Michelin City

This was a training site set up to go room to room for building clearing. They took a post and dropped old car tires around the post. These stacks in a row formed the walls of the "city." Inside the tires and post, sand or dirt was pored. A row would form a wall. Four walls, a room. No ceilings.

1985 or 1986, Alpha company was there for training. The soldier who threw the Frag grenade in watched it bounce back and as he told his team to retreat, the grenade went off. Each soldier got bits of fragment in back, thighs, and biceps.

I suppose it bounced back because his throw was too forceful? Maybe. His toss hit the wall and the angle returned it to where his troops waited.

A metal cylinder bounces off a rubber surface? Really? How could that happen?

My sarcasm rears its ugly head when I speak of the U.S. Army in Berlin. We had good people – Tim Lindsey, George Partridge, Jack Sax, Darryl Bryant, Richard Lozano – to name a few. But we also had some of the worst assholes: Keirn C. Brown, Wendall or Weldon Kavecki, Andrew Burris. Racists – show fits; hypocrites – applies to all.

SGT Micah, NBC NCO

I was and still am a very naïve person. I remember on the first floor at the end of the hallway, SGT Micah had his room in the barracks. He was our NBC NCO. Nuclear, Biological, and Chemical.

He was listening to a spoken word record. I could hear the inflection and cadence of the words, but not the words themselves. It sounded like a preacher. I asked, "Is that Richard Pryor?" Micah said, "no, that's Doctor Martin Luther King."

I was so embarrassed. Mortified. Lesson to self – listen first.

At CSU in 1988, Professor Daniel Melnick asked us to read, "The letter from Birmingham Jail" written by Dr. Martin Luther King, Jr. on April 16, 1963. It should be required reading for Junior high and high school. Since 1988, I have used the internet to print copies to people I have met. Is that to compensate for my ignorance in the 1980s? Perhaps. I use the same rationale to ask people if they know who Emmett Till was. When they say, "No," I say "google his name."

American Education System

I grew up in the Mentor, Ohio school system. I went to Rice Elementary, Ridge Junior High School, Saint Joseph High School, Lake Catholic High School, Mentor High School and Painesville Harvey High School.

Not one of those educational institutes ever mentioned Doctor King, Malcolm X, Harriet Tubman, Frederick Douglass, Emmett Till, Marcus Garvey and this partial list goes on and on. And I keep adding more names to the list.

Black Lives Matter... I bought these DVDs and shared them with friends because they are that important: "Selma," "Green Book," Blackkklansman," "My Best Enemy," "Hidden Figures," "Harriet," "Just Mercy," and "Queen & Slim."

Growing up in the Mentor Ohio school system, somehow I understood that the governor of Alabama was a racist. His name was George Wallace – but not until the movie "Selma" did I grasp to what extent. How extreme.

April 4, 1968, in Memphis, Tennessee, I was seven years old in second grade. There was no moment of silence. Why?

In Fairness to Saint Joseph High School, the religion department played the film "Night and Fog" about the

Holocaust. That film showed bulldozed bodies into mass graves. It showed the ovens and gas chambers. Kudos to Saint Joe's for educating us catholic boys about the Holocaust. Aww Shit - Failure about blacks, women, native americans, Asians and Latinos.

Thank God, that CKLW played Motown. But that's not the point.

The K through 12 education curriculum was lacking. Unless it's changed, the topics were all about old white men.

"Bury My Heart At Wounded Knee" by Dee Brown should have been there.

"Night" by Elie Wiesel should have been there.

"If they come in the morning: Voices of resistance," by Angela Davis should have been there.

"Soul on Ice" by Eldridge Cleavor should have been there.

"The Ghetto Code" by Gil Scott-Heron from his album "The mind of Gil Scott-Heron" should have been included.

And the content of the TIME Magazine: 100 Women of the Year should have been included. I bought the magazine for Lynn's niece's daughter Annabelle. Annabelle has an amazing mind. I hope she memorizes all the women who were great and goes on "Ellen" DeGeneres and tells the world about all these amazing women who were never lauded or covered in the history books.

Sure hate it for ya, part two (I mentioned this earlier)

There was an idiom in Berlin among the soldiers that I'd never heard before.

It often was muttered after someone was called to the platoon leader's office or the First Sergeant's office or the Company commander's office. And on occasion the Lieutenant Colonel's office. LTC Brown was our acting Battalion commander.

If you got called down, it meant you were getting an Article 15.

Chris Reddish excluded, all officers in Berlin would wait until they had perhaps two weeks left of their time with the platoon. Then they would hand out Article 15s like they were Halloween candy.

Officer evaluation form gets bonus points for "Discipline" if they punish the troops. So an Article 15 can reduce rank, reduce pay and eliminate favorable action like medals and awards.

To the Nay sayers, I say, "prove me wrong."

An officer starts as a lieutenant. They are staff until they have a platoon. After the platoon, they are staff again until as a Captain, they have a company. Then they are staff again until they are promoted to LTC (lieutenant colonel) and have a battalion.

How it works is usually an eleven-month stint in charge, and then years as a staff pencil pusher. Enlisted are field duty as a private, then NCO, and there is no end.

Someone had been taken to see the C.O. (company commander – the captain).

I heard a soldier say, "Sure hate it for ya."

I asked what he meant by that. He said, "It means, he's getting fucked over… but at least it's not me this time."

I said, "this time?"

He said, "Yeah, I've been fucked over twice in the past. NCOs don't stick up for us. We're sacrificial pigs." That was life for a soldier in the Berlin Brigade. Leg Land overseas. The ossifers were sheltered by the distance. No scrutiny by DC or the Pentagon.

Field Grade Article 15

When LTC K. C. Brown signed off on it., it was also supposed to mean "No favorable action for three years." Effective March of 1985. Lasting until March of 1988. My ETS was 18 November 1986.

Transcription.

Certificate of Achievement

4th Battalion 502nd Infantry

Berlin Brigade (Infantry)

Is awarded to

Specialist Four Clement Ross

For

Meritorious achievement while assigned to Company A, 4th Battalion, 502nd Infantry during the Wildflecken Major Training Exercise conducted from 6 MAY 1985 to 30 MAY 1985. His outstanding performance and sincere dedication to duty contributed significantly to his unit's mission accomplishment. Specialist Ross's achievements are in keeping with the finest of military tradition and reflect great credit upon himself, the swift strike battalion, and United States Army.

01 JUNE 1985

Signed LTC Keirn C. Brown.

I have the certificate to prove this. Why did I get this? I have no recollection of why.

I do not recall one detail of the Wildflecken exercise. My Ranger Battalion certificate of achievement are not documented here. Should they be?

Department of the Army

The Army Achievement Medal

To: Clement J. Ross

For:

Meritorious achievement while serving with company A, 4th Battalion, 502nd Infantry, Berlne Brigade from 1 October 1984 to from 30 September 1985. Specialist Ross demonstrated exemplary professionalism, and unparalled proficiency in the performance of basic soldierly skills. He distinguished himself by attaining a 300 score on the Army Physical Readiness test, 92% on the Skill Qualification Test and and qualified as an expert Marksman, earning the commanding General's Silver TRIAD Coin for individual excellence. This accomplishment reflects uncommon ability and dedication and serves as a standard for all to emulate. Specialist Ross' achievement were in the finest military tradition and reflect great credit upon him, the Berlin Brigade and the United States Army.

And...

Department of the Army

The Army Achievement Medal

To: Clement J. Ross

For:

Meritorious service as a Squad Leader and Team Leader while assigned to the Scout Platoon and Company A, 4th Battalion 502nd Infantry from June 1983 to November 1986. Throughout his tour, Sergeant Ross displayed only the highest of standards of *professionalism and dedication to duty. He excelled as leader and trainer. As a Squad Leader he effectively led his men through two arduous Annual Training Evaluations completing assigned missions with high marks. He further distinguished himself with flawless personal performance during a Spandau guard change-over. Sergeant Ross's achievements reflect great credit upon himself, the Berlin Brigade and the United States Army.*

Signed 16 November 1986

LTC Lawrence White

Inf Commanding, And

And John O. Marsh,

Secretary of the Army

I also had two good conduct medals for 1983 and 1986. The later was also during the "no favorable action" time frame.

Ramon Godoy

Ramon deserves to have his name as a chapter or section of this book because he was such a good sport about so many things.

He was Mexican-American. A sergeant, E-05.

One day, I started to fuck with him and I said you're not really Mexican. You're French. Look at you. Light brown hair, blue eyes. Your last name is most likely pronounced Guh-dwah.

Ramon's car

I had my international driver's license. When Ramon got word that his car arrived, he asked me to go with him to get his car.

When Ramon saw how I was dressed, he said, "For real? That's how you're going to go?" By this time, all my clothes were German, Berliner. No one thought I was American. And I wore what was called a Helmut Schmidt Mutze. A north sea fisherman's cap. Red pants and black robin hood boots.

Memories are like wheels of fortune. I'm certain about some of the letters. But I look at the blanks and have to give a best guess.

I remember when we arrived to get his vehicle. I can't tell you how we got there. Duty train to Frankfurt and then other trains to the coast? Maybe. I can't recall.

We arrived and Ramon got the paperwork for his SUV. The paperwork said that a rear tail-light was missing the red plastic cover and that the vehicle would not be released until that cover was replaced. Ramon said, "that's such bull. All the lights front and rear were intact when I delivered the vehicle to be shipped."

The clerk shrugged shoulders.

I said, "So what do you want to do?"

He said, "let's drive around the parking. Someone took part of my tail light. I'll just take one off another vehicle." And that's what we did. We drove around until we found an SUV of the same make and model. He popped out and replaced the plastic part and they released us to drive back to Berlin.

Alert with Ramon

There was one night after an alert and we were once again filling sandbags and building defensive fighting positions at Doughboy City.

It reminded me of "Cool Hand Luke." Spreading tar on the road.

Remember when Luke was out there saying "Yah mule Yah" and urging the men to push themselves. Fuck the guards, fuck the warden. Do it because you had integrity. Right, Sisyphus?

Ramon would sit in the wheel barrel on top of the sandbags and I'd grab by the handles and run to the cinderblock building. Back and forth. Beyond sheer exhaustion. I almost dumped him once because I was laughing.

Ammo NCO

I was the Ammo NCO who had to do the inventory inspection… that was weird because I was an E-04 following my demotion to Specialist Class Four.

They tried – the Leg ossifers – to write me up again because I missed a scheduled inspection. I was in the west driving Ramon's car back to Berlin.

That's how fucked up the Army in Berlin was.

I think they dropped it because they realized it made them look overly stupid.

Look stupid? They were stupid.

The universal adjective

When I studied German grammar, I learned that in English a gerund is when you add "-ing" to a verb. I didn't learn that in American English classes – or if I did, I had long since forgotten it.

At some point, I realized that I was losing my English vocabulary because the gerund "fucking" was replacing all descriptive words.

I went to the PX and bought an American Heritage Dictionary. I read it from A to Z. Literally. I liked this dictionary over the others because it included etymological origins.

I am not normally a self-conscious person. Well, that's not true. When I was a teenager, totally different. But rangers and Berlin, I had a self-confidence that I lacked before. But noticed that people would notice me and study me. I supposed most people who pull out a dictionary, look up one word and put it back. I was reading and turning pages like someone reading Sherlock Holmes.

If someone had ever asked, what are you doing? I would have answered, I'm reading the dictionary. I wanted to replace the vocabulary I'd lost.

My second assignment of duty at Spandau Prison

Summer of 1986. Back at Spandau Prison.

The lieutenant in charge came to me in a panic. He said there is a German flashing a gun.

The Lieutenant was an officer; I was an enlisted E-04. He spoke not one word of German. By this time, I was moderately fluent.

I was supposed to confront the threat.

The threat was a Bavarian man on Urlaub (Leave). He was drunk and happy and waiving a pistol and wanted to volunteer to kill Rudolf Hess. He wanted to kill the Nazi. He wanted to do us and the world a favor.

I walked out and listened to him. Then I said, "I'm with you." He said, "I want the Nazi dead."

I said if I could kill him I would. He said, "I'll do it for you and for Germany."

I eventually talked him out of it. He wandered off and I went back inside the prison.

That time at Spandau, I stole a brick.

We rotated in shifts. Eight hours in the tower, eight hours sleep, and eight hours on stand-by – that meant ready but idle. Sitting watching videos. Eating when chow was served.

In the tower meant, rotating clockwise or counter-clockwise? I don't recall. But it was for eight hours. That was crazy.

Spandau Bricks

On my last shift. I stole a brick. We were on our way out. There was a pile of bricks. Bricks used to build Spandau prison.

I stole one.

They were probably repair bricks. I stole one.

Twenty or so years ago, I offered it to the Naples Holocaust Museum. They said no thank you.

In 2020, I offered it to the Cape Coral museum of military history. They said yes and thank you.

Bonnland – 4th of the 502nd

I had two deployments to Bonnland. The first with the scouts and the second with Alpha company.

Bonnland was a small village in West Germany. During WWII, Hitler ordered the people to evacuate the village and relocate. Who knows where they went. But he used the village to train his Wehrmacht Soldaten for in-city fighting. And the post-WW II allies continued this tradition.

We would take the duty train to Frankfurt. Then another train to the closest town to Bonnland. Then road march to Bonnland. It wasn't bad. But I learned that during the second visit, former Ranger school instructor SFC Steve "no-go"

Rondeau was now with 4ᵗʰ Battalion and decided to show off by humping a 50 cal.

In Ranger school, you were graded on patrols as either a "go" or a "no-go." SFC Rondeau got the nickname because he would start his intro with a pencil that was half red and half blue. Red was bad. He'd break it in half and throw the blue part over his shoulder. Hence the title.

I heard that humping the 50 cal smoked his ass. The gun was 84 pounds. The M67 90 mm that I carried in the Rangers was 35 pounds. I can only imagine.

In 2014, I met Steve Rondeau again in Savannah. It was the 40ᵗʰ anniversary of the 1ˢᵗ Battalion, 75ᵗʰ Infantry. Mike Hall was also there.

French Translator

When we were at Bonnland, we had a platoon of French soldiers assigned to our company. We learned that this platoon were fresh recruits, basic trainees. Like – yesterday, they could have been civilians with long hair smoking hash and rebelling like normal teens do.

The CO (commanding officer) of Alpha company, a tab-wearer named CPT Wiles. He decided that since I studied French in 1974...; therefore, the French platoon could have me as translator. Whiskey Tango Foxtrot. I was proficient with "Come" and "Stop" when we were maneuvering. But that was about it.

This is the telephone game... one of the French soldiers. Sorry Buddy, I forget names. I had it written down. It's gone.

Anyhow, he spoke German. When classes in English were taught, I would translate into German and he would translate into French. I have no idea how the results were received.

During the training for in-city fighting, we'd run to a new building and to call them I'd say "Vien avec moi" (come with me). When we stopped I'd say "Arrestez." They complied so I can only assume they understood. My buddy who spoke German was not with us when we "invaded" Bonnland.

Back to Reggie Richards

He became the NCOIC of the new Snipers of Combat Support Company.

Good for Reggie. I love him like a brother which he is. We still had our talks and our tea.

Reggie told me about a conversation that he had with CPT Donald Cox. I wish Mike Roof had been there. But Reggie held his own. He told me CPT Cox said what happened to SGT Ross with Kaveckie was so wrong. Cox, admitted to Reggie that he didn't know the story, didn't know enough of what it was all about. And that he agreed it should not have happened. But he also never tried to learn the story.

Yeah, Donald Cox was SF, Green Beret. But he sold out a Ranger. To a leg. Not just any leg, but a douche bag leg who was a drunk and a racist. Way to go, Donald. Many happy fucking returns.

Those in the Rangers and those in SF – we need to watch each others' backs. Because the Legs are not going to do it for us.

But I qualify that… the mechanics at LOG 213 – they had my back better than an SF captain or Ranger qualified LTC. I loved those mechanics.

Tim the armorer and "Michelle"

One night after drinking on deployment, Tim the armorer and I were in a basement. I told Tim I knew he was gay and that Michelle was actually Michael.

He was paranoid. How did I know? How did it show?

I told Tim it did not show. I told Tim a tale of James Kennedy. Then he felt comfortable that a ranger knew that he was gay.

I had two glossy photos of David Bowie from 1976 from Newberry's in the 1970s and gave them to him.

The next time I was in their apartment, the photos were framed and hanged on the wall in their foyer. Why didn't I think of doing that? The photos looked great and honored Bowie.

"Der Dschungel"

David Bowie owned a night club in Berlin. The name was the translation of the Jungle into German. I knew it was on Ku'furstendamm (Ku'damm), but I didn't know where. One night I found it. Keep in mind, this was before the internet or google.

Open from 15 OCT 1978 until 31 MAY 1993 (that came from google). I was there in Spring or early summer of 1986. It was after the separation from Michaela Becker. So I was free to galavant. Bowie did his albums with Iggy Pop and Brian Eno from 1977 to 1981. "Low," "Heroes," and "Lodger." I liked Low the best as an album, but the single song, "Heroes," was divinity for the ears.

"Heroes" in my interpretation was about a man and a woman attempting to escape east Germany by crossing the Wall. There was not one wall – there were two. And in between was a no-man's land. Traps were laid, dogs were trained, towers with conscripts who were under orders to shoot.

Bowie's narrative was about two who tried to escape. I interpret it that she got shot. She died. You never knew his fate. Captured or killed by the Border patrol. The song has this angst. It tears at the soul. Patti Smith wrote a poem about it that was published in Creem Magazine. Her poem emphasized being overwhelmed. I could relate. I had not even been to Berlin yet and it overwhelmed me.

Back to der Dschungel...

It was dark and the wait-staff were known as the "fantasy girls."

By this time, I wouldn't call David a "dandy" as Ian Hunter did after his death. He was a musician married to Iman. But the fantasy girls were transgender. Some even had the adam's apple shaved off. Each one looked like a Victoria's Secret model.

They were beautiful. I was horny. But suddenly...

I ordered a beer and as I sat there, Christian Pauels came up and sat beside me. We greeted one another as friends, family and then he said jokingly, you "know" what they are? He was referring to the fantasy girls. Christian was straight without a bi-bone in his body.

I departed shortly thereafter. I was tempted and did not want Christian reporting that back to the Pauels family.

I was the hypocrite who mocked Boy George singing, "Do you really want to hurt me."

Tommy's Kneipe

After Michaela and I ended. I did not want the company of women. Too many nights I came to the apartment where I paid the rent. A Friday night and I was there to deliver my salary to the mother of Julian. Until we were divorced, she was my wife.

Countless nights, I came to the apartment. Pitch black. No lights. The infant in his crib, afraid and crying in the dark. I picked him up and held him until he calmed down. "Ruhe, bitte, Ruhe... Alles ist okay. Ich bin hier. Keine Angst zu haben. Ich halte Dir fest. Und ich geh nicht weg." The last part was a lie. I did go away. To America.

Michaela would eventually come home. Drunk. I was surprised that she didn't have a companion soldier.

Julian was traumatized enough. I spoke in a calm voice.

"You left him alone." Der war ganz alleine in der Wohnung. Not a one-time incident. Too many times to count.

I had friends at this bar called Tommy's. It was off limits. My friends always looked out for me.

If the Military Police (M.P.s) came in for a routine inspection, my friends covered for me. I looked like a Berliner with my leather jacket and Helmut Schmidt Mutze.

Who knew? The MPs may have been looking for me. James Kennedy frequented the "Dunkel Zimmer." He also met a curator of the art museum in Munich. We had great conversation about expressionism and degenerate art during the Nazi era.

Tod Ross and I and Wall Patrol

Tod Ross and I met when I was in the scouts.

When I was close to ETS (expiration time in service) he wrote me a Haiku. I have to ask him to complete it.

Tod said the first line was "The winter's cold descends upon us."

God' is gone.

Who will tell the Tell?"

"The Tell" is an allusion to a Mel Gibson "Road Warrior" movie. I've never been paid so high a compliment.

Tod went on many Wall Patrols with us. He was like the unofficial/official member of the Scouts. And he joined us to run the entire length of the Berlin Wall. Tod got the certificate. I never did. Alpha company did not accept CSC timed slots. I had to run the entire distance with Aco. Politics. I should ask Tod to do a color photo copy of his for me.

Wall Patrol and assisting an East German

Wall Patrols were conducted along the American Sector of the Berlin Wall. We had 5.56 mm rounds for the M16s, we had 7.62 mm rounds for the M60s. We had smoke grenades.

The concept was that if an East German was attempting to cross the No-Man's-Land and escape to the West, with smoke and bullets we were to provide aid and assist to that escapee. Never got the chance. I say too bad and I also say thank God.

I would have loved the chance to help an east german citizen to escape. That was my job. But we never got to practice "rules of engagement." Ossifers said, "Battalion S-3 develops the subjects and objectives for training."

Call me stupid -- you've got 19-year-olds with M16s that have full auto and an M60 machine gun. Now the M60 was jeep mounted so it would not have been a factor unless the operator detached it and carried it up the steps to the platform. Typically, the M60 gunner stayed with the jeep. Can you say, "international incident"?

We were overly confident that there would not be a citizen trying to escape and evade. We should have planned the contingency that there would be.

Up to this point, all wall patrols started at 0830 hours or so. But at some point, we got report that a successful escape happened at night at Check Point Charlie.

Whoever the platoon leader (lieutenant) was at that time, said we need to do wall patrol at dusk or night. It may have even been 1LT Rodgers or 1LT Burris. I don't recall. Tod may have to refresh my memory.

But prior to my demotion to Spec 4, we did wall patrol at night.

Christmas 1985

Alpha company had this arrangement with a local orphanage. The soldiers bought Christmas presents for all the kids. Each soldier volunteered and a child was assigned based on age and what gift they wanted.

Ironically, I was never told about this program to be a participant. I would have gladly been. Instead, I was asked to be Weihnachtsmann. That's the German name for what American's call Santa Claus. I was the only one in our company who spoke German. The orphan kids did not speak English.

The day came and I was given the Santa costume. I duct taped two pillows front and back. I would not need to do that now at age 59. The costume came without boots. I wore my army boots. I thought no big deal.

Our day room was used as the location.

The kids and the soldiers were present when I arrived. I didn't know if "Ho, Ho, Ho" was how the German Santa Claus spoke, but I used it any way.

Each child sat on my lap. I would then say, "Bist Du nett gewesen?" Have you been nice? I never said "Oder Boese?" Or Naughty?

Each child told me that they behaved really good.

THEN!

… there was this little girl. Nine, perhaps? I don't know. She studied me. Scrutinized is a better word. Her facial expression was that she was puzzled and wanted to solve the riddle. I was the riddle. She said in German, "Weihnachtsmann, why do you have the same boots as the soldiers here at the barracks?"

Remember the Grinch and how he thought up a lie and thought it up quick? That was me. I said, "Meine Kleine" – endearing term for little one – "Where do you think the soldiers got their boots from? I brought them."

I will never know if she believed me or knew that I was full of shit.

But I will never forget that young girl. She was intelligent and observant and deserved the Sherlock Holmes award.

PFC Maurice

Army is not for everyone. I have close friends who are LGBTQ. Frank in basic training was risking a lot… but never got caught. Perhaps Frank gravitated toward Darden, DeGedio and me because he instinctively knew, we would protect him.

I remember when Frank told us that he had sex with Private Wolf. All three of us were saying "Oh, man…" We were disappointed. Not because of the act that Frank and PVT Wolf committed. We weren't judging that and could care less. We were disappointed because he could have gotten caught and that would mean a court martial. 1980 in the Army or anywhere in the military, "abomination" was synonymous. Fuck Leviticus. He was a sexist homophobe. And a hypocrite.

In Berlin, Maurice drew attention to himself.

He was the most meticulous, and paid the most attention to detail of any soldier I knew. Back in the 1980s, we wore yellow running suits for PT. Maurice would starch his PT uniform and show up with starched creases. Seriously.

In the company, everyone wondered. The name, "Maurice," isn't that too cliché to ever be applicable?

Maurice was a tall slender black man with an extra long head. He had fuller lips than most black men (or women).

Maurice had something in overdrive and one night he cast off the shackles of inhibition and Army regulation.

Maurice was seriously fucked up. Sexually and Socially. When I heard about this situation, my reaction was to say, oh my God, Maurice – what got into you?

An NCO… he was red neck through and through. That meant southern culture, family all served, and he carried on the tradition. He was ultra-squared away. Should have been citadel or another academe.

I loved him like a brother. We competed in achievements. He belonged in a ranger unit. Same with a soldier we called Sea-Dog. Sea-Dog and I trained for the Berlin marathon running 15 miles a night. Meanwhile I was still smoking Marlboros, one pack a day.

One night, Maurice was perched like a bird on the end of the bed of the red neck NCO. He balanced on the lower portion on his feet like a bird. His large hard erection was being stroked by his hand. He was naked. And masturbating.

My NCO friend from West Virginia would have and almost killed Maurice.

He kept screaming, "No… no… no…" Like he did not want to believe it was true.

He told me later… "if that fucker would have ejaculated on me…"

I think Maurice was stockaded and confined. I felt bad for Maurice. My first question was who damaged him? It wasn't a matter of being gay. Gay men don't stalk and jerk off to non-gays. There are too many willing participants.

Cascades

Jump ahead to 2009 or so… I don't have the date. I was managing the Cascades. A Home Owner Association (HOA) with 614 single family homes. We had a gated system with a tele-entry call box. There was this one owner. She was British. Based on the details she provided it seemed as if she was in the bunkers when the nazis bombed London. She was shell-shocked and could barely leave home.

She came to the office crying. Her sister wanted to visit and couldn't get in. She was trembling in my office. I looked up her code for family. I said it's "key, key, zero six four two nine nine" which matched her address. She was shaking her head no.

I said, "May we walk out to the tele-entry call box? I'll go with you and we can do it together."

She said that would be nice.

She held my arm as we walked to the gate. I remembered the movie "Damages" with Jeremey Irons. I said to her, "You know. All of us. We are all damaged. Some more than others. You're not alone." The last line was from David Bowie.

I do have occasional original lines. But that time, I borrowed from two amazing sources.

I demonstrated the code and then asked her to do the code again so she could see. She did the code and successfully opened the gate solo. She was so happy.

1986

1986 meant my ETS (expiration time in service). It would not come until November 18ᵗʰ so I had to be patient.

LaBelle's

LaBelle's was a nightclub in Berlin. Berlin women would go there to meet American men. What I didn't know is that ex soldiers – American soldiers – ex African-American soldiers – they did the screening. LaBelle's was in walking distance from where I lived with Michaela. A lot of guys from my company went there on a regular basis.

April 5ᵗʰ, 1986. LaBelle's disco in Berlin got bombed by the Libyans. LaBelle's was a bar that was bought by two Americans who did a "European Out." That was the term used to describe when soldiers ETSed in Europe. That meant opted to stay in Europe. I had planned to do the same. Until I learned of Michaela's numerous fuck partners while I was in the field. JAG told me that if I were to do a European Out, the German Courts would rule in favor of Michaela regardless of the circumstances.

I don't think the Libyans cared about race. The Libyans picked a bar that was popular among Americans. And they planted a bomb in LaBelle's that killed many Americans.

Kenneth Ford was my Assistant Squad Leader. He was blown up. I pray for him every Memorial day.

I also pray for Marlin Maynard. He was my assistant gunner in the Ranger Battalion. He died in Grenada. October 1983. His gun jeep was hit with an RPG-7 round. He died with Randy Kline, Mark Yamane, and Mark Radamacher.

After the bombing of the LaBelle's disco, we pulled guard duty on the PX and Commissary for the next two or three months.

LaBelle's was right down the road from where our apartment was. I suggested one evening, let's go see what it's all about. Berlin women knew about it and raved.

When we got to the door, the black American said in English, "She can go in – you can not." I said, "She's my wife." He said, "I don't give a fuck. She can go in. You can not. Club rules." We walked back home.

Moving back to McNair Kaserne

I never felt "home" at the apartment on Schmiljan Strasse. Home. Strange concept. There were two times we got a letter from the landlord that the rent was overdue. I gave Michaela all my money from the Army except what I needed for cigarettes (cartons of Marlboro were $2.00 at the PX). Twice she failed to pay the rent because she went out and bought clothes with the rent money. She partied with the money.

And what I later learned from soldiers at McNair, she went out and partied with American men and took them home to the apartment to have sex.

June 1985 – we got married in Denmark. May 1986 – we were separated in Berlin. I spent the summer delivering my salary as a soldier. As a husband and as a step-father. I loved Julian.

I re-established a presence in McNair Kaserne. After I returned to the barracks, Reggie Richards would visit me. Like Tod and me, we were best friends. In Berlin, the two soldiers I loved the most, trusted the most. One was jewish and one was black. I wouldn't have it any other way.

Too many whites were racist. White NCO in my company, he was a huge fan of the Scorpions – the hard rock back from Germany who sang in English. In the company of other *white* soldiers, he didn't hide it. The arrogance of assuming skin color meant sharing the same sentiment.

Here's a good question: the racist whites hated "niggers" (apologies for the n-word). I have to ask, "why?" I would say that most were more athletic than whites. Latinos, Asian and Native Americans were also better. Better athletes, better runners. Better marksmen. Consider the marathons when a Kenyan athlete comes in first. That's not by chance.

I have been accused at times that I try too hard. My black friends tell me back off. They say, it's like you're over-compensating for something.

I say, yeah because my father was worse than Archie Bunker. Bunny made Archie Bunker look like a saint.

Sadly, I even found racism in the rangers. Nowak and Stahl. Bringing KKK comics back from Detroit. So they liked Dale Kennedy and Howard Mullen. Were they less racist than Kavecki in Berlin? No. Ignorance isn't bliss. Ignorance is a stupor denying facts and questioning nothing.

Reggie told me that some soldiers from other battalions came to see him. They knew Reggie and I were friends. They were scared shitless.

They were convinced this Ranger from America would kill them. He said the American soldiers picked Michaela up mostly from the Ku'Dorff. Went to the apartment and had sex. The next day, there were pictures of me on the walls. They made their exit. Bravo Michaela.

I told Reggie, I'm not having sex with her anymore so it doesn't matter. We will get divorced when I'm back in the States. Tell the guys who fucked her, I hope they whatever reason. had a good time. She was a bad lay. I sought romance. She sought fucking for one night.

Michaela Becker

One evening, EARLY ON -- I took her to the Pauels home. Dagmar had found all these clothes at the German equivalent of Good Will.

She couldn't wait to show me a t-shirt for Julian that read, "Freschdachs." We translated it as "cheeky young rascal." It was an inside joke with the Pauels and me. They called me "Freschdachs." I was now and then impudent. Not in a mean way.

My Latina friends call me "Travieso" – mischief maker. That would be Freschdachs.

Michaela was embarrassed. She rejected the clothes and thought the Freschdachs comment was insulting. Who was she to be a snob? She wasn't better than them or anyone.

I had never lived with a woman before Michaela. Previously, I saw how Mark and Mitzi were; I saw how Eric and Denise were. Michaela and I were different. Most of the time, I was in the field Monday through Friday. Sometimes on deployment.

I made dinner on the weekends and when I wasn't in the field. What she did during the week was a mystery. How wrong of me to assume, that her priority was her son.

When I was home, after household chores were done, I was typing at my typewriter. Harlan Ellison inspired me to write short stories. I was in my early and mid 20s. I didn't know if they were good or drivel. I followed Harlan Ellison's approach. It began with "What If…"

Michaela was… I don't know. Jealous of my typewriter? Forty years later, I'm doing the same thing (albeit non-fiction) and Lynn is okay with it.

Reggie Richards read some of my work of fiction. Afterwards he said to me, "I don't ever want to have your nightmares."

Bill Stevens

Around 1996, Bill Stevens allowed me to read his draft for "In Barcelona." I would never write fiction or attempt to write fiction ever again.

Literature freaks call it the "Canon." It's the body of collective works that comprise what Literature as a whole is. A contribution to the Canon must add something new. No fiction from me ever contributed to the Canon. My fiction was contrived, condescending, trite. But I believed in my poetry. I published it in 2016. It was worthy.

My old fiction sits on a shelf where it will remain until tossed out with the trash.

Bill's fiction was the best he had ever written. "In Barcelona" was the most brilliant – no, the most eloquent manuscript I'd ever read.

I have checked Amazon over the years.

Shame on his family. They should have published it.

It was THAT good.

Brigade Headquarters Guard Duty

I lost the dates. Alpha Company had guard duty at the Berlin Brigade headquarters building. Clay Allee across from the PX and Commissary.

The first time chow was brought to us, First Sergeant Dawson told me, "No chow for you, Ross. You're married and on separate rations." I said fine, I'll get my own food. He then says, "You're on duty here. You can't leave the compound." I said so how am I to get meals? He said, "That's your problem."

He was a dick. I suspected he was a racist when he accused Tod Ross of being a racist. He asked me to support his allegation – I refused. Tod was no racist. A Jew in Germany? Are you kidding? I think when Dawson didn't get my support, he joined the ranks of those who wanted me busted.

I called Michaela and asked her to bring me canned vegetables from the pantry at home. Spinach, baked beans. She complied. But she also brought a box of brownie mix. I asked her, "were you going to bring eggs and milk and an oven so I could bake them?" The blank expression. I'd seen it before. The cliché is "doe in the headlights." I loved her mom. I loved her sister, Undine. They were smart, sharp as tacks. What happened to Michaela? I've used this idiom before… she turned her brain off. Her father? I'm not so sure about.

I'd like to point out, I'm not a snob. I do not think I'm better. Rodney Norris taught me that. He was better than me because his values were superior.

Lynn taught me and showed me that at IBM, they had signs that read, "THINK." What an innovation. Unless trademark, I think all businesses should incorporate that as a motto or at least a motivational sign.

Detlef, her dad -- there was something weird about him. Probably the "you're pregnant, show me your tits" thing. That never settled with me.

He once told me that American soldiers were mean to him when he was a child. I get that. Bullies are not limited to one country or culture. Based on how many nazis got killed by the war or executed by trial, there were probably more American bullies at that point in time.

At some point, when I thought about the marriage to Michaela,… it wasn't a marriage, it wasn't a partnership; it was a sham.

Sham means different things in different languages. It told me this is not going to work. I moved back to the barracks at McNair. Only then did Reggie tell me about her extracurricular activities.

We had free reign of the Clay compound while on guard duty there. Supposedly, in the tile of the main lobby under the carpet was a huge swastika. I did not explore to find out.

I did discover a storage closet with a guide-on with campaign ribbons. That's a USA flag with long colorful nylon sections of material that are embroidered with Army campaign activity. I found the one for Grenada and removed it. Berlin didn't deserve it. I eventually sent it to Roland Crawford. He was there in October of 1983.

The Cramps

April 14, 1986. I saw the Cramps concert at the Metropol. It was my first time seeing them live in concert. I had been a fan since I first bought their first 45 in 1978. It was "Human Fly" backed with either "the way I walk" or "Lonesome Town." The other 45 was "Domino" with the other track on side two.

The tour was to promote the album, "A date with Elvis." Nick Knox was still drummer. He was Mike Metoff's cousin. Mike was in the Pagans back in Cleveland.

At one point, Lux asked (in English) if anyone had a request. I was in the front row and shouted, "Human Fly!" He said we don't do that one anymore. It actually became one of their encore songs.

Tchernobyl, April 26, 1986

When the incident occurred, I thought about three-mile island from when I was in high school. In 1978, Doug Enkler did these t-shirts with the cones that looked like they wore girdles. The motto in print on the shirt was "Three Mile Island – hate to say I told you so."

He had another t-shirt from 1979. It said, "52 dead in Iran – hate to say I told you so." Doug did that.

After Tchernobyl, we had summer weather in Berlin. It wasn't right. Berlin had one more year of winter for the five-year cycle.

I stayed in-doors as often as I could. Consequences? Would Tchernobyl give me leukemia in my 60s? We will just have to wait and see. Vietnam vets of the 1960s had to wait until the 1990s when Agent Orange was finally confirmed as a cause of their condition.

In September of 2020, Lynn and I watched a mini-series on DVD from Netflix called "Chernobyl." The fire fighters who arrived on scene the day of the accident ended up hospitalized and their decay rapidly caused their deaths. The soviets buried their coffins in concrete.

Any one with Netflix, I highly recommend it.

Quick Reaction Platoon (QRP).

When I got to Alpha Company, all I heard about were the "Gate Babies."

QRP – quick reaction platoon -- was duty rotated. There was a Humm-V fully loaded. One soldier had guard duty to protect the Humm-V due to ammo on board.

One guy on guard duty, I recall his name was Steve. He bragged about getting a blow job through the chain link fence from a gate baby.

Gate Babies were underage girls who sought American soldiers to become brides and go to America.

They were perhaps 13 or 14 years old.

Soldiers attracted to them should be prosecuted as pedophiles and put in prison.

Why was an "alleged" adult sexually attracted to a child? The yuck-yuck immature answer is "any port in a storm." Bull shit. Or Quatsch.

But I have to ask, this was the city that produced, "Wir Kinder vom Bahnhof Zoo." Child heroin addicts around the subway station for the Berlin Zoo who traded sex for cash to buy the next fix. Christiane F. wrote the famous book.

Does every famous city have site where pedophiles acquire badges of dishonor? I'm from Cleveland and it was Detroit avenue around West 89th.

At some time in 1986... summer as I recall...

Michael Quinlan came back. He was in the scouts as a Specialist class four. He rotated to the 101st Airborne Division, "Screaming Eagles." He was now an E-06. Staff Sergeant.

Quinny now out ranked me. Quinny was not surprised that I was still an E-05. That was my second time as an E-05. I got to do it twice.

Later that year, I was walking on base in the direction of the NCO club and there was SSG Champaco from 3rd Platoon, 1st 75th (RGR). He was now SFC (Sergeant first class). He called out to me, "Punk Rock Ross!"

It was a greeting of endearment. My running cadence became a trademark.

Rick Knight once asked me… "we heard that in Berlin, you went insane."

That was likely mostly true. The army fucked me up. The betrayals.

"Who was 'we' white man?"

Not The Army. The douchebag NCOs and Ossifers. My God, they were so fucked up.

They actively sought ways to fuck over soldiers. If they could fuck someone over, it made them look good.

Read that statement again – how fucked up is that?

Urinalysis Tests

Berlin staff did urinalysis tests all the time. Probably because of Geraldo Rivera.

A close friend of 1LT Andrew Burris told me that his sample was removed every time to avoid detection. He never got caught.

In Berlin, if we wanted to get high, we did microdot. It might have been similar to LSD.

I don't know what the LSD of the 1960s was like. I never had an option. In the late 1970s and 1980s, it was called microdot and basically, you laughed for eight hours.

Nachttierhaus

In late 1986, a group of us dropped acid (microdot) and of all places, we went to the Berlin zoo. If you've never dropped acid and then went to a zoo, it is the BEST place to go. The animals? You will love how expressive they are of emotions. Gorillas stick their tongues out and say nah-nah-nah-nah.

The "Nacht Tier Haus" – nocturnal animal house – fascinated me. Moreso than ever on acid. They had an exhibit meant to look like a barn's attic. It was filled with bats.

My friends said that I knelt down and watched. And two hours later, they came back and found me in the same position watching the bats. I loved it that much.

If you want to do acid, I highly recommend – go to the zoo. It will be an experience you'll never forget.

1986 German-American Volksfest – "Broadway in Berlin" was the theme

I took 30 days leave in July 1986 and worked at the Volksfest. Normally, thirty days leave was only granted for those going back to the states. They called it CONUS. Continental US. I just wanted no part of parade season my last year in Berlin.

Jim Brown had taken a European Out and lived with his wife Beatrix. He learned about the Volksfest needing workers and he contacted me. The main guy wanted someone who could do New York City style graffiti with spray paint. He also wanted large hand-painted renditions of Broadway posters. He hired me. I did "Singin' in the Rain" and "Cats." I have photos of the posters I did. Five by eight feet enlargements. The original was usually 1" by 1". Painted on Plywood boards. Then mounted around the Volks Fest grounds.

To steer clear of the barracks, I slept at Sophia's apartment. She was Rex Barkeley's Greek girlfriend. Rex and I were in Alpha Company together. I did not take enough socks. Sophia ended up putting my running shoes in the hallway – they stank that bad. Don't ever wear tennis or running shoes without socks. God knows how she tolerated my feet and their stench.

One day I went to the barracks. At the CQ desk a lot of my black comrades were gathered. I didn't realize how dark I had tanned. Must be due to my Native American blood. My black brothers were racing up to me to place their forearm against my forearm and shout, "Whoa!" "You're darker than he is!" Many of my light skinned black comrades were lighter than me.

I was never like that hippy in Doonesbury seeking the perfect tan. I never laid out. This was really the first time.

While working at the Volksfest, there was one day when Jim and I each had ONE beer at lunch. Context: the German workers drank German beer all day long and they were up on scaffolds sixty to eighty feet in the air.

Jim and I were toasted. Worthless the rest of the day. To this day I don't know how those German guys did it and functioned.

Leda

Sophia had a friend who visited her from Greece. They were both teachers. Leda and I spent one evening together. We went to dinner and then arms clenched tight, we walked along Kurfurstendamm. People saw us and tilted their heads and said, "aww." It was very romantic. Superficially. No one would have guessed it was a one-night stand. I didn't know it was a one-night stand. I was naïve. Leda was smart, funny, we had great conversations, and I really liked being with her. She was someone I could stay with. I wanted to stay with.

We had just met and yet we were like a couple who were romantically involved for years.

We made love like passionate dancers. It was a whole-body exercise. Every pore, every inch. And when she orgasmed, she arched her back and lifted me off the bed. It was the first time I was with someone who had multiple orgasms simultaneously. After she caught her breath, she asked me why I hadn't cum. I said because I'm not using protection. She told me that it was okay because she had protection.

I wanted to have a relationship with Leda. We had a great rapport. She was smart. And the sex was unbelievable.

The next time I talked to Sophia, I said where's Leda? I wanted to continue what we started. Sophia said, she's moved on. I never saw her again.

Walter Mudrie and the Klo Kneipe

Walter and I were in the Klo Kneipe. Klo is slang for toilet. The craziest things happened there. Rubber spiders dropped from the ceiling. Shots were served in test tubes.

[So many people are going to say, "Dude, you forgot my name?"]

This medic showed up with his German girlfriend. Sorry. I forgot your name. He was GQ and she was Victoria Secret. We told them that we had dropped acid.

That was all he needed to hear. He took me on a ride on his motorcycle doing 120 MPH on the freeway. Walter was left behind with the medic's girl.

When we returned, I was sober. Speed erases acid. I should not have gone. Wasted trip. It exited my system on the bike ride.

Walter later told me that I was an asshole for leaving him with this gorgeous German woman alone.

DLAB and the Defense Language Proficiency Test for German

I wanted to do the 4187 (personal action request form) to go to DLI (defense language institute) in Monterrey California and study Russian and Arabic.

Tod Ross and I took the DLAB. Defense Language Aptitude Battery. The education instructor told us most do not pass the test the first time.

Tod told me his mom was poor and so she could only afford one letter "D."

The test was designed to assess your ability to learn a language. It gauged your skill with a made-up language. It was a test to see if you could recognize and understand patterns in language. I scored minus one. Tod scored minus one. No one else had ever done that.

Tod reminded me that each of us missed a different question. They could not accuse us of cheating because we each missed a different question. [Thanks to Tod for reminding me of that.]

After that, I took the Defense language proficiency test for German. I scored one below native speaker. To me that meant the test was easy. Not that I was that good.

Both tests and results were turned in with my 4187 -- personal action request form. I was coming up on my ETS – expiration time in service. 18 November 1986.

I wanted to remain in the Army. But I wanted to use my brain and not my back. Captain Eaves, the battalion surgeon at 1st Batt told me that the crushed disk -- L4 or L5 -- in my lumbar area would put me in a wheel chair if I stayed in Battalion.

I seemed to have a knack for languages. I studied French in junior high and two years at Saint Joes. My skills with German were even better than my French skills.

The aforementioned 4187 was a request for DLI – Defense Language Institute in Monterrey, California. My goal was to become a Russian and Arabic linguist. Then if my body was still functional, do the Q-course for Special Forces. Seemed like a good plan.

The Defense Language Proficiency Test for German resulted in weekend duty as a translator. Tempelhof USAF base was one such incident. It was the annual "Open Door" weekend. While I was there, Michaela showed up with Julian. She offered him to me to hold. I refused. The child was not mine. After all the nights when I went to the apartment and found him alone, crying in the dark. That was too much.

Another time it was on our parade practice field -- asphalt area adjacent to the barracks of McNair Kaserne. Orientation of the German Politzei of American weapons. No one taught me how to say, "grenade launcher" in German. All of the specific jargon about weapons and equipment – I never learned the German equivalents. That wasn't why I learned the German language. I learned German to connect to the people.

When I talked to the Politzei, I'd say, "Das heisst, L.B.E. fuer "Load bearing equipment. Aber keine Ahnung wie es auf Deutsch heisst." Meine Wortschatz fuer militaeristischen Woerter ist lehr.

More on O-03 Wiles...

CPT Wiles wore a Ranger Tab. Infantry officers get to pick two schools after they get commissioned. If they are combat arms, especially infantry, they typically pick Airborne and Ranger. Rangers called them "tab-wearers." Not Rangers.

Army has three main groups: Combat Arms – infantry, armor, artillery; Combat Support – field medics, engineers; and Service support – PAC paperwork and payroll, hospital, and supply.

In the fall of 1986 I learned my 4187 (personal action form) had been rejected. I requested an audience with CPT Wiles.

PAC told me that my 4187 got rejected because I had reassignment orders for the dollar ninety-seven at Fort Benning. That's the 197th infantry. The orders had a reporting date in December of 1986. My ETS (expiration time in service) was 18 NOV 1986.

I told CPT Wiles, the orders are bogus. The reporting date is after my ETS. Let's rescind the orders and I'll resubmit my 4187 and re-enlist for DLI.

He said, "we can't. The orders have been at Brigade HQ for over 60 days. If you re-enlist, you have no choice but to go to Fort Benning."

In so many words, I said, so the Army invested the money and time to train me for Airborne, Ranger, Pathfinder, Jungle Expert... and they are willing to let me go -- over a technicality?"

He said, "regular infantry isn't that bad..."

I cut him off. "Fuck that noise, Sir. Leg land sucks. The officers are assholes, the NCOs are all limp dicks, and the troops have no morale and no motivation. I will never serve in a leg unit ever again."

CPT Wiles dismissed me. We never had another conversation.

Jim Brown had joined a band called "Les Cretins."

Beatrix was the love of his life.

He told me that making l love to Beatrix was like being in a pornographic movie, but it was for real. The passion was real.

Jim joined a band called Les Cretins. He played saxophone.

Berlin Wall Graffiti

The night before I left Berlin, Jim and Beatrix and I painted Graffiti on the Berlin Wall.

I painted a Ranger Tab. Black and Gold. Then added "Iguana Paradox." Jim painted, "Les Cretins." Beatrix painted, "I hate this."

It was amazing how much paint the Wall sucked in. I would have thought that all the prior years of graffiti would have added sufficient layers of paint to form a base or primer coat. Each spray had to be recoated to apply enough paint for the image to remain.

The next day, I flew back to America.

In Mentor, Ohio, 1986

Jim Brown asked me to video record MTV – the latest music videos and mail them to him. When my personal property got delivered to mentor, three items were missing: my television, my VCR and my typewriter. The guys who packed up my property stole them. I eventually bought a new VCR from J. C. Penny's.

But my parents had an old Magnavox. It *played* videos. But did not record.

I also learned that the American system was called NTSC. European videos were PAL or SECAM. So even it I could have recorded the videos, they would not have played on a European TV Set. Sorry Jim.

PART FOUR: AFTER WARDS

Bergen-Belsen

Written on September 19, 1989
Blatant reason; as I stood
Defenseless amidst foundations
Without each its home above
Providing any inkling at all:
Amassed, 700 Toten –
Strangers to us, entombed...
Bonded victims, interred.
Somewhere, in one of those,
Anne Frank lies still
Making earplugs from candlewax
For all her old friends
Who never numbed themselves.
Rains came, not from heaven;
Nature alone pursues to restore
Balance keeping flowers fresh.
I remembered a prior visit
Where, in East Berlin,
The soviet army had buried
Their own in such similar
Mass graves for fallen Heroes.
Then I thought of the parades

Held to honor the living;
They never invited Elie Wiesel...
Blatant reason, as I stood;
Looking heavily down
Between my feet into the murk
Of a puddle casting me back.

POST ARMY...

Concerts 1990s

1993?		Social Distortion	Phantasy	Solo
1995		David Bowie & NIN	Blossom Music Center	Lise
1997		Fiona Apple	The Odeon	Karen Cuiskelly
1997	20-Nov	The Cramps	The Odeon	Karen Cuiskelly and Lisa the librarian
2001	28-Sep	Neil Diamond	Value City Arena, Columbus, OH	Patti and Megan
2003	11-May	The Cramps	Carrboro, NC	Solo
2010	19-May	Michael Franti	Tampa, FL	Lynn

Add to that, Laurie Anderson with Paul Harrigan, Michael and Holly when I lived in Ohio City. Possibly 1998? And Anita Baker at Blossom Music Center. Don't remember the year and don't care.

JFK to Fort Dix

I had just landed. It was November of 1986.

At JFK. I approached the clerk at Herz and said my mom rented a car for me. It was November 1986. He said I have no record of that.

I rented a Herz.

The clerk said how much do you have for the deposit. I said ninety dollars. He said that would be enough.

I got into the rental car and after loading my baggage it was an "aw-shit" moment. New York has tolls. But I had this check for $75.00. A treasury check

I went to a bank to cash it. The teller said, "Do you have an account with us?" I said, I've been in West Berlin for the past four years. She said, "If you don't have an account with us, we can't cash it." It felt like a Catch-22 nightmare.

But this was my saving grace. A black woman, perhaps in her 40s, tells me "go to the post office... they will cash a treasury check." I said thank you. She even gave me directions. God bless her. I wish I had her name to thank her.

I found the post office and cashed the treasury check and had cash for the tolls. I drove to Fort Dix.

Drive from Fort Dix

Fort Dix had me sign my name a hyperbolic amount of times. When they released me, I drove north. I reached somewhere around Allen Town and took a highway west. It bi-sected PA east and west. At some point, I stopped for dinner at a Perkins and called home. I told them where I was and that I was enroute.

When I arrived in Mentor... perhaps 11:00 p.m. or so?, Bunny had a glass of whiskey waiting for me.

I could view that as make amends. I could view that as make it all go away. I arrived in 1986, October. ETS was 18 Novemebr 1986 but I took what was called Terminal Leave.

There were times I tried to broach the subject of the past. I was no longer a terrorized child. There was an evening when I recalled, retold tales from memory... nightmares that plagued me. Painful events. They are recorded in this book. I asked "Why?"

The Bunny said, "You must have dreamt that... Those things never happened."

Futility. I cannot discard them as futility.

Bunny had a friend from High School, Ralph Bush

Ralph would come over from time to time. Ralph and Bunny were beer buddies. One day Bunny said that Ralph took a liking to my mug from the Berlin bar the Ku-Dorf and wanted it.

I said no and I still have the mug. I should send it to Jack Sax. He loved the Ku-dorf. Must I say it?

CSU Graduation status March 1991

I graduated from Cleveland State University March 1991 with a 3.68 GPA. The Bunny wanted me to rent a cap and gown so he could take pictures. He even offered to pay for the rental fee. I said no. He didn't come to my Ranger School graduation. That would have been meaningful. Ranger school was harder than CSU.

The Ranger List Server

In the 1990s, a ranger from 2nd Batt, Stephen "Peter" Parker aka Spider-man created the list server. If you joined, when you sent an email, it got replicated to everyone who subscribed. Likewise, when they sent an email, you got a copy.

Spider-man said his motivation came due to a ranger who was alone and committed suicide. His thoughts were that if there would had been the listserver, he would have had resources.

In the 1990s, I was constantly on the listserver. I even wrote a series of didactic tidbits called "iguana's fables."

The 1999 Ranger Reunion at Fort Benning was a blast because of the listserver. Yes, I saw Mike Hall and Doug Droesch. And I also saw so many new friends from the listserver.

My Berlin story reached hundreds of rangers.

One was at the Pentagon who told me that Keirn C. Brown was an even fatter fuck warming some new chair over there.

Another ranger told me that Lt Andrew Burris was killed while sleeping in his fart sack when a Duece and a half (aka 2-1/2 ton truck) rolled over him as he slept. It's kharma or kismet.

One down, two to go. And I won't need to lift a finger. The furies will do my bidding for me.

There is a hindu adage. It says, "if you wait by the river long enough, the bodies of all your enemies will float by."

By the way, I wish no ill on CPT Donald Cox. He seemed more like a captive yet silent prisoner and observer. Yet for a former Green Beret, he had no balls. In leg land, the elites need to fuse a bond. It doesn't matter the circumstances.

If I ever see Donald Cox again, I would ask him, "would you send an 11B to motor sergeant school?"

1995 Christmas – when the whole family was last together

I drove to Mentor. When I arrived, Cyndy said, "You should leave."

Chuck plodded his way downstairs and said, "Where is this piece of shit?" Cathy trailed behind him. I said, "don't be a Neanderthal, let's discuss this as rational human beings."

Chuck was still "mad" because mom and me cleaned his room and his closet.

Perhaps this needs to be clarified. Cyndy cleaned her room. I cleaned my room.

Chuck and Cathy never cleaned their rooms. That was someone else's job (mom's). Privileged spoiled brats.

I was being held back by Cyndy, mom and the Bunny. Chuck threw three punches that connected. His knees were my first targets. But I restrained. Adams's apple was second.

Rangers don't "box" – they eliminate the obstacle in the path.

He was stupid. Is stupid. That won't change.

His objection? In 1994 while Lise and I were separated, my mother and I cleaned his former bedroom to make it a guest room. We neatly boxed his personal property and stored it in one closet while freeing up the other closet for overnight guests. When we stripped the bed to wash the sheets, there was beach sand all over the sheets. He left for San Diego in 1987 after he graduated from Mount Union with a GPA of something ridiculous like 1.87. Seven years later, my mom and I cleaned his bedroom. By the way, we also did the same thing for all of Cathy's and Cyndy's personal property that they left behind. I used copy paper boxes from BP. Neatly packed and stored in the hallway closet.

1997 – Raleigh Trip... Karen Cuiskelly and I drove to Raleigh. Cathy loved that I got on the floor and played with Audra. She said Chuck never does that.

1996 Restraining Order

There was a day in Mentor. The Bunny presented mom with a restraining order. He - the perpetrator of all the abuse. Did the Mentor Sheriff serve it? It's only official if he did.

Lise did the same to me at Manor Park in 1996. I showed up with a U-Haul to take my property and she handed me a restraining order. I had to turn around and take the U-Haul back. I didn't know it wasn't official unless it was delivered by the sheriff or a process server. Lise counted on my ignorance of the law and my trust of her that she was complying. She cost me for a U-Haul that I had to take back. She was a bitch and a fucking cunt. There. I said it.

I never said that about her. Now I did.

Mom had to move out by 12 noon. And the Mentor Sheriff would be there to ensure it happened. His grounds for the restraining order? One night she threw a lamp or vase at him. They were both inebriated. In the later years, they both drank wine in the living room. He would watch TV ignoring her. She would ramble on about all the abuse she suffered. Just like he told me – "you must have dreamt that – because it never happened." Bunny, Bunny, all stuffed with fluff. And no substance.

Lucky for mom, she had become friends with a dental patient who had a moving company. Her friend came to her rescue and moved her and all her furniture out of the house at 7398 Lakeshore Blvd. That night, she slept on the couch in the living room of the house in Lakewood where Lise and I lived.

Mom got an apartment in Mentor and a job at a nursing home in Mentor.

Lise and I and our separation

August of 1986, Lise and I separated to be finalized with divorce. It was a Friday night and I was working late at BP America. She started an argument while on the phone.

The conversation was banal and insipid. I realized that this was the end. My softball team was having an overnight out in Westlake. I took the bus to meet them

Some people are going to say, "You? On a softball team?" Jim Frederick was on the team and got me the application to join. I totally sucked at softball. But the team were great friends. After games we'd meet at the bar who sponsored us and drink beers and have laughs. Mike Peruzzi and I became friends. He loved the Buzzcocks and the Dead Kennedys.

The evening was filled with BBQ and Beer. I slept in someone's tent after staying up until about four ayem.

The next day, I moved in with mom. My marriage to Lise was over. I lived with mom in Mentor for perhaps two weeks. I then moved to Ohio City.

Cathy and Chuck forgot about the restraining order. Conveniently. With Bunny all was always forgiven. The two of them punished mom in different ways. I suppose they considered it payback for allowing me to join the army and for allowing Cyndy to go to Hiram.

1997 – Divorce of Audrey and Clement Sr Ross.

Lake County, Ohio. Never get divorced there. Move south, west or east. Negotiations of a divorce go back and forth with the magistrate, until the magistrate steps in and says enough is enough. Now he's going to dictate the terms and if the judge signs off on it it's final.

The magistrate took mom's GROSS salary and compared it to Bunny's NET salary and said the difference is only $13,000; therefore, there will be no spousal support. The idiot wrote it as part of the record. What's more, the judge signed off on it.

Does anyone need a math lesson here? Gross is before taxes and net is after taxes.

Look it up if you don't believe me. Lake County divorce records are public record.

I want 60 seconds in a room with that magistrate asshole. His adam's apple is a goner.

Cathy and Chuck "forgot" about the magistrate's decision. Conveniently.

Dunderhead and Princess forgot about a lot of things.

Me, the scoundrel, believes that they thought they would become heirs of a fortune. Unfortunately, the Bunny and mom spent combined $600,000 in legal fees. Oops.

So much for inheritance and loyalties rewarded.

BP & Amoco

BP bought Amoco in 1998 and at first we thought the Cleveland staff would have new "former Amoco" colleagues. Instead, London decided that Chicago had greater international recognition than Cleveland. The Headquarters was moved from Cleveland to Chicago. I spent six months training my replacements. Ironically, my counterpart was a gent named David Clement.

David had a staff of five reporting to him.

I trained them to do Share Appreciation Rights (SARs), Executive Share Option Scheme (ESOS), deferred compensation (Bonuses deferred until retirement) and Long-Term Performance Plan (older bonuses with a longer distribution schedule). QDROs, qualified domestic relation orders, was still up in the air. One woman staff member was so overwhelmed, she quit.

1999 Ranger Rendezvous at Benning

The list server told us about a ranger rendezvous at Fort Benning in August 1999.

Mark Ross was a ranger with Aco 75th Infantry at Fort Hood. We met on-line. Thanks to Peter Parker and his ranger listserver.

I drove from Cleveland to Indiana University where Mark was a student. At his dorm room, I coin checked him. He pulled out a coast guard coin.

Mark was smart and funny.

We drove to Benning. We checked into the hotel I had reserved. It was the one with the group rate.

At Benning, we couldn't find the WWII barracks. When Mark and I each went through Ranger school, we were in barracks from WWII.

They were gone. Torn down and ripped apart. We drove on post and found the new ranger school compound surrounded with chain link and concertina wire.

I met Gil Berg and his son at the awards ceremony. Gil was General Greb. His last name spelled backwards. He was the OPFOR commander. OPFOR was "opposing forces." Gil was a master sergeant who was tasked with creating training scenarios for the rangers. "What if?"

CSM Mike Hall was there and 1SG Doug Droesch. So very cool to see them both again. Mike introduced me to his son. I told him how proud I was to have served and and been trained by his father.

I opened my hotel room to list server rangers. Coyne was there from Second Batt. Coyne brought acid. I bought two hits.

We ventured to a strip club on Victory drive.

At some point I was staggering walking back to the hotel. Two rangers – based on the hair cut walked past me and made a derogatory comment about the fucking hippie. I stopped and shouted, "First Battalion." Why did they think I was a hippie? Because I wore a leather vest?

I was a punk rocker from Cleveland. Never a hippie.

Even though… I could sing "Dream a little dream of me" by Mama Cass, "Bridge over troubled waters," by Simon and Garfunkel, and "Me and my Bobbie McGee" by Janis Joplin and match the singers' vocals note for note. I got bragging rights. My singing voice was THAT good.

Mark and I agreed that the Ranger Battalion had become weight-lifters with gym cards. What happened? Reliance on gummint issued toys? Range estimation was a skill taught, not a gadget.

But I digress… change is inevitable. The qualifiers of quality are too quickly dismissed before being considered and weighed into the equation.

Five women and one Great Woman.

First…

Michaela Becker

Reggie Richards broke the news to me. Every time I went to the field, she went to the Ku'Dorff and took a GI home and fucked him.

Guys would wake up in the apartment and see a photo of me and say, "oh shit, I gotta get out of here" --- he's a ranger and he'll kill me." That was the summer of 1986.

In Mentor my divorce attorney said she told the German courts I was Julian's father. I said she was five months pregnant when I met her. Julian's father was a soldier from Detroit named Gary Scott. At least that's what she told me. But it's true that she was pregnant when I met her. She had the belly of a pregnant woman. And she fucked me the first night we met.

Kathy Blumers

Second...

She played guitar and flute in "Black Diamond." Our band. 1977 – 1978. I was the vocalist, Kathy played guitar and flute, Joe Zbaznick was lead guitar and Tom Kunst on drums. Tom's last name is the German word for "Art."

I met Kathy again after the army in 1987. She was the DJ at a bar on 615 under the overpass. Gatzby's? Perhaps that was the name.

Kathy was my dream woman. I thought I was out of her league. She was that gorgeous. But mostly, Kathy was smart, fun, witty, and delightful to be around.

While in Black Diamond, she was Tom Kunst's girlfriend. We became a couple and did the "harmonic convergence" with her roommates.

But in the end, she concluded I would break up with her the moment I finished college. Based on that presumptive logic, she broke up with me in 1987 -- the year I started college at Cleveland State. She broke my heart.

Lise Stevens

Third...

Wife #1. Married 1988 to 1996. Comments would only provoke a war. There was severe wrong on both sides. 'Nuff Said. No heart to give.

Her father Bill Stevens was a writer and the best novelist, best prose writer that I've ever read. His prose was so eloquent that I knew I could not compete with his fiction. Harlan Ellison taught me I can write fiction if I can come up with a "What If" scenario. Bill taught me that's not good enough. I read his manuscript for "In Barcelona." The standard of quality has never been higher.

I check amazon regularly for the published book "In Barcelona." It was the most brilliant prose I've ever read. I could never compete with that.

If you can't contribute to the canon, you do not apply.

Anna Van Der Meulen

Fourth...

Anna was Doug Enkler's girlfriend at some point. Doug introduced me to Anna when he came home to Cleveland while I was at BP.

Anna was single with two children who I fell in love with.

We talked about me becoming the stay at home parent. I was going to lose my job at BP when they moved to Chicago and Anna worked for an attorney downtown.

It seemed like the perfect plan.

I met Anna in December of 1999 (during Doug Enkler's visit). We spent new year's eve at Rudy's – a Gay bar on West 25th.

Anna's sister, Wiebke was murdered by a psycho stalker in the bad lands. Memorial Day was the anniversary.

Prior to that, Wiebke's two sons and I cleaned out the soot from LTV Steel from the attic of the rental property that Anna owned on Kenilworth in Tremont.

Anna told me do what you wanna do on the nights when we were apart. What did that mean?

Wiebke's loss was too painful. I miss Lou and Alaska. I went insane when Anna broke it off.

After she broke it off, she asked if I was "watching" Nikki and her from the woods. Nikki was her friend from Australia.

No, I never did. I could not come to Euclid or any where near there. It hurt too much. Ask Mark. He'll tell you.

Patti Glasser

Fifth…

Wife #2. Met in the Summer of 1999. Divorced in 2001. Family never came first.

One day, I went to kroger. I filled the shopping cart with groceries for the weeks ahead. I had $300 in my checking.

The check out woman said "your card has been declined. Insufficent finds." When I got back home I asked Patti, did you use my debit card for anything?

She said I bought a Bob Mackie Barbie doll on line.

It cost $300.

That's all I need to say about Patti.

<u>Lynn Ann Frick</u>

Sixth....

My actual first wife. We met on October 5, 2004 at the WCI employee expo. I knelt and felt the surge of lightning. Lynn said I scared the shit out of her. But we moved in together on Memorial Day 2005 and got married on March 24, 2010.

We have been happy ever since. Mark Vocca told me that after meeting Sarah, he realized that all his years prior to that were all about fucking. Not making love. With Sarah, it was all about making love for the first time in his life. I said that's the same with Lynn for me.

NEXT CHAPTER...

2006 – Bunny Died

I don't know the date. It came and went and I slept through. I did not miss a thing.

My father died and I did not attend the funeral. He was east side of Cleveland. Possibly Willowick. I was in Florida.

"Of all sad words of tongue or pen,

"The saddest are these: it might have been."

-- James Whittier

I wonder at times, if I had been asked to speak a eulogy, what would I say.

I am named after my father. I had to struggle to come up with good memories of the Bunny for this book.

I'm the Seventh Son. That's why people should read this. The sins of the father run unto the son for seven generations. The seventh son breaks the mold.

After Word

I'm fifty-nine as I write this. I quit smoking in 2006. My gut has grown and now... I weigh 250 pounds. My pants went from 32" by 34" to now 40" by 32". Shirts from Large to 2XL.

I am not a toad. I am the Seventh Son. The one who breaks the mold.

My email address is clementross@yahoo.com

I am the sum of all my parts. I will answer all emails that I receive.

You now have 85%. Of the remaining 15%, some I can't recall due to amnesia and some due to selective and deliberate omission.

Funeral Service

If I could plan my funeral…

There would be no service in a church. I learned that at Karl Strmen's funeral. The Church rep talks about the deceased like he was his closest bosom buddy. I writhed at Dr. Strmen's funeral and Lise scolded me and chastised me for it.

Nothing in the church. At home, I want friends and (select) family to eat, drink and tell stories and lies.

Music – David Bowie, Iggy and the Stooges, Mott the Hoople, Roxy Music, New York Dolls, Lou Reed, Michael Franti, Pink, Velvet Underground, the Ramones, Frank Zappa and Prince.

Open Bar. White Castle and Skyline.

Five Beatles songs – in this order.

1. In my life (for Lynn)
2. Strawberry Fields Forever.
3. I am the walrus
4. Come Together
5. The End (from Abbey Road).

That pretty much sums it up.

"That's the way the cookie crumbles."

Grandma Ross used to say that all the time. I learned it to mean, that's the way things turn out. We can't control our world. We have to accept that shit happens, we can't control circumstances and sometimes, it is what it is.

"Things fall apart," by Chinua Achene.

What if – I said I made this whole thing up? Then I would be a toad in the Lithuanian sense. You can't make this shit up.

The End

Suicide

I pang, I delve, I despair.
But in the end, I lack.

The answer finds repair
As option null and black.

I wait. The path: appear
And I will know it then.

As just and lacking fear.
And time will answer when.

But doubt and confidence
Combat each other fierce.

For bit of common sense,
Does loudly scream in ears.

So deeper, dank and down;
I have no cry for help.

This stupid fool, this clown.
This whimper dog who yelps.

But bite my tongue and stay.
Prevent more words of clay.

12/16/2024